SIR ROBERT MORIER

SIR ROBERT MORIER
by Franz Lenbach

Sir Robert Morier

*Envoy and Ambassador
in the Age of Imperialism
1876–1893*

AGATHA RAMM

OXFORD
AT THE CLARENDON PRESS
1973

Oxford University Press, Ely House, London W.1

GLASGOW NEW YORK TORONTO MELBOURNE WELLINGTON
CAPE TOWN IBADAN NAIROBI DAR ES SALAAM LUSAKA ADDIS ABABA
DELHI BOMBAY CALCUTTA MADRAS KARACHI LAHORE DACCA
KUALA LUMPUR SINGAPORE HONG KONG TOKYO

© *Oxford University Press 1973*

Printed in Great Britain
at the University Press, Oxford
by Vivian Ridler
Printer to the University

PREFACE

IN 1911 Mrs. Rosslyn Wemyss, as she then was, published two volumes of the life of her father, *Memoirs and Letters of the Right Hon. Sir Robert Morier, G.C.B. from 1826 to 1876*. It related the events of a young man's life, passed in the cramping, dynastic diplomacy of the German courts, but in contact with the commercial and political questions of the world outside them. Further volumes were to have described his career when, in the prime of life, he discharged the duties of minister at Lisbon and Madrid and then of the Queen's ambassador—in those days she had only five of them—at the court of the Emperor of Russia at St. Petersburg. One may surmise that this part proved more difficult to write, though all the materials for it were in Lady Wester Wemyss's hands. Not only was it like writing part of her own life, but she may have felt her knowledge of the small intimacies of the diplomatic world to be as much a hindrance as an aid to the objective treatment she wished to give her father's work. Moreover, the war of 1914–18, when (1917–19) her husband was First Sea Lord, was an inevitable interruption. Nor was there in the thirties any longer a public for the ample, leisurely treatment that Lady Wester Wemyss had been able to give to her theme in the first volumes. When she died in 1945 she had, however, drafted eight short chapters covering 1876 to 1878. Her own daughter, who had worked a little with her mother on the papers, in 1951 gave over the task of completing the life to a young outsider, whose only qualification was that she had published one small piece of diplomatic history. What follows is her attempt to pick up Lady Wester Wemyss's story without retelling any part of the events narrated by her and to present the rest of Sir Robert's work as part of the history of British foreign policy.

A. R.

Somerville College, Oxford
March 1971

ACKNOWLEDGEMENTS

I HAVE been able to make use of material in the Royal Archives by the gracious permission of Her Majesty the Queen. I have to thank the Registrar of the Royal Archives and her colleague for assisting me in using them. I am indebted for kind services to the officials of the Foreign Office Library, the Public Record Office and the British Museum, to the Librarian of Christ Church, Oxford, to the Librarian of the School of Oriental and African Studies, to Mr. Alan Bell of the National Library of Scotland, to the archivist of the County Record Office at Ipswich, and to the Librarian of the Dundee Public Library. I am grateful to Miss S. E. Crowe who lent me letters of her father, and to Miss N. E. Johnson who supplied me with a number of references to Morier.

The Hon. Mrs. F. H. Cunnack, granddaughter of Sir Robert Morier and herself a historian, made this book possible, and to her is due the author's deepest gratitude.

CONTENTS

Introduction	1
1. India: the Goa Treaty, 26 December 1878	23
2. The Eastern Question	50
3. Africa: the Lorenço Marques Treaty, 30 May 1879, and the Congo Treaty	73
4. Principles of Policy	113
5. Assessment	144
6. Madrid, October 1881 to January 1885	160
7. St. Petersburg, 1885 to 1893	195
8. Bulgaria and Batum, 1885 to 1887	208
9. Central Asia, 1885 to 1887	252
10. Morier and Bismarck	270
11. Siberia	305
12. Persia and the Pamirs	330
Bibliography	365
Index (with details of persons mentioned in the text)	371

LIST OF PLATES AND MAPS

Portrait by Franz Lenbach. *Frontispiece*
  Reproduced by the kind permission of the Master and Fellows of Balliol College, Oxford.

Map. 1. The Goa Railway. *p.* 32
  From *Parliamentary Papers* (1880), lii, p. 633.

Map. 2. The Transvaal, 1875–6. *p.* 79

Map. 3. The Western portion of the Congo and the adjoining coast. *p.* 96
  From R. J. Anstey, *Britain and the Congo* (1962), p. 32, by the author's permission.

Letter to Sir Henry Ponsonby, January 1878. *between pp.* 124 *and* 125
  Reproduced by the gracious permission of Her Majesty the Queen.

Map. 4. The Russo-Afghan Frontier. *p.* 257

Map. 5. The Kara Sea. *p.* 307
  Based on Morier's sketch-map printed in *Parliamentary Papers* (1888), cix, p. 379.

INTRODUCTION

Robert Burnet[1] David Morier came of Swiss trading stock, but among his immediate forebears a Dutch grandmother was important. She was Clara, the eldest of a number of remarkable daughters of David van Lennep, who was Dutch consul and head of the Dutch Factory at Smyrna at the beginning of George III's reign. She married in 1778[2] Isaac Morier (1750–1817), when she was eighteen and he was twenty-eight. Fourteen years before, Isaac had been left fatherless at Vevey in Switzerland. He had gone to a brother settled as a calico printer in London and further improved his prospects by going out to Smyrna to an uncle who belonged to the trading community there. When the uncle died Isaac joined the van Lennep household as a clerk (1772). In the following year he was naturalized a British subject, so that he might become a member of the British Levant Company. After Isaac's marriage the British connection became increasingly important. In 1785 the second van Lennep daughter, Emily (Tonissa), married Captain the Hon. William Waldegrave, who in 1800 was raised to the Irish peerage as Baron Radstock. The third daughter, Annette, married in 1787 the comte (later marquis) de Chabannes La Palice, who came as an *émigré* to London. The three sisters educated their sons in England and played their part in London society.

Clara had four sons of whom three entered the British foreign service and the fourth the British navy.[3] Two of them attained distinction: James Justin Morier (1782–1849), who served at Teheran, wrote *The Adventures of Hadji Baba*, a gentle satire about an engaging rogue, which still makes lively reading

---

[1] He was called Burnett by his wife, but he himself when giving his full name wrote Burnet. He was Uncle Burnie to nephews and nieces.

[2] I have adopted this date from an entry by Isaac Morier in his Bible. The full date was 17 Feb. 1778. Lady Wemyss wrote 1775.

[3] This fourth son was William. To his, younger part of the family also belonged three daughters: Emily, Ann, and Maria. The eldest son was John Philip (born 21 Nov. 1778).

and has recently been reprinted; David Richard Morier (1784–1877) was British minister in Switzerland and was notorious for his quarrel with Lord Palmerston who dismissed him. David Morier was the father of Sir Robert who was born in 1826. His mother was Anna, youngest daughter of Robert Burnet Jones, Attorney-General of Barbados and lineal descendant of Bishop Burnet. His childhood home was the Hübel, near Berne. He was brought up there in an atmosphere of straightforward Anglican piety, what he later called 'positive religion'. After an indifferent schooling in England at two successive country parsonages, he went up to Balliol in October 1845. He took a second in Greats in November 1849.

Oxford meant much to Morier. Benjamin Jowett, later Master of the College, then a young tutor of three years' standing, exercised a strong influence upon him and they continued to correspond for the rest of their lives,[1] both dying in 1893 within a few months of one another. Morier was himself also conscious of the influence 'of the old ethical discipline of the unreformed Oxford Schools'.[2] He was up when the core of the work in philosophy was still Aristotle's *Ethics* and in history Thucydides' *Peloponnesian War*, but the reforms of 1847–8, broadening the curriculum, were beginning to take effect. Jowett had begun to lecture on the history of philosophy and to impart to Balliol men his own interest in English philosophy from Locke to Mill. The Examination Statute of 1850 first introduced the *Republic* of Plato into the curriculum, but Jowett had already begun to give to his pupils his own Hegelian interpretation of it. Morier later described to Max Müller, his friend as an undergraduate, how under the influence of his reading of contemporary philosophers, including Auguste Comte, the doctrinal structure of his religion fell away bit by bit.[3] Yet he came down from Oxford a man of a forceful rather than reflective habit of mind: a man noted for his intellectual

---

[1] Geoffrey Faber in *Jowett* (1957), p. 307, argues that Morier shared with Florence Nightingale the position of the friend who eclipsed all others.

[2] To Benjamin Jowett, 29 Oct. 1879. All references without a source are to letters preserved in the Morier papers at Balliol College, Oxford. This letter is preserved only in a typed version.

[3] To Max Müller, 13 July 1879, preserved as a typed copy in the papers put together by Lady Wemyss for her account of Morier's work in 1879. The same letter describes his view in 1879 as one of 'disbelief in our unbelief'.

energy. He had a broad faith in humanity, unmarked either by the high Anglicanism of one section of the University or by the liberal Anglicanism of another. His circle of friends had included men of as different outlooks as Matthew Arnold, James Anthony Froude, the historian, and Arthur Hugh Clough.

He already wrote a vivid, fluent, and copious English full of gallicisms, near-slang expressions, and elaborate metaphors. His dispatches were always to be too long and seldom as a result to make the mark that their best points warranted. They were never dull. Something of his style may perhaps be traced to the influence of Carlyle, which was strong among the Balliol men of his day. It may explain his over-frequent use of the term philistine for pretentious, ignorant people and his doctrine of the great man, who alone could make the opinion of a nation effective, as well as the declamatory note that crept into his letters and dispatches.

He came down from Oxford, eager to enter the world of affairs, ambitious, exuberant, at times imperious and yet a young man of great charm. He had a short career as clerk in the Privy Council Office and was also engaged as correspondent for the *Morning Chronicle*. This post he never took up. Much to his delight the fall of Lord Palmerston opened the diplomatic service to him. In 1853 he was nominated unpaid attaché at Vienna. He was then 27. In 1858 he was appointed paid attaché at Berlin and then from 1866 to 1876 served in turn at Frankfurt-with-Darmstadt, Stuttgart, and Munich. In 1876 his appointment to Lisbon made him head of a first-class mission.

The Europe into which Morier now stepped as a fully responsible diplomatic agent comprised countries different from each other in much more varied ways than they are today, yet at the top, through their ruling classes, with their common classical education, their bookish and reflective traditions, more closely knit together. It was a Europe that could take for granted, whether it measured this in industrial progress or by the criteria of its own cultural tradition, its superiority to the rest of the world. Nor would the assumption be challenged. The minds of those who shaped the relationships between the European countries were thus accustomed to work in a narrow and well-defined intellectual field. In the seventies and eighties this intellectual field was broadening and its frontiers loosening.

The intrusion of Europe into Africa and Asia confronted men of Morier's generation increasingly with the problems of non-European peoples.

Morier's response to these problems was typical. He accepted Europe's 'civilizing' mission and he was impatient with anyone who was not 'progressive' and eager to seize the opportunities to further economic development that he believed his generation was offered. He was inclined to equate civilization with trade and progress with railways, shipping lines, and banks. Trade, tariffs, and railways were to bulk large in Morier's future career. He had inherited a commercial tradition, but he also brought to Lisbon some commercial experience: since, while he was at Berlin, he had been sent to Vienna to help to negotiate the Anglo-Austrian commercial treaty of 1865. He belonged, moreover, to a circle of men who were proud to call themselves disciples of Cobden and he was himself in 1866 a founder member of the Cobden Club.[1] In 1872 he was still a member of its committee. Sir Louis Mallet, John Morley, Thomas Huxley, and Sir Henry Maine formed a circle at the Athenæum among whom he was welcome when in England. Nor was it without significance for his interest in free-trade economics that his wife was born Alice Peel.

When Morier arrived in Lisbon he claimed also to be an imperialist in foreign policy. By this he meant to express his belief in the need to maintain and assert the power of Great Britain and of her empire in India and elsewhere. That he was not an imperialist in an annexationist sense is made clear by his letter to Lord Salisbury of 18 January 1879 (see below, pp. 83, 85–6). Another club in London to which he belonged—indeed, had founded, in 1850[2]—was the Cosmopolitan, and it expressed his imperialist interests. The circle of which he was there the centre included Chichester Fortescue, Ralph Lingen, Lord Arthur Russell, and Austen Henry Layard, all of whom had notable official or diplomatic careers; W. C. Cartwright, a liberal M.P. (1868–85) and a landowner of independent means who had been in Rome at the time of the Vatican Council, was to write

---

[1] This was the name given in 1866, after the death of Cobden, to the reorganized Political Economy Club, founded in 1821.
[2] 'For the young duke of Nassau and Roggenbach', see Morier to Sir Henry Ponsonby, 6 Feb. 1889, R.A. I 57/16.

INTRODUCTION

a book on the Jesuits, and had something of the journalist's flair for being at interesting places at the right moment, though he was nicknamed Cartwrong by his friends; and Henry Reeve, the editor of the *Edinburgh Review*. The chief friend among those who shared Morier's belief in a strong foreign policy was Lord Odo Russell, the brother of Lord Arthur. Their mother was that Lady William Russell who influenced so many men of the mid-Victorian generation and was the friend of Morier's father. Lord Odo Russell was the closest of Morier's diplomatic friends and the only one of all his correspondents whom he addressed by Christian name;[1] he was 'dear Odo' or 'dearest Odo'. In temperament Lord Odo, the graceful man of the world, and the ebullient, tempestuous Morier had little in common; but they respected each other's knowledge of Germany and Europe, and Morier's long letters had a patient and sympathetic reading from Lord Odo, both when he was at Rome and later when he was ambassador at Berlin. He once expressed the opinion that Morier was 'the first man in our profession'.[2] Finally, there was George Goschen (then a banker, but later chancellor of the exchequer), another friend, who once told him that they two were the only men in England who combined faith in economic principle with imperial feeling.[3] Morier's imperialism led, however, to a breach with the Cobden Club in 1878.[4]

To understand Morier as he was when he arrived in Lisbon, one more subject must be faced. Morier saw his life as a battle with Bismarck and the assertive Prussianism associated with him. It is difficult to know how seriously to take this antagonism. From Morier's side, it becomes more easily intelligible if one understands that his outlook was as much European as English. He was at home in almost any continental country and spoke

---

[1] Morier's letters to Lord Odo Russell were kept by Lord Odo with his personal archive preserved at Woburn Abbey and now deposited in the Public Record Office; see F.O. 918/55. See also G. Blakiston, *Lord William Russell and his wife* (1972).
[2] Jowett so reports him in writing to Lord Rosebery, 11 Apr. 1876, Rosebery papers, box 63. [3] To Jowett, 27 Jan. 1878; see below, p. 122.
[4] I cannot establish this date, since I cannot find a complete set of the Club's published *Proceedings*. The only set reported to be complete (that of the Dundee Public Library) turned out to have a gap between 1876 and 1883. My conjectural date is based on evidence that he was not a member after 1881 and on the correspondence of 1878 over the eastern question.

French and German as easily as English. Moreover, he knew Germany extremely well. His special knowledge of German affairs had been shown in writings on the Schleswig-Holstein question, Hessian land tenure, Prussian land reform, and Prussian local government, and on the *Kulturkampf*. It was acknowledged when he was employed by Lord Granville in 1870 to report on the state of feeling towards Germany in Alsace-Lorraine.[1] And politically Morier was a liberal.

The battle becomes more easily intelligible from Bismarck's side if one understands his hostility to the Crown Prince and above all to the Crown Princess, Victoria, the eldest daughter of Queen Victoria; Morier had enjoyed since their marriage in 1858 the affection and esteem of this young couple. 'Bismarck hates Morier', the Crown Princess had written to her mother in 1867, 'because he knows that you are partial to him and that Fritz and I like him—and also for political reasons.'[2] The fact was that Morier belonged to a liberal, anti-Bismarckian circle in Germany, which included Baron von Stockmar, the Prince Consort's counsellor and friend, his son Ernst von Stockmar, Baron von Bunsen, son of a former Prussian minister in London, Baron von Roggenbach, the liberal minister of the Grand Duke of Baden and the creator of Strasbourg University in its late nineteenth-century form, and Professor Heinrich Geffcken, who had been a fellow student with the Crown Prince at Bonn and was later representative of the three Hanseatic towns at Berlin and then London, becoming Professor of Jurisprudence at Strasbourg when their separate diplomatic representation ended. More loosely attached to the group were General Albrecht von Stosch, Walter Baron von Loe, and the novelist Gustav Freytag. The circle had connections, through Roggenbach, with the Princess of Wied, of whom Roggenbach was the secret husband only acknowledged on his deathbed. Her daughter was the Queen of Rumania, wife of the Hohen-

---

[1] *The Dano-German Conflict and Lord Russell's Despatch of 1862* (1863), anonymous pamphlet; *Parliamentary Papers* (1870), lxvii, 'Reports of H.M. Representatives respecting Tenure of Land in the Several Countries of Europe', pp. 737–71; *The Agrarian Legislation of Prussia during the Present Century* (1870) and *Local Government in Germany and England with Special Reference to Recent Legislation on the Subject in Prussia* (1875), both pamphlets published by the Cobden Society; 'Prussia and the Vatican . . .', *Macmillan's Magazine*, xxx (1874), 464, 559; xxxi (1874–5), 72, 261.

[2] The Crown Princess to the Queen, 11 Sept. 1867, R.A. Z 20/41.

zollern king. It was Morier who recommended to the Crown Prince Dr. Hinzpeter, to be tutor to the future William II. Hinzpeter was regarded by Morier as also a member of the group. The circle revolved round the Crown Prince and Princess. The latter denied that it was a ' "Faction" to overthrow B[ismarck]', but admitted that it was

a set of *wise*, superior, *intelligent*, *independent* men deeply devoted to Germany who *studied* and watched his affairs with *deep interest*—criticizing it is true—what appeared to them mistaken—but never actively interfering in anything. [There was] a simple interchange of opinions,—in which the Emperor Frederick [she was writing in 1888] took part, or not—but which was not a *regular* or *continued* practice.[1]

In this letter-writing Morier certainly had a part. Much of it seems to have been conducted over pseudonyms and with circumlocutions. Roggenbach was Ryebrook, a translation of his name, and Morier was Emmschen in writing to Ernst von Stockmar, his dearest Anna—one cannot think with the hope of baffling any serious censor, but perhaps with the idea of foiling passing curiosity. Bismarck was Z or Zornebock, 'a great Pomeranian Giant who had no hair on his head and made everybody uncomfortable'.[2] After Ernst von Stockmar died in 1886, Morier wrote fortnightly letters to his widow. They went in the diplomatic bag from St. Petersburg, where by now Morier was stationed, to Berlin, and at Morier's request were always conveyed to her by hand.[3] A curious air of conspiracy hangs over the members of this group.

Morier's first serious clash with Bismarck occurred the year before he took up his appointment at Lisbon. The occasion was the war scare of 1875. Morier's part is difficult to judge, since it is not really known and probably cannot be known how much deliberate purpose there was behind the panic, and what the direction of that purpose was. Morier's appointment by Lord Derby immediately afterwards to Lisbon may have given a colour of justification to Bismarck's resentment. Rumours of

---

[1] The Empress Frederick to the Queen, undated, bound with letters of 1888, R.A. Z 280/18.
[2] To Lord Odo Russell, 7 May 1875, F.O. 918/55.
[3] See Sir E. Malet to Lord Salisbury, 14 Apr. 1888, and the Queen to Salisbury, commenting on it, 20 Apr. 1888, Salisbury papers, A/61, fo. 245 and A/45, fo. 65.

war arose out of the high language that Germany had used to Belgium and France, first over the pronouncements of their bishops about the German *Kulturkampf*, and then over alleged military preparations. France gave back accusation for accusation. Apprehension and disquiet were astir all over Europe when Morier, then chargé d'affaires at Munich, received a letter from Dr. Geffcken, who at Strasbourg was in a good position to report war preparations. The letter was dated 27 March 1875 and warned him of the imminence of danger and of the likelihood that Bismarck would seek to extricate himself from the difficulties of the *Kulturkampf* by plunging Germany into another war; not directly, for Germany would need to seem to be attacked, but by an attempt to destroy Belgium. Morier passed this warning on to Lord Derby, then foreign secretary. Derby should have received his letter on the last day of March or the first of the new month. On 5 April the *Kölnische Zeitung* denounced the increase in French armaments and on the 8th the Berlin *Post* published the article, ending with the question 'Is war in sight?' It was also announced that the Emperor of Germany had abandoned his intention of visiting the King of Italy. On the 12th Derby delivered the first of his pointed warnings to the German ambassador, Count Münster. In London Morier's was not the only letter, nor its contents the only information, which led Derby to tell Münster that French fears of a German attack were justified; for Derby could draw his own conclusions from a series of incidents in German-Belgian and German-French relations, all of them reported in the newspapers. But Morier, meanwhile, had drawn attention to his sympathies by breakfasting with the Crown Prince and Princess on Munich railway station (13 April—the Prince and Princess were passing through on their way to Italy)[1] and shortly afterwards visiting them at Innsbruck[2] (8 May—they were on the way back from Italy). He adjured the Prince to use his influence to prevent such a terrible calamity as another European war. Between 13 April and 8 May Morier had received further letters from Stockmar and Geffcken (4 May), now putting Belgium in the background and bringing forward the possibility of a direct German attack on France. Again

[1] To Derby, 14 Apr. 1875.
[2] To Derby, 9 May 1875; cf. to Odo Russell, 7 May 1875, F.O. 918/55.

Morier passed on the warnings to Derby together with Geffcken's plea that Derby should 'seek to convince Count Peter Shuvalov, the Russian ambassador in London, that Russia and Britain must unite all their efforts to secure peace'.[1] The letter may have been received by Derby on the morning of the 7th, and on 8 May official instructions went to Lord Odo Russell for combined diplomatic action with Russia in Berlin. But Derby already on 3 May had inquired of Lord Odo Russell whether any reliance could be placed on the intervention of Russia, and on the 5th had written to the Queen about action with Russia, and on the 6th to Disraeli.

However important, or unimportant, Morier's intervention was, it was known and it drew upon him Bismarck's ill will. At the least, Morier had helped to spread suspicion that Bismarck entertained notions of a preventive war and had helped 'in the arraignment of the Chancellor before Europe' and before the German royal family, which was the way the Russian and British representations at Berlin were described at the time. Both these actions were resented by Bismarck as unjust, either because they were so, or because he deluded himself that they were, or because he wished to delude Europe that they were. On a different interpretation of events, Morier had helped to foil Bismarck's design of releasing war or the threat of it upon Europe yet once again.[2] In any event, Morier rather than Lord Odo incurred Bismarck's ill will, since he had so officiously associated himself with the Crown Prince and the advice the latter shortly afterwards probably gave at the German court.

Morier's appointment to Lisbon, in place of Lord Lytton, who was made Viceroy of India, was thought by his daughter to be due to the 'gratitude' of Lord Derby for Morier's services in the crisis of 1875. But he already stood high in Derby's esteem, and Morier's wife[3] was an intimate friend of Lady Derby and brought her husband into a close-knit social circle. Lady Derby, who had married Lord Derby as her second

---

[1] Lady Wemyss's draft of her continuation of the *Memoirs and Letters of the Right Hon. Sir Robert Morier, G.C.B.* (1911).

[2] See W. Taffs, 'The War Scare of 1875', *Slavonic Review*, ix (Dec. 1930), 335–49, and Lady Wemyss, *Memoirs*, ii. 323 ff.

[3] She was the daughter of Lady Alice (*née* Kennedy, daughter of the Marquis of Ailsa) and General Peel (younger brother of the great Sir Robert).

husband, was Lord Salisbury's stepmother. The appointment perhaps needs no further explanation than the appreciation by his chief of Morier's abilities, without—given the personal friendship and confidence—that fear of appointing an overzealous agent which was to hold Lord Granville back from appointing Morier to Constantinople in 1884.[1] His daughter was to remember Lisbon, where she spent five years of her girlhood as a period of great happiness, where there seemed little work and, except occasionally, little pressure. Certainly the appointment gave Morier pleasure and a sense of security.

'It is an immense boon', he wrote to Sir Louis Mallet, in the first flush of pleasure,

> to jump into a *first class* mission (1,300 a year pension instead of 900) and thus to get rid once for all of any chance of being sent to Buenos Aires, Copenhagen, Stockholm and the rest. Now they *can* only offer me America (which I would like) Spain or an Embassy. Beginning diplomacy at 27, I have now not only caught up but [out]distanced all my competitors and can look quietly forward to my Embassy as a certainty, unless I make some grievous fiasco.[2]

He had, however, been too long the big fish in the small pond of German dynastic politics easily to make the transition that was demanded of him in the second part of his career that now opened. He thought himself more important in European and world politics than in fact he ever became.

Morier arrived in Portugal on 20 April 1876. The Prince of Wales had been touring India during the winter of 1875–6, and on his way home was to pay a visit to the King of Portugal. Morier, therefore, hastened to take up his post and present his credentials before the Prince's arrival. On 28 April he was received in audience by the King and Queen of Portugal and the Algarves.[3] He remained at Lisbon during the Prince of Wales's visit through a series of brilliant court festivities, but on 7 May embarked with him on board the *Serapis* to return to England.[4]

---

[1] Granville to Gladstone, 15 Aug. and 14 Sept. 1884, A. Ramm (ed.), *Political Correspondence of Mr. Gladstone and Lord Granville, 1876–86* (1962), ii. 227, 256.

[2] To Sir Louis Mallet (permanent under-secretary at the India Office), 14 Mar. 1876.

[3] To Derby, nos. 54, 66, 68 confidential, 20 and 28 Apr. 1876, F.O. 63/1034.

[4] To Derby, nos. 75 and 76, 7 May 1876, F.O. 63/1034.

The health of his father, who in the preceding winter at the age of ninety-two had suffered from congestion of the lungs, his return to Germany to fetch his family and pay good-bye visits to his innumerable friends and finally a severe attack of gout, which for many weary weeks of a hot summer laid him up in Paris—detained him longer than he had expected, so that it was only on August 12th 1876 that he and his family arrived at Lisbon.[1]

The staff which then served him in the Legation comprised only three men—no clerks, no private secretaries and, needless to say, no typists. There was a secretary of Legation, G. F. Gould, brought from Stockholm at Morier's request, to change places with R. G. Watson in October 1876. Gould was replaced, when he went as minister to Belgrade in July 1878, by Dudley E. Saurin. There was a second secretary, in turn, Sir G. F. Bonham until December 1877, the Hon. W. J. G. Napier, and A. G. Vansittart (1879). When Napier was temporarily employed in the Foreign Office in 1879–81 and Vansittart, who was by rank only a third secretary, took his leave, Walter Baring was added as the second man. And there was a translator, J. C. Ff. Duff. Saurin had a high notion of the prerogatives of a first secretary and caused much trouble by refusing to do his share of copying and cyphering when there was pressure of work in the chancery. Both Saurin and Morier appealed to Lord Granville, by 1880 foreign secretary, Morier asking that Saurin should be promoted to be head of the chancery of a first-class embassy.[2] But he did not go until March 1882 and Morier himself was promoted first. Five years of fruitful activity were to pass before this.

As for other practical things: in 1876 neither minister nor Legation staff lived in the Legation building, where the chancery and rooms to receive callers were, but each man had his separate house.

Lord Lytton's magnificent ideas and romantic imagination had caused him to plan grand additions to the Legation. A huge banqueting hall and extensive reception rooms were in the course of construction, but the Treasury grant being small and the incapacity of the Portuguese masons, charged with the execution of these vast

[1] Lady Wemyss's draft of her continuation of the *Memoirs*.
[2] To Granville, no. 138, 11 Nov. 1880, F.O. 63/1094; from Granville, no. 1103. 27 Nov. 1880, F.O. 63/1092.

designs, great, the unfinished buildings after the autumnal rains stood under water, while the drains were out of order and the roof leaked. The house being thus uninhabitable until the necessary repairs could be carried out, Morier and his family had to take refuge at Cintra, where they rented the Quinta Vianna, a picturesque old country house which was to be their much loved home for many summers to come.[1]

'Cintra is very beautiful and the walks and the donkey rides about it lovely', Morier wrote to Jowett in the course of the autumn. 'We have a large garden or rather park, there being about forty acres of the noblest wood, trees of every kind . . . I do not dislike my work here. There is more of it than I expected and it is real work, not mere dilettante work like my work in Germany, which only consisted in writing general views on the situation.'[2] At the end of October, Morier and his family moved into the Lisbon Legation house for the winter until the following March.

When Morier took up his post, King Luis, a second cousin of Queen Victoria, had been on the throne for fifteen years, having succeeded his elder brother in 1861. A kindly, well-intentioned monarch, imbued with all the traditional Coburg reverence for parliamentary institutions, he had also a somewhat anti-clerical bias acquired as the son-in-law of King Victor Emanuel of Italy. King Luis was to have no fewer than five ministries during Morier's five years at Lisbon. In 1876 his government was headed by António Maria de Fontes Pereira de Melo as president of the council. General Fontes had gone into politics from the army. Morier wrote of him, he 'has a great Parliamentary reputation for his quickness in debate, his ready repartee, and his mastery of tactics. He likes the dramatic side of politics and is restlessly active in the way of public meetings, railway station ovations, and the like'. He

[1] Lady Wemyss's draft; cf. to Derby, no. 138, 28 Sept., and no. 141, 11 Oct., no. 142, 16 Oct. 1876, F.O. 63/1035. The two wings, built out into the garden, that on the river side containing a drawing-room (or ball-room) and smoking-room and that on the other side a banqueting-room, still stand. The wings were linked by a covered way so badly placed as to shut out the light from the existing dining-room.

[2] To Jowett, 2 Nov. 1876; the letter was begun on 31 Oct.; it exists in a typed version only. I quote an earlier part of the same letter on p. 53 below and a later part on p. 18 below.

cared for popularity, his manners were cavalier and his temper domineering. He liked show and was given to brilliant schemes. He disliked work and steady application and little ever remained of his brilliant schemes but a large amount of political corruption. His strength lay 'in his conformity with the national type'.[1] Very different was his political partner, João de Andrade Corvo, in charge of both foreign and colonial affairs. From his first interview Morier liked Corvo, an 'intelligent man with a frank manner'.[2] Later he described him as a professor, 'a literary and scientific man of real intellectual power', who kept in the background and had little taste for parliamentary life. He rarely left his study but, when occasion demanded, was 'a very powerful and eloquent orator'. He cared little for personal popularity and more for actuality than for show. He was given to probing to the bottom of superficially confused and difficult situations and in a clear-headed way to finding solutions.[1] In short, and in Morier's recollection, he was 'one of the finest, most patriotic and most unselfish men I have ever had the privilege of knowing'.[3] António de Serpa Pimentel was minister of finance. Serpa, a mathematician and economist was the third element of strength in the cabinet. These three were 'certainly the ablest and most energetic statesmen now in Portugal'.[4]

Their party, the *Regeneradores*, had an overwhelming majority in the Chambers. The Opposition was composed of the *Histórico* and *Reformista* parties which, in September 1876, soon after Morier arrived, effected a fusion and created the *Progressista* party. Though reputed to be against tariffs and generally pro-British, it failed to formulate any serious programme or to concentrate its parliamentary forces for any seriously calculated attack. On the contrary, on the occasion of the opening of the new parliamentary session of 1877, the party absented itself from the Chamber of Deputies and remained away for another three weeks.[5] There was in Portugal no notion of an Opposition

[1] To Lord Salisbury, no. 68 commercial, most confidential, 20 Dec. 1878, F.O. 63/1083.
[2] To Derby, no. 133, 14 Sept. 1876, F.O. 63/1035.
[3] To Jowett, autobiographical letter of 1889.
[4] To Derby, no. 14, 3 Mar. 1877, F.O. 63/1062.
[5] To Derby, nos. 128 and 133, 11 and 14 Sept. 1876, F.O. 63/1035, no. 3 Mar. 1877, F.O. 63/1062.

whose function was to provide an alternative government. Parliamentary politics were 'frothy and unreal'.

The so-called parties in this country [wrote Morier on a later occasion] are all of them offshoots of the great liberal coalition which defeated Dom Miguel and established definitely in Portugal constitutional, in opposition to absolute, forms of Government. The result is that under the name of parties they are really mere political coteries under the leadership of the coterie chiefs, the object of the coteries being to come into power and the business of the chief to distribute the prizes of office to the followers who have helped him to power. Whichever coterie is in office represents the conservative element of politics, whichever is in opposition deals in the commonplaces of radical reform.[1]

The normal political business of the country was conducted in the political clubs without the outside world being let into the secret of what was transacted in them.[2] There was always the danger that the so-called parliamentary Opposition, being too long deprived of the fruits of office, would become a revolutionary group and aim at overthrowing the dynasty as well as the ministry, or at least conspire to do so.[3] The political reality in 1876 was not the strength of the Opposition, but that Fontes, Corvo, Serpa, and their colleagues had already been in office for five years, were tired of power, had exhausted their political strength, and did not wish to continue in office much longer.[4]

At last, on 3 March 1877, the Fontes–Corvo–Serpa ministry resigned, although it retained the support of parliament and public—a not unusual happening in a country where elections were 'made' by the Ministry of the Interior.[1] It was succeeded by a stop-gap ministry under the Marquis (in 1878 Duke) de Ávila. He was president of the Chamber of Peers and the leader of the most powerful and active group in it; a man with a reputation for political sobriety and dislike of extremes. His function was 'the recognised one of being ready at any moment to form a ministry when no other combination' was possible. Morier believed that the retiring ministry hoped de Ávila would carry two difficult measures of theirs through the

[1] To Salisbury, no. 35, 3 June 1879, F.O. 63/1084.
[2] To Salisbury, no. 23 commercial, 7 June 1879, F.O. 63/1091.
[3] To Salisbury, no. 37 most confidential, 29 Apr. 1878, F.O. 63/1075.
[4] To Derby, no. 133, 14 Sept. 1876, F.O. 63/1035.

Chamber of Peers, where he commanded a majority and they did not, and then let them come back.[1] De Ávila was joined by two men of ability: Carlos Bento da Silva (for Finance) and João Gualberto de Barros e Cunha (for Public Works).

Morier proved a true prophet. After nine months Fontes, Corvo, and Serpa duly returned to power with new discipline and cohesion among their supporters.[2] At the end of January 1878 Fontes became president of the council and minister for war, Corvo minister for foreign affairs, and Serpa for finance. But Tomás António Ribeiro Ferreira now joined the government as minister for colonies. He had been for some time director (permanent under-secretary) of the Ministry of Justice as well as a member of the Chamber of Deputies, zealously supporting Corvo. He was a poet of some merit, but was chiefly known as a notorious anglophobe and denunciator of the 'ancient alliance'. Fontes accordingly went out of his way to assure Morier that his appointment, 'far from throwing obstacles in the way of that friendly co-operation in the work of placing our colonial relations on a more satisfactory footing than they had hitherto been', would assist, since it had been made a condition that the impressionable and imaginative Ribeiro should heartily identify himself with Corvo's policy, of which 'friendly co-operation with Britain was an essential part'.[3] Other ministers were António Rodrigues Sampaio (Interior), Augusto Cesar Barjoma de Freitas (Justice), and Lourenço António de Carvalho (Public Works).

The Fontes–Corvo–Serpa group did not, however, return with such promising prospects as they had hoped. This was due to the malice of Barros e Cunha, who exposed, during the debate which preceded de Ávila's fall, the corruption which had prevailed when they were last in power.[4] Moreover, although 'an advanced liberal and reformer', he refused to allow himself to be captured by the *Progressista* and like de Ávila strenuously resisted identification with them. The mediocre Braamcamp remained undisputed leader of the *Progressista* and the Fontes–Corvo–Serpa administration could not succeed the de Ávila

[1] To Derby, no. 16, 3 Mar. 1877, F.O. 63/1062.
[2] To Derby, no. 94, 25 Nov. 1877, F.O. 63/1063.
[3] To Derby, no. 144, 31 Oct. 1876, no. 149 most confidential, 19 Nov. 1876, F.O. 63/1035; no. 16 confidential, 31 Jan. 1878, F.O. 63/1075.
[4] To Derby, no. 15, 31 Jan. 1878, F.O. 63/1075.

ministry as *Regeneradores* succeeding *Progressista*. It is clear now, as it was not to Morier, that these were all men essentially disliking party politics and thinking of themselves not as party leaders, nor as national leaders, but as ministers of the King, appointed to do the King's business and to take what rewards were available for themselves and their friends. Something like the Spanish system of *turnismo*, described below, existed. Morier himself wrote: 'By a kind of tacit agreement which has of course never been expressly formulated, the coterie that has had its fill of the loaves and fishes of office is bound to make room for another and thus to allow of an alternation taking place which shall keep the professional politicians tolerably satisfied all round.'[1]

Morier, like any other diplomatic representative—though he regarded it as his peculiar misfortune—was liable to have his work spoilt by a change of government. He began at Lisbon with men, like Corvo, nominally of the *Regeneradores* or, like de Ávila, of no party. With them Morier brought his work to some sort of conclusion in the shape of the signed Goa and Lorenço Marques treaties. But before these treaties could be put into effect, they had to be ratified. Their ratification he was obliged to secure from a fresh set of men belonging to the *Progressista* party—the opponents of the ministry with whom he had so far co-operated. This last, the second Fontes–Corvo–Serpa ministry, fell on 30 May 1879.[2] The eight years of *Regeneradores* rule had brought to Portugal not only roads and railways but also a growing budgetry deficit. Serpa, Morier believed, had broken under the attacks made upon him for offering palliatives, instead of imposing drastic measures of financial reform and additional taxation. He had 'thrown up the cards'. Corvo had joined Serpa in wishing to resign, since he believed drastic measures were necessary. The two men had then prevented Fontes from simply reconstructing the ministry. A fourth man, Lourenço de Carvalho, simply wished to resign before his maladministration of the Ministry of Public Works was exposed. He had been appointed, Morier reported,[1] as a means of bribing his father-in-law, Count Ribeiro, to drop his anglophobia, and had proved incapable of managing a department.

[1] To Salisbury, no. 35, 3 June 1879, F.O. 63/1084.
[2] To Salisbury, no. 35, 3 June 1879, and telegram, 30 May, F.O. 63/1084.

INTRODUCTION

So the Braamcamp ministry succeeded. On 30 May 1879, Anselmo José Braamcamp, 'a very second-rate minister',[1] 'an aged, amiable and anaemic mediocrity',[2] was appointed president of the council and minister for foreign affairs and thenceforward acted the part of prime minister. Shortly afterwards the Chamber was dissolved, but the elections did not shake the new government; for, as was indicated above, whoever controlled the Ministry of the Interior normally won a general election. The new men held power for nearly two years, from 30 May 1879 until 21 March 1881, and it was with them that Morier had to complete the work he had begun in 1876. But this government in turn fell before the work was finished, brought down by the ignominy of the anti-British disorders of Sunday, 13 March 1881. When the Braamcamp administration had come in, a reversal of the policy of 'truckling to Britain' was expected of it, but it too had been drawn, whether by Morier's skill, or by its own interest, as head of a small power, in not alienating the government of a powerful neighbour, or by a calculated readiness to pay the price for maintaining the 'ancient alliance', into the work of dispelling the haze of traditional claims and formulating, in treaty terms, real relationships with its colonial neighbour. The disorders of 13 March happened when a public meeting to protest against the ratification of the Anglo-Portuguese treaty about Lourenço Marques—a republican meeting—had forcibly broken up another meeting—a monarchical meeting—convened to protest against the policy of the government as a whole. The incident was said anyhow to have been provoked by the government itself, because it was anxious to find in a hostile public opinion ground for not ratifying the treaty.

António Rodrigues Sampaio now took power, and formed the fifth of the ministries that succeeded each other during Morier's period at Lisbon. It was a *Regeneradores* ministry from which Fontes and Corvo, the leaders of that party, held aloof. Morier asserted that Fontes inspired and directed it all the time from behind the scenes. Sampaio was a 'plain-spoken man, who bears the reputation of straightforwardness and honesty', but without any knowledge or pretensions to knowledge of foreign

---

[1] To Derby, no. 15, 31 Jan. 1878, F.O. 63/1075.
[2] To Salisbury, no. 69 slave-trade, 6 Oct. 1879, F.O. 84/1538.

affairs. He was, like Fontes, Corvo, and Serpa, a member of the Chamber of Peers.[1] For one month, Miguel Martins d'Antas, summoned from London where he was Portuguese minister, was foreign minister until 1 May 1881. But in that year Morier's mission ended and he was moved to Madrid.

In 1876, Morier, with characteristically exaggerated professionalism, sought firm ground from which to begin his new task as one might seek to base an argument on some indisputable premiss. He formulated at the outset of his mission the essential elements in the Portuguese situation. The first of these was that Portugal was a small power. He must, therefore, as he later said, 'avoid as much as possible questions of *la grande politique*' in his intercourse with her.[2] A large part of his work was concerned with things such as Maçao slave-labour at San Thomé or the Lindsay claim. However much his head buzzed with ideas on the eastern question, he seldom alluded to it officially and was content to give vent to his views in private correspondence. His second proposition was that Portugal was bound to Britain by an 'ancient alliance' which neither state could afford to allow to lapse. Its solid basis, in nineteenth-century terms, he believed, was Portugal's need of defence against Spanish designs of Iberian union and Britain's need to have free use for her fleet of the mouth of the Tagus and the harbour of Lisbon. It meant, in short, 'independence for the Portuguese patriot and protection for the lords of Gibraltar'. 'The alliance with England', Morier had written to Jowett, 'is the sheet-anchor of Portugal's position and as we never could afford to allow anyone but a small country like Portugal which we can depend upon to hold the Tagus (which is the only station for our fleet this side of the Mediterranean) we have all the elements of a good ménage.'[3]

For the requirements of our everyday life [he wrote on another occasion] Portugal is more useful to us than Belgium—the Tagus more necessary to the Channel Fleet than Antwerp. On the other hand, the fulfilment of our international obligations and Treaty obligations towards Belgium is hardly conceivable except at the cost

[1] To Granville, nos. 80, 31 Mar., F.O. 63/1130, and 82, 3 Apr. 1881, F.O. 63/1131.
[2] To Derby, no. 23 most confidential, 13 Mar. 1878, F.O. 63/1075.
[3] To Jowett, 2 Nov. 1876, see above, p. 12, n. 2.

of a maximum expenditure of National Force. The protection of Portugal against the only conceivable danger which threatens her, the daydreams of Spanish adventurers, would require a minimum expenditure of National Force—no more than perfectly decided language consistently held from the first dawning of impending danger.[1]

Fear for her fleet and for Cuba would be sufficient to restrain Spain.

Morier's third proposition was that Britain and Portugal were, in Africa and India, neighbours, and not only neighbours, but the only white rulers and so to all intents and purposes joint rulers. That the two nations divided white power in India between themselves—in however unequal shares—was a fair, if unusual, observation.[2] It needs, however, an effort of the imagination to recall the situation before the partition of Africa, only ten years later, in order to accept as not wholly inaccurate for black Africa Morier's description of Britain and Portugal as the 'two appointed guardians' of Africa, 'this rich and interesting ward' as to the management of whose property and education they 'ought to be of one mind'.[3]

This part of Morier's formulation of the facts of the situation led him, not to a territorial, but to a commercial line of thought. When Morier wrote to Louis Mallet of his pleasure in his appointment, he had added: 'But more than all this I cannot but hope that at Lisbon I may be able to take up our commercial policy and work it to some purpose. Of course this sounds chimerical . . . *but* there are some very important things the Colonial Office want from Portugal and I shall take my stand on the do ut des, facio ut facias and say *I must have an equivalent to offer* and won't get things done by bullying.'[4]

The first proposition had indicated to Morier what he should avoid, the second proposition looked to contingencies, to possibilities rather than actualities. It was the third proposition which was the starting-point for policy-making. Morier believed he was met here more than half-way by Corvo, in whose hands he saw taking shape a policy of opening the

[1] Memorandum, Baden-Baden, 6 Apr. 1876, part of Morier's reflections on his conversation at Baden-Baden with Derby, before taking up his post.
[2] To Derby, no. 23 most confidential, 13 Mar. 1878, F.O. 63/1075.
[3] To Derby, no. 43 consular, 14 Sept. 1876, F.O. 84/1447.
[4] To Mallet, 14 Mar. 1876.

Portuguese possessions to European trade—'a colonial policy altogether different from anything which has before been known in Portugal'. In 1876, 'hermetically sealed to the rest of the world by prohibitive Tariffs, exclusive rights of navigation for Portuguese ships which had no existence, and impotent monopolies, the vast possessions of Portugal in Africa [and her small enclaves in India, he might have added] were lost to mankind'. Instead of this absolute seclusion 'the treasure-houses' of Africa and India were to be thrown open 'to the competitive energy of cosmopolitan commerce'.[1] This was the starting-point of Morier's African and Indian policy.

At the time when Morier took up his mission, Britain was not especially popular in Portugal, and her unpopularity increased. African travellers attacked in virulent language, in their books, the Portuguese African administration. The newspapers of the British African colonies were openly hostile and covetous in their attitude to the Portuguese. Portuguese ministers suspected that the assurances of support and adherence to the 'ancient alliance' would not be made good if in the *casus foederis* British interests should chance not to be engaged. Even Morier was apt to lecture Corvo on the duties of white men to black men.[2] There exists, among Morier's drafts of his dispatches, an exceedingly long dispatch (thirty-five foolscap sheets closely written on both sides) about British unpopularity, dated September 1878, written not as a draft on the right-hand half of the page only, but as a fair copy straight across the sheet, but presumably not sent—wisely, since Morier's imaginative writing (he purported to be reconstructing a Portuguese argument) had escaped control and had no longer any obvious stopping-place. It began by attempting an analysis of the grounds of this unpopularity and ended in an invented Portuguese indictment of Britain's particular misdemeanours in Africa. 'The general soreness which prevailed in Portugal on the subject of the inter-colonial relations of Great Britain and Portugal' was especially strong among those most eager to cultivate the traditional friendship. It was partly due to the natural antagonism 'between workers and dreamers, between a nation bent upon making the most of the present and the future and one living wholly on the

---

[1] To Salisbury, no. 4 slave-trade, 18 Jan. 1879, F.O. 84/1537.
[2] To Derby, no. 23 most confidential, 13 Mar. 1878, F.O. 63/1075.

recollections of the past and *fainéantise* of a morbid introspection'. 'There were', he wrote, 'on the [British] side toilers and moilers, gold diggers, sheep farmers, stock breeders, explorers and missionaries with an eye to business—on the [Portuguese] side a procession of images decked out in mediaeval trappings, Dons Enriquo, Bartolomeos de Dias, Vascos da Gama, de Castros, with tattered worshippers burning incense before them and holding aloft the ghostly semblance of the banner which, three centuries ago, swept the Indian Seas.' Against this antagonism, which accounted for nine-tenths of the soreness between Britain and Portugal, he believed nothing could be done. It was a poison in the air whose disappearance could only be hoped for, when the intercolonial relations of the two countries had been actually improved. The remaining one-tenth of the soreness had nothing, he believed, to do with Europe, but only with Africa. As far as sentiment went, it arose from the chauvinism of the British colonial politicians and press and the habits of British missionaries, 'who made the Portuguese the villains of the piece in the sensational missionary dramas acted at spring meetings for the benefit of Exeter Hall in which Portuguese vice is used as the foil to enhance the lustre of negro virtue'. As far as acts went, it arose from the British failure to recognize the Portuguese claims to the Congo territory between 8° and 5° 12′ south. 'By the threat of broadsides', Morier imagined the Portuguese saying, 'from your monster ships we are kept out of property which as undoubtedly belongs to us as the Isle of Wight belongs to the British Crown'. Britain argued that only actual occupation gave a right, refusing to admit Portugal's *de jure* claim. She prevented her from achieving *de facto* rule but, nevertheless, whenever atrocities happened made Portugal responsible for them. As far as acts went, the soreness arose in the second place from the incident at San Thomé—the Portuguese possession on the equator at the mouth of the river Gaboon—where Morier believed that Britain had unjustifiably accepted negro, to the exclusion of Portuguese, evidence and wrongly assumed that slave-labour and the slave-trade existed there.

It was not, however, until 1880 that the tide began to set seriously against Britain in Portugal and 'the excessive demonstrations of intimacy and friendship' for Portugal from the

French Republic began to influence Morier's negotiations with the Portuguese government.[1] In 1877 the French minister at Lisbon, Count Armand, a Bonapartist, resigned on the retirement of MacMahon and was replaced by de Laboulaye, an ardent republican; but as long as the *Regeneradores* were in power de Laboulaye had little personal standing. The advent of Braamcamp and the failure to ratify the Lorenço Marques treaty, the breakdown of the Congo treaty negotiations, and the attacks on the British of Mariano de Carvalho—the *Progressista* leader in the Chamber of Deputies—brought him to the fore. He used his influence in turn against Corvo and the English alliance and Morier's colonial treaties. By 1881 he was using it successfully. Morier thought of his mission when it was over, since it should be measured in terms of the improvement or deterioration of Anglo-Portuguese relations, as on the whole a failure. He was right, and some of the blame for the failure lay unhappily with himself.

[1] To Granville, no. 121 confidential, 7 Oct. 1880, F.O. 63/1094.

1

INDIA: THE GOA TREATY
26 DECEMBER 1878

AT the outset of his mission Morier was concerned to clarify the meaning of the 'ancient alliance'. This was indeed ancient, but the common interests underlying it were still discernible in 1876. The link forged between the English and the Portuguese kings by the marriage of João I to Philippa, daughter of John of Gaunt, in 1387 had even then been strengthened by the common political interests of two small trading kingdoms. Both were safe towards the Atlantic but vulnerable towards the east and south. Portugal was always in danger of conquest by Castile, her eastern neighbour; England was only secure in the Atlantic or Channel if she could curb the power of the rulers of Castile or, later, of Spain. The first of the treaties of alliance customarily referred to in the nineteenth century was that signed by Richard II and João I in 1386, the year after João had routed the Castilian forces at Aljubarrota, freed Portugal from Castile, and inaugurated her century of greatness. But already in 1380 Richard II had allied with Fernando of Portugal against Castile. This alliance in turn renewed former treaties. The second of the treaties customarily referred to was signed on 23 June 1661 at the time of the marriage of Charles II to Catherine of Braganza. It was the year after Portugal had won her twenty years' struggle to recover the independence she had lost when Philip II of Spain made good his claim to her throne (1580). This treaty, too, confirmed earlier alliances including those of 1641 and 1642. It was distinguished from that of 1386 because by 1661 Portugal had acquired a colonial empire to which it also applied. Both the medieval and the modern treaties committed each ally to defend the territory of the other; that of 1386 mentioned domestic rebels, that of 1661 mentioned colonial territory. 'It is by this secret article', so ran the text of 1661, 'concluded and accorded that His Majesty of Great Britain . . . shall promise and oblige himself . . . to defend and protect all conquests or colonies belonging to the crown of Portugal against all his enemies.'[1] Both the great continental wars which Britain had fought, the War of the Spanish Succession and the Peninsular War against Napoleon, were occasions for the reaffirmation of the alliance and for its effectual working. It provided Britain with a means of ingress into the continent and to the heart of her enemy. It gave Portugal a means of saving her national existence. The alliance had been reaffirmed by Canning in 1826 and more recently by Granville (1873), but both had only spoken of the alliance in general terms. Moreover, Canning had repudiated any obligation for the colonies and Granville left them unmentioned.[2]

Morier had asked Lord Derby for an interview before he went to Lisbon in April 1876, since he was to pass through Baden-Baden where Lord and Lady Derby then were. They met accordingly and Morier asked what he should say to the Portuguese about the 'ancient alliance'.[3] The Portuguese were to be discouraged, answered Derby, from hopes for a fresh guarantee additional to those of 1386 and 1661 or

for a state of things which would in the matter of *positive* engagements place them towards us on a precisely analogous footing to that on which Belgium stands. Short of such positive treaty engagements the Portuguese Government is to be unequivocally assured that they may count on the hearty co-operation of Britain to resist any filibustering attempts of Spain to tamper with the integrity of the Portuguese crown.

In his first audience of King Luis in April 1876 Morier accordingly observed that Lord Derby 'had particularly instructed me to state unequivocally that the independence and integrity of Portugal were matters which England would not cease to consider as essential elements of her policy and that the Portuguese Crown would always be able to rely upon the co-opera-

---

[1] *Parliamentary Papers* (1871), lxxii. 520, but cf. I. Bains in *Bulletin of the Institute of Historical Research* (1942–3), p. 95.
[2] H. Temperley and L. M. Penson, *Foundations of British Foreign Policy* (1938), pp. 341–3; G. P. Gooch and H. Temperley, *British Documents on the Origins of the War* (1927), i. 94.
[3] Memorandum of conversation with Derby, 6 Apr. 1876.

tion of Great Britain in resisting unjust encroachments upon its integrity', and he made pointed allusion to the projects of Iberian union cherished by Spain.[1]

In September 1876 Corvo drew Morier's attention to talk in the Spanish newspapers of ambitions for Iberian union and observed that he had reason to believe Germany was egging Spain on in schemes of aggrandizement and ambition. Morier sought to dispel his fears with a long lecture on Bismarck's methods. He told how Bismarck left his agents to talk in the way they thought he would wish, so that he might disavow them if he chose. They were not necessarily to be believed. He said that Britain would 'always take care that the Spanish Government should not be left in doubt as to the views which prevailed in England on the subject of any schemes of the kind', and reminded Corvo of the assurances given by Granville in 1873, adding that he considered himself 'perfectly authorized to say that the views of Her Majesty's present Government in no way differed on this subject from those of their predecessors'.[2] In October the King and his foreign minister reverted to the subject and owned to a real fear of a Spanish attempt to absorb Portugal, in the event of a European war resulting from the eastern question. Morier said that Spain was preoccupied with the Cuban insurrection, which had entailed the organization of an expedition of 50,000 men under General Martinez Campos (the man to whom King Alfonso was said to owe his throne). But King Luis and Senhor Corvo replied that precisely here lay the danger: General Campos would return triumphant and seek to crown his Cuban success by an invasion of Portugal. Morier then repeated the assurances he had given in September. The Portuguese fears of Spanish aggression, he however commented, seemed like those of children 'who on a winter's night tell ghost stories to each other' and then, 'frightened at the sound of their own voices . . . mistake the rattling of a mouse behind the wainscot for the tramping of legions on the march'.[3] Morier again took opportunity to refer to Bismarck's methods and described how he created rumours by inserting a paragraph in some obscure provincial newspaper which the national

[1] To Derby, no. 68 confidential, 28 Apr. 1876, F.O. 63/1034.
[2] To Derby, no. 136 most confidential, 20 Sept. 1876, F.O. 63/1035.
[3] To Derby, no. 143 most confidential, 20 Oct. 1876, F.O. 63/1035.

papers then copied. On 8 November he repeated the assurance yet again, saying he was authorized by Lord Derby to assure Portugal 'that Great Britain would not view with indifference an attempt on the part of Spain to force Portugal into an Iberian Union and that H.M.G. considered the independence of Portugal as a question of European importance'.[1] A week earlier he had remonstrated in strong terms against an article denouncing the English alliance which, though over a pseudonym, was known to be written by Tomás Ribeiro, then director of the Ministry of Justice and a zealous supporter of the government in the Chamber of Deputies. The article had appeared in the *Commercio de Porto*, according to Morier 'the best written and most influential journal in Portugal'. As a result of his remonstrance a reply appeared in a paper identified with Corvo repudiating Ribeiro's doctrines.[2]

Over a year later, at the end of February 1878, it seemed as if the alliance might be appealed to by Portugal in order to gain representation at the congress that was already thought likely to meet to settle the eastern question; for the rumour was current that the United States (later Greece and Holland as well) intended to claim representation there.[3] D'Antas in London in fact addressed himself to Derby, and submitted the wish of Portugal to be invited to the prospective congress if it assumed a general character.[4] Morier, in discussing with Corvo Derby's friendly reply, had taken occasion again to give assurances. The temper of the British nation, he said, was such as to brook no attack upon Portugal, and he advised her to rest with confidence on the British alliance. He believed it, he reported,

to be of very great importance to us that Portugal should continue to feel that it is to the English alliance, and not to a collective European instrument that she owes her immunity from Spanish aggression. The circumstances under which we should be able to use the all important station of the Tagus for our fleet would be very different if we could only claim a joint right with other guaranteeing Powers to the hospitality of the Lisbon harbour. The present rela-

[1] From Derby, no. 68, 23 Oct. 1876, which crossed with no. 143 to him, F.O. 63/1033, and to Derby, no. 145 confidential, 8 Nov. 1876, F.O. 63/1035.
[2] To Derby, no. 144, 31 Oct. 1876, F.O. 63/1035.
[3] To Derby, no. 21 most confidential, 18 Feb. 1878, F.O. 63/1075; cf. from Derby, no. 12 confidential, 22 Mar. 1878, F.O. 63/1074.
[4] From Derby, no. 7, 1 Mar. 1878, F.O. 63/1074.

INDIA: THE GOA TREATY

tions wrapped up, as they are, in a kind of indefinite historical haze are more advantageous to us than any other combination that could be suggested.[1]

Nothing, of course, came of the notion of Portuguese representation when the congress assembled eventually at Berlin. More important were the Indian and African negotiations. In both, the 'ancient alliance' figured, and it became plain, even to Morier, that Britain was a great deal more hesitant to stand by it in this context than in its European setting. Morier later recalled in writing to Jowett how he arrived at his

new post full of vigour and ambition and strong in the belief that by basing one's policy upon strict principles of justice and equity—in a word that by applying to practical politics all that you used to teach me was contained in the words $\phi\rho\acute{o}\nu\eta\sigma\iota\varsigma$ and $\sigma\omega\phi\rho\sigma\sigma\acute{v}\nu\eta$—I would carry the world before me and inaugurate a new era in the handling of international subjects (how bitter the disillusionment). Within the first few weeks of my being there I mapped out the work which I set myself to accomplish during the limits of my stay. I found three great organic malformations—one in reference to our relations in Goa and the Portuguese possessions in India; another relative to Lorenço Marques and Delagoa Bay; the third having reference to the Congo. The two latter were aggravated by perpetual conflicts in connection with the Slave Trade.[2]

Morier's predecessor at Lisbon, Lord Lytton, had already addressed himself to 'the Indian malformation' in Anglo-Portuguese relations. On 23 November 1875 he had proposed to the Portuguese government a comprehensive settlement of all pending commercial difficulties in India and hinted that Britain might be prepared to buy Portugal's Indian colonies— Goa, Damão, and Diu in the Bombay Presidency. Bombay had been small when originally ceded to the British Crown as part of Catherine of Braganza's dowry, but had grown so as to engulf all remaining Portuguese territory. Portugal, like 'a grand seigneur who would rather starve in the workhouse than sell his old ancestral castle', had spurned this hint, made 'in

[1] To Derby, no. 23 most confidential, 13 Mar. 1878, F.O. 63/1075.
[2] Autobiographical letter of 1889. I have taken my quotations, here and on pp. 13, 28, and 33, from a typed, undated version which prefaces the material put together by Lady Wemyss for her account of 1876.

our brutal shopkeeper kind of way',[1] but welcomed the offer of a settlement of commercial difficulties.

Portugal's main grievance was the suppression of a privilege which her Factory at the British port of Surat had enjoyed since 1774. It had allowed her subjects to import goods into Surat at the same rates of duty as those paid by Indian and British residents importing goods for their own use. Portuguese merchants had abused it by importing wine and spirits into Surat and re-exporting them into adjacent parts of British India, so that they escaped the British Indian tariff with a resulting loss to the revenue estimated at £150,000 a year. The Indian government had accordingly, in 1872, suppressed the privilege. The Portuguese government had protested and claimed compensation, which had been refused.[2] The Portuguese had a further grievance in that the British Indian tariff differentiated against port in favour of burgundy and claret. The British Indian authorities on their side had grievances about the customs and excise duties levied at Goa and Portuguese India generally and, above all, about the manufacture of salt in Portuguese India and its smuggling thence into British India, where its sale was a government monopoly.

In the autumn of 1876 Morier was given an important commission by Derby, when he was instructed to bring these matters to a settlement by a commercial treaty. Morier was to prepare the way, but the actual negotiation of the treaty was to be the work of a conference between Portuguese and Indian government representatives at Bombay.[3] Morier, however, annexed the negotiation to himself and gave the affair a political importance which the Foreign Office had not intended. He was not prepared merely to fit into a pattern of ideas belonging to his predecessor, Lord Lytton, who, now Viceroy of India, intended to transfer to his new field what he had begun at Lisbon.

Morier, looking back on these events in 1889, saw himself as breaking a deadlock and setting negotiations going, by his

[1] To Jowett, autobiographical letter of 1889; cf. to Cranbrook, secretary of state for India, private, 21 May 1879.
[2] Lytton to Salisbury, then secretary of state for India, no. 193, 28 Sept. 1876, printed copy, sent to Morier by Derby on 14 Nov., is in F.O. 63/1081; for proceedings to the end of 1875, see F.O. 63/1080.
[3] From Derby, no. 17 commercial, 14 Nov. 1876, F.O. 63/1081.

inventiveness and vigour, that others had failed to bring to a conclusion and yet others persistently obstructed. He *was* inventive and did succeed in gaining a settlement, but it is important to know precisely what he contributed, so that his case should not suffer by his own strong need to justify himself. He contributed three important ideas. One was excellent. Since the Indian government was adamant in refusing compensation, Morier proposed to replace the word 'compensation' by 'substitution'; so that no acknowledgement of Portuguese 'rights' would seem to be made. The Portuguese agreed to a settlement in which a commercial treaty about customs and excise levied at Goa should be 'substituted' for the privilege suppressed at Surat.[1] Secondly, Morier contributed a large and characteristic phrase with which to describe what the Indian government had proposed as an assimilation of the customs duties of Portuguese and British India to each other. In Morier's wording this became 'a customs union' or 'Zollverein' and 'the suppression of all customs frontiers by land and sea between the British and Portuguese possessions'.[2] The Indian government protested that this was more than it had intended. Morier insisted and got his way. The final treaty established a customs union, abolished all customs duties, suppressed the customs frontier and created a common tariff against the rest of the world (articles 7 and 8). He was not, however, allowed to use the more ambitious phrase, 'commercial union'.[3] Morier's third contribution was a mistake. In investigating the long-standing grievance of the Portuguese about discrimination against port wine, he had come to an over-hasty conclusion. He reported home that Britain was in the wrong and the duties levied in India constituted 'in equity' a breach of the most-favoured-nation

[1] To Derby, nos. 60 and 62 commercial, 28 and 29 Nov. 1876; India Office to Foreign Office, 11 Dec. 1876, F.O. 63/1081; 'substitute' was used in the preamble.

[2] From Derby, telegram, 12 Dec.; to Derby, telegrams and nos. 75 and 76 commercial, 14 and 15 Dec.; to Corvo, 15 Dec.; from Corvo, 17 Dec. 1876, F.O. 63/1081.

[3] To Derby, telegram and no. 63 commercial, 1 Dec. 1876, F.O. 63/1081, and final text of *Treaty of Commerce and Extradition between Her Majesty and the King of Portugal with reference to their Indian Possessions, Parliamentary Papers* (1880), lxxix. 395. The memorandum of proposals presented to Corvo which Morier sent home has the phrase 'commercial union' marked off in red ink (? by Salisbury); correspondence between India Office and Foreign Office in Dec., F.O. 63/1081, and Jan., F.O. 63/1082.

clause of the Anglo-Portuguese treaty of 1842. Derby thought 'there was a good deal in' what Morier said. But it turned out that most-favoured-nation treatment by that treaty was to be extended to Portugal by Britain *and her colonies* and that no one among the Foreign Office staff or the legal advisers of the Crown could be persuaded that India was a British colony.[1] Morier quietly dropped his view and no one would suspect from his own papers that he had been found wrong.

Other parts of the proposed treaty were contributed by the Indian government. They related to (1) the excise duty on spirits to be levied in Portuguese India according to the system by which a similar duty was levied in British India; (2) the suppression of the manufacture of salt in Portuguese India in return for the payment by British India of two lakhs of rupees (later four, or £50,000) annually to the Portuguese authorities. Lord Lytton had begun to carry out a scheme for equalizing the salt duties throughout India.[2] The suppression was part of this plan as well as a means of ending the smuggling. Finally from the Indian side were proposals relating to (3) the extradition of criminals and (4) the prohibition of the import of arms into and the export of opium from the Portuguese ports.

What mostly caught Morier's imagination was, however, certain further proposals which came from the Portuguese side. When Morier first acted upon Derby's instruction of 14 November, Corvo told him that there was 'an English syndicate represented by a Mr. Frederick Campbell now at Lisbon who proposed if they could obtain the necessary concession from the Portuguese Government to undertake the building of a railway line from Murmagoa', the port of Portuguese India, to the British Indian frontier.[3] Morier had not known of Campbell, but he at once took up the plan and pushed it for all he was worth. What had been begun as a negotiation about Surat—

[1] To Derby, nos. 61 and 65 commercial, 28 Nov. and 6 Dec. 1876; Derby's remark is on the back of no. 65, F.O. 63/1081; to Derby, nos. 11 and 13 commercial, 4 and 7 Feb. 1877, with minute by T. V. Lister of 14 Feb. and memorandum by G. March on the application of the Anglo-Portuguese treaty of 1842 to India ending 'Mr Morier is entirely in error as to the conclusion he has come to on this point', 19 Feb. 1877; the matter was submitted to the Law Officers on 6 Mar. 1877, and Morier corrected in a dispatch, no. 8 commercial, 4 May 1877, F.O. 63/1082.
[2] Lady B. Balfour, *Lord Lytton's Indian Administration* (1899), pp. 461 ff.
[3] To Derby, no. 64 commercial, 1 Dec. 1876, F.O. 63/1081.

the papers on which were filed under the heading 'Surat Duties' —became a negotiation about the Goa railway and the heading of the file had to be expanded. What was originally a tariff treaty emerged as the Goa Railway treaty, signed in Lisbon on 26 December 1878. It became a basic element in Morier's grand project for Anglo-Portuguese overseas co-operation. It was not surprising that a government preoccupied with the eastern question should not have shared Morier's vision, and it was his personal success that he signed the treaty in that form. But to procure its execution he participated in a task of company promotion that was an altogether unprecedented activity for a British diplomatic representative.

The position in December 1876 was that the Portuguese wanted a subvention from the Indian government for the building of a railway from Murmagoa, the port of Goa, to a place in British India.[1] The building was to be done by a private company under a concession from the Portuguese government for the Portuguese section of the line. It was to connect with the British Indian system at Bellary; so far as it ran within British Indian territory (beyond the British-Portuguese Indian frontier, that is), it would be built under authorization by the Indian authorities. The Indian government from 1845 to 1875 had a consistent practice over railway building.[2] It exercised a strict control, since all plans needed its authorization and its help in securing land, overcoming engineering difficulties, and importing skilled labour and raw materials. It was not, however, its practice to build state railways. All the early railways, the Madras Line, the Great Indian Peninsular Railway, the Bombay, Baroda and Central Railway, the Great Southern Indian Railway, were built by private companies. Yet it did provide a 5 per cent guarantee on an unlimited amount of capital; indeed, on capital up to whatever amount the railway cost to build. Thus shareholders in Britain were assured of a 5 per cent return on what were virtually gilt-edged investments. Neither Indian capital, nor Indian resources, except navvy

[1] To Derby, no. 64 commercial, 1 Dec. 1876, and memorandum enclosed, F.O. 63/1081.
[2] W. J. Macpherson, 'Investment in Indian Railways', *Economic History Review* (1955–6), p. 177; see also the annual 'Report to the Secretary of State for India in Council on Railways in India', *Parliamentary Papers* (1874), xlix. 311, with table of amounts actually paid in guaranteed interest at p. 335.

labour, were involved, though the Indian taxpayer contributed to the making good of the deficiency when profits fell short of a 5 per cent return. Indian capital, indeed, was simply not available. When in 1881 the South Mahratta Railway Com-

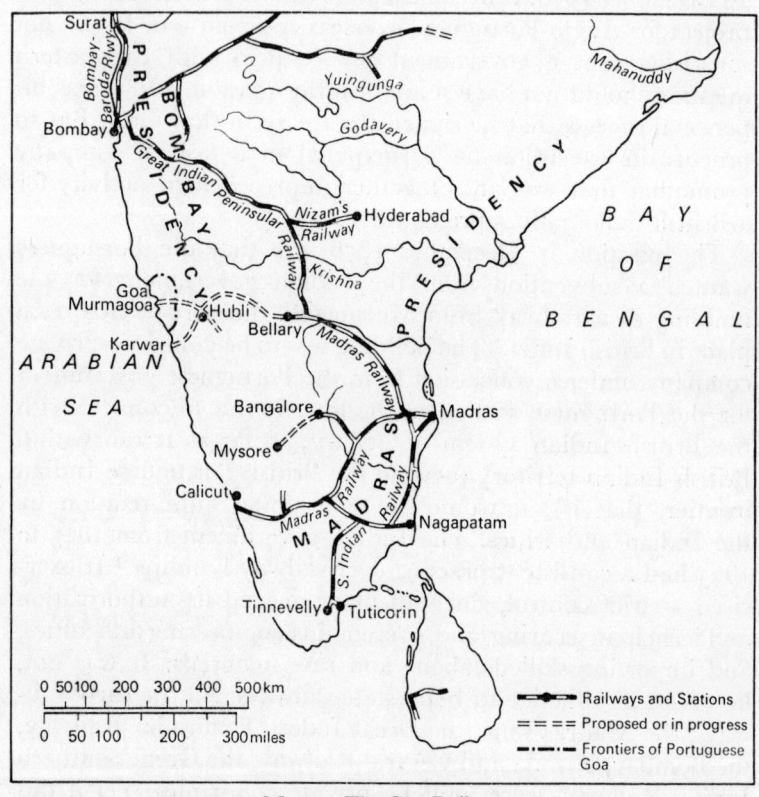

MAP 1. The Goa Railway
(as shown in a map of the Railways of India in 1880)

pany, for example, offered £500,000 in shares on the Bombay stock market, none was taken up, whereas in London the capital was subscribed several times over.[1]

Lytton's Viceroyalty saw the inauguration of a new practice. This was not, however, fully working until after the famine of 1877. The government of India then embarked upon consider-

[1] Sir James Fergusson to Cranbrook, private, 6 Aug. 1881, Cranbrook papers, T. 501/96.

able expenditure on public works, which included railways as well as irrigation and roads. It was the policy of opening up the backward districts—to use the language of those days. By 1881 the government of India had railway schemes in hand costing a total of £20,000,000. Most of them it planned to build by private enterprise. When a private company undertook a scheme, the Indian government now offered a guarantee of 3½ per cent interest to investors on their investment for fifteen years. When private companies did not come forward, the Presidency governments (Bombay, Madras, Bengal) were authorized to spend as much as was economically possible out of the Presidency budget.¹ Since the negotiation of the Goa treaty lasted over the period of changing practice in India, it was not surprising that the crux of the negotiation became the Portuguese wish for an Indian subvention or, at least, guarantee and the Indian government's counter-proposal of a Portuguese guarantee.

The Indian government at first refused to authorize a line going beyond Hubli, which was over 200 miles short of the junction at Bellary; for it wished to keep open the possibility of developing the port of Karwar, a port in British India some twenty miles south of Goa, and linking *it* rather than Murmagoa with Bellary. It gave way before Morier's persistence on this, but it steadily refused any subvention or guarantee. In the draft treaty, which was the basis of discussion during 1877, the Indian government simply declared itself 'ready to permit the construction by a private company, without a guarantee, of a railway from Bellary to the Portuguese frontier, if, after due examination by a joint commission, it was proved that the Murmagoa–Bellary route was more advantageous to commerce than the already surveyed Karwar–Bellary route'.²

A second proposal came from the Portuguese side and this too caught Morier's imagination. The Portuguese desired that a renewal of the British territorial guarantee of the Portuguese colonies (1661) should be included in the treaty. Lord Lytton was prepared to treat on this basis,³ but the Foreign Office jibbed at this political matter being taken out of its hands and

---

[1] Fergusson to Cranbrook, private, 6 Aug. and 2 Dec. 1881, ibid.
[2] To Jowett, autobiographical letter of 1889; draft treaty in Morier to Derby, no. 3 commercial, 10 Jan. 1877, F.O. 63/1082.
[3] Viceroy to India Office, telegram, 1 Jan. 1877, F.O. 63/1082.

the Viceroy's sanction was not communicated to Lisbon. Sir Edward Hertslet, librarian of the Foreign Office, was instead required to draw up an account of Britain's obligations to Portugal and of recent occasions when she had renewed them (1815), acted upon them (1826) or shown readiness to act upon them (1873). In the memorandum[1] he accordingly drew up, he reminded Derby that these old treaties with Portugal belonged to an age which had long passed away and might be dismissed as Lord Howden in his dispatch no. 6, 7 January 1856, had dismissed similar treaties with Spain: 'a mass of useless, conflicting, superannuated and even impossible stipulations'. He also reminded Derby that the House of Commons had narrowly defeated a motion to annul them in 1872 and that successive failures to act on them in east and west Africa had shown that they were 'inoperative in Africa'. In the draft treaty that Morier sent home on 10 January 1877 the reference to the alliance was restricted to the preamble and to articles 11 and 14. The Portuguese were not satisfied with this and wished for an explicit renewal. Hertslet, however, in a covering minute submitting his memorandum, doubted whether it was politic even to make the allusion, as the preamble did, to the 'amitié et fraternité mutuelles qui ont inspiré et maintenu inaltérable pendant des siècles la plus intime et fidèle alliance entre les deux couronnes'. 'It is so easy', wrote Hertslet, 'to quote a Clause from any of the old Treaties which read by itself appears to have a very binding effect, but which if read in connection with the remainder of the Articles is very considerably modified.' He went on to point out that in the memorandum in which the Portuguese asked for the renewal in the full way in which they wished to have it, an article was quoted apparently obliging Britain to defend Portuguese India, but the unquoted part of the article 'went on to say "from the power and invasion of the States of the United Provinces" which shows that it had reference to the peculiar events of that day. But', Hertslet finished, 'the Portuguese Mem. carefully omits this part of the article.'[2] Sir Julian Pauncefote, who supervised the negotiation

---

[1] Dated 10 Jan. 1877, F.O. 63/1082.
[2] Minute by Hertslet, 17 Jan. 1877, F.O. 63/1082; the treaty was drafted and negotiations conducted in French but the final texts were in English and Portuguese.

in the Foreign Office, proposed, and Lord Derby agreed, that 'the reference to the old Treaties should be quietly dropped'.[1] The members of the Foreign and India Offices, with whom the Portuguese negotiator conferred in London in February 1877—this conference will be explained presently—were not able to insist on the modification of the preamble as it stood in Morier's draft nor upon an omission of a direct reference to the treaty of 1661 in article 14 of the draft.[2] Here it was stated that the armed forces of the one party should only enter the territory of the other for ends specified in certain articles of the treaty of 23 June 1661. They were, however, able to gain its rewording in more general terms so that it finally read: 'for the purpose specified in former treaties'. Derby, who relieved Britain of the newly made Luxemburg guarantee in 1867, was extraordinarily vigilant in keeping her obligations so limited that she could fulfil them. He was running true to form in this negotiation and Portugal never had a chance of gaining the explicit renewal or extended reference for which she wished.

The whole meaning of the treaty for Morier was in the railway and in his vision of the prosperity it would bring to Goa. He had the support of Lord Lytton and of Sir Louis Mallet, the permanent under-secretary at the India Office. But for both of them all the parts of the treaty—tariff, salt duties, and railway—were equally important. Mallet (then head of the commercial department in the Board of Trade) and Morier had been colleagues in negotiating the commercial treaty of 1865 with Austria. But Morier was imprudent in assuming that they were now allies in opposition to most of the civil servants in London and India.

Morier summed up the mood in which he thought they acted when he wrote to Mallet: 'the only good that is ever done in the world is by two or three persons with real convictions and a spark of the *feu sacré* working together as conspirators against the powers of darkness as Guy Fawkes bent on blowing up the citadels of chauvinism.'[3] Mallet, in an effort to prevent

[1] Minute by Sir J. Pauncefote, 18 Jan. 1877, marked 'I agree' by Derby, F.O. 63/1082.
[2] See Lister's memorandum of the meeting with Soares at the Foreign Office and correspondence between Lister and Mallet, 5 and 6 Feb. 1877, F.O. 63/1082; the final text of the preamble recorded 'the desire to draw closer the ancient ties of friendship which unite the two nations'.
[3] To Mallet, 17 Jan. 1879.

confusion and irritation arising from Morier's exuberance, had earlier told him: 'write dry, short businesslike despatches to F.O. and send your real views in your own way to me and I will send them on to Lytton.'[1] There was official opposition to the building of the railway led by Sir R. Temple, Governor of Bombay, and strongly supported in London by Sir Andrew Clarke, who as an engineer spoke with authority, and in India in the Viceroy's Council by Sir A. Arbuthnot, and 'General Sir M. Kennedy, another army engineer'.[2]

A diplomatic representative was, after all, at the serious disadvantage that he could not hear all the views which made themselves heard to the government in London. Morier was not wise in writing and acting as if he could. The engineers had a serious objection, based on the cost of tunnelling through the mountains between Hubli and Murmagoa. Morier was wrong, too, in assuming that Temple's stand was adopted out of prejudice or pigheadedness. Temple argued that if the Murmagoa–Hubli–Bellary line was built rather than the Karwar–Hubli–Bellary one, British capital and British credit 'would be devoted to improving Portuguese territory [Goa], while next door [Karwar] Britain would leave British territory unimproved'.[3] Temple did not yet know of the other provisions of the treaty, but it is clear that when he did, he still did not think them sufficient to warrant the sacrifice of Britain's interests in India to her interests in Europe, in so far as these were involved in Anglo-Portuguese friendship. Nor was Temple alone, for his successor as Governor of Bombay, Sir James Fergusson, spontaneously wrote a long private letter to the secretary of state, deploring 'how utterly Indian interests have been mistaken and disregarded' in the preference of Murmagoa over Karwar.[4] Morier would have replied that general prosperity was more important than British Indian prosperity; but it was not self evident that general prosperity would be the result of the railway.

There was certainly no especial enthusiasm in the Foreign Office for the railway part of the treaty, which had come from

[1] From Mallet, 1 Jan. 1877.
[2] From T. C. Hope, 1 Aug. 1879.
[3] Temple to Cranbrook, private, 12 June, and extract, 1 Nov. 1878, Cranbrook papers, T. 501/55, and 28 Sept. 1879, ibid., T. 501/14.
[4] Fergusson to Cranbrook, private, 2 Apr. 1881, Cranbrook papers, T. 501/96.

INDIA: THE GOA TREATY

Portugal. Nor did the officials there see the negotiation as a whole as anything more than a piece of useful tidying up. It was one among many contemporary negotiations and not the most important. In January 1877 Mallet warned Morier of a hostile minute written by T. V. Lister and endorsed by Lord Tenterden, the permanent under-secretary, and by Lord Derby. 'It has been a revelation to me and makes it vital that we should proceed with great circumspection. Enough to say that Lister is doing all he can to discredit you and trip you up.' 'Lister', he unjustly wrote, 'is a worthless official who hates work and men who do work and commercial business of all kinds is his detestation. He has ruined the commercial department at the F.O. [originally built up by Mallet in the Board of Trade and recently transferred to the Foreign Office] and is trying to get rid of the whole thing.'[1] Morier could not know that Mallet's letters to Lister created the same atmosphere of conspiracy—but with Lister a conspiracy to keep Morier 'who had shown too much zeal . . . quiet'.[2] Mallet, however, certainly did all he could to stir the Foreign Office to action, especially during the time when the secretary of state for India, Lord Salisbury, was away at the Constantinople Conference in January 1877, and later to win over Lord Cranbrook, who in April 1878 had succeeded Salisbury as secretary of state for India, and to impress on him the advantages of the treaty.[3] A little earlier Mallet had complained of the Calcutta Foreign Office—'a vulgar imitation of the Downing Street institution'—and told Morier that 'the kind of international considerations to which you appeal are matters which have never entered the mind of the Anglo-Indian official to whom British India is the whole world and the British Civilian the only inhabitant thereof who need claim attention.'[4] Morier in his turn complained to Mallet 'of the ineptitude and imbecility of the F.O.' as 'something that passeth man's understanding'.[5]

[1] From Mallet, 1 Jan. 1877. It is not possible to distinguish to which of Lister's many minutes Mallet's strictures apply. Lister's minutes are cautious but not hostile.
[2] See Lister to Mallet, 13 Nov. 1877: 'Morier gave me the impression of having shown rather too much zeal in the Goa Com[municatio]n[s] and particularly on the Portuguese side. Your letter gave me the impression you thought so too and wished him to be kept quiet', F.O. 63/1082.
[3] See for example Mallet to Cranbrook, private, 1 Oct. [1878], Cranbrook papers, T. 501/93. [4] From Mallet 26 Dec. 1876.
[5] To Mallet, 13 Jan. 1877.

This might be dismissed as mere 'blowing off steam' between friends, if Morier's complaints of 'the clerklings' had not been so frequent. His daughter went so far as to speak of his 'feud with the Foreign Office which was only to end with his death', and of 'a narrow-minded bureaucracy, insular in outlook, antiquated in method, totally devoid of sympathy with any scheme not of its own inception, belittling every success and magnifying every failure, and well-fitted to drive so sensitive and high strung a temperament as that of Morier to the verge of desperation'.[1] Her recollection was coloured by Morier's later convictions, after the Bazaine incident had embittered the whole relationship. Yet her language, even when toned down, shows what Morier came at least to believe to be true of his earlier relations. During the Lisbon period the burden of his complaint was that his policy of bargaining on equal terms was seldom accepted and that he was too often expected to get more than he gave. On their part, Tenterden, Pauncefote, Sanderson, Currie, Lister, and Kennedy in the Foreign Office, with justice, believed that Morier took on the colouring of the country where he lived, was more Portuguese than the Portuguese, and was led by his enthusiasm to make mistakes and confusion.

The draft treaty having been agreed upon in Lisbon and the Indian government having agreed to it in principle, negotiations were to continue in Bombay between a Portuguese representative and Sir A. Arbuthnot and the Hon. T. C. Hope, as representatives of the Indian government. By January 1877 the meeting-place had been changed to Calcutta and Duarte Gustave Nogueira Soares, a free-trader and head of the commercial department of the Portuguese Foreign Office, had been appointed Portuguese representative. It was agreed that he should go to London on his way to Calcutta. At the same time it was agreed that although the negotiations should be completed in Calcutta, the treaty, owing to the semi-political character which the reference to the old treaties of alliance had given to it, should be signed between the Portuguese and British, not the Portuguese and Indian, governments.[2] On 1 February

---

[1] Lady Wemyss's draft.
[2] Foreign Office to India Office, 9 Jan. 1877, and India Office to Foreign Office, 15 Jan. 1877, F.O. 63/1082.

1877 Soares saw Mallet at the India Office and a day or so later conferred at the Foreign Office with Lister, Mallet, and A. W. Moore (the head of the political section of the India Office). At the India Office he was mostly concerned with the railway and at the Foreign Office with the reference to the ancient treaties of alliance. The final wording of the preamble and article 14 was settled after further correspondence on 5 and 6 February, and discussion then moved to the Portuguese-Indian tariff and the wine duties. By 16 February Soares had left London. There is no need to follow the course of the negotiations in Calcutta. Suffice it to say that by August 1877 the negotiations had broken down—from the Portuguese side and on the railway question. The Indian government were ready to give authorization for the building of the line, but continued to refuse any guarantee and insisted on not so binding their hands that the alternative, easier line to Karwar should be excluded. In Portugal meanwhile the less friendly de Ávila ministry had come into office (March 1877) and the annexation of the Transvaal in April 1877 had created a wave of anglophobia. The high hopes for a diplomatic success stirred in Morier by Derby's instructions of November had been dashed. In the summer his spirits were low. He had suffered a personal loss in the death of his father on 13 July; he went to England and remained there, away from Lisbon until 24 August 1877.

The year 1876, then, saw a promising beginning, but 1877 was a blank in the history of the negotiations. They began again only in the summer of 1878 after the European negotiations on the eastern question were over. By now Fontes and Corvo were back in power—they had returned in January 1878. Salisbury, now foreign secretary, reopened the negotiations on 10 August 1878 and sent T. C. Hope to Lisbon 'to give information'.[1] Lord Lytton in his telegram of 15 August raised objections which Morier interpreted as directed against the initiative in the renewal of negotiations being taken by the British, since it was Portugal who had broken them off the previous summer. Morier answered that Corvo on returning to office had made a declaration to him acknowledging the

---

[1] From Salisbury, telegram, 10 Aug. 1878, F.O. 63/1083. The draft of the telegram is in Salisbury's hand.

largeness and liberality of the Indian government's offers of 1877.[1] On 23 September, before Morier had had a chance (owing to the India Office's objections) to act on Salisbury's instructions of 10 August, Corvo of his own accord had instructed the Portuguese minister in London to approach Salisbury. This d'Antas did in October.[2]

Indeed Portugal in 1878 was pressing the negotiations forward. The explanation is that negotiations had also been opened for the building of a railway from the Transvaal (now annexed to Britain) to Lorenço Marques. Here Portugal could give facilities which Britain was anxious to have. She hoped Britain might buy them by giving her the facilities—and the guarantee—for the railway she wanted in British India. Salisbury telegraphed to Morier on 25 October that d'Antas had applied for a renewal of the Goa negotiations on the basis of the draft treaty of 1877 and that the British government had assented. The concluding passage of the telegram which Salisbury added in his own hand ran: 'If possible at the same time commence and conduct *pari passu*, negotiations for Lorenço Marques railway referred to in your despatch of the 3^d inst.'[3] It is difficult to tell what precisely Salisbury meant by the phrase *pari passu*. If, though this is unlikely, it had no precise meaning for him, it may have been a reflection of his awareness that there was a clause in the draft Goa treaty allowing the transport of troops and war material along the Portuguese portion of the line, as if the same were in British territory, and that an equal provision for this was the essential basis of the Lorenço Marques treaty. But of course the phrase as he used it should have applied to the steps of the negotiation and not to the content. I shall return to this matter in Chapter 3.

Morier began at once, without waiting for the formal and full instructions which were being sent to him by the messenger leaving on 30 October. He later described how for three days, from 25 to 28 October, he laboured with Corvo until they had reached provisional agreement on all questions of principle. He omits to say that he did not wait to begin for the assistance of

---

[1] To Salisbury, no. 47 commercial, confidential, 29 Sept., 1878, F.O. 63/1083.
[2] D'Antas to Salisbury, 19 Oct., enclosing Corvo's note to him of 23 Sept., 1878, F.O. 63/1083.
[3] From Salisbury, telegram, 25 Oct. 1878, F.O. 63/1083, F.O. 84/1524.

T. C. Hope who had been sent out to Lisbon. The Foreign Office demurred at this haste, but Salisbury defended Morier. One reads: 'I cannot understand why it should have been necessary to act with such extreme haste about a matter which has been hanging about for two years. T. V. L[ister] N. 11.' 'Because Mr. Hope had to come away. S[alisbury].' The Portuguese gained concessions in this phase of the story. The provision was dropped from article 5 for a joint Anglo-Portuguese survey of the two routes (Bellary–Marmagoa and Bellary–Karwar) to determine which of the two was commercially better. In the redrafted treaty this provision would only come into effect if Campbell, to whom the Portuguese had promised facilities if he formed his company within a reasonable time, failed to do so. The second concession to Portugal was that the two lakhs to be paid annually as compensation for the suppression of the manufacture of salt in Portuguese India were raised to four. On the other hand, it was now agreed that this money should be used to enable *the Portuguese* to provide the guarantee for investment in the railway. This was a Portuguese suggestion made already in 1876.[1] It removed the principal stumbling-block to the railway part of the treaty. Another small gain for Portugal was the association of Portuguese with British officials in the enforcement of the British salt monopoly. Morier and Corvo initialled the treaty on 9 November, Morier's instructions, dispatched on 30 October, still not having arrived.[2] Meanwhile Frederick Campbell returned to Lisbon to negotiate for the facilities from the Portuguese that he was assured of in British India. Morier was told 'to give him such unofficial assistance as you can properly afford in carrying out the object of his journey',[3] and he came with a letter of introduction to Morier from the Foreign Office.

There was a sudden recrudescence of Portuguese opposition led, according to Morier, by Soares, the negotiator of 1877, who refused his co-operation and that of his department. On the very day that Morier's full powers to sign arrived, the prime minister, Fontes, called on him. Repeating 'parrot-like the stereotyped objections of Senhor Soares', he said the railway and

[1] To Derby, no. 64, 1 Dec. 1876, F.O. 63/1081.
[2] To Salisbury, telegram, 9 Nov. 1878, F.O. 63/1083.
[3] To Morier, commercial, separate, 23 Sept. 1878, F.O. 63/1083.

the salt articles required consideration. 'I replied', Morier reported, 'by expressing my unfeigned astonishment ... The negotiations ... had now lasted rather more than two years, and ... had been brought to a satisfactory conclusion more than a month ago ...' The initialled draft had been approved. 'My Full Powers had arrived that very morning and, His Excellency could see, were lying on the table at which we sat ... I thought it my duty ... to tell him in the most positive manner ... that I refused to re-open the negotiation or admit of the discussion of one jot or one tittle of the draft as now finally rédigé.'[1] An appeal to postpone the signature on the ground of cabinet division over the treaty was met with equal firmness. Morier was rewarded when he learnt that Corvo had offered to resign if the treaty were not signed, since his good faith was so much involved in it. By 16 December Fontes had withdrawn his opposition and ten days later (26 December 1878) the treaty was finally signed.[2] An additional article was signed on 10 March 1879.

The last round had still to be won. The treaty had to be passed by the Cortes. It was held back in the hope that it might be presented simultaneously with the Lorenço Marques treaty. Its presentation became more and more urgent and still there was no move.

This in part at least arose from the difficulty of creating a company to build the line. Campbell had been too sanguine. The Portuguese had been ready to sign the contract with him in 1876 provided that by February 1877 he presented a list of men who would form a company and furnished the Portuguese Government with their collective declaration that they had found, or would find, the necessary capital to build the Murmagoa–Hubli section. He had failed to fulfil both these conditions. He had, however, come back to Lisbon in December 1877 supplied even then with a letter of introduction from the Foreign Office to Morier, whom he told that he was in treaty with the Indian Government for a contract to build the Hubli–Bellary section. Campbell's purpose was to secure an extension of time in which to form his company and provide the collective declara-

---

[1] To Salisbury, no. 68 commercial, most confidential, 20 Dec. 1878, F.O. 63/1083.

[2] To Salisbury, no. 69 commercial, 25 Dec. 1878, F.O. 63/1083.

INDIA: THE GOA TREATY

tion. Since Gonnear and not Corvo was then minister for the colonies, Morier had no hope of Campbell's gaining the contract on the old conditions. Morier's ingenuity, however, gained for Campbell his extension of time. He cleverly substituted a provision for the prior signature of Campbell's contract with the British government for the condition of the list of capitalists and their declaration. It gave the Portuguese what they wanted since 'they felt certain that the F.O. would not sign a contract except with persons whose solidity and respectability were beyond question',[1] and it cost them nothing. On these terms Morier had secured for Campbell a year from 27 December 1877 in which to form his company. Morier's part had extended even to the drafting of the letter which constituted the new engagement. But Campbell had failed yet again. After the Goa treaty was signed he had returned to Lisbon (December 1878) with the intention of getting the contract signed, so that he could take it back to London and use it to induce capitalists to help him to form his company. Morier accused him of seeking to gain his ends by sharp practice, but nevertheless if he was prepared 'to state frankly, truthfully and straightforwardly how matters' stood and the reasons which had, for a second time, made it impossible for him to fulfil or to try to fulfil either of the conditions, Morier would try to gain him a further prolongation of time.[2] A scene occurred between them,[3] but in the end Morier made terms for him with the Portuguese government and once again drafted the letters which constituted the understanding.[4] The Portuguese renewed their promise of the contract and gave Campbell until 27 April 1879 to fulfil either of the two conditions. Campbell had, at least, a list of names and now had only to obtain their formal declaration about finding the capital.

The unfortunate Campbell had returned at once to London (12 January). He failed yet again to form his company. His failure brought a second man on to the scene, for Campbell made an arrangement with the engineer, Robert Francis Fairlie. (He was the inventor and patentee of a type of railway engine.)

[1] To Campbell, draft 2 Jan. 1879, letter sent dated 3 Jan.
[2] To Campbell, 2 (3) Jan. 1879.
[3] To Mallet, 14 Jan. 1879.
[4] Drafts by Morier of Campbell to Ribeiro, 10 Jan., and reply, 12 Jan. 1879, Morier to Campbell, 17 Jan., and Campbell to Morier, 24 Jan. 1879.

Fairlie took on the task of company promotion on the understanding that, if he got a company together by 27 April 1879, he might have both the contract with the Portuguese government, promised to Campbell, and the contract promised by the Indian government for £20,000. When Morier heard of this, his anger welled up against 'a promoters' company having for its main object not the construction of the line but the selling of the engines'.[1] Morier all along, in the spirit of John Bright, Sir Thomas Bazley, Sir Louis Mallet, and the whole circle of Manchester men, had conceived of the railway as serving a public purpose. To facilitate the transport of cotton,[2] and by trade to open up southern India to development, were recognized public purposes, apart from Morier's more particular professional concern of improving Anglo-Portuguese relations. He was determined that the railway should not be deflected into what he called private profit-making. Before Fairlie could get his company going, the time-limit expired, and without Morier's assistance no further prolongation was possible. Fairlie, like Campbell, encountered the insuperable difficulty that no one would back a company unless the Portuguese guarantee were extended to cover not only the Portuguese section but the whole railway to Bellary; for investors would not lend without it.

Morier now obtained two months' leave, and during April and May 1879 was in London. From *tabula rasa*[3] he himself mustered a committee, 'every member of which', he claimed with some exaggeration, 'was selected by myself'. He obtained from them full powers to act in their name and dictated their letters to the Portuguese government.

The committee consisted of five men: the Duke of Sutherland,[4] William Mackinnon (chairman of the British India Steam Navigation Company), Henry Green (senior partner in R. and H. Green & Co.), Frederick Youle (chairman of the London County Bank who was well known in Portugal and

[1] To Cranbrook, 21 May 1879.
[2] Cf. *Parliamentary Papers* (1863), xliv. 83.
[3] To Cranbrook, 24 May 1879. Morier writes to Mackinnon from Sandringham on 16 Apr. He left for Lisbon on 24 May, see Mackinnon to Morier, 9 May.
[4] The third Duke, 1828–92, the original of the Chairman of the North South East West Diddlesex Junction Railway, in *Thespis* (the first Gilbert and Sullivan opera); *Country Life*, xviii (Mar. 1971), 626.

was Sutherland's confidant), and Sir Douglas Forsyth (a retired Indian civil servant and director of the most important of the Indian railway companies).[1] Frederick Campbell had already gained promises of support from Green, Forsyth, and Mackinnon, whose names had figured on the list he brought to Morier in January 1879,[2] but it was Morier's success with the Duke of Sutherland and his arrangement about the salt (see above p. 41, below, p. 47) and, above all, the extension of the guarantee that made the new committee important. The Duke of Sutherland's name carried weight with the public. But Mackinnon was the source of strength in the new undertaking. At this time he was known as a shipowner, who had made a fortune by trade in India (1847–56) and then founded his shipping-company (1856). He was known to cherish a general interest in opening up the world by the development of steam communication by river, sea, and rail. He was known as a self-made man— he had begun by keeping a grocer's shop in Campbelltown—with wide business interests. Morier's means of persuasion with him had been the chance that the Goa railway offered of helping on the Lorenço Marques treaty, for Mackinnon was already deeply interested in south and east Africa.[3]

Mackinnon had insisted on the Portuguese guarantee being given for the British as well as the Portuguese portion of the line, and Morier was on close enough terms with Corvo at once to telegraph to ask for this and to gain an assent by telegraph to negotiate about it.[4] The committee was prepared to pay preliminary expenses out of its own pocket, creating a fund, made up of £1,000 from each member, for the purpose, and to organize a company and invite investment on the open market, without charging the usual promoters' fees or seeking profit for themselves or any others. The crux of the new negotiation in Lisbon was the extension of the Portuguese guarantee to both the Portuguese and British sections of the line. Morier induced in the Portuguese sufficient confidence in the committee for them to guarantee a 5 per cent return on the capital invested in the whole railway using the four lakhs of rupees as backing for the guarantee.

[1] From Mackinnon, 10 July 1879.
[2] Morier's draft of Campbell to Ribeiro, Jan. 1879.
[3] To Viscount Duprat, 16 Apr. 1879.   [4] To Corvo, 25 Apr. 1879.

Morier's first venture into concession-hunting imperialism was eminently successful. The committee met at Stafford House on 8 May 1879 and agreed to the conditions on which they were ready to sign a contract with Portugal.[1] Morier had persuaded Corvo informally to accept them. Corvo and the committee officially proposed them to Braamcamp, the head of the new government, in June 1879 after Corvo fell. Thus in the summer of 1879 presentation of the Goa treaty to the Cortes became urgent, because a company was in process of formation which would be dissolved if the treaty were not ratified.[2] Morier always spoke later on of the three weeks' ultimatum which he had induced the Stafford House Committee to present to the Portuguese.

He had originally intended that the Lorenço Marques treaty should make the Goa treaty palatable to the Portuguese Cortes. But since the former was not signed until 30 May and since it contained a provision postponing ratification until British relations with the Transvaal had been reviewed, it proved impossible to present both treaties at the same time. The Indian railway thus became the only means of recommending the Goa treaty. Morier had to guard against the suspicion that, because the treaty involved the construction of a very considerable stretch of railway on British territory under Portuguese guarantee, it was a 'mere diplomatic feint to obtain from Portugal the very great concession of a monopoly of the Goa salt works and the presence of British excise officers in Portuguese territory',[3] and a trick to gain, by means of the customs union, the practical absorption of the Portuguese territory in British India.

Morier had to be able to argue effectively that, if the government refused to present the Goa treaty to the Cortes then in session, it would lose the railway, and that the treaty, if it then eventually passed, would pass without what was to the Portuguese its one redeeming feature. It took him a fortnight of unremitting pressure to get his way. He began by engaging the new minister, Braamcamp, who knew nothing about the

[1] The Duke of Sutherland, William Mackinnon, Henry Green, Frederick Youle, and Sir Douglas Forsyth to Morier, 31 May 1879.
[2] To Salisbury, no. 23 commercial, 7 June 1879, F.O. 63/1091.
[3] To Sir Henry Ponsonby, 1 July 1881.

INDIA: THE GOA TREATY

business, to get it up by discussion with Corvo. He then himself had an exhaustive conversation with Braamcamp, who evaded responsibility by saying that everything depended on his party's majority in the Cortes. Morier next, therefore, saw Fontes, the party leader. Rumours then began to spread that the Cortes would be dissolved before the treaty was passed, and Morier had further unsatisfactory interviews with Braamcamp and the ministers for colonies and finance. Striking his characteristic dramatic and humorous note, Morier reported that he finally saved the situation by appealing to the Duke de Ávila's gratitude for the advice he gave him 'in the great sardine controversy with Spain' (see below, p. 148), and that he so secured the votes of his party for the treaty.

Thus on 18 June 1879 the treaty passed the Cortes with the support of the Opposition as well as of the Government. The zeal of the Opposition in supporting a measure which a fortnight before they had prepared to oppose meant that they might do even more than the Government to secure its execution.[1]

Morier took great credit to himself both for inventing the conditions, which he persuaded the Stafford House Committee to present to the Portuguese government, and for inducing the Portuguese ministers to accept them. They included (a) the Portuguese guarantee, for the whole line from Murmagoa to Bellary, of a return of 5 per cent on the capital invested by the construction company to be organized by the Stafford House Committee, the Portuguese taking profits up to 6 per cent and profits above that being shared equally between the Portuguese and the company; (b) an understanding that the four lakhs of rupees to be paid to the Portuguese by the Indian government for the suppression of the salt manufacture should be used to defray the costs incurred by the guarantee; (c) an understanding that after twelve years (the original proposal of thirty years had to be dropped since the commercial and extradition treaty was for twelve years only in the first instance) the concession thus granted by the Indian government to the company to be organized by the Stafford House Committee should become the property of Portugal; (d) an assurance from the Indian government that it would not authorize a branch line

[1] To Salisbury, nos. 24, 27, 31, and 34, all commercial and confidential, 7, 8, and 18 June 1879, F.O. 63/1091; treaty finally ratified 7 Aug.

to Karwar until the Murmagoa line had worked long enough to show whether there was enough traffic for both; and (e) an agreement that the Stafford House Committee and the Portuguese government should share equally the expenses of a preliminary survey of the Zimern Ghat and harbour of Murmagoa (the route and terminus respectively of the railway) to determine the cost of construction and therefore roughly the amount of capital on which the Portuguese were to guarantee the 5 per cent interest; if the survey was unfavourable to the whole project, the Portuguese government undertook to reimburse the Stafford House Committee.[1]

Sir Douglas Forsyth came out to Lisbon to negotiate a contract on these conditions with the Portuguese government on 24 July 1879, but by 13 August his negotiations had broken down. The Portuguese capitulated and in September negotiations were renewed in London. It took two more years' work in Lisbon and London before the contract was at last signed in Lisbon between the Portuguese government and the Stafford House Committee at the end of April 1881.

The shares were immediately afterwards offered to the British public. 'So thoroughly sound', wrote Morier in 1881, 'were the financial bases which I had been able to give to the enterprise that the capital was subscribed *eleven* times over in three days, and that the shares are now at 10 per cent premium.'[2] The works for the West of India Portuguese Guaranteed Railway were begun by July 1881 with the intention of finishing in four years. In fact the railway was not completed until 1888, though most of it was open by 1886.

Morier, who never went to India, claimed that the Goa treaty, even before the railway was built, had changed a city of splendid ruins into a flourishing commercial town. By 'the customs union' Goa had ceased to be a city of ruined palaces, the habitat of cobras and monkeys, a nest of reptiles with a starving population. When the railway was built, it would start forward at the rate of progress in Birkenhead in 1850 and in half a generation her wealth would have to be counted in millions. 'Now I need not say that the boon I have thus conferred on

---

[1] See to Mackinnon, private and confidential, 28 June, 8 and 11 July 1879, Mackinnon papers, 171, fos. 9–23.
[2] To Ponsonby, 1 July 1881.

Portugal is one of an altogether extraordinary and unparalleled kind and that you might search the annals of diplomacy in vain for a case in which a British minister in his *private capacity* has been in a position to confer such a boon on the country to which he was accredited.'[1]

Lord Salisbury's language was milder. 'I am very glad', he wrote, 'to hear that the Murmagoa Railway is becoming a reality. Somebody will lose heavily. I trust it may be the Portuguese Government, and not the much squeezed shareholder. But in either case India and England will gain and for that result both are greatly indebted to you.'[2]

'You will be glad I think to hear', wrote the more sanguine Theodore Hope to Morier from the Public Works Department in India on 11 November 1886, 'that the whole railway is now completed except about 12 miles of the Ghat, for which another year is necessary—and not merely the whole railway, as you and I intended if from Murmagoa to New Hubli and Bellary, but infinitely more in several directions.' He went on to describe the working of the arrangements in relation to salt, extradition, and tariff and concluded: 'Altogether I think the Treaty is a success: to us it has been a vast advantage . . . to the Portuguese it has brought increased revenue and considerable opportunities by which, however, they seem unlikely to profit much.' Nevertheless, the treaty itself was abrogated in January 1891.[3]

[1] To Ponsonby, 1 July 1881.
[2] From Salisbury, private, 5 June 1881, answering a letter from Morier.
[3] This was 'a terrible shock' to Morier, to Salisbury, private, 7 Feb. 1891.

2

THE EASTERN QUESTION

ALTHOUGH so much of Morier's energy was given to the Goa treaty, he was throughout 1876 and 1877 in a fever of excitement over the eastern question. Morier's wife, when the news arrived in Lisbon of a prospective European conference at Constantinople at the end of 1876, had written without her husband's knowledge to Lady Derby urging his suitability to be named a plenipotentiary. 'Now we know', she wrote, 'and the F.O. must know that there is more in him' than the mere ability to manage 'the private affairs of Princes' and a small 'post like Lisbon'.[1] He had, indeed, knowledge gained from journeys in Serbia, Bosnia, and Montenegro in 1856; he was the friend and correspondent of Sir William White, then at Belgrade, but later (1886–94) British ambassador at Constantinople; he had an independent point of view; he believed Britain should abandon the *idée fixe* that she had to be hostile either to Turkey or to Russia, and this view was in the long run vindicated. Soon after Morier took up his post, Corvo passed on to him a communication about Anglo-Russian cooperation from M. de Glinka, the Russian envoy in Lisbon—made 'solely with the view of being passed on to me and thus reaching' the British government. Glinka had descanted on the difficulties of Russia in the Balkan peninsula and on the Tsar's desire for peace. 'The only hope', he had said, 'of extrication out of a position which seemed otherwise hopeless lay in a loyal understanding between Russia and Great Britain arrived at directly by the two Powers themselves without the officious intervention of a third Power, an allusion which Senhor Corvo had no doubt was aimed at Germany . . .' He was unable to say whence the message came but convinced Morier that 'it emanated from the bosom of the Imperial Family'. The episode has

[1] Mrs. Morier to Lady Derby, Lisbon, 1876.

little meaning except as an indication of Morier's reputation for connections with the English royal family and for interest in the Ottoman Empire, and as a pointer to what was thought to be the likely drift of his own views.[1]

Morier had observed nationalism as a cohesive force in the shaping of a united Germany. In the European part of the Turkish empire, which still nominally covered the whole Balkan peninsula, he watched it work disruptively. He was, as he later wrote, 'bound Prometheus-like to my Cintra rock with Portuguese tomtits pecking at my spleen'[2] when the revolt, which had begun in July 1875 among the peasants of Herzegovina, spread, and he was torn by anxiety lest the British government should misunderstand what was happening. The European Powers had at first acted together, notably in the so-called Andrássy Note— a note drafted by the Austro-Hungarian foreign minister. It summoned the sultan to execute certain reforms in his dominions. The note failed to have any effect. As the ferment grew worse, the six Powers moved towards military intervention and the next proposed summons to the sultan, the Berlin Memorandum, communicated by Germany, Austria-Hungary, and Russia to Britain, France, and Italy, contained a sting in the tail. If the proposed reform measures failed, it would be necessary, the Memorandum concluded, 'd'ajouter à leur action diplomatique la sanction d'une entente, en vue des mesures efficaces . . . pour arrêter le mal et en empêcher le développement'. Whereas France and Italy adhered to this note, the British government not only refused to do so, but on 24 May acted independently and sent the fleet to Besika Bay. This step put an end to concerted European action and quickened the pace of disruption in the Ottoman Empire. In the early summer of 1876 the principalities of Serbia and Montenegro declared war upon the sultan and the Bulgarian peasants rose in revolt. The Turks failed lamentably to deal with either eventuality. The massacre of Bulgarian Christians by irregular Turkish troops, Circassians, and Bashi Bazouks raised in Britain a cry against the Turks. The outcry was vigorously supported by Gladstone's campaign of speeches and his well-known pamphlet, *The Bulgarian Horrors*

---

[1] To Derby, no. 134 most confidential, 20 Sept. 1876, F.O. 63/1035.
[2] To Lord Odo Russell, 14 June 1878, F.O. 918/55 and copy in the Morier papers.

and the Question of the East. On the other side, as the insurrection grew more desperate, the Turks claimed that the Christians, instigated by the Russians, perpetrated atrocities quite as bad.

Nationalism also operated in Russia. In the shape of Panslavism it rendered her policy assertive, acquisitive, and unreliable. Looked upon with scant favour by the St. Petersburg government, the movement was too firmly rooted

> in religious and nationalist soil, with, however, the revolutionary germ clearly discernible, to be opposed. The authorities deemed it, therefore, more politic to divert it into an external channel and considered the Balkan peninsula . . . a safer outlet for Panslavist activities and agitations than would be the interior of the empire. The peninsula was, therefore, honeycombed with Panslavist agents; the majority of the Russian consuls were Panslavists and General Ignatiev, Russian ambassador at Constantinople, was one of the most prominent of their leaders.
>
> The declaration of war on Turkey by Serbia and Montenegro evoked boundless enthusiasm all over Russia, where in every town committees were formed to raise funds and organise relief for the Slav wounded while volunteers from every class and province of Russia flocked to the aid of 'the little brothers'. The situation was becoming every day more menacing; for should the Serbian army commanded by Chernayev, a Russian General though not any longer in the Russian army, and composed, despite a recent ban on volunteering, very largely of Russians, suffer decisive defeats, Russia was expected to intervene.[1]

Morier's anxiety arose from the fear that the British government would commit itself to some strong policy which, not being based on a real understanding of Balkan nationalism or the limitations of Russian Panslavism, would begin in illusion and end in empty gesture. He was thus led to praise Derby's calmness and to condemn the emotion of both the denunciators and defenders of Turkey and to pour scorn upon Disraeli and Gladstone alike. 'Indeed', he wrote to Lady Derby on 5 October 1876, 'it seems to me that the race hatred between the great Jew and the great Christian and the political atrocities it is not unlikely to bring about in the British Commonwealth bear a curious analogy to the animosities of the Turk and Christian in Bulgaria!' The pamphlets and speeches of Gladstone,

---

[1] Lady Wemyss's draft.

Lowe, Argyll, and, above all, Fawcett appeared to him to be the progeny of 'the vilest spirit of faction'. He had no word of good for Gladstone, 'the most voraciously ambitious man that ever lived', all the more dangerous because 'his underlying faith in the sanctity of his motives' wholly blinded him to his own ambition. Desperate efforts by the British government to hold back the Turks and the Serbs failed, and at last General Ignatiev on 31 October presented an ultimatum to the Porte and Russo-Turkish war was expected. Morier, before news of Turkey's acceptance reached him, wrote to Jowett a characteristic letter.[1]

I do not know what Cassandra's state of mind was when the news was brought to Priam that the breach was practicable and that the Greeks would be all over the place in a few minutes. My impression is that it must have been one of unmitigated relief at the thought that now at last the Trojans would see for themselves what was the real state of the case and that she would be no longer called upon to prophecy the horrors which she must have thanked God had at last come. I must confess to having experienced something of this feeling in reading your letter. For years I have insisted that everything connected with our foreign relations was rotten from top to toe, not only our Foreign Office and diplomatic machinery but, what was far worse, the elements out of which a public opinion on foreign politics and statesmen capable of dealing with foreign politics could be elaborated—and you have never ceased to regard this opinion which was the serious outcome of a carefully generalized experience as the mere result of impatience with my career and of a habit of criticising the chiefs I worked under. Even when you have had glimpses that matters looked bad you have always asserted that all would come right the moment an able man turned up somewhere and that he would be sure to turn up. Now it is against this that I have protested and do protest.

Given a public opinion that knew what it wanted and wanted the right thing, Morier believed, the able man did turn up, for he was simply the man who gave shape and utterance to what all the other Englishmen meant and wanted. But when as then, in 1876, there was

no consensus of opinion in any one direction, your able man when

---

[1] 2 Nov. 1876; Jowett's reply, 27 Jan. 1877, is in the Jowett papers at Balliol College and partly printed by E. Abbott and L. Campbell, *Life and Letters of Benjamin Jowett* (3 vols., 1897), iii. 82–3. My quotation is from a typed version in the material collected by Lady Wemyss for her account of 1876.

he turns up is either drawn into some foolish side current and invests a momentary paradox with the appearance of vitality, or he gives to some negative platitude the dignity of a general principle. If he really did get hold of a creative consistent policy he would place before the eyes of the nation . . . something which it would be perfectly incapable of appreciating or understanding. It would be Phidias making statues at the court of Dahomey.

Both Derby and Gladstone were in a position where they could 'concentrate into a focus the will of the nation' if it had one, but they had made 'a precious mess of it', Derby in part at least because he would really like to shut up the Foreign Office, Admiralty, and War Office altogether, Gladstone because of his 'linendraperism', his habit of going hat in hand to foreign Powers, mixed with sheer demagogy, stumping the country to regain his lost hegemony. Returning to this subject again at the end of the letter, Morier likened Gladstone, who had known for a long time the kind of atrocities perpetrated in Turkey, and that they were no worse than they had been, to a doctor who went into hysteria at the sight of a compound fracture. He had gone on, after his first reference to Gladstone, to describe the conclusions he drew from his journeys during three weeks in Serbia, Bosnia, and Montenegro in 1856.

The fact which got fast hold of my mind was that we [had] made a radical mistake in having as consuls throughout those countries men who were thoroughly good *Turkish* scholars but who knew nothing of the people amongst whom they lived . . . The Russian consuls of course, knowing the language and being of the same religion, had it all their own way and intrigued to the top of their bent[1] but our men not having the slightest knowledge of the language could not even find out what was going on under their noses.

A second fact had struck Morier equally forcefully. 'There was', he continued, among the southern Slavs

the greatest distrust of the Russians and the greatest wish to find some Power they could lean against and . . . we were the very Power that they would have wished to lean against. Here then was the most splendid opening for a policy. With our blood and treasure spent in the Crimean War we had bought the right to interfere, to interfere as it could be done in those countries by an able Ambassador, a first class set of subordinates and a clear policy directing the

---

[1] A view substantiated by modern research; see B. H. Sumner, *Russia and the Balkans* (1937), p. 130.

whole—and no one could have suspected us of any other but honest intentions.

The clear policy would have been to use an honest pasha to put through a programme of British-designed reforms—the policy of 'educators of the Christian populations by the use of Turkish machinery'. His only reward for urging his policy upon Lord Clarendon and his successors had been that he was labelled in the Foreign Office a 'dangerous man'.

He now elaborated his constructive view, however, once again for Derby, through the latter's wife. To her he wrote to urge that the only way was to build up British influence among the Slavs through the right men at the key points with full knowledge of the Slav languages and ways.

This is still the only chance for the Christian provinces. To anyone who knows the country, to talk of autonomy at present, or for twenty-five years to come, is simply absurd. They require to be educated up to it, and they can only be educated up to it within the framework of the Turkish Empire.

Of course I should be tarred and feathered if I said so in England, but as I am safe at Cintra I have no hesitation in expressing my belief that the very best form of government that could be given to Bulgaria would be a Pasha, such as we could still find (though I doubt whether there are very many of them) with an Ambassador strong enough to keep him unmoved at his post for ten years, and a man like White[1] on the spot to keep him up to his work; a thoroughly well drilled police of the Irish Constabulary type, Christian for the Christian villages, Turkish for the Turkish villages; a radical reform of the land laws (I do not know what these are in Bulgaria, but in Herzegovina and Bosnia nine tenths of the mischief arose from the feudal forms of villeinage pure and simple, which had remained stereotyped under Mussulman lords of the manor; an evil quite capable of being radically cured); a large amount of self government as regards the economical side of self government, I mean the making and repairing of roads, school houses etc.,[2] but, for the present at least, a minimum of political self government, if

[1] Sir William White, born 1824; educated at King William's College, Isle of Man, and Trinity College, Cambridge; Consul at Danzig 1864–75; Belgrade 1875–9; British representative at the Constantinople Conference 1876; minister at Bucharest 1879–85; ambassador at Constantinople 1886–91.

[2] What could be done in this respect had been shown by Midhat Pasha's government of the Danube vilayet, see H. Temperley, 'British Policy towards Parliamentary Rule and Constitutionalism in Turkey (1830–1914)', *Cambridge Hist. Journal*, iv (1932–3), 156 ff.

any at all, i.e. self government as at present understood, viz. by *elected* vestries—(elected magistrates are the root of all evil, in every country and every climate, but elected magistrates in countries like the Slav provinces of Turkey would be the . . .[1]); for the administration of justice, Christian tribunals in the Christian villages, with some code like our Indian Code to be approved of by the guaranteeing Powers; Turkish tribunals in the Turkish villages, with the Koran to judge by; in mixed cases a mixed tribunal with the president, a Christian, trying with the Christian Code where the accused was a Christian, and vice versa; for the keeping of the machinery of Justice and Administration in working order a High Commission sent straight from Constantinople, holding a circuit and assizes in each province at least twice a year, and hearing appeals both in judicial and administrative cases—in fact the 'Comites missi' of Charlemagne or the 'Judiciarii errantes' of Henry III [of Germany]; these measures and the forced emigration into some purely Mussulman portion of Asia Minor of the Circassians who have been located in Bulgaria within the last twenty years, would constitute, I believe, a very workable programme and get the country on more rapidly in the next ten years than any conceivable autonomy, worked as it would have to be, by autonomous cats and dogs. The institution which, I believe, might be made most productive of good would be my wandering High Commission. As its members would have to be selected at Constantinople, under the pressure we could bring to bear there, the very best men procurable would be obtained; of course it would have to consist half of Mussulmen and half of Christians, but in addition to this, we should insist upon the Porte selecting one or two members from among a certain number of persons presented for selection by the guaranteeing Powers. In addition to this the Consuls of the guaranteeing Powers should sit as assessors without a vote, and without the right of interfering directly in the conduct of the business, but so as to take cognisance of every case that came up, and thus to act as a European gallery established locally *en permanence*. Then as the British public is so very anxious to show its sympathy, I would guarantee a loan of ten millions to rebuild churches and schools, smoke out Circassians, build roads, improve the country, etc. but every farthing of the loan would have to be spent under the direct control and supervision of British Commissioners. It always seemed to me that it was an outrageous thing this not having been done in the case of the former guaranteed loans. I should very much wish to see this proposal made, as it would be a good test of the earnestness of all this howling and tall talk, and, in the next place, if we do not show some readi-

[1] The dots here are Morier's. He has, presumably, omitted 'devil'.

ness to back our opinions by a sacrifice, we shall not only appear ridiculous, as we are doing now, but ineffably mean; and, lastly, the spending of this English loan in the country under the direct supervision of British Commissioners would give us an immense purchase over the country and establish a brilliant counterpoise to Russian influence, as Russia could not compete with us, not having the credit for such an operation. The interest might be guaranteed on the revenues of the province, which would give us a voice in the taxation . . .[1]

Morier's proposals amounted to a characteristically British scheme alike in its capacity for gradual development, its absence of dogma, and its sharp contrast with French and Russian plans and with actual Turkish reforms since the Crimean War. The French saw as the goal 'a fusion of races, to be achieved through the sincere application of administrative uniformity and civil and political equality'. The extreme liberals among the 'Young Turks' held similar views. The Russian alternative was decentralized autonomy, such as would accord with the fact that the Ottoman Empire was indeed an amalgam of religious and national communities. Each of the peoples within the empire should be offered 'des garanties *spéciales*, en mettant à profit les institutions religieuses et communales déjà existantes et en s'efforçant avant tout d'adapter ces dernières au principe *national*'.[2] The proceedings at Constantinople since 1856 had, by contrast, been directed towards a new and efficient centralization, more nearly approaching the views of the French. Christians were still not admitted to the army or to the navy and their evidence was still not taken in the courts, but by 1876 they were admitted to the civil service and high offices of state. This was to be the beginning of an administrative uniformity that would end by fusing all Christians into an Ottoman nation. It was followed meanwhile by the proclamation (23 December) of a central constitution with a parliament (a Senate and a House of Representatives) for all Turkey elected by all the subjects of the empire. The intention of its Young Turk framers was falsified, when the electoral system was so contrived as to produce a permanent Mussulman majority in the Lower House. Young Turk influences with the sultan,

---
[1] To Lady Derby, 5 Oct. 1876. My quotations are from a typed version in the material put together by Lady Wemyss for her account of 1876.
[2] B. H. Sumner, *Russia and the Balkans* (Oxford, 1937), p. 105.

personified by Midhat Pasha, were simultaneously able to stimulate a purifying and revivifying of the administrative and financial machine by punishing from the centre the negligence and inefficiency of local pashas. The constitution was accompanied by a series of reforms aimed at the fusion of races and centralized efficiency.[1] No British government had ever pressed for the grant of parliamentary institutions or for constitutional limitations upon the sultan's absolutism, but the habit had been rather to seek to improve the lot of the Christians by using his absolutism and depending upon his strength and his authority over the local pashas.[2] The British stood apart then from the French, the Russians, and the Young Turks, but at this date, 1876-7, while clear about the general drift of the reforms that were needed, they were less precise than Morier about the steps necessary to obtain them.

They were certainly not ready for the degree of British stimulation, even responsibility, which Morier took for granted. Disraeli might have been ready, but he could not have carried his cabinet with him. Morier also sent to Lady Derby information which reached him from his liberal friends in the circle of the Crown Prince and Princess, who were in their turn connected with the Hohenzollern rulers of Rumania. Charles of Hohenzollern-Sigmaringen, prince of Rumania, was married to Elizabeth of Wied (see above, p. 6). Morier's liberal friend and frequent correspondent, von Roggenbach, was *amicus curiae* of the Neu Wied family and 'its friend and counsellor for the last thirty years', and was in Bucharest in the summer of 1876 in attendance on the Princess of Wied, Elizabeth's mother, whom, as has been already said, he later secretly married. She was also connected with the Russian royal family.

Roggenbach wrote to Morier on 11 November 1876 a letter whose prophecies were not far off the mark and may have strengthened and stimulated his own ideas. It was this which he forwarded to Lady Derby. Roggenbach first bewailed the British passivity after the failure of the Berlin Memorandum, believing, as Morier had already asserted, that the Bulgarians, Greeks, Serbs, and, above all, the Rumanians were all ill-disposed to dependence upon Russia and would welcome the

---

[1] B. H. Sumner, *Russia and the Balkans* (Oxford, 1937), p. 243.
[2] H. Temperley, op. cit.

protection of any European Power or Powers against her. Britain, he wrote, should then have exerted sufficient pressure 'on the Ottoman Government', as her fleet, already at Besika Bay, enabled her to do, 'to obtain of [*sc.* from] it the autonomy of the provinces north of the Balkans [so] that all the merit of [these] liberations would have been hers after Russia had proved herself unable to do anything for [their] liberty'. Autonomy for these peoples should have been founded, not on the Andrássy Note or the Berlin Memorandum, but on the old Rumanian capitulations which had guaranteed the self government of Moldavia and Wallachia in the fourteenth century. Roggenbach went on to predict a Russo-Turkish war. The Bulgarian atrocities had so worked on Russian public opinion as to make the war inevitable, although it was certain 'that the Emperor and all who know how the things are standing' [who were aware, that is, of Russia's political weakness and military inefficiency] 'are looking' upon the outbreak 'of war as an immense calamity and the beginning of a shameful disaster'. Roggenbach's letter also contained the dangerous prophecy of a Russian military defeat and victorious Turkish resistance, backed by many plausible arguments. Rumania, however, he believed, would most likely maintain her neutrality against the Turks rather than against the Russians. Since she was not strong enough to prevent the passage of both, she would try to prevent the passage of the Turks rather than that of the Russians, acting under the influence of Bismarck, whose policy it now was to bring Russia and Austria together, on the basis of 'a second partition of Poland in Bosnia'. He still believed Russia would be defeated.[1]

In sending Roggenbach's letter to Lady Derby, Morier further clarified his own ideas and defined another step in his own programme. This was the plan for a joint Anglo-Russian occupation of the disturbed parts of the Ottoman Empire.[2] He developed it more soberly in a letter to Sir Louis Mallet on 2 December 1876 and, at the same time, returned to his proposal of a loan, already elaborated in his letter of October to Lady Derby. Mallet sent Morier's letter to Salisbury, his immediate chief at the India Office and British

[1] From Roggenbach, 11 Nov. 1876, preserved only in a typed copy among the papers collected by Lady Wemyss for her account of 1876.
[2] To Lady Derby, 5 Dec. 1876, typed copy.

plenipotentiary at the Constantinople Conference where representatives of the European Powers were then discussing the measures to be instituted by the sultan for the reorganization of his empire. Morier's plan had a hearing at the right moment.

Looking at the question from this long way off [he wrote to Mallet] and knowing it only as the man in the street knows it, I should, if I were asked to give a professional diplomatic diagnosis of it, say that it presented one difficulty and one only. Everybody is agreed that the integrity of Turkey is to be maintained and her independence destroyed, in so far at least as it is prejudicial to the interests of the population subject to the Porte. Everybody agrees that this is to be done by setting up a Government that shall represent the interests of the governed and not those of the hitherto governors. How this is to be done is a question of very difficult detail but still not one which will drive negotiators back to their tents to arm.

The next question is that of guarantees. Here there is more difficulty but I cannot believe that it would be impossible or even very difficult to obtain unanimity on the *principle* that the only guarantee possible is a limited occupation. The Syrian precedent[1] is too crushing to allow I think of [its] being persistently resisted. The fact of the Porte disliking it I estimate very cheap. Whatever the six Powers decide short of the dismemberment of Turkey she must and will submit to. The only *real* difficulty . . . I take to be as to *who* shall occupy. Everybody has been proposed in turns either singly or jointly—France, Italy, Austria, Russia, England, I believe even the United States, and now people seem to be drifting into a kind of fatalistic belief that the only possible occupiers are the Russians. The only solution which I have never seen propounded and which seems to me the only possible one and the one that would solve *all* difficulties is a *joint English and Russian occupation*, small in point of force, 5,000 men each, and strictly limited as to time. Such a proposal made by us would checkmate any ulterior plans of Russia if she has any whilst it would give her the amplest satisfaction for all legitimate desires. It would be the fullest possible guarantee to Turkey that the troops of occupation were not settling down there indefinitely, and that their presence there would have for its sole object the bringing about of an amelioration of the state of the country which must conduce to the welfare of Turkey herself. The presence of English troops alongside the Russians would further give for the three or four or five years it lasted perfect repose to Europe who would look upon the Eastern question as set to sleep

[1] An allusion to the proposed Anglo-French occupation when disorders occurred in 1860.

during that time by the beneficent paralysis of the two rivals whose rivalries are the real cause of disturbance. In fact from whichever side it is looked at, it presents advantages without my being able to detect a single objection.[1]

The second part of Morier's scheme was, it will be recollected, a loan. He now proposed a more modest sum of four or five millions, its interest secured on the revenues of Bulgaria; for its purpose was to make the part occupied, called for convenience Bulgaria, though the Constantinople Conference was still to fix frontiers, a model province during the occupation. It would be used to rebuild villages, make roads, furnish schoolhouses, and transplant the Circassians.

The application of this loan [continued Morier] should be vested in a commission, half of which, say two or even one member, should be English officials. By this means we should get the power not only of completely building up the country again materially and furnishing it with the organs of life, but as the mortgagers we should obtain direct influence with regard to the taxation of the country which if properly used might enable us to determine once for all the whole system of administration.

The result Morier pictured to himself with the confidence, characteristic of his day, that Britain excelled in creating prosperity for subject peoples. The occupied territory would fall into two halves: one, the English, in six months 'a kind of paradise'; the other, the Russian, with the population, whether Christian or Turkish, wishing them well out of the place. He recalled his experience of the yearning of the southern Slavs 'to lean on England and to find safety in her arms from the offensive embrace of Russia'.[2] Something not very different, in fact, was to happen in Egypt. Egyptian indebtedness was to lead after 1882 from control over taxation to the re-creation by a reluctant Britain of an Egyptian state. It has been one of the chief grounds for accusations of self-aggrandizement, made at the time and since, against Great Britain. Morier's initial proposals for Turkey, and the professional interest in creating good government which they reflect, are typical of the motives behind British imperialism.

[1] To Mallet, 2 Dec. 1876, preserved in a typed copy in the papers collected by Lady Wemyss for 1876.
[2] Ibid.

The scheme which Lord Salisbury actually secured at Constantinople comprised, not Anglo-Russian occupation, but international supervision by an international commission and a Belgian *gendarmerie*; not elected village vestries or councils with powers over roads and schools, but an elected provincial assembly; not a radical reform of the land laws and Christian courts, but some administrative and judicial reform and a Christian governor; and the idea of a loan, though renewed for Asia Minor in August 1878, was for the present, and in this context, dropped. It was a scheme more ambitious than Morier's in its European implications, and less ambitious in its local effects. It was designed for a north–south oblong of Bulgarian territory that never took shape; the whole plan, indeed, was stillborn.

Any satisfaction for Morier was of a very superficial kind; for there was no sign that Salisbury was anywhere directly influenced by his ideas. His plans encompassed the increase of British influence among the Balkan peoples. Nothing that Salisbury had gained would have enlarged this. Salisbury's scheme had anyhow no sanctions behind it and nothing but the spontaneous co-operation of the Turkish sultan could have put it into effect. It was this which caused Morier to be so critical of what was done.

It has lowered my notion of Lord Salisbury's statesmanship [he wrote][1] that he should have apparently consented to go to Constantinople with no better weapon in his hand than the harlequin's wooden sword of a *withdrawal of the Embassy* in case of failure. There are certain simple rules in international intercourse, just as in chess or any other complicated combination, from which results are to be evolved, which cannot be disregarded but which our F.O. seem absolutely to have lost all sense of. The only possible conditions on which we could get a satisfactory result out of the Conference, but on the other hand by which we could make *quite certain* of getting the results we wanted, were: if Russia put forward exorbitant demands, to be ready to assist Turkey in resisting those demands *by force* if necessary. If on the other hand we could agree with Russia and the rest of Europe on certain minimum reforms then equally to insist on these *by force* if necessary. What the deuce is the use of *force* unless it is to use its *potentiality* in such a way as to secure its not having to be had recourse to in its *essentiality*—in other words, why,

[1] To Mallet, 15 Jan. 1877, typed copy.

loving peace, do we spend millions on the largest navy in the world if not to have it in our power by threatening a war *in posse*, to prevent a war *in esse*?

Instead of joining the Conference [he went on to complain] as a member of a European Areopagus bound to enforce its *dicta* by force, if necessary, and called to sit in judgement on the maladministration of Turkey, we went in as if we had been mediators between Russia and Turkey, two parties not at war! And the notion was that if we did not succeed in mediating then we should just have to let them go to war! Whereas in so far as Russia is moderate she is *one of us* and anything more absolutely unfair *by her* than to say: if Turkey refuses what we i.e. Europe determine to be a minimum which we i.e. Europe have a right to demand of her then *you* Russia are at liberty to go to war with her and force her to do what Europe demands *but no more*—cannot be imagined. If Russia under these circumstances does go to war then she is perfectly justified in saying, if I am to make war on my own hook and at my own expense I shall make it for *my* purposes and not *yours* and if I succeed you have no right to interfere with my gathering up the fruits of my victory into my barns, not yours. But to allow the war between Russia and Turkey *à eux deux*, a war the most savage and barbarous that imagination can paint, and necessarily involving the ruin for generations and generations of the populations on the theatre of war for whom we profess such unbounded love and sympathy will be a disgrace to Europe and *specialiter* to *us*, the like of which we have not seen in our generation . . . Of course if the faculty of knowing how to use our force *potentially* has died out within us then Manchester is right and we had best sell off our Ironclads, pawn India, and give up being a Great Power, but in that case I would apostrophise myself in Barbier's words 'tourne-toi sur ton flanc et crève comme un chien'.

Of all Morier's suggestions the notion of Anglo-Russian combination alone proved to be the seed of further ideas. It seems to have germinated with both Mallet and White and perhaps even with Salisbury himself. Yet it was a notion that could equally well have been entertained by each of them independently. Mallet's reply to Morier's scheme of joint occupation described an idea that originated with Sir James Hudson[1] and had 'wide and powerful support . . . some months since but was stopped I expect in high quarters'. This was the idea that the Duke of Edinburgh and his Russian wife might create from the

[1] See below, p. 71, n. 2.

British and Russian royal houses a new dynasty to rule the Ottoman Empire. He thought it a real solution 'but too heroic for these days of parochial statesmanship'. Mallet then told how he had written to Lord Salisbury,

> that while I firmly believed that the best policy, and perhaps the only chance of enduring greatness for this country, lies in the direction of non-intervention in the politics of Europe, as a part of what you and I understand by the Cobdenic policy, yet that our possession of India, and our self-incurred obligations in that quarter have so compromised our position, that practically it was useless to talk about it. Neither Cobden nor Bright, nor anyone else, has ever even attempted to show how a system of policy can be constructed by which we can govern England as these men would have desired that it should be governed—and play the part of a great Asiatic despotism at the same time in India.
>
> ... Whether in any event [he continued] the attempt on the part of a country like England with 30,000,000 people to be at once a great European and a great Asiatic power, can be successful, may well be doubted. But I am sure of this, that the game can only be played by supreme skill and by availing ourselves of every possible resource within our reach. Neither in Europe, nor in Asia can we succeed without allies. We cannot fight the battle of civilization and order, against the vast forces arrayed against us, single-handed. Still less can we enlist on our side, in this campaign, the great forces of barbarism, which it is our mission to subdue and control. This would soon land us in the merited and hideous failure which awaits all violations of great natural laws.
>
> Now it seems to me that not only is Russia a suitable ally for this purpose—but the only possible ally. She is the only power besides ourselves at once European and Asiatic. In Europe closer relations with England are the one thing needful to help Russia forward in civilized progress, and to prevent her from falling back into anarchy, while in Asia to make her a friend instead of a rival, is to convert a senseless dream of barren dominion into a fruitful work of practical civilization . . .[1]

This was to be a theme to which both men were constantly to return. Meanwhile a few weeks later Morier received from White a letter from Pera recounting 'the secret history' of the Conference from which much the same lesson was to be learnt and reporting that Salisbury had indeed sought to draw nearer to

[1] From Mallet, 25 Dec. 1877, typed copy among the papers collected by Lady Wemyss for 1877.

Russia. White had been sent to Constantinople to assist Salisbury in the Conference which was then coming to an end. 'Lord Salisbury', he wrote,[1] 'during his diplomatic tour to Continental Courts [i.e. on his way out to Constantinople] has convinced himself that no Power is disposed to shield Turkey—not even Austria if blood has to be shed for the status quo and H[is] L[ordship] came here determined to prepare for a new line of policy . . .' After some gossip about Salisbury's relations with the regular ambassador, Sir Henry Elliot, he went on:

> Bismarck is aiming at upsetting every pacific solution and involving Russia in an expensive and dangerous war; he will continue to use Andrassy as his tool and he will thus prepare two great results: the weakening of Russia and the partitioning of Turkey. If he can bring all this about, and for this there must be war, he will find it easy to isolate France permanently and to make some rearrangement of the map of Europe which will in his opinion strengthen and consolidate the *Reich*.
>
> The question for us is firstly to preserve peace on fair terms advantageous to the populations of this Empire—secondly, if this fails, to watch over such portions as bear on our interests. It is certainly most important for us to prevent Bismarck from having altogether his own way in Europe but to do this we must, while keeping well with France and Austria, draw nearer to Russia—this has been Ld. Salisbury's object—he has been thwarted by the Premier at home and to some extent by some parties here. He is not likely to forgive all this *apparent* failure.

Morier saw with increasing dismay that the development of events between the dispersal of the Constantinople Conference and the presentation of the London Protocol of 31 March to Turkey on 6 April steadily diminished the power of Britain to influence what might happen in the Balkan peninsula. Russia, by the negotiation in London of a fresh scheme of reforms which Turkey was to be invited but not obliged to accept, masked her real work. This was to ensure, by the negotiation of the secret agreement of Budapest with Austria-Hungary (January 1877) and the convention with Rumania, that when she acted in isolation, as she did on 24 April, she would do so in the most favourable circumstances for herself.

---

[1] From Sir William White, 16 Jan. 1877, typed copy among the papers collected by Lady Wemyss for 1877.

Morier knew nothing, of course, of Russia's proceedings, but he prophesied a Russo-Turkish war and rightly saw that it was unlikely to be easily won by Russia. He wrote to Jowett from Lisbon, on 2 March 1877:[1]

I am truly glad that your Hall and other buildings [at Balliol] have succeeded, especially if, as you say, the success is *architectural* as well as social and academical. I do not see much chance of the days we live in producing anything excellent in painting and sculpture but I do not see why within the next thirty years we should not considerably improve architecture not of the highest kind, for we do not believe enough either in Zeus or the God of the Athanasian Creed to build them fitting habitations and neither the Parthenon nor Seville Cathedral can ever come to life again. But we believe in man rather more than was ever done before and I do not see why in time we should not construct habitations for him at least as good in their kind as some sorts of snails have succeeded in doing. I wish I had been at the symposium. I have never yet assisted at one such College Feast. One, I mean to come to, even if I have to come from the ends of the earth to it and that will be the Silver Wedding of your Mastership. Let me know some time before when it will be that I may make preparations in time. Fancy my not recollecting the date of your succession to the stool of Saint Jenkyns![2]

I do not understand (you see I am writing as a Christian ought to do with your letter[3] before me and taking your subjects seriatim) why in your table of precedence of the States of Europe you put the Turks first and the Russians last—still less why you put the Russians after the English. About the position of the latter there can be no doubt—some hundred fathoms below Greece or Monaco. But it is the to-do that is made about the Turks that puzzles me most, or rather does not puzzle me because it is only a proof of the very patent fact that we have entirely lost in England the power of measuring and gauging these questions of international politics. That the Turks would refuse to submit to the dictation of the Conference was what anybody might have foretold who knew that in inviting Europe to ascend the judgement seat we had duly warned the offender that, whatever were the sentence passed under

---

[1] Typed copy, among the papers collected by Lady Wemyss for 1877.

[2] Richard Jenkyns, Master of Balliol College, from 1819 to 1854. Jowett did not succeed him until 1870. Both Morier and Jowett had been undergraduates under Jenkyns. Neither lived to see the Silver Jubilee of Jowett's Mastership.

[3] From Jowett, 27 Jan. 1877; Morier alludes to the paragraph beginning 'This country has sunk rather low . . . the relative position of European nations seems to be . . .', Abbott and Campbell, *Life and Letters of Benjamin Jowett*, iii. 82.

no circumstances would it be put into execution. The fallacy seems to me to be this: that because the Turks committed atrocities in Bulgaria, they are barbarians and because they are barbarians their political conduct is not guided by the same rules as the political conduct of non-barbarians. Whereas the real state of the case is almost the reverse. Because the Turks have remained barbarians with the traditions and some of the prestige of a great barbarian Power that has held its own for centuries against civilized nations, they have retained the traditional *savoir faire* of the *grande politique* (never mind my French: I'm not writing to print and if I take too much trouble in choosing my words I will never end this letter) far more than other European Powers who in the process of civilization have lost their traditions. Above all they have by a kind of hereditary instinct retained the power of never losing sight of the *simple rules* of the great game of politics (a power which we have lost absolutely and beyond recovery) so that I shall have no hesitation in saying that in a great international chess tournament like that lately played out at Constantinople anyone who knew what he was about, would have from the first day put his money on them against the field.

Now among the simple rules of the game of international politics the simplest is the one that you must know whether you mean to fight and if you do, when, where, and against what odds. Of all the infernal nonsense English statesmen have got into the way of talking that of 'moral influence' as something different from fighting *in posse* is the most absurd and suicidal. The art of international politics, or in other words diplomacy, is the art of so employing the force 'fighting in posse' as to prevent the employment of the force 'fighting in esse' and of course the excellence of the artist will consist in concealing from the spectator the working of the machinery by which his masterpieces are brought about. Of course too the diplomatic artist will not only know when *he* means to exchange the pen for the sword but he will know exactly when his partners and above all his adversaries mean to do so.

Well, one thing was obvious, which was that the Turks (considering the very great straits they were in: that *pluck*, moral and political as well as mere fighting pluck, is the quality they have *never* been deficient in: that they had already repudiated [interest on their debt] and therefore that they had no credit to lose) would look upon a single handed war with Russia as the least of the evils with which they were threatened. For the odds in such a war are by no means so unfavourable to Turkey as '*Our William*'[1] and his 'people'

---

[1] i.e. Gladstone.

imagine. As a question of strategy all experts are agreed that to make a *certainty* of a victorious march upon and conquest of Constantinople *two* conditions are necessary, a movement by an overpowering army across the Balkans and a flank attack by sea in support. But by the destruction of Sebastopol, whose *raison d'être* was this flank movement, this combination was destroyed and Russia has not had time to rebuild her great arsenal or her fleet, whereas the Turks have spent a good portion of the money they have extracted from our idiotic country clergymen and officers' widows[1] in creating a fleet capable of sweeping the Russian fleet off the face of the waters and holding the Black Sea. There only remains therefore the unsupported march across the Balkans and nobody knows better than the Russians what this means against 200,000 Turks who mean fighting. Have you forgotten that in the winter of 1853–54 the garrison of Silistria with three Englishmen to lead them kept the whole Russian army at bay for five months and that 40,000 Russians lie rotting there at this moment? Consequently good diplomacy ought to have known that a duel with Russia in which she would be pretty sure of being left alone and of no one interfering on either side would be what Turkey would on the whole consider the least evil for her to choose and that such a duel therefore never could be held out *in terrorem* of Turkey as the *Sanction* which would enforce the decision of the Conference. In a word the strength of Turkey's diplomatic position at the Conference lay in her having quite made up her mind that she would fight Russia if Russia was to be the only enemy she had to meet in the field. Now good diplomacy ought to have known this from the first and played its cards accordingly. The *one* thing it was bound not to do was to let Turkey know that recalcitration to the decisions of the Conference would have as its worst consequence this Russo-Turkish duel because this was to invite recalcitration. If we could not make up our minds beforehand as to what we were to do (and to have a policy with an outlook of 48 hours is what we have ceased to be capable of) and if joint coercion was a sin against the Holy Spirit of non-intervention which we would not commit, the least we could do, if we meant the Conference to have a result, was to keep the *Sanction* wrapped up in mystery to the last and to lead the Turks to believe that joint coercion was one of the possible consequences of recalcitration. But instead of this, *Oh sancta simplicitas!* what do we do? Without apparently consulting the other Powers (in itself a great indecency for you have no business to invite people to join in an act which you doom a priori to a ridiculous *fiasco*) we tell the Turks whatever happens and however much they may

[1] An allusion to the people investing in the nearly gilt-edged security of the guaranteed loan of 1856 to Turkey.

recalcitrate we shall not coerce. Now, as under the given circumstances of the case, our refusal to join in coercion necessitated the neutrality of Austria and Germany, what we said was: the only sanction to the decisions of the Conference, however unanimous these may be, will be the very duel with Russia which is what you have made up your minds is the best thing on the whole that can happen to you. When Mr. Nightingale driven by hunger to desperation made up his mind to commit an act of highway robbery he compromised with his conscience by attacking Tom Jones with an unloaded pistol, but he did not write the day beforehand to let Tom Jones know that his pistol would be innocent of powder and shot. To make matters quite logical and to paralyze our action in every direction we told the Russians that nothing would make us fight *for* the Turks against them. Thus having all the trump cards in our hands and the most magnificent chance of settling the question in the way that it ought to be settled viz. by preventing the Russians from effecting a lodgment either military or political South of the Danube and by extorting from Turkey a maximum of concessions for the Christian populations, we played our game so as to secure as far as bad diplomacy could secure it, the one issue that we should from the first have guarded against—an issue so horrible to contemplate that I should have thought no one could have entertained the thought of it without instinctively crying out: anything rather than that, even the risk of a few bluejackets being killed and wounded and an ironclad or two indented! I mean a single handed fight protracted perhaps for a year or two in the Balkan Peninsula amidst all those populations for whom we have been lashing ourselves into such furies of philanthropy, between fanaticized Russians and fanaticized Turks. Yet I am sorry to say this was the issue which our Olympians of the F.O. regarded with the greatest complacency and as on the whole the best thing that could happen. Now all this sickening mismanagement and ineptitude arose solely from the fatal fallacy of believing that there is such a thing as *moral influence* in international politics as something distinct from and independent of fighting *in posse*; in other words that you can set diplomatic machinery in motion *without a motive power*. You have only to bear in mind the situation as it was when we had got the Conference together (our doing remember) and then to imagine the action of British diplomacy acting with a motive power instead of without one and you will at once see how the results were to be obtained. A man like Ld. Palmerston would have known that Russia could never face a coalition between Turkey and England, nor Turkey one between Russia and England, and before calling the Conference together or moving a step in that direction he would have told the Turks: if Russia demands what we consider would be dangerous to your integrity and what you cannot grant we will assist you against her. But in return for this prospective assistance we demand such concessions in regard to the Christian populations as will secure them against your misrule and these concessions must be of the widest and most drastic kind. To Russia we should have said: we will resist any demands which will further your projects for approaching Constantinople but if you drop these and only demand bona fide guarantees for the Christians we will join with you in *forcing* the Turks to grant them. These were the rules of the game and no two Powers understood the rules better than the Turks and the Russians. I have no hesitation in saying that there never was a finer game to play *or an easier one* than England had at the opening of the Conference. Nor is this an afterthought. I had it all down in black and white and placed before Ld. Salisbury before the Conference began but *cui bono*?

Of course I shall be told if Ignatieff's memorandum succeeds and he finds a bridge for Russia to retreat by out of her present position, that our diplomacy has been a magnificent success—that we have prevented a European War etc. etc. My answer is this is all fudge. The F.O. never for one moment believed that Russia would not fight. They have been more astonished than anyone at the collapse— every step they took led us nearer and nearer to the duel and it is no fault of theirs that we are not being dunned at the present moment by societies for the relief of wounded Cossacks on the one side and wounded Bashi Bazouks on the other.

Cintra, 28th March 1877

Thus far had I got at the beginning of the month when I was interrupted by a ministerial crisis which has played the devil with many matters I was successfully carrying out here and which with our emigration to Cintra has kept my hands in full work and prevented my finishing. And now appears your second letter[1] heaping coals of fire on my head. There is enough in these four sheets to serve your turn for a while so I will now set to work to answer your number two. I agree with much of it but naturally have a somewhat less abstract way of viewing these European politics than you have, a mason viewing buildings more in concrete detail than a landscape painter. The great and important habit for an *homme de métier* in politics to form, is, the exact mean between too much generalising and too little of it. On one or two points, however, I consider you

---

[1] From Jowett, 14 Mar. 1877, Jowett papers, part printed in Abbott and Campbell, *Life and Letters of Benjamin Jowett*, iii. 83–9.

wrong in your premises. I believe it to be a fatal miscalculation to look upon France as in any way desirous of war or the least equipped with those heroic sentiments you credit her with. I have taken immense pains to come to a correct opinion on this subject and have exceptionally good means of verifying the results I have myself come to and my conviction is that the war of 1870 has taken the fighting out of her to an extent very little known generally. France will not fight unless she cannot possibly help it unless with such extraordinary odds in her favour (a Russian-Austrian coalition or the like) that she could see Alsace-Lorraine falling into her mouth with no more risk on her part than just opening it. French politicians know this very well and their art consists in not letting the world find it out. France is very rapidly getting the disease which we have been more slowly and surely dying of—a fatty heart, brought on by wealth, by wealth-making on a national scale. The dangerous element in Europe is not Germany but Bismarck. He is getting just as dangerous as Napoleon I was after Austerlitz. I therefore quite agree with you that it is the danger from that quarter we have got to guard against and it could quite easily be guarded against if England had retained the power of playing a rational political part in Europe. The thing is infinitely easier than you seem to fancy because these things are not done by *formal leagues* but by informal exchange of views, but as no English Foreign Minister can be brought to have a *view* which he cannot expound in Parliament at 24 hours notice it is useless to speculate on what might be if England was still for practical purposes a Great Power. That she has it absolutely in her hands to prevent a great war and to secure that period of peace which would ensure all the nations of Europe getting the disease of the fatty heart which might bring about a general disarmament, is my most firm conviction and that no Power ever had such a position for effecting a maximum of international good (given the peculiar way in which the various Powers are at present balanced against each other)—but it is impossible—so there's an end of it. It is one of the *Bon Dieu*'s bad jokes that He always puts the power of doing good in hands that won't use it. You ask me if I know of anyone fit to replace Elliot[1] [at Constantinople]. My answer is that if there was a fit man, in the true and high sense you mean, his fitness would be a fatal bar and disability to his being employed. Sir James Hudson[2] was for six years (I do not know whether he

[1] Sir Henry George Elliot (1817–1907) was withdrawn from Constantinople and replaced by Sir A. H. Layard on 31 Mar. 1877. He was afterwards ambassador in Vienna until he retired in 1884.
[2] Sir James Hudson (1810–85), British representative in Turin 1851–63. He left his post some six years before he reached retiring age.

would be up to it now) to be had for the asking. We never produced a diplomatist so exactly fitted for the post: yet the F.O. whichever party was in, would have appointed the last shoeblack rather than him. The candidates most *talked* of in London at the F.O. and the clubs, have been myself and Thornton . . . I do not however believe that there is *now* the least chance of my being the victim, though there was some time ago. Such qualities as I may have for the post are just of the kind as would unfit me in the eyes of the F.O. and the qualities that would fit me, knowledge of the East, an easy pleasant ambling official action etc. are just the qualities I have not got. I should like nothing more than a post of this kind with a *MAN* at my back . . .

3

AFRICA: THE LORENÇO MARQUES TREATY, 30 MAY 1879, AND THE CONGO TREATY

IN east Africa Great Britain had both territorial and economic disagreements with Portugal. She contested—on the ground that David Livingstone had actually discovered it—Portugal's claim to sovereignty over Lake Nyasa. She claimed for herself a share in the control of the rivers which flowed through both British and Portuguese territory, and refused to accept the Portuguese claim to monopolize the steam navigation of the rivers Shiré and Zambesi (denying that the first flowed wholly through Portuguese territory). She objected to the Portuguese monopoly of the coasting trade and the high tariff which prevented British economic penetration of Portuguese Mozambique. Portugal answered by 'showing the intense soreness of people who feel themselves put upon but who feel too weak to show their teeth otherwise than by a ghastly endeavour to smile pleasantly', and by asserting 'a determination to abide by a dogged *non possumus*'. Portugal maintained the monopoly on the Zambesi, preserved the Mozambique tariff, and limited the coasting trade to Portuguese registered ships, thus shutting 'up 1000 miles of coast to every flag except that of the non-existent Portuguese ships'.

Morier opened his campaign for better Anglo-Portuguese relations in Africa by raising the question of the east coast. He told Corvo:

> I cannot guarantee you against the fire-eaters and the Hotspurs of our religious societies. If the British Lion gets a religious fit, still more if that fit tends in the direction of fresh markets for cotton goods, *il est capable de tout*. But what I can do for you, is to fight your battles, when you are clearly in the right and to defend you, when

you are unjustly and unfairly attacked. I feel very confident that during such time as I may be Minister here, no British Government will annex Lake Nyassa or found a colony there and your just rights and just susceptibilities will invariably find in me a zealous exponent.[1]

He asked in return that Portugal should 'throw every barrier down, give me the lowest tariff on the Dark Continent, tear down the cabotage on the coast, open every port and creek and inlet to the flags of all nations, uncork the Zambesi'.

This was pretty well what he got. Within a year the Mozambique tariff had been reformed. The decree enacting the new tariff was drafted by Serpa and Corvo, and issued by the de Ávila ministry of 1877. As a result duties were levied in Mozambique at a uniform rate of about 6 per cent *ad valorem* 'instead of 40 per cent or 400'. These were lower than those levied in British Natal, a little further down the coast. This reform Morier claimed was made at his instance and owing to his initiative. At the same time the customs regulations were revised, and transit dues for goods going to Lake Nyasa and elsewhere in the interior were established at 3 per cent.

Next, Morier attacked the monopoly granted for thirty years to the Portuguese company of Anhory and Zagury[2] for the steam navigation of the rivers Shiré and Zambesi.[3] He poured out his doctrine of 'the general get-at-ableness' of colonial territory with torrential force in a letter to the Portuguese minister. It is a superb statement of the conviction which lay at the root of late Victorian imperialism: that the economics which were good for Britain were equally good for the rest of the world.

He began by repudiating any pedantic adherence to international law; it was not there, but in a much more elevated region that they should seek for a rule of conduct, the one towards the other; it should be in memories of centuries-old political intimacy and in the common interests which above all dictated in so many respects a policy of harmonious solidarity.

---

[1] Morier so reports his language in a long private letter to Salisbury, 18 Jan. 1879, which reviews Anglo-Portuguese relations in east and west Africa, see below, pp. 83, 85-6.

[2] A company with a capital of only £20,000 and possessing only two steamers, see to Corvo, 20 Oct. 1876, enclosed in Morier to Derby, no. 49 consular, 20 Oct. 1876, F.O. 84/1447.

[3] See to Salisbury, no. 12 slave-trade, confidential, 14 May 1878, F.O. 84/1504; no. 4 slave-trade, 27 Jan. 1879, F.O. 84/1537.

He went on to claim as the principal argument against the monopoly an alleged agreement between himself and Corvo to pursue an identic policy in Africa whether in relation to the natives, to the slave-trade, or to commerce. He showed its practical results in the tariff and the custom-house regulations and went on to urge that it only remained to reach an accommodation in regard to the coastal and transit trade. 'Libre-échangiste', he continued, 'jusqu'au bout des ongles, la vue d'un douanier me donne des crispations nerveuses telles que l'on peut s'imaginer ressentait au moyen âge un Inquisiteur à la vue d'un Juif, ou, à l'heure qu'il est, un Serbo-russe quand il flaire le Turque.'[1] He then contrasted the British system of accessibility with the Portuguese system of impenetrability ('imperméabilité'). After expensive wars such as those which she fought with China, after diplomatic triumphs such as those which she celebrated against Japan, Britain had never claimed exclusive privileges, but had worked for others as much as for herself. In the same way Britain's work of policing the rivers and coasts of Africa had opened the trade of Africa to all. As for Portugal: 'partout où il peut se fixer et établir sa forteresse je vois mon douanier avec son sabre prêt à fermer l'entrée au marchand légitime qui ne veut ou ne peut pas partager avec le fisc, les profits de son pénible travail, partout des droits si élevés qu'ils tuent le commerce sans enrichir la colonie; partout des tracasseries et des pédanteries encore plus nuisibles que les droits élevés.'[2] The closure of the coastal trade even to the British, who admitted foreigners to the coastal trade of the United Kingdom, he likened to the closing of the pores of the skin which brought disease in its train. Morier drew, towards the end of his letter, a vivid picture of an imaginary trading enterprise, about to bring enormous profits to Portuguese Africa under concessions from the Portuguese government, stifled by the Anhory–Zagury firm, and

---

[1] 'Free-trader to my finger tips, as I am, the sight of a customs officer sends nervous shudders down my back, such as one might imagine an inquisitor felt in the middle ages at the sight of a Jew or a Serbo-Russian nowadays when he scents a Turk.'

[2] 'Wherever [Portugal] has been able to lodge herself and establish a fortress, I see my customs officer with his sword ready to close the entrance to legitimate merchants, who do not wish to or cannot share with the Treasury the profits of their arduous labour; everywhere duties so high that they kill trade without enriching the colony; everywhere annoyances and pedantic restrictions even more injurious than high duties,'

closed with a hint that, since Africa was becoming a matter of ever greater popular interest in Britain, focusing alike the idealism of missionaries and the realism of traders, British opinion would turn against Portugal unless she broke absolutely and 'd'un coup hardi' with her traditional system. Finally he asserted that Portugal had not the means of inducing her own nationals to develop her African colonies. 'Ouvrez-les,' he appealed, 'et le capital et le travail étrangers y entreront et en première ligne le capital et le travail anglais; les affaires marcheront; les colonies se développeront; une fois florissantes les Portugais s'y rendront par milliers comme ils le font maintenant au Brésil . . . Nous sommes faits pour s'engraisser à côté l'un de l'autre [sic] par l'échange de nos produits.'[1] Morier had deliberately chosen the formal mode of communication by letter, written in French, so that he could gain 'a better chance of placing my observations before the eyes of those other members of the cabinet who might be accessible to such representations'.[2] The immense length of the letter may not, however, have helped him to do so.

Yet he won his success. The coastal trade was opened to the flags of all nations and the monopoly was withdrawn. Morier's policy seemed by the end of 1876 to have succeeded in establishing on the east coast the mutual confidence he desired.

The situation was then entirely altered by the British annexation of the Transvaal in April 1877. It raised immense excitement. The Portuguese papers, Morier reported,[3] 'are filled with Anathemas against the devouring ambition of the British Crown'. Many 'otherwise sane and estimable' Portuguese firmly believed that Britain acted only out of revenge for the arbitration of President MacMahon which, in 1875, had assigned Delagoa Bay to Portugal. This conviction was the more bitter, since their triumph had recalled the past, 'when the galleys and carvels of Vasco da Gama and Castro swept the

[1] 'Open them, and foreign capital and labour will come in, especially English capital and labour; business will thrive; the colonies will develop; once they prosper Portuguese merchants will go there in thousands as they do now to Brazil . . . We are made to grow rich side by side by the exchange of our products.'
[2] See to Corvo, 20 Oct. 1876, enclosed in Morier to Derby, no. 49 consular, 20 Oct. 1876, F.O. 84/1447; see also F. Latour da Veiga Pinto, *Le Portugal et le Congo au xixe siècle* (Paris, 1972), pp. 128–32.
[3] To Derby, no. 30, 15 May 1877, F.O. 63/1061.

Indian Ocean and distributed rewards and punishments along the coasts of Africa and India to the friends and foes of the Portuguese Crown', and stimulated dreams of 'golden harvests' which were to be reaped by exploiting the need of 'the leaden inhabitants of the Transvaal' for transit through Portuguese Africa to an outlet on the coast. Morier sought to allay the excitement by an explanation to the King and by a series of three letters published above the signature 'Anglicus philolusitanus' in a Lisbon newspaper. To the King he explained[1] that

for twelve months everything had been done by us in the way of warning, encouragement, and even the promise of support to save the Republic, which, torn to pieces by internal dissension was bent on an aggressive policy towards the native population, whilst offering to the warlike tribes by which it was surrounded the tempting prize of a helpless and disorganised white community ripe for attack. All our efforts have proved fruitless.

The threat of Zulu attack combined with the call for annexation by 'the wealth, intelligence and respectability' of the Transvaal community had been the immediate cause, and no other, for annexation. It was 'a necessary measure of self-preservation, and that not merely as regards the British population in Southern Africa, but . . . the whole white population in those parts, including His [Portuguese] Majesty's subjects'.

Morier's longer defence of the annexation in the three letters[2] is even more interesting. Although he received frequent letters from Captain Frederic Elton, consul at Mozambique until his death in March 1878, he had had no material officially supplied on which to base it. He was also in correspondence with Lord Carnarvon, but he did not receive and did not need instructions. He had only to set out his own thinking on events as they happened to make a better defence of the annexation than Carnarvon, the colonial secretary, made in the House of Lords or J. Lowther, the under-secretary, in the House of Commons.[3] The strength of late Victorian policy in Africa was the

[1] To Derby, no. 33 confidential, 17 May 1877, F.O. 63/1062.
[2] See Lady Wemyss's draft for her continuation of the *Memoirs* where they are typed in full in English. There are also English drafts in Morier's hand. They were published in Portuguese.
[3] The government at home left a voluminous Blue Book of dispatches to speak for itself. Carnarvon made the bare statement that the Transvaal was in chaos and it was likely that war with the natives would spread. Lowther made the debating

consensus of opinion in the political nation in Britain behind it. Men brought up in the long tradition of old families and old institutions arrived spontaneously, by however different routes, at the same terminus. Though Morier's was not on one side an old family, he wrote from within the tradition.

Morier's three letters recounted the history of the annexation, as he interpreted it, with great clarity and simplicity. His first claimed it was a mistake to have allowed the refugees from Cape Colony to plant their new states (the Orange Free State and the Transvaal) in a wilderness peopled by fierce Kaffir tribes whom they had to fight in order to exist at all. It went on to describe a second mistake: that of allowing the Boers to build what he called a breakwater against black invasions *without any control*, merely to save Britain expense. Next, Natal had developed as a new independent colony on the coast, divided from the Cape to the south by British Kaffraria and divided from Portuguese Mozambique to the north by the powerful Zulu kingdom. This had been followed by the appointment of a British High Commissioner for South Africa in order to hold together the policy of the two colonies, the Cape and Natal, on matters where they had common interests, especially those concerning the black Africans. The flood of white men to the gold and diamond fields in the interior increased his responsibilities.

The problem everywhere was the precarious safety of a small white minority surrounded by a black host—the figures Morier gave were 14,000 white people in Natal, 400,000 Kaffirs, and a Zulu army of 40,000—and the answer was to confront the solidarity of the native races with the solidarity of the European race. Carnarvon's object, Morier explained, was to attain this solidarity by uniting the white colonies and the Republic of South Africa (as the Transvaal was called before annexation) into a Confederation, or Federal Union, in which each colony or state should retain its full autonomy for internal affairs, but conform to a common policy in whatever affected its external safety or welfare. Before the negotiations for federation were complete, the Transvaal went to war and its forces

---

point that Shepstone's action, being taken with only a bodyguard of 26 policemen, could not be called aggression, but did not argue the real issue of whether war with the Kaffirs and Zulus would spread or not. *Hans. Parl. Deb.* ccxxxiv, 353–5, ccxxxvi, 974–80 (debate on South African Confederation).

collapsed before the Kaffir host of King Sekukuni. This defeat made it necessary to save it from destruction by covering it with the British flag.

Morier's second letter described the position of the Transvaal, hedged about by disputed frontiers and surrounded by tribes

MAP 2. The Transvaal 1875-6

outside, which were connected with British subjects *inside* by 'ties of blood, intermarriage and ancient clanship'. To the south-west lay the frontier which the Keate Award had failed to settle; to the south-east lay the Zulu kingdom, whose king claimed suzerain rights over the tribe of the Amaswasi inside the Transvaal; to the north-east lay the dangerous triangle between the Oliphant, Steelpoort, and Limpopo rivers, excluded from the Transvaal in a map of 1868 and included in that of 1875; to the west lay the territory of King Sekukuni and Lydenburg, the centre of the gold-diggers. Inside the Transvaal, to the south of the triangle, was the kraal of Sekukuni's brother and enemy.

In a third letter Morier described the forward movement of the Boers in all three of the disputed areas, from the time of the proclamation of 15 August 1875, which took over the territory assigned to the Transvaal by the Keate Award, to the assertion of undivided power over the Amaswasi and the declaration of war on Sekukuni in May 1876. The drift of the story was to show that British interests were deeply compromised, especially those of the colonists of Natal to the south-east and the community of British gold-diggers to the north-west; so that annexation was unavoidable. The concentration of Transvaal forces on the military campaign against Sekukuni in the north left them exposed to an invasion from the Zulus in the south. The Kaffir war ended ignominiously in August 1876 when the citizens of the Republic generally deserted the colours and, abandoning their President, returned each to his own homestead. Troops were at once sent from England when the news reached home in September 1876, and the high commissioner, Sir Theophilus Shepstone, who was then in England, was sent back to the Transvaal. Shepstone found matters in the Transvaal even worse than he expected to find them: the Republic in a state not far short of anarchy and impending civil war, its finances not disordered only but hopelessly bankrupt, its military organization non-existent; a violent war party insisting on the resumption of hostilities without men or money; a crushing war tax which the citizens refused to pay; the Kaffirs on all sides gathering together to swoop down upon their prostrate victims; the prestige of the white man dangerously compromised. There was but one chance of salvation: the hoisting of the British flag over the tottering ruins of the Republic and with it the symbol of white unity under the humane guidance but with the irresistible force of the imperial power of Great Britain. Morier forestalled the modern verdict that 'annexation probably saved the Transvaal'.[1]

The conclusion of the letters was yet another plea that cooperation and not rivalry should guide the policy of Britain and Portugal in Africa.

In 1878 Morier's policy of improving Anglo-Portuguese rela-

[1] D. M. Schreuder, *Gladstone and Kruger* (1969), p. 27.

tions was threatened from another quarter and Portuguese fears that the British were bent on driving them out were renewed. Scottish missionaries had established themselves, in honour of Livingstone, on the Great Nyasa Lake immediately behind Portuguese Mozambique. Their only waterway to the sea lay down the Zambesi through Portuguese territory.

They combine [Morier wrote], quite rightly, trading operations with Christianity and deal indiscriminately in Gospel truths and cotton prints, receiving in return baptizable infants and ivory. They were placed very directly under my protection and I had to obtain for them every kind of facility from the Portuguese Government including everything for their settlement and *all their merchandise* free of Custom House charges. Nothing could have behaved better than the Portuguese Government did. There were a few hitches by the local authorities which were set right as soon as ever they were reported here and all the settlers ever suffered was the having to deposit part of the Customs' duties at Quilimane until Lisbon could be communicated with.

In May 1878 one of their number, E. D. Young, was reported to be preaching a crusade against the Portuguese,

saying they ought to be turned out of the country, that they are one and all villains and scoundrels, that they charged 28 per cent on all the mission goods, that the descendants of Livingstone's negroes had established themselves firmly on the Shiré at its entrance into the Zambesi, that they would shoot down every Portuguese who attempted to get up to the Lake ... The Portuguese in Lisbon were much excited and the matter was raised in the Cortes.[1]

Morier was especially discomfited because he had used the Nyasa settlement as a justification for his pressure to get the reforms in the tariff, the opening of the coastal trade, and the lowering of the transit dues. E. D. Young's speech at Cape Town in which he indicated 'that Englishmen could make everything of the country and of its inhabitants and the Portuguese nothing and that therefore the sooner the one was substituted for the other the better' was the most offensive. Meanwhile Young had written to Morier a letter which showed his animus against the Portuguese and made it difficult for Morier to deny that the Nyasa settlers were making common cause with native tribes against the Portuguese, were furnishing

[1] To Mallet, 1 June 1878, typed copy.

them with arms and ammunition, and using them effectively to bar the Portuguese from the interior. Morier said something of this in his reply to Young and sent both letters home.[1] To the Portuguese he had explained the Cape Town speech as Young's private folly, but the impression, he believed, remained 'of a settled purpose on the part of Great Britain to establish British communities as the *nuclei* of future colonies to the rear of the Portuguese dominions' with the object of driving them ultimately into the sea. Morier feared the lasting ill effects on Anglo-Portuguese relations. This was particularly dangerous, since the Nyasa settlement was likely to increase in importance because it would bring in its train the rapid commercial development of the interior and 'with this importance it will grow and with its growth will necessarily come British jurisdiction, and with British jurisdiction and the unfurling of the British flag, British territorial Rights and Sovereignty'.[2] When that time came, delimitation of frontiers and territorial arrangements would have to be determined between the two governments. In these arrangements Portugal, by possessing the seaboard and part at least, therefore, of the waterways which give access to the interior, would be at an advantage. It was eminently in the British interest to prepare for this future by building good intercourse now. This purpose Morier's policy was directed to achieve, and Young's antics—'the pyrotechnic displays of bombardier missionaries'—calculated to foil. Morier showed characteristic far-sightedness. It was something of a handicap to a man acting as the mouthpiece of a government that liked to let the future take care of itself. His government was unlikely to back him in seeking to anticipate the struggle to define and clarify African territorial rights.

The British annexation in 1878 of Walfisch Bay on the west coast of Africa added yet another reason for Portuguese mistrust. The report of the commissioner responsible for the annexation, W. Coates Palgrave, was made to the Cape government and published by them.[3] It was especially irritating, since it

[1] To Salisbury, no. 13 slave-trade, confidential, 15 May 1878, F.O. 84/1504.
[2] To Salisbury, no. 12 slave-trade, confidential, 14 May 1878, F.O. 84/1504.
[3] See *Report of W. Coates Palgrave, Esq. Special Commissioner to the Tribes North of the Orange River of his Mission to Damaraland and Great Namaqualand in 1876*, presented to both Houses of Parliament by H.E. The Governor in 1877, copy in the Morier papers.

made it clear that the annexation amounted to shifting the allegiance of the local chiefs from Portugal to Britain. The annexation was said to be made at the solemn request of the native chiefs of the entire country which was undoubtedly Portuguese. The annexed territories comprised 'sixty miles of Portuguese coast, and this be it noted', Morier wrote, 'not coast merely claimed by Portugal, but coast which in two solemn treaties (1815 [sc. 1813] and 1817) we have recognised as Portuguese'. Morier, over this as over so much else that was controversial, took the side of the Portuguese.[1]

While causes of difficulty with Portugal were thus accumulating, the government at home had come to the decision to open negotiations with her for certain safeguards, at Portuguese Delagoa Bay, for the Transvaal. One of these—the control of the import of arms and ammunition through Lorenço Marques —was not likely to be difficult; since Portugal in October 1876 had already professed herself willing to prohibit it and had offered to negotiate a formal agreement. The offer was not accepted as long as the Transvaal was at war with the Kaffirs. But at the next critical time—during the Zulu War, January to February 1879—Portugal effectively prohibited arms reaching the Zulus through Lorenço Marques. The second safeguard— that for Transvaal trade—was equally unlikely to offer difficulties. Portugal was ready to agree with Britain on an arrangement for the unhindered passage, without excessive customs dues, through the port of Lorenço Marques of goods brought to the coast for export from or import into the Transvaal. All turned on the third safeguard—that for the improvement of communications between the Transvaal and the coast, that is on the prospective Delagoa Bay Railway. The British object was to induce Portugal to bear a share of the cost of whatever scheme was adopted, and it was proposed that, if a tariff at Lorenço Marques could be agreed upon, the proceeds might be used to pay the interest on the whole or part of the capital needed to build the railway.

The Delagoa Bay Railway was indeed no new idea. A contract had been signed between the Portuguese government and the then independent South African Republic for the building of a railway from Lorenço Marques into the interior.

[1] To Salisbury, private, 18 Jan. 1879.

A tax of thirty shillings per farm had been levied to meet the cost, and railway material to the value of £90,000 had been purchased by the Transvaal. In the autumn of 1876 materials for building the railway had actually been shipped to Lorenço Marques, but in the preoccupations of war no one had done anything to use them. After the annexation the tax had been appropriated to other purposes and the material allowed to rust, for Natal was interested in preventing the Transvaal's access to the coast. The contract itself, on the pretext of legal flaws, was repudiated.[1] The Portuguese minister for foreign affairs in 1878 repeatedly urged upon Morier the importance which Portugal attached to the railway and his wish to revive the contract. Morier had replied that he would encourage it if, when the time came, Portugal would enter into such arrangements 'as would enable Lorenço Marques to fulfil its natural destiny' and become the port for the Transvaal, as Goa was to become that for southwest India.[2]

By the autumn of 1878 Morier appears to have caught Lord Salisbury's interest. When, in October,[3] he was instructed to open negotiations for these safeguards, Salisbury wrote privately to him,[4] acknowledging and regretting lost opportunities in Britain's relationship with Portugal.

> Partly that evil results [he wrote], and I freely confess it, from our neglect at the F.O. We have been too much in the habit of passing on the demands of the C.O. without considering their bearing on general policy. And this has specially been the case with regard to Portugal, because almost all the points at which the C.O. and Portugal touch, concern Africa: and Africa (barring Egypt) must be looked upon as one of England's bad debts. It is lamentable to think of the amount of energy and money which have been expended on various points of that vast continent, with no return whatever in the way of Power, and little enough in the way of commerce. But, in order not to make a total loss, we have to go on spending more and more.

[1] To Granville, no. 38, 6 May 1880, a retrospective and self-justifying account; see also pencil notes on it in the margin, F.O. 63/1101.
[2] To Granville, no. 79A, 17 June 1880, reviewing the history of the question, F.O. 63/1101.
[3] From Salisbury, telegram, 25 Oct. 1878, F.O. 84/1524, see above, p. 40.
[4] 24 Oct. 1878.

Morier agreed with the description of Africa as a bad debt—
'it expresses in a short and epigrammatic form my entire *credo*'
and an idea to which he had adapted his whole policy. He
deplored the absence of any general policy to end this situation.
Britain had once had an African policy, one which 'flowed
logically from a great, and on the whole, noble humanitarian
élan . . . the national *sic volo, sic jubeo* to put down the Slave
Trade'. This had been exhausted when the American Civil War
brought the transatlantic traffic in slaves to an end. Nothing
had replaced it except 'a kind of morbid and unnatural love of
the black race because it is black and not white'—a 'hopeless
hotchpotch of cross purposes and unclear ideas, of vacillations
between weakness and violence, of movings forwards and
movings backwards, of the finest general phrases and the
meanest local jealousies'.[1]

The new policy, for which Morier claimed he stood, had an
economic objective as its sole governing principle. Africa was
to be made available for commercial purposes by the application of the rule of equal access for ships of all nations to the
coastal trade, by the abolition of monopolies, by the reduction
of tariffs and the abolition as far as possible of tariff barriers,
and by the building of railways.

The reasons behind the policy must be given in Morier's own
picturesque language.

We ought in my opinion [he wrote to Salisbury], to give up,
once for all, all idea of African Empire, a dream stirring in many
foolish heads; all idea of colonisation; all idea of annexation; all
idea of sovereignty over black subjects with wool on their heads.
When 'Natural Selection' peopled Africa with Blacks, 'Natural
Selection' clearly expressed its intention that it should not be a
habitat for whites. Of course Cape Colony is an exception, which
cannot be helped. But it does seem to me that with the acquisition of
the Transvaal, we might be well content to stop, and that now, if
ever, the Imperial Government should put down its heel and say
'thus far and no further' . . . This much for the things we ought
not to do.

What we ought to do, is to use our utmost endeavours to make
Africa available for the purposes which an all wise 'Natural Selection' intended, i.e. that of the nearest and largest storehouse of
tropical produce, and of the only kind of labour available for the

[1] To Salisbury, private, 18 Jan. 1879.

purposes of tropical production. If we can make Africa available for commerce throughout its length and breadth, and free negro labour available not on its native soil alone, but in all European tropical settlements, for the purposes of tropical production, we shall have done all we need do and be our own benefactors and those of the rest of mankind.

For these purposes we should insist *per fas et nefas* on the absolute get-at-ableness of every portion of Africa, on the removal of all artificial restrictions and on the free play of commercial enterprise from coast to coast. We should especially insist on all the great inland waters and the great arterial rivers being free to the navigation of every flag... As regards the labour question we should... by means of international treaties and arrangements, set up rules and machinery to enforce those rules by which Africans might instead of being hecatombed at the court festivities of their native Kings, be made available under free contracts as labourers, wherever 'Natural Selection' makes their labour the best if not the only available labour.[1]

Just before Morier received Salisbury's instructions to negotiate for the three safeguards, Corvo, in a conversation on 2 October 1878, had given him opportunity to reopen the subject of the railway, speaking of his hopes of better relations when once the questions of Goa and Lorenço Marques were settled, and those ports had become the termini of two British railways bringing the British and Portuguese communities 'into the close contact of mutual good offices' and cementing their relations 'by common material interests'. Morier had at once asked whether Corvo meant that Britain might accept the free and untrammelled use of Lorenço Marques in military as well as commercial matters and Corvo had replied that he did.[2] Soon afterwards Morier told Corvo that he had received instructions on 25 October 1878 to negotiate an agreement. Corvo was ready cordially to co-operate but unable, owing to his preoccupation with the Goa treaty,[3] to negotiate before December.

The Portuguese were full of goodwill. They put Lorenço Marques at Britain's disposal for the use of troops passing to Zululand when war was imminent. This had the drawback that Britain would be morally bound to defend the Portuguese if, as

[1] To Salisbury, private, 18 Jan. 1879.
[2] To Salisbury, no. 41 slave-trade, confidential, 3 Oct. 1878, F.O. 84/1504.
[3] See above, pp. 40–2.

a result of the transit of her troops through their territory, they were in turn attacked by Cetewayo.[1] Morier's vigilance, however, avoided the abuse of the privilege, and troops were not landed at Lorenço Marques, nor was the Delagoa Bay territory used as a base from which to march directly into Zululand, which abutted on it to the south. As it turned out the assurance which Corvo gave on 2 October and the prohibition of the import of arms more than satisfied the Colonial Office.

In December 1878 conversations between Morier and Corvo on the three safeguards duly began. The proposals on which they were based came from the Colonial Office; so after these conversations Morier submitted an account of them to Sir Bartle Frere, who was under the Colonial Office as high commissioner for South Africa until his supposed responsibility for the Zulu War caused his recall by the Gladstone government in 1880. Frere returned the account with his initialled comments in the margin. In the conversations Corvo had been quick to seize his opportunity. In India, Britain wanted customs facilities and the Portuguese a railway; in Africa, Britain wanted a railway and the Portuguese had the capacity to withdraw customs facilities. 'In the one case as in the other, Corvo saw the customs facilities were the complement of the railway and the railway the complement to the customs facilities.' Morier incidentally reminded the Foreign Office that, owing to the reform of the Mozambique tariff, any attempt to put the British and the Portuguese African tariffs in equilibrium would mean lowering the Natal tariff since it was now higher than the Portuguese. Corvo and Morier evolved a scheme (a) for bonded warehouses at Delagoa Bay, to be managed by British agents, into which all merchandise intended for the Transvaal should go, being taxed under Portuguese surveillance, but being sealed at Delagoa Bay and unsealed on a station to be erected in the Transvaal by the joint act of British and Portuguese customs officials. They evolved a second plan (b) to create a fund from the duties levied at Delagoa Bay, out of which the cost of building the railway should come. Sir Bartle Frere commented, 7 February 1879, that he 'entirely agreed in the general views of [Morier's report of the plan] and

[1] From Salisbury, no. 48, 5 Nov. 1878, F.O. 63/1074; to Salisbury, no. 76, confidential, 25 Nov. 1878, F.O. 63/1075.

considered the suggestions of the greatest importance to the future peace and prosperity of the Transvaal, and to the development of its resources'. Corvo had reminded Morier, in the course of one conversation, that under the earlier contract with the Transvaal, before its annexation, Portugal had agreed to pay a considerable subvention 'without any prospect of direct returns and merely in view of the advantages likely to accrue to the [Portuguese] colony [of Mozambique] from the scheme'. Frere promised more accurate estimates of the costs of construction than the Portuguese had, and added: 'Even if the Railway only crossed the low coast country, it would give an immense impulse to commerce, both in the Portuguese possessions and the Transvaal as that part of the line is, at present, a far greater obstacle to cheap transit than the mountain chains.' To the section of Morier's report on the equalization of tariffs Frere added the warning that the Cape tariff was even higher than that of Natal. On the commercial side as a whole, he wrote, 'I think this is all we can desire and much more than I expected.' Finally he agreed with Morier's conclusion that, if the railway did not at first pay for itself, Britain should make good the Portuguese deficit out of her customs revenue from the Transvaal, since this was likely to be much increased when the railway increased trade.[1]

Morier continued to negotiate, convinced that Britain could not get the Goa treaty (which had now been signed) ratified without a Lorenço Marques treaty, that she would never again get the latter on such favourable terms, and that she would never again see parliamentary circumstances so favourable in Portugal to the simultaneous passage of both treaties. Thus the Lorenço Marques treaty took shape. It was drawn up at the end of January 1879 in general terms, the details to be filled in after technical discussions between Sir Theophilus Shepstone, now administrator of the Transvaal, and a commissioner to be named by the Portuguese in Africa.[2]

[1] To Frere, 19 Dec. 1878; from Frere, 7 Feb. 1879. In the papers collected by Lady Wemyss for 1879 there are in addition a letter to Morier written by Frere's daughter on her father's behalf commenting on Morier's 'wonderful success' (4 Feb. 1879) and a typed copy of Frere to Morier 6 Feb. 1879 with further comments.

[2] To Salisbury, nos. 3, 4, and 6 slave-trade, 18 and 27 Jan. 1879, F.O. 84/1537. No. 6 enclosed the draft treaty.

The first three articles of the draft followed those of the Goa treaty[1] with the addition of a provision for the maintenance of the navigation of the Zambesi, free from all restrictions in the way of exclusive concessions and monopolies. In the later version article 1 was dropped, 2 became 1, 3 became 2, and the provision about the Zambesi was put in as article 3. Article 4 secured to Britain the free use for commercial and military purposes of the harbour of Delagoa Bay. Article 5 covered the joint construction of the railway from Delagoa Bay to the Transvaal border and provisions for the exemption of British goods in transit through Portuguese territory from all dues and charges, the plan of the bonded warehouses, and the fund for the joint construction of the railway. A number of articles dealt with technical concerns, the eleventh with a common system about the sale of arms; the twelfth, taken from the Goa treaty, dealt with the extradition of criminals and the thirteenth with the suppression of the slave-trade.

Morier had just sent the draft treaty home when he suddenly received (5 February 1879) a totally unexpected communication from the Foreign Office. The Colonial Office had decided after all not to negotiate. This decision had been taken as long ago as 16 January. Satisfied with Portugal's good offices over the arms traffic, Sir Michael Hicks Beach, colonial secretary since March 1878, decided it was not worth while negotiating about the tariff and the railway. He was wholly unaware of Morier's grand vision of Anglo-Portuguese co-operation in Africa and India. Even worse, he knew nothing of Salisbury's instruction to Morier to negotiate *pari passu* the Lorenço Marques and Goa treaties. Worst of all was the Foreign Office failure: it sent on the Colonial Office decision by sea, not by telegraph, and without any attempt to reconcile it with its own instructions of October 1878.[2]

The incident suggests two reflections. Co-ordination of cabinet policy in Disraeli's cabinet was known to have been slipshod where the prime minister was not himself interested. He was not interested in black Africa. This Portuguese incident may

[1] See above, p. 29, note 3; article 1 provided for reciprocal freedom of commerce, navigation, and transit; article 2 for equality of rights in trade and industry for the subjects of one state in the territory of the other; article 3 for the reciprocal opening of the east African coasting trade.
[2] See above, pp. 40 and 84.

have been an example of bad co-ordination. Salisbury may, however, have simply held back the Foreign Office view out of consideration for Morier. Salisbury certainly believed the mistake to be entirely on Morier's part. When Morier vigorously defended his draft treaty,[1] Salisbury replied by telegram (6 February) that whereas the British government was prepared only to *authorize* the building of a railway (i.e. as in the Goa treaty), Morier had committed his government to paying for it. 'I am afraid you have misunderstood our instructions,' Salisbury telegraphed, and the draft is in his own hand,[2] 'I have carefully examined all the correspondence that has passed: and I can find nothing that even provisionally commits H.M.G. to anything more than was agreed to by the Indian Government in the case of the Goa Railway. I certainly never meant to convey to you any intention on the part of H.M.G. to pay for the making of a railway and I cannot find any words that imply it.' This would need parliamentary sanction, which would not be given except after a careful survey. 'Article 5 of your draft Treaty is quite inadmissible.' Secondly, the incident reminds one that what to Morier was a matter of high policy was to the cabinet at home—its readiness for assertion limited to the Mediterranean and to India, and to Africa as seen from the Mediterranean—much less important.

Morier wrote a further defence of his conduct on 7 February which crossed with Salisbury's dispatch expanding the telegram of 6 February.[3] In this Salisbury made it clear that he had meant by the *pari passu* telegram a treaty similar in content to the Goa treaty, but he did not allude specifically to the phrase. The situation was plain: since Morier had told Salisbury that article 5 was the crux of the whole treaty, he had to submit to the suspension of negotiations until he had satisfied the home authorities. Morier's eventual response was to draft a revised version of the treaty. Nothing more was heard of the general condemnation of his action or of the Colonial Office's decision to break off negotiations; nor, be it said, did Morier ever mention his mistake in committing his government by article 5.

[1] To Salisbury, telegram and nos. 10 and 11 slave-trade, 5 Feb. 1879, F.O. 84/1537.
[2] From Salisbury, telegram, 5.55 p.m., 6 Feb. 1879, draft in F.O. 63/1084.
[3] To Salisbury, no. 15 slave-trade, 7 Feb., F.O. 84/1537; from Salisbury, no. 17 slave-trade, 7 Feb. 1879, F.O. 84/1537.

He proceeded and was able to redeem his word to the Portuguese government. The revised version of article 5, instead of making a plain engagement to construct the railway, provided merely for a joint commission to survey possible routes from the Transvaal to Delagoa Bay, estimate the cost along the best route, determine the works necessary at Lorenço Marques in order to make it into an adequate railway terminal, estimate their cost, and report about the possibilities of traffic and freight. It provided further that if this report established that the estimated income of the railway in addition to the estimated customs revenue at Lorenço Marques would be enough to pay for its construction, this would be begun as soon as possible; alternatively, if it established that it would be insufficient, then the two countries would apply to their respective parliaments for an advance of the necessary funds.

On 12–13 February came the British defeat at Isandlwha on the Zulu frontier. This was the occasion for Corvo to express his regret that Britain had not taken advantage of the Portuguese offer of Lorenço Marques as a port for the disembarkation of British troops. He dwelt on the advantages which preparations for common action might have had in preventing the Zulu rising and described the reinforcement of the garrison at Lorenço Marques. He ended by saying 'that the moment was more than ever favourable for concluding the treaty, the delay in the negotiation of which he greatly lamented'.[1] Corvo's attitude further encouraged Morier to attempt to continue negotiations. The British defeat by the Zulus and accusations bandied about between the newspapers of Britain and Portugal caused Corvo to repeat that he was ready to conclude an agreement with Britain for common action to deal with the traffic in arms.[2] This provided yet further encouragement. The death of Mrs. Morier's father, General Peel, and Morier's own wish to go to England in connection with the Goa treaty, but reluctance to do so if there was a chance of proceeding with the new treaty, led him to appeal to the Foreign Office to let him know by telegraph what his position was. He wanted positive authority to go on. The defeat, he telegraphed, made direct access to Zululand

---

[1] To Salisbury, no. 19 slave-trade, 15 Feb. 1879, F.O. 84/1537.
[2] To Salisbury, no. 20 slave-trade, 16 Feb. 1879, F.O. 84/1537.

—whether we annexed, disarmed, or whatever—and the military and commercial use of Delagoa Bay 'on terms which for all practical purposes would assimilate it to a British port', once only a desirable object, now 'one of imperative necessity'.[1] Morier's appeal brought, on 12 March, a telegram from the Foreign Office which made it plain that the Colonial Office was now willing that negotiations should recommence. But, alas, the Foreign Office had new reasons against the negotiation. No answer to his appeal could have been more irritating. 'Events in South Africa', the telegram ran, 'have made conclusion of treaty for Lorenço Marques railway impossible for the present as explained in my private letter. The security of persons and works during construction and after it could not be guaranteed possibly for many years.'[2] Morier was undaunted. He decided to go on leave to England. Here he arrived by the end of March 1879. Salisbury had by then received a dispatch in which 'at the risk of appearing importunate' Morier urged the reconsideration 'of a decision which ruthlessly destroys results at which I have unremittingly laboured since I have had the honour to represent Her Majesty at Lisbon'.[3] This appeal Salisbury passed on to Hicks Beach (who was now ready for negotiations to continue, agreeing that the revised article 5 would have made the draft acceptable had it not been for the Zulu War) together with an intimation that Morier was in England and available for consultation.

Morier now brought all his guns to bear, sending through the Foreign Office a memorandum, dated London 4 April,[4] detailing the negotiations so far and setting forth once again the reasons for bringing them to a conclusion. His most telling argument was that the real grievance of which the Boers had to complain was the persistent manner in which Britain had resisted all their attempts to gain access to the seaboard. 'The refusal to go on with the railway,' he wrote, 'which they believed had been secured under President Burgers, is consequently one of the most real and effective causes of their present disaffec-

[1] To Salisbury, no. 22 slave-trade, 8 Mar. 1879, F.O. 84/1537.
[2] From Salisbury, telegram, 12 Mar. 1879, F.O. 84/1537.
[3] To Salisbury, no. 32 slave-trade, 14 Mar. 1879, F.O. 84/1537.
[4] See F.O. 84/1538. See also Morier to Salisbury, private, 5 and 7 Apr., 15 May 1879, answering a letter from Salisbury and carrying further the process of agreement on a draft, Salisbury papers, volume of letters from Morier, fos. 3, 5, 7.

tion.' He was convinced that to go on with the treaty would be 'the most effective measure of conciliation which could be devised'.

Morier's persistence and verve proved irresistible. 'I broke the ice', he wrote later[1] to Lady Derby, 'at the dinner at Kensington Palace where I managed to have a preparatory talk [with Lord Salisbury]. I then got an appointment and came all prepared with the practical facts to show that the thing must be done, and if it were not done there would sooner or later be a very ugly day of reckoning for the Govt. *as such* and not merely the C.O.' Surprisingly, he found Salisbury 'very quick at apprehending and seizing the points' but 'absolutely deficient in the consecutive grasp of his subject. It was all harum-scarum,[2] just a toss up whether he could keep any view persistently before him, and with a sense that he might go off at a tangent any moment. An absolutely un-English mind... He ended by saying the thing clearly had to be done.' Morier refused a joint conference and insisted that Salisbury should win over the colonial secretary. Within twenty-four hours Salisbury saw Hicks Beach and afterwards proposed certain modifications in the draft treaty which Morier accepted that same evening. On the following day it was agreed to resume negotiations. Morier had gained what he wanted, and on 12 April he was able to write privately to Corvo from London that he would be authorized to renew the negotiations and able to send him the draft treaty, now in a form acceptable to the British Colonial and Foreign Offices. He was subsequently able to telegraph that modifications suggested in the draft by Corvo had been approved and to warn him to prepare for signature.[3] The end had been quick but left Morier uncomfortable.

I have been completely and absolutely successful [he had written to Lady Derby[4]]. It gratifies my vanity by a triumph, and it enables me to succeed in a work to which I have devoted incredible labour and trouble for a long while past, but it is on the other hand so deeply humiliating to me as a man and an Englishman that I really

[1] 14 Apr. 1879, typed copy among the papers collected by Lady Wemyss for 1879.
[2] It is interesting that Mallet in writing to Morier should have used the same expression about Salisbury's mind, to Morier, 29 Dec. 1878.
[3] To Salisbury, no. 48 slave-trade, confidential, 28 May 1879, F.O. 84/1538.
[4] 14 Apr. 1879, the beginning of the letter quoted above.

don't know whether the sense of general shame and the feeling of dread as to what is to happen next, if this is the way the country is governed, does not destroy the sense of personal gratification. Indeed I feel almost ashamed of my victory.

Salisbury himself later admitted that the treaty was hardly a 'triumph for the administrative qualities of either F.O. or C.O.'[1]

Morier returned to Lisbon on 27 May 1879 with power to conclude a treaty 'determining general principles but postponing details until the restoration of peace'.[2] He was authorized to sign what had been drafted,[3] but the ratification was to be postponed 'until the political and economic relations between Great Britain and the South African colonies are more definitely adjusted' and until the assent of the local authorities had been gained. An exchange of notes effected agreement on this point and the draft treaty was signed. It bore the date of 30 May 1879. This was the day the Corvo government resigned—for the second time during Morier's mission.[4] In these circumstances it was apparently a notable success to have got the treaty safely signed.

The treaty, however, remained to be ratified, and a formidable agitation developed against this. Ratification became linked with the third imperial disagreement which divided Britain and Portugal. This related to the boundary of Portugal's possessions on the west coast of Africa. Britain contended that these did not extend even as far north as Ambriz and went only as far as 8° south latitude. Portugal claimed that they extended north of the Congo and so included the mouth of that river itself.

The threefold justification for Portugal's claim to the coast

[1] From Salisbury, 5 June 1881.
[2] From Salisbury, no. 72, 12 Apr. 1879, F.O. 63/1084.
[3] The old articles 2 and 3 were now 1 and 2; the Zambesi part of 2 became separate 3; article 4 provided for (a) the exemption of goods in transit from dues and charges and (b) the British right to land troops and munitions of war at Lorenço Marques and their free passage through Portuguese to British territory; article 5 was the revised railway article; article 7 contained provisions for levying the same tariff on all goods at Lorenço Marques whether on the British or Portuguese account and for its adjustment according to the requirements of the single fund into which the proceeds would go; article 10 prevented the arms traffic, article 11 provided for the extradition of criminals, and 12 and 13 dealt with the slave-trade (all this as before). [4] See above, p. 16, and below, pp. 157–8.

between 8° south and 5° 12′ south—the area from Angola to the north shore of the Congo river—is explained by Roger Anstey in *Britain and the Congo in the Nineteenth Century*. The Portuguese had discovered the coast in 1483 and had held it strongly during the heyday of their empire and intermittently afterwards. To prior discovery and actual occupation Portugal could add the recognition—implied or explicit—of her claims by Britain in treaties of 1810, 1813, 1817, and 1826. The same author explains the British commercial stake (the trade of British merchants and investors might be valued at some £2,000,000) in the Lower Congo territory and the position of the two missionary societies (the Baptist Missionary Society and the Livingstone Inland Mission) which had missions in the area and the support they could command at home. He also shows why both interests were opposed to the Portuguese claims: the one because the restrictive, monopolist policy of Portugal would prevent the development of trade and curb its potential; the other because it had committed itself in part to Leopold of the Belgians' International Association of the Congo.

Lord Palmerston was responsible in 1856 for the formulation of the British attitude to the Portuguese claims on the Congo coast. This attitude prevailed until 1876. It was summed up in a minute (1867) by W. H. Wylde, then head of the Slave Trade Department in the Foreign Office. If the Lower Congo and adjoining coast 'were to fall', he wrote, 'into the hands of the Portuguese it is needless to say that the trade would be trammelled to such an extent that there would be little chance of the River becoming as it someday surely will, one of the main channels of Trade into the interior of Africa'.[1] In 1875 Portugal, prompted by Commodore Hewett's expedition against piracy to the Lower Congo, renewed her claim to the coast and requested negotiations for its recognition (December 1875). Derby was not prepared blindly to renew the Palmerstonian stand. He was characteristically inclined to mistrust manifestations of assertiveness[2] and was about to repudiate (February 1876) a British protectorate which Commander V. L. Cameron had proclaimed (28 December 1874), in the course of his journey across Africa, over the Congo Basin.

[1] R. Anstey, *Britain and the Congo in the Nineteenth Century* (1962), p. 53.
[2] See above, p. 35.

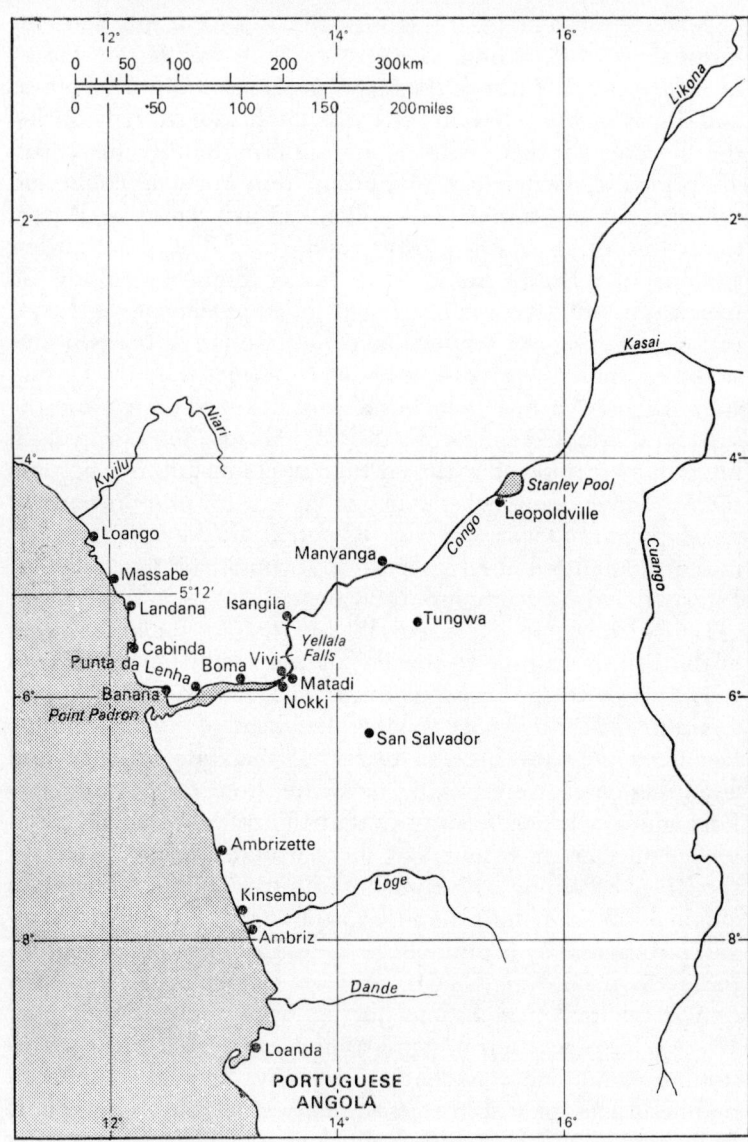

Map 3. The Western Portion of the River Congo and the adjoining coast

One of the first tasks that Derby set Morier was to draw up a statement of the facts in relation to the British attitude to the Portuguese claims. At this stage (the beginning of April 1876) Derby still had an open mind.[1] He told Morier that while Britain did not put forward counter-claims to the mouth of the Congo she 'resented their claims because the presence of the Portuguese flag at any port or any seaboard was the signal of every species of commercial restriction and chicanery. Our policy at first sight had a dog in the manger look, but was in fact the reverse'. He referred to a Foreign Office memorandum on the subject[2] which cautiously advocated a settlement, but asked Morier to draw up one of his own. This Morier submitted on 17 August 1877. Dr. Anstey summarizes and prints part of this memorandum. I quote his summary. 'The Portuguese claim was stronger than the Foreign Office had hitherto assumed, and Britain had no tenable basis for resisting it. Even if she had, more harm than good would probably result from the continued absence of a responsible European jurisdiction on the Congo.'[3] Morier recommended a settlement by negotiation and urged that in such a negotiation the following considerations should be kept in mind: the importance of the Congo, in his words, 'as the great arterial communication from the west with the centre of Africa', the impossibility of allowing an absence of jurisdiction to continue, and the danger of letting 'the river get into other hands than ours'.

It must be borne in mind that by 1877 the whole African picture had changed owing to Stanley's having followed the Congo from its source to the coast, King Leopold's foundation of the International Association of the Congo, and de Brazza's treaties which established a French protectorate on the Upper Congo. For Morier the meaning of the negotiation would lie in what Britain was to gain in return for recognizing the Portuguese claims. We should in return make them, he wrote, 'cede the portion of the territory claimed from the mouth of the Congo to 5° 12' [just north of the mouth], a short strip of territory, but which would give us the right bank of the Congo

---

[1] Morier's memorandum of a conversation with Derby. The date of the memorandum is 6 Apr. 1876, but the conversation took place some days before.
[2] Drawn up by Sir E. Hertslet, 23 Mar. 1876, F.O. 63/1116.
[3] Anstey, p. 84.

and the full command of its mouth . . . We could in the same treaty make the Portuguese engage to regulate the whole of their traffic and commerce along the coast by the rules we laid down for our portion of the coast'.

While Morier was preoccupied with the Goa and Lorenço Marques treaties, he did not refer to the Congo question and the Portuguese did not renew their request for negotiations. It was thus with Salisbury and not Derby that he eventually took it up. At the end of March 1879 (see above, p. 92), Morier went to London in order to explain to Salisbury the Lorenço Marques treaty and win his approval for it and to promote his company to build the Goa Railway. In the course of their discussions Morier was asked his opinion of what should be done about the conclusion by the Portuguese of treaties with certain native chiefs in the disputed Congo territory.[1] Morier replied that 'a radical solution' on the basis of his memorandum of August 1877 should be attempted and that the conclusion of the Goa and Lorenço Marques treaties would provide a favourable opportunity. In April there was actual friction between the British and Portuguese on the Congo coast, and Salisbury thought that the matter would have to be taken in hand seriously when the new Braamcamp ministry had settled down.[2] Just before Morier left London in May he sent Salisbury a copy of his memorandum of 1877, 'confident that [he would] agree . . . that the state of things therein described should . . . be remedied'.[3]

It will be remembered that it was with the Braamcamp ministry that Morier had to negotiate the ratification of the Lorenço Marques treaty. The Cortes had, however, been dissolved and the new Cortes which would have to ratify the treaty would not be elected until October 1879.[4] Meanwhile there was no sign that the national feeling against the treaty had disappeared; nor any improvement in the general prospect of railway building in South Africa. As Salisbury wrote:[5]

If the Transvaal ever possessed anything in the shape of accumulated resources or peaceable population they have disappeared

---

[1] Anstey, p. 90.   [2] Cf. Anstey, p. 91.
[3] To Salisbury, 23 May 1879, Salisbury papers, volume of letters from Morier, fo. 9.   [4] To Salisbury, no. 69 slave-trade, 17 Oct. 1879, F.O. 84/1538.
[5] From Salisbury, private, 24 Sept. 1879.

[in the Zulu War]. What remains is not of the kind that produces revenue or makes railways a profitable venture. It will be hard enough to get the money for a survey. I am told that the lower part of the railway will be very easy to make—but that it will be a formidable piece of engineering when the Drakenberg is reached.

Morier's eyes, however, were fixed upon the ratification and especially upon Tomás Ribeiro, whom he believed to be behind the agitation against the treaty, not upon the prospect of its ever being executed. In order to check Ribeiro's influence Morier pleaded with Salisbury to allow him 'to state "en temps et en lieux et à qui de droit" as from myself and not as speaking from H. M. Govt. that with a friendly ministry and one desirous of co-operation with us I have every reason to believe that H. M. Govt. would not refuse to take a settlement of the Congo question into their consideration'. This was a proposal to use the recognition, or partial recognition, of the Congo claims as bait to fish for the ratification of the Lorenço Marques treaty; it was supported by a lengthy argument in which Morier put the settlement of the Congo question forward as the aim towards which he had been working since his arrival in Lisbon, and explained at length why he had not returned to it after his memorandum of August 1877. When the election results came in they showed as usual that the government in power was normally able to win. Braamcamp now had a strong parliamentary majority prepared to follow his lead. Salisbury did not write again to Morier until 22 November, when he picked up in two places the thread of his last letter of 24 September. Thus he virtually ignored the way Morier presented the Congo question in the letter of 26 September, which must have reached him about 7 October,[1] yet he gave Morier something. He telegraphed some time in October or November authorizing Morier to use the prospect of the Congo negotiation as a bait for the Lorenço Marques ratification.[2] 'D'Antas', he wrote in the letter of 22 November, 'has not been to me again on the subject of the Congo territory —nor do I think he will come for some time [at his last visit he

---

[1] Morier describes Salisbury's letter to him of 24 Sept. as reaching him on 5 Oct.
[2] To Salisbury, private, 26 Nov. 1879; Morier refers here to this telegram, but I cannot find it.

had intimated that he would have a proposition to make about the Congo] . . . But of course I will inform him, if he does come, that we can take no step with respect to the Congo territory until the Lorenço Marques affair is finished.' The rest of the letter must have dampened any inclination Morier may have had to be optimistic; for on the Congo, Salisbury hinted that the Portuguese might be less eager for recognition than they had been ('they are difficult people to deal with—these Portuguese: their one desire in January is their pet aversion in October'), and on Lorenço Marques he reverted to the impracticability of the railway, though he recognized that the treaty contained other things that were valuable to Britain.[1]

During the next months there was a struggle beneath the surface. Braamcamp sought to establish that he would do his best to get the Lorenço Marques treaty ratified, if negotiations about the Congo were opened—negotiation first, then ratification. Morier sought to hold the position that, if the treaty were ratified, negotiation *might* follow. Dr. Anstey has described the resulting confusion. The position was at least clear when in Britain the Conservative government fell; for at the end of March 1880 the British ratification of the Lorenço Marques treaty was sent to Lisbon. Braamcamp then engaged that 'the treaty should be forthwith submitted to the Cortes [with the certainty, as he assured Morier, of its being accepted] in return for the engagement that *after* it is ratified I shall enter into negotiation respecting the West African claims with the sincere desire on the part of H. M. Govt. to arrive at an equitable settlement of this long pending question'.[2] The British instrument of ratification had been sent out as the result of a protest from Braamcamp that Britain asked for certainty from Portugal while leaving everything uncertain on her side. Britain having satisfied him, Braamcamp, Morier believed, was committed by his own protest to managing the treaty and getting it through the Cortes before it was prorogued. Prorogation was due on 15 April 1880 but was postponed to allow the treaty to be presented. Morier always referred later to Braamcamp's 'engagement' of 28 March.

Meanwhile, matters had moved in relation to the Congo.

[1] From Salisbury, private, 22 Nov. 1879.
[2] To Salisbury, private, 31 Mar. 1880; and no. 20, 26 Mar. 1880, F.O. 63/1100.

On 27 January 1880 Salisbury had formally instructed Morier to open negotiations for the recognition of the Congo claims and had invited him to send home an outline of the basis on which he proposed to act. But Morier found it hard to respond to this invitation. 'My great difficulty', he wrote to Salisbury,[1] 'is that the more I look into the case, the worse it appears to me to be on our side . . . The Sovereignty of the Portuguese Crown over the districts in litigation is indisputable.' The British repudiation of Portuguese sovereignty in 1856 was, he believed, utterly unjustified. He, therefore, proposed to frame a treaty on the assumption, not that Portugal had no rights, or that her rights had lapsed, but that Britain, through her activities in suppressing the slave-trade, had *acquired* rights. These would be surrendered in the treaty, or rather shared with all states, Portugal included. This idea he used in article 5 of the treaty he actually drafted in April 1881. His draft is discussed below. The idea also explains why he there describes the whole west coast from the Congo mouth to the southern frontier of Angola as the area over which Britain recognized Portuguese sovereignty and did not single out the disputed part of it. The idea was, however, too much for Salisbury. It had, indeed, an element of fantasy.

On 3 April Salisbury forbade any immediate action over the Congo. Dr. Anstey, who did not, I think, know of Morier's fantastic idea, writes: Salisbury 'does not appear to have been opposed to [action on the Congo] in principle but was, rather, reluctantly obliged to prohibit the opening of negotiations because of the Conservative defeat at the polls and the impropriety of committing his successor, in whose hands, he told Morier, the decision must lie'.[2] But Salisbury's glimpse of the way Morier's mind was working may also have had something to do with the halt he called to negotiations. Morier began, next, vigorously to press his Congo policy by private letter, and eventually in July 1880, when he again went to London, by word of mouth, upon Granville, the new foreign secretary. On this occasion Morier had allies in the Foreign Office. Tenterden

[1] To Salisbury, private, 12 Mar. 1880, Morier papers; and Salisbury papers, volume of letters from Morier, fo. 22.
[2] Anstey, p. 95, which is based on a minute by Salisbury of 3 Apr. This provided the substance of a telegram on 6 Apr. and was amplified in a dispatch on 21 Apr., F.O. 84/1801.

raised the matter with Granville on 25 May; a junior official raised it with Tenterden two days later. Both had in mind that Morier believed that Congo negotiations would facilitate the passage of the Lorenço Marques treaty; but also that a policy would have to be deliberately adopted by the new foreign secretary: 'it would never do for the Govt to pledge themselves to enter negotiations which it was not intended seriously to pursue.'[1] By June Tenterden had drawn up a memorandum generally favourable to the proposal. Pauncefote had concurred: 'the more I examine the Congo question, the more convinced I feel that provided we secure our established trade from injury and the free navigation of the Congo, we should abandon the attitude hitherto maintained, especially if the Lorenço Marques treaty is ratified.'[2]

Meanwhile, however, the Lorenço Marques treaty, on 20 April 1880, had in fact been submitted to the Chamber of Deputies.[3] Opposition to it in Portugal continued. The political cartoonists gave it point. 'Antonio Maria' of the Lisbon *Charivaria* showed Corvo as a shabby and obsequious waiter (at once recognized in the Foreign Office as a caricature of Morier himself and at once recognizable as such to any modern eye that has also seen Morier's portrait) offering Lorenço Marques on a dish to the gorged representative of Great Britain—Morier without disguise. The journalists and writers, celebrating the tercentenary of the death of Camoens, found excellent material in the treaty for barbed phrases contrasting the sixteenth and the nineteenth centuries.[4]

The treaty was debated at length so that the Chamber's prorogation had to be delayed until the end of May 1880 to let it pass. For a few days Morier believed that Braamcamp, stiffened by himself, was threatening his followers with the government's resignation in order to gain its passage. But on 3 June 1880 Morier telegraphed that Braamcamp was

[1] Minutes attached to Morier to Granville, no. 46 most confidential, 20 May 1880, F.O. 63/1101; see also memorandum on the Congo negotiations by Morier, 26 June 1880, printed by the Foreign Office, 29 June 1880, with extensive comments by Kimberley, Morier papers.
[2] Memorandum and minute dated 3 June 1880, F.O. 63/1101.
[3] To Granville, nos. 31, 32, and 33, 21 and 22 Apr. 1880, F.O. 63/1100.
[4] To Granville, no. 39, 8 May 1880, and no. 46 most confidential, 20 May 1880, F.O. 63/1101.

'behaving ignominiously', conciliating rather than threatening his rebellious followers. Morier had demanded categorically that the session be further prolonged—as it was until 7 June—and the debate pushed to the issue of a formal vote.[1] But this only led to a further scene, lasting three hours—'the most painful scene which my diplomatic experience has to record'[2]—with Braamcamp who, when it was clear that the vote would be against the treaty, prepared to offer his resignation to the King. For an hour and a half out of the three hours, Morier told Granville, he struggled to persuade Braamcamp that this was simply evading the fulfilment of his engagement of 28 March. Braamcamp, nevertheless, offered his resignation to the King; the King refused it; a vote was not in fact taken. On 5 June the Chamber of Deputies simply shelved the treaty by referring it to a committee. The result was a strong sense in Morier and the Foreign Office of a debt due to them from the Portuguese government.

Nor would the British government let the treaty drop, but prepared to try again for ratification when the Chambers reassembled in 1881. They were, indeed, now as eager for the railway as the Portuguese had been before. The Colonial Office on 1 July urged upon the Foreign Office that every effort should be made to secure the eventual ratification,[3] for owing to the prospect of South African confederation, which had again opened out, the railway had become more important. During July 1880 discussions took place in London between Granville, d'Antas, and Morier, home on leave.[4] As a result it was agreed to modify the treaty in order, it was hoped, to make it acceptable to the Cortes. Morier in his combative way had begun by refusing all idea of amendment and insisted that the claim for amendment was a political manœuvre. Equally characteristically, he found a way to surmount the difficulties raised, and carried the negotiations forward in two conversations after his return to Lisbon, on 17 August and

[1] To Granville, telegram, 3 June 1880; cf. to Granville, no. 50 most confidential, 27 May 1880, and nos. 52, 53, 54, 57, and 58, 28, 29, and 30 May 1880, F.O. 63/1101.
[2] To Granville, no. 63 most confidential, 5 June 1880, F.O. 63/1101.
[3] Colonial Office to Foreign Office, 1 July 1880, F.O. 63/1101.
[4] Granville to d'Antas, 4 Aug. 1880, and to Morier, no. 72, 4 Aug. 1880, F.O. 63/1102.

17 September 1880.[1] Impasse was reached again on 7 October 1880. Morier, as usual dramatic, believed it was deliberately reached and found an explanation in the intrigues of Mariano Carvalho. Still in character he found the wording which provided the way out.[2] By 31 December the Portuguese were satisfied with an additional article providing that the treaty, with necessary exceptions in article 5, should last for twelve years only, a protocol providing that when the railway or system of roads had been constructed, the passage of troops through Portuguese territory should cease to be 'unconditional' and conditions be imposed upon it by a convention, and two modifications in the tariff and slave-trade clauses strengthening the safeguards of the equality of the two signatories.[3] But the ill fate which dogged the Lourenço Marques treaty continued.

By January 1881 when the Cortes was next in session, the Boer insurrection in the Transvaal had begun. By 2 February Morier was again accusing the Portuguese government, because it had still not put a bill for the Lourenço Marques treaty before the Chamber of Deputies, of having failed to act upon its engagements. The Portuguese, however, published a white book to provide the Chamber with material for its debate. This was the occasion for Morier to send a long dispatch of self-defence and self-exculpation to Granville.[4] During February 1881 he was continually at Braamcamp's elbow trying to counteract the effect of meetings of protest against the treaty

[1] To Granville, nos. 104, 105, and 106 most confidential, 17 Aug. 1880; no. 107, 24 Aug. 1880, enclosing a minute of the conversation of 17 Aug. 1880; no. 114, 17 Sept. 1880, enclosing a copy of a memorandum left with Braamcamp; and no. 115 enclosing minute of conversation held on 17 Sept. 1880, F.O. 63/1102.

[2] To Granville, nos. 124 confidential and 132, 11 and 26 Oct. 1880, F.O. 63/1102.

[3] To Granville, no. 116, 18 Sept. 1880 forwarded the additional article. From Granville, no. 87, 5 Oct. 1880 protested against the 99 years' provision for the railway article; to Granville, no. 122, 11 Oct. 1880 described the sudden change in the Portuguese attitude which led to the impasse Morier claimed to have overcome, F.O. 63/1102; to Granville, no. 133 confidential, nos. 134, 135, 5, 8, 9 Nov. 1880 describe the ministerial crisis which made the conclusion of the protocol negotiation urgent; from Granville, no. 95, 12 Nov. 1880, and telegram, 19 Nov. 1880 deal with a Portuguese protest in London against perpetuity and tell Morier to abandon it; from Granville, nos. 106 and 119, 1 and 25 Dec. 1880 are final instructions; to Granville, nos. 156, 158, 159, 162–6, 14, 23, and 30 Dec. 1880 report final stages and signature, F.O. 63/1103.

[4] No. 12 confidential, 22 Jan. 1881, F.O. 63/1130.

and demonstrations of sympathy with the Transvaal. At last on 24 February 1881 the debate began and the treaty was actually passed by the Chamber of Deputies on 8 March 1881. This was the signal for new demonstrations and for the cry to be raised again against the alleged surrender of Lorenço Marques to the British. On 21 March 1881 the ministry fell without having taken a vote on the treaty in the Chamber of Peers. The new ministry under António Rodrigues Sampaio was a *Regeneradores* ministry without the leader of the party (General Fontes), but acting under his direction (see above, p. 17).

Morier now once again linked the treaty with the Congo question. Unfortunately for British African policy and for his own future in Lisbon, he put himself into a thoroughly false position in doing so.

As a result of his discussions with Granville in the summer of 1880, Morier had obtained an assurance that he and Kimberley, the colonial secretary, were ready for the opening of negotiations on the Congo as soon as the Lorenço Marques treaty was ratified. On 18 March 1881, in order to persuade the new ministry to push the treaty through the Chamber of Peers, Morier asked for a public declaration in parliament that the British government would open the Congo negotiations immediately after its ratification.[1] A fortnight later (3 April)[2] Morier proposed to reverse the order of events: Congo negotiations should be begun in order that the ratification might follow. He thus would have yielded—when it was to prove too late— the position he had so strenuously defended against Braamcamp the year before. The outcome was that Morier sent home, on 20 April 1881, at Granville's request a hastily drafted Congo treaty in seven articles.[3]

The draft was so devised as to carry into effect a particular and personal policy of the envoy,

> that of admitting the claims of Portugal which are the most valid of any that have been put forward, and to use these claims in the way I propose for establishing a permanent British influence on that portion of the African coast which without entailing the burdens

[1] To Granville, telegram, 18 Mar. 1881, F.O. 63/1130.
[2] To Granville, no. 82 most confidential, 3 Apr. 1881, F.O. 63/1131.
[3] To Granville, no. 101 and enclosure, Draft Congo Treaty, F.O. 63/1131; summarized by Anstey, pp. 96–7.

or dangers of annexation would enable us to obtain all the safeguards we require for the development of legitimate commerce and the putting down of such small remains of the slave trade as still remained.

Morier's original idea had been, it will be remembered, to recognize the Portuguese claims in return for the cession to Britain of the strip of coast at the actual mouth of the river. This he had now improved on somewhat fantastic grounds.[1] Article 1 proposed to recognize, and to use Britain's influence to induce others to recognize, Portuguese sovereignty along the west coast from latitude 18° south to north of the Congo—that is from the *southern* frontier of Angola, where no one ever thought of disputing Portuguese authority. This extension of the area of recognition Morier proposed to turn to advantage as the rest of the articles showed. He would use it to impose limitations upon Portuguese sovereignty, in the undisputed and disputed area alike, such as would ensure the opening up of all Portugal's west African empire like her east African possessions to international trade. The commercial relations of the two Powers on the section of the coast not already occupied by Portugal should be determined by a separate convention (article 2). There were further to be three joint commissions: to consider the rights of the native tribes and the established interests of the European inhabitants of this unoccupied west coast (article 3); to manage slave-trade affairs for a period of twelve years along all the coast from 18° south—thus bringing Angola's 700 miles of coastline within the scope of British anti-slave-trade measures (article 4); to control the navigation and policing of the Congo itself (article 6). Article 7 linked the treaty with the Lorenço Marques treaty by providing that ratifications should be exchanged on the same day as ratifications were exchanged for the latter, and arranged that the treaty should last for twelve years, but be renewable for a further period of twelve years. Dr. Anstey has pointed out the signs of hasty drafting here and elsewhere in the treaty.[2] Morier himself regarded article 5 as the central article of the treaty, since it not only announced Britain's intention to safeguard her own rights, but also her right to act 'as trustee of the civilized world claiming free and unhindered access to Africa'.

[1] See above, p. 101.   [2] Anstey, p. 97.

The King of Portugal [the article read], whilst maintaining his rights of sovereignty over the coast from the mouth of the Congo to 8 degrees fifteen minutes South latitude [i.e. to the *northern* frontier of Angola] during such period as the present treaty lasts, engages to exercise the said rights in common with the other Governments whose subjects possess recognised commercial establishments within the region on the right bank of the Congo to which His Most Faithful Majesty lays claim.

Such governments were to be invited to settle with Britain and Portugal the means of such international sharing in Portuguese sovereignty. The article bears eloquent witness to Morier's valuing trade more than territory.

Next, on 27 April the new Portuguese government made a plea that the Lorenço Marques treaty might be withdrawn from the Chamber of Peers and its discussion adjourned. Granville with Kimberley's concurrence, but against Morier's strong advice, accepted this plea. A week later, and not until then, Morier received Granville's reply dated 25 April 1881 to his request of 3 April (received in London on 11 April) to be allowed to open the Congo negotiations. This reply told him that Granville and Kimberley thought 'it would not be desirable to take any step at the present time in regard to the Congo question'.[1] Thus the government put an end to both treaties for the time being.

Morier had, however, gone forward without authorization and already put pressure on the Sampaio government to abandon its plea for adjournment and to put the treaty through the Chamber of Peers before the Cortes went into recess. He was only justified in competing with the Portuguese opposition to the treaty for the ear of Sampaio if he was right in thinking the opposition was not genuine. There had been two demonstrations on Sunday 13 March, a 'republican' to protest against the Lorenço Marques treaty and a 'monarchical' to protest

[1] From Granville, nos. 50 and 52, 25 and 30 Apr. 1881, F.O. 63/1104. The man responsible for this decision was Kimberley, not Granville, see Kimberley's minute, 22 Apr., on Foreign Office to Colonial Office, 20 Apr. 1881, and for the minute, 27 Apr., C.O. 291/13. Kimberley may well have been influenced in his opposition to the Congo negotiation by Morier's over-complicated (not to say fantastic) draft treaty. Cf. D. M. Schreuder, *Gladstone and Kruger* (1969), pp. 192-4, where 13 is printed for 30 May and the passage of the treaty through the Chamber of Deputies is mistakenly said to have completed its ratification.

against the general policy of the government, and Morier disparaged them both. If his judgement was wrong, successful pressure on Sampaio would only cause the defeat of the government and put him and Britain in the wrong. Granville saw this and already on 29 March had held Morier back from a categorical demand on Sampaio that he should take a vote in the Chamber of Peers on the treaty before the end of the session.[1] On 26 March the Chambers were adjourned until 26 May.

There was much to be said for Granville's caution. The opposition in Portugal was far from artificial: Sampaio was inclined to consider the treaty as a pet scheme of Corvo and to assert that his party was not committed;[2] the position in the Transvaal was uncertain; and finally d'Antas had proposed in London, just before he went to Lisbon to take up the position of foreign minister in Sampaio's cabinet, that the present treaty should be abandoned and a new negotiation begun when the Transvaal Commission had finished its work.[3] Even if Morier had been authorized to do what he wished and begin the Congo negotiations in order to get a vote in the Chamber of Peers before the end of the session on the Lorenço Marques treaty, the possibility remained that the Chambers might be dissolved before they reassembled on 26 May and the British minister would then have been plainly and publicly duped. Accordingly Granville refused to sanction the course proposed by Morier on 3 April. The dispatches of 25 and 30 April 1881 dropped both the Lorenço Marques and the Congo treaties for the time being.[4] Morier had failed, and his failure was all the more sour because he had secured, just before Granville's dispatches reached him, an engagement from Sampaio to allow the Lorenço Marques treaty to take its course in the Chamber of Peers.[5] But d'Antas resigned four days later and returned as envoy to London. Much to Morier's irritation, he said he resigned because he had failed to induce Morier to co-operate with him in persuading the British government to agree to postpone the vote on the Lorenço Marques treaty until

[1] To Granville, no. 62, 22 Mar. 1881, F.O. 63/1130; from Granville, no. 42A, extending telegram, 29 Mar. 1881, F.O. 63/1104.
[2] To Granville, no. 80, 31 Mar. 1881, F.O. 63/1130.
[3] From Granville, telegram, no. 10, 29 Mar. 1881, F.O. 63/1104.
[4] From Granville, nos. 50 and 52, 25, 30 Apr. 1881, F.O. 63/1104.
[5] To Granville, telegram, 27 Apr. 1881, F.O. 63/1131.

1882.¹ D'Antas now brought pressure to bear directly on Granville,² and on 18 May 1881 categorical and final instructions went to Morier to let the two treaties drop.³ The arguments of Morier against yielding to d'Antas which Granville received four days before, 14 May, went unheeded.⁴ The Lorenço Marques treaty was only ratified after Morier had left Lisbon, and the railway only reached the Transvaal frontier in 1889.

But the Congo treaty, which Britain might have gained in Morier's form and when Morier wished to negotiate it, she sought between 1882 and 1884 to gain under quite different circumstances and was ignominiously compelled by domestic opposition and the action of Germany and France to drop. A British and a Portuguese initiative practically coincided to revive the Congo negotiation. On 19 October 1882 Walter Baring, who was acting as chargé d'affaires at Lisbon—Morier having been promoted to Madrid—reported that Portugal was likely to reopen the Congo question. The Portuguese overture came in a dispatch from Serpa to d'Antas communicated to the Foreign Office on 22 November 1882. But already, some time before 9 November, the British government had on its own account decided to reopen it.⁵

On both sides the cause of the initiative was the same: France threatened to take the mouth of the Congo. De Brazza had returned to Europe and in August 1882 the treaty he had signed with the African chief at Stanley Pool had been published. This was the famous Makoko treaty of 3 October 1880. The Foreign Office had already received news of it through the Baptist Missionary Society, but it was not until October that its efforts to find out from Paris whether it was genuine and whether it was likely to be accepted by the French government bore fruit.⁶ Granville rightly regarded this treaty as marking

the complete revolution of the condition of the African continent. The successful efforts of Livingstone, Stanley and other explorers [he wrote] have brought within the limits of practical knowledge the geography and ethnology of the vast regions of Central Africa,

---

¹ To Granville, nos. 107 and 108 most confidential, 1 May 1881, F.O. 63/1132.
² D'Antas to Granville, 7 May 1881, F.O. 63/1132.
³ From Granville, telegram, no. 18, 18 May 1881, F.O. 63/1132; cf. from Granville, no. 52, 30 Apr. 1881, F.O. 63/1104.
⁴ To Granville, nos. 114–17, 6–7 May 1881, F.O. 63/1132.
⁵ Anstey, pp. 101, 104.   ⁶ Anstey, pp. 100–1.

the nature of the watersheds and the utility of the rivers which bring the central districts into communication with the coast. An important field of commerce has been opened up.[1]

Britain was prepared to acknowledge the Portuguese claims to the coast including the right bank of the Congo and as far south as Angola, not as of right but as a new departure. Nothing was now said of Morier's idea of including the whole coast as far as *southern* Angola. Portugal had no anxiety about the extension of French control from the Gaboon to Stanley Pool by the Ogoué, north of the Congo, but she was anxious to prevent France from getting to the right or north bank of the Congo and reaching Stanley Pool by the Niari. On 18 November a bill was introduced into the French Chamber of Deputies to ratify de Brazza's treaties, and at the same time a supplementary credit was requested to assure their execution. There was much stir in Britain about the danger of an exclusive, monopolistic commercial policy if French rule was established. There were questions in the House of Commons and memorials from shipowners. Granville now requested Kimberley's concurrence in reversing the previous denial of Portuguese right. He advanced three reasons: the argument that Portugal could not suppress the slave-trade was no longer valid; it was not worth sacrificing Portuguese friendship to maintain a pedantic correctitude; the extension of France appeared to threaten monopolies detrimental to British commerce. This scarecrow policy of recognizing the rights of some other Power in order to keep the French out was to become characteristic of Britain's attitude to Africa. She recognized Italian claims on the Red Sea coast for the same purpose.[2]

In the new draft treaty nothing was of course said of the condition of an international share in the exercise of Portugal's sovereign rights on the coast. Portuguese sovereignty was to be absolute. But Granville planned to exact in return the cession of the Portuguese enclave, Whydah, on that part of the Gold Coast later known as French Dahomey. Traces of Morier's influence may be seen, however, in three proposals: first, in the provision for freedom of navigation on the Zambesi without

[1] Granville to d'Antas, 15 Mar. 1883, reviewing the history of the negotiations, F.O. 84/1804.
[2] A. Ramm, 'Great Britain and the Planting of Italian Power on the Red Sea Coast', *English Historical Review*, lix (1944), 223.

monopolies as provided for in the still unratified Lorenço Marques treaty (base 2). Safeguards were also to be obtained for free access to the Congo trade and navigation, without monopolies or river tolls or dues (base 2). Secondly, Morier's influence may have been responsible for the provisions for a low maximum of customs duties (base 3), for reserving the rights enjoyed by British subjects under treaties with native chiefs (base 4), and for the suppression of the slave-trade (base 5). Thirdly, his influence may be seen in the proposal for securing Britain most-favoured-nation treatment for trade. The Colonial Office modified the Gold Coast surrender, so that it included all Portuguese claims to that coast between 5° west and 5° east and added a provision by which Portugal disavowed any claim to territory on the west coast south of latitude 18° and on the east coast south of latitude 26° 30′. This last eventually became the substance of a separate declaration, which also contained the repudiation by Portugal, for those districts where her sovereignty was recognized on the coast, of its extension 'further up the rivers or into the interior than the points actually occupied' by her. By December 1882 Morier had jogged Granville's memory about his own contribution, Granville having sent to him at Madrid the draft treaty for his comments.

Morier, however, seems to have had no influence on the course of the negotiations. These took shape when d'Antas submitted on 10 January 1883 a Portuguese counter-draft, dated 26 December 1882.[1] This modified the provisions in regard to the tariff and added a provision placing British subjects on an equal footing with the Portuguese in relation to the sale and leasing of land and religious worship instead of leaving this to be covered by the reservation of British rights under treaties, of which the contents were unknown to the Portuguese, with the native chiefs. The counter-draft omitted the cession of the Gold Coast territory. D'Antas kept in reserve a possible sixth article covering this and including also a *quid pro quo* to enable, it was said, the government to carry the treaty through the Cortes, in the shape of a British guarantee—harking back to the ancient alliance—of Portuguese possessions

---

[1] Anstey, pp. 107–12; cf. F. Latour da Veiga Pinto, *Le Portugal et le Congo au xixe siècle* (Paris, 1972), pp. 186–210.

described in the treaty or, failing that, a promise to use their good offices in helping Portugal to resist 'contestations' of her rights on the coast. The treaty was not finally signed until 26 February 1884 and was never ratified. It was then a much stiffer treaty and much more strictly drafted. It was the first brain-child of Percy Anderson, who began in February 1883 to shape Britain's Africa policy.

Dr. Anstey has described the course of the negotiations and vividly traced the building up, at the instigation of King Leopold of the Belgians, of an opposition to the treaty in Britain.[1] Leopold had the interests of the International Association of the Congo in mind. He could exploit the commercial fears and missionary ideals of James Hutton and Sir William Mackinnon for his purpose. The opposition in the House of Commons and the country was powerful.[2] But Granville would probably not have yielded to it, had there not also been difficulties with the Great Powers. France, Italy, and Spain had shown themselves hostile. But it was Bismarck's blunt refusal on 7 June 1884 to recognize the treaty that was decisive. He gained its withdrawal and the submission of the whole territorial question to the Berlin West African Conference. Here the principal victor was Leopold of the Belgians whose African Association was recognized as the Congo Free State. But Britain gained territorially all she had sought by the Congo treaty, since Portugal's sovereignty on the coast was established. The mouth of the river, however, went to the Congo Free State. Britain was obliged to give up the Anglo-Portuguese Commission to supervise the navigation of the Congo in favour of an international commission, but she gained when the Franco-German *entente* failed to survive the Conference. But the victories of prestige were all German. From this point of view neither Morier nor Granville could look back with any satisfaction on the story of the Congo treaty. Morier would add it to the case he was steadily building up against Bismarck.

[1] Anstey, pp. 113–67; cf. Latour da Veiga Pinto, pp. 194–205.
[2] Cf. A. Ramm (ed.), *The Political Correspondence of Mr. Gladstone and Lord Granville* (Oxford, 1962), ii. 42–3, 121–2.

4

PRINCIPLES OF POLICY

In the winter of 1877–8 everything seemed at a standstill: the Goa negotiations were broken off, the Lorenço Marques negotiations could not be begun until the reverberations of the annexation of the Transvaal and of the antics of the leaders of the Nyasaland colony had died away; the Russians had declared war upon the Turks, but their advance had been arrested at Plevna and active fighting was suspended until December, when that fortress fell and the Russians were able to cross the Balkan mountains. In these circumstances Morier's most interesting dispatches were devoted to the Catholic question—a question which in its German aspect he had already analysed (see above, p. 6). 'There is here as elsewhere', he wrote in May 1877, 'a zealous and uncompromising Vatican party ready at any favourable opportunity to push to the front and seize such advantages as may be within their reach.'[1] It could count on the sympathies of the Marquis de Ávila, but neither the *Regeneradores* nor the King lent it their support. Portugal, alone of the Catholic monarchies, had not published the papal decree on infallibility. Public opinion had been much agitated when, at the time of the de Ávila ministry, the Vatican party had tested its strength. Rumours had circulated: an ultramontane civil governor of Lisbon city would be appointed, the Cardinal Archbishop of Lisbon would head a pilgrimage to Rome on the occasion of his proceeding there to fetch his cardinal's hat, and this would be given an anti-Italian colouring. A committee headed by the Archbishop and including members of some of the oldest Portuguese families sponsored the pilgrimage. Morier irreverently made fun of the contrast between its solemnity and the huckstering tone in which the Cardinal then applied to the Portuguese government to advance the cost

[1] To Derby, no. 28 confidential, 11 May 1877, F.O. 63/1062.

price of his cardinal's hat and the amount of his travelling expenses; Morier believed that the Vatican party had received a sharp check when the King saw to it that the Cardinal was told that he must pay his own expenses if he wished to associate his journey to Rome with the display of the pilgrimage.[1]

In view of the expected death of Pius IX—it happened on 8 February 1878—Morier sent home a voluminous account of the history of the Portuguese King's claim to exercise, like the rulers of France, Spain, and Austria, a veto on any candidate for election to the papal see of whom he disapproved. He reported that it dated back to the reign of João V (1706–50) who had used every endeavour to induce 'the Roman Curia to give to Portugal the *status* of a Catholic Power of the first class. The palatial monastery of Mafra, built with a view to throw the Escurial into the shade, the Patriarchate of Lisbon, the title of Most Faithful Majesty are all of them monuments of the King's efforts in this direction and of their success.' It was claimed that he had succeeded in gaining 'all the rights and privileges enjoyed by the three Catholic Powers of the first class—the Empire, France and Spain—and that the right of exclusion is one of these rights'.

Morier recounted how the veto, though it had never been exercised, had equally never been denied, and described one significant recent instance of Portuguese intervention. On the day before the election of Cardinal Braschi as Pius VI, on 14 February 1775, the Portuguese ambassador had announced that he would make no objection to the election. The gratitude with which the announcement was received by the anti-imperialist and Bourbon faction allowed the deduction that the Portuguese exercise of the veto had been expected.

Morier pointed out that some significance attached, in the circumstances of 1878, to Portugal's making good her claim. First, she was an 'Old Catholic' or liberal Catholic country, and second it was especially important that her relations with the papacy should be cordial. King Luis was the son-in-law of Victor Emanuel and his representative, Count Thomar, was a possible go-between for the Quirinal with the Vatican. Count Thomar, appointed Portuguese envoy in 1870, had been left in charge of Italian interests when King Victor Emanuel

[1] To Derby, no. 28 confidential, 11 May 1877, F.O. 63/1062.

broke off diplomatic relations with the papacy during the crisis in which Italian troops entered Rome. Thomar had been responsible for the detaching of an Italian brigade to protect the Vatican and had won the confidence as a result of both King and Pope; his wit had since taught him how to retain it. Pius IX was said to resent his visits to the Quirinal. 'J'apprends que vous avez été au Quirinal', he is reported to have said in no pleasant humour on the first occasion of its being known that Count Thomar had visited the King of Italy. 'Pardon,' replied Count Thomar, 'je n'ai pas été au Quirinal; j'ai été dans la maison du beau-père de mon roi.' Finally, Corvo had well prepared the way for Portugal's playing a moderating and conciliatory part in the diplomatic mizmaze likely to precede the election of a new pope. In 1874 he had made it a principal feature of his policy to assert the position of Portugal as a liberal Catholic Power determined to exercise the right of veto if need be, and so prevent the election of an ultramontane successor to Pius IX. He had taken occasion to submit the Portuguese claim to do so to the papal secretary of state who, after investigation, had acknowledged its validity in conversation with Count Thomar. Finally 'Corvo shortly before he quitted office addressed a note to the Curia placing the claim of Portugal on formal record. To this note no answer has been returned and the Portuguese Government interprets this silence as equivalent to the negative assent, which is all the Curia has ever vouchsafed to the veto of the other Powers.' While, Morier concluded in this part of his report, it was doubtful whether the circumstances of the next conclave would give opportunity for a Portuguese veto, it was obvious 'that the mere fear of the complications likely to arise from her attempted use of this right might . . . give her a considerable ground of vantage in a divided Conclave'.

The last part of Morier's long dispatch recounted Corvo's preparations with the European Powers. Already in full accord with Italy, he had also entered into confidential communications with Austria and found 'a hearty response to the overtures made by him'. The two courts had reached complete accord on the policy to be pursued at the next election. During 1877 communications had also been opened with Germany— 'of the most confidential kind, they have not passed through the ordinary diplomatic media of communication . . . [but] were considered as having led to a complete understanding upon the question between Germany and Portugal'. Negotiations with France had been opened but dropped when it was found that the French candidate was Cardinal Sforza, an ultramontane.[1] Spain had assured Portugal that she wished to co-operate 'in the "manufacture" of a liberal Pope'.[2]

The policy initiated by Corvo seemed safe despite the change of government. Count Thomar was advanced to the rank of ambassador and France was added to the number of Powers with whom Portugal reached agreement. Thomar saw Waddington (then minister for foreign affairs) in Paris on the way back to Rome to take up his new rank and it was agreed that the conclave should meet at Rome, no foreign candidate should be put up, and an Italian cardinal not belonging to the *Zelanti* be elected. Portugal's position suddenly deteriorated when the Pope insisted that Count Thomar should break off relations with the Quirinal before taking up residence at the Vatican, since the position of ambassador, who unlike a minister or envoy represents the monarch personally, was incompatible with the preservation of relations with the Pope's enemy. (After the completion of Italian unity by the entry into Rome and the Pope's refusal of the Law of Guarantees, diplomatic relations between the papacy and the Italian government were not renewed until 1929.) 'King Humbert came to the rescue by taking the initiative in saying that he would see no discourtesy on the part of Count Thomar in discontinuing his visits to the Quirinal.' Thus a few days before the death of the Pope, good relations with Portugal had been restored and ultramontane intrigues to destroy the strong position she held had been foiled.[3]

In the event the election of Leo XIII commanded a singular consensus of opinion and the conclave, one of the shortest in the history of the papacy, proved to be well prepared against ultramontane influences. Leo XIII came of a military family, and was a fine scholar of the eighteenth-century type, and one who had kept silent throughout the debate on infallibility.[4] He was

[1] He was not in the end a candidate.
[2] To Lord Derby, no. 100 most confidential, 12 Dec. 1877, F.O. 63/1063, the substance of which I have summarized or quoted from p. 114 onwards.
[3] To Derby, no. 17 most confidential, 6 Feb. 1878, F.O. 63/1075.
[4] E. Soderini, *Il pontifico di Leo XIII*, i. 218–19; only 2 votes were taken, on 19 and

well suited to quiet the controversies that Pius IX's pontificate had witnessed.

The struggle between ultramontane and liberal Catholics created, indeed, much more stir and agitation than its power to influence events warranted. This had been illustrated by the King's language to Morier in 1877 at the time of the ministerial crisis in France. On 16 May 1877, President MacMahon had addressed to the prime minister, Jules Simon, a letter about their differences over a new press law and a law making sessions of municipal councils public. Whereupon Simon had resigned. But it was known that the real reason for this virtual dismissal was the incompatibility of an ultramontane president and a radical prime minister at a time when the French bishops and ultramontanes (provoked by the introduction of a bill into the Italian parliament) were petitioning their government to rescue the Pope from subjection to the temporal authorities of Italy. The French ultramontanes had chosen bad ground on which to fight; since Mancini's bill merely sought to make it an offence for ecclesiastical persons to publish writings threatening the security of the state. Of course much could be read into this general ban, but it was obvious that the ultramontanes' agitation was largely factitious, and it was not surprising that the French Chamber, just before Simon's fall, had passed a resolution condemning their activities. Thus after 16 May the president and the new prime minister, the duc de Broglie, stood on one side as conservative and Catholic and the Chamber on the other as radical and anti-clerical. The Chamber was led by Gambetta with the cry 'le cléricalisme—voilà l'ennemi'. On 23 May the King of Portugal, drawing Morier aside after a dinner he had given in honour of Queen Victoria's birthday, asked him his opinion on these events. Morier in reply said that he thought the greatest danger was the effect they might produce in Germany. He could not, it is true, shake off a habit of viewing Europe from Germany, but he also showed in this reply a characteristic mixture of quick penetration and ready simplification.

He was probably not far wrong in attributing to Bismarck great influence on the Continent and in recalling the war scare

---

20 Feb., Cardinal Pecci already carrying 19 first votes as against 6 for the candidate with the second most votes.

of 1875 to prove his proposition, but he was less near the mark in simplifying Bismarck's motives and reducing them to an anti-ultramontane impulse; the history of the Prussian *Kulturkampf* was more complex than Morier appreciated. 'The accession of the duc de Broglie to power', he said to King Luis, 'and the rupture between the President and the Chamber immediately after the strong anti-clerical vote of the latter might therefore not impossibly lead to one of those crises of nervous irritability across the Rhine which in the present electrical condition of relations between France and Germany were so much to be deprecated.' This was because 'rightly or wrongly' Bismarck believed 'that the accession to power of Governments with ultramontane tendencies meant the mobilization of the forces of the Vatican against Germany'. King Luis, for whom danger came from the radicals and free-thinkers and whose fears were lest *they* should be provoked by the ultramontane reaction, was less realist and more alarmed. The ejection of Jules Simon was 'a most auspicious event', for 'he had positive reasons for believing that M. Jules Simon had been carrying on active negotiations with the revolutionary party in Spain with a view to establish a republican form of government in the Peninsula'. When Morier expressed doubt, the King

repeated that he could completely rely on his secret sources of information, and that he was convinced that in this instance they were correct. He added that one of the King of Italy's Ministers, Signor Mancini, was equally keeping up relations with the revolutionary party in Spain and, as I understood His Majesty, in collusion with M. Jules Simon. His Majesty added that he also knew for certain that the late visit of the Paris Municipality to London had for its real purpose, not the visiting of underground railways and hospitals but the taking counsel together with the French *Communards* residing in that Metropolis.[1]

The French Chamber, before its adjournment for a month pending the fate of the president's request, then before the Senate, for a dissolution, passed a resolution condemning the Broglie ministry. The Senate by a narrow majority granted the dissolution. The fate of France lay with the French electorate.

[1] To Derby, no. 39 most confidential, 24 May 1877, F.O. 63/1062.

Henri Blowitz, *The Times*' correspondent, wrote to Morier from Paris on 16 June:

Now all is lost and poor France will return to the incessant struggles which have lasted for ninety years. Nobody knows for which party to pray. If the Marshal had waited a fortnight longer J. Simon would have fallen himself and Europe would have then applauded the advent of the conservatives. Instead of which the world has been surprised and the Left has been afforded a pretext to cry out against reaction, violence and treason. What will be the answer of the country no one knows and this country is too ignorant to know itself.

The ultramontane *velléités* of Marshal MacMahon were much less pronounced than was generally thought, as is shown by his letter to Victor Emanuel of 23 May reassuring him after Simon's dismissal. The elections, however, returned a strong republican majority, caused Marshal MacMahon to resign in January 1879, and showed the weakness of the ultramontane party; but although their anti-clericalism continued to be the one thing that bound the French radicals, in all their diversity, together, it was not a very good political bond and did as much to weaken them as a political force as it did to bind them together as a group. Morier's reports from Lisbon and afterwards from Madrid might be expected to contain a good deal on the continuing antagonism between Catholics and liberals or radicals. But there was a notable falling off of his interest in observing Catholic politics and of the significance he attached to them after 1878.

The eastern question continued throughout 1877–8 his chief preoccupation. The fall of Plevna had broken the spell and the Russian armies advanced on Adrianople and towards Constantinople. On 5 January the Russians occupied Sofia and on 20 January Adrianople. An agreement was signed there which formed the basis of the Treaty of San Stefano of 3 March 1878 that concluded the Russo-Turkish war. Morier, who, of course, knew nothing of the steps which led to the strengthening of British policy, continued, as long as Derby was in power, to bewail the impotence of Great Britain.

Yesterday [he wrote to Jowett][1] brought *The Times* announcement

[1] 4 Jan. 1878.

that H.M.G. had *approached* the Czar with a view to bringing about negotiations for peace. I cannot tell you with what a sinking of the heart I have read this announcement. Absolute immovability is bad enough and fraught with dangers of all kinds but from the first opening up of this Oriental Question we have never yet taken one single diplomatic step which was not a blunder or which failed to place us in a worse position than we were in before. (Let me here put in a parenthesis on the question of pessimism and let it be the last word on the question. I completely and from my heart subscribe to all you say about the unhealthiness of a querulous habit of mind, and you only preach to a *convert*.[1] I also quite feel and appreciate your kindness in wishing to warn me about a bad habit—only I must make this observation. You are the only person I can speak or write to absolutely and entirely without reserve. I am anxious to avail myself of the exceptional advantage offered me by this 'temple of friendship' to record systematically my impressions on political matters as far as they come within the sphere of my craft—but as, the present state of the British political cosmos being such as it is, my record cannot but be an unfavourable one and you must expect to meet with strong language of condemnation. If each time I use such language I am to expect a sermon I shall lose the freedom which alone will give value to my letters to you. On many occasions I have refrained from telling you things or rather expressing opinions *based on positive knowledge* because I have known it would elicit a stricture on seeing things in black. Had my habit of mind been pessimist and querulous I should at the first rebuff from the F.O. have crossed my arms, drawn my 2000 a year and sulked, instead of going on fighting cheerfully till I gain my points. When you hear that I am complained of for doing nothing (instead of abused for doing something) or for writing querulous despatches then apply the rod and I will kiss the hand that smiteth. The really important fact to seize is that the whole of our administrative system is in a state of dangerous chronic disease and that apparently the existing parliamentary apparatus is wholly incapable of furnishing a remedy. The business of each of us is of course to see how we can in our way stay the disease. Crying and howling will certainly not stay it—but neither will educating oneself into an artificial habit of looking at things optimistically and *couleur de rose*. The first thing is to have a correct *diagnosis* and to register the symptoms and this is what I propose to do in my letters to you.)

[1] See from Jowett, 28 Dec. 1877, original in the Jowett papers at Balliol College, printed in Abbott and Campbell, *Life and Letters of Benjamin Jowett*, iii. 89–92. A compact existed between Morier and Jowett that each would return his letters eventually to the other, and Jowett alludes to it in this letter.

After this long and characteristic digression Morier returned to *The Times*' announcement of the British approach to the Tsar. He complained that the Foreign Office acted only to satisfy 'the gallery of on-looking British Philistines', and without regard to the international effect.

What I fear then is that impelled by the belief that they are expected to do *something* they have hit upon the device of bawling out to Europe that they have had the pluck to undertake the business of postman between the belligerents and that beyond this they have no plan of action.

Now a country like England cannot act as postman and both Russia and Turkey have a right to expect that if we undertake this task there is more behind. Is there more behind? I doubt it. Are we going to act as mediators? If so have we realised what is the business of a mediator? I am absolutely convinced that we have not. These are the rudimentary principles of diplomacy of which the F.O. has not so much as an inkling. There are but two kinds of mediation possible. One where *both* parties ask you to mediate from which if you cannot satisfy both parties you can retire *re infecta* without disgrace. The other where one party only asks you to mediate in which case if you accept the office you tacitly undertake to impose your mediation on the party which has not asked for it and from which therefore you cannot retire *re infecta* without discredit.

Now both parties have certainly not asked us to mediate. And the only role possible for us therefore, if we accept Turkey's prayer to act on her behalf, is to settle with her what we deem equitable conditions of peace and then to propose these to Russia as our own and Turkey's. But this of course presupposes our being ready to fight for these conditions if they are refused: and that the Ministry as at present composed should have made up their minds to this, I cannot believe.

(I have written to Lady Derby today saying I dreaded lest we had offered mediation in the same way as we entered the Conference viz., with a clear intimation that nothing we said was to be taken *au sérieux*.)

In my opinion, however, the present moment is one not for bawling through the columns of the 'Times' but for the lowest whisper *en tête à tête* of which diplomacy is capable and where there is a *will* behind the whisper it is wonderful what can be done by whispering. It is to Russia that the whisper should be addressed—a conciliatory, courteous whisper, to the effect '*thus far and no further*'.[1]

[1] This was the course Salisbury took when he succeeded Derby as foreign

One step beyond the line we mark out for you and even at the eleventh hour we join the Turks. It will then be a question of honour for you to take Constantinople, and Constantinople, even the broken remains of the Ottoman Empire, the *'reliquiae Danaum atque inmitis Ignatieff'*,[1] backed by the whole power of Great Britain, can hold out against you world without end AMEN. I will now proceed to tell you the grounds which make me believe that such a course would be perfectly successful . . .

27 Jan. Thus far had I got at the beginning of the month and was interrupted. Since then all manner of things have happened. Amongst others a correspondence elicited by a letter from an important individual.[2] In my answer I touch upon most of the points I mean to touch on in my letter to you. As it is carefully written so as to avoid all indiscretions or strictures on Ministers and the like I send you a copy which I should much like you to send to Goschen. He is the only man viz. statesman with whom I instinctively feel I am in sympathy. I had a letter from him some time ago in which he said he believed we were the only two men in England who combined faith in economic principles with Imperial feeling. It was very interesting to me therefore that you should have chanced to suggest him as 'a person to submit my lucubrations to'. I wish you would send the letter to him confidentially telling him it is mine and that he is to return it to you.

Morier then took issue with Jowett on the advisability of a country's acknowledging its fault when it had been in the wrong. 'Whether or not the U.S. arbitration [on the Alabama case in 1873] was a case in point, whether the results have been so satisfactory as you say, is what I am not in a position to judge of.' He also differed from him about the future of France, taking a more hopeful view.

I think the success of the Republican party and the self command by which it has been obtained is the brightest spot which has appeared in European politics since I have had to do with them. When the fresh clash between France and Germany comes (not that I believe in its necessary imminence as you do) I do not believe that it will be under the banner of either real or sham catholicism that France will fight. *À propos* of France and humiliation I have no hesitation in admitting the immense advantage to a nation of a humiliation

secretary in Mar. 1878, and it led to the Anglo-Russian agreement of 31 May, see below, p. 136.

[1] Virgil, *Aeneid*, 1. 30, 3. 87: 'Troas, reliquias Danaum atque inmitis Achilli', 'The Trojans, all that were left by the Greeks and the harsh Achilles.'
[2] See below, p. 124.

which has been accompanied by great national efforts to avoid it, in which the sentiments of honour and self-respect have been preserved, such as that which France underwent in 1870–71 . . .

He agreed, however, with remarks Jowett had made about the harm done by Cobden and Bright, and continued:

My quarrel with Cobden is his want of logic. The solidarity of the human race, our all being members of *one* family, economic harmonies as a scientific basis for the duty of co-operation on the part of all mankind in each other's interest as the best way of securing their own, this is his doctrine and that which gave him the right to the designation *l'homme international*. Yet having got hold of this great and true idea he sees its truth only in the limited sphere of exchanging cotton for grains. He does not or will not recognize the fact that man being such as he is and human society being such as man being such as he is, has made it, to refuse co-operation by force if need be, for the great ideal object of the solidarity of the race is the grossest of selfishness and the negation of the general principles he starts from. We are to be all in all to our neighbour till he requires the aid of a strong arm to save him from having his head broken: if he prays for help the most we can give him are some tracts on the currency something under the cost price.

Morier then, leaving common sense behind, went on to assert that had Britain not been influenced by Cobdenite doctrines of non-intervention,

we might very likely have had a united Italy without war. We could certainly have stopped the Franco-German war (though France would have been the loser as I verily believe by missing the chance of renovation through humiliation) or had we not stopped it we might certainly have prevented the annexation of Alsace-Lorraine or at least of the French part of Lorraine—and lastly we might absolutely have prevented the horrible butcheries of the present war and the destruction for generations to come of Bulgaria. All this without in practice having once had to fire a shot . . . The absurdity, however, of the matter is that the idea of non-intervention on the part of a country like England is simply *nonsense*. Our mere size and the fact that we are the only people with a first class position in Europe, Asia, America and Africa, prevents the possibility of our non-intervening. *Our very presence is intervention.* You might as well say that you would drive a coach and four down Regent's Street at five o'clock in the afternoon during the season without intervening with the other vehicles that crowd that thoroughfare. You may do your best to get out of the way of A.B.C. but by so doing you must get into the way of D.E.F.

I think that of all the ghastly proofs of decaying power, of the *decadence* of Great Britain, the way in which the newspapers and the *anthropomorphised* Times-leading-article Lord Derby, pointed to the discomfiture of Europe at our refusal to join the Berlin Memorandum as a proof that the prestige and international power were as great as ever, is the ghastliest and at the same time the most instructive. Our refusal to accede to the Berlin Memorandum without at the same time preparing some alternative plan to re-establish the European concert and solidarity which we had broken up was the starting point of all our blunders. Yet Ld Derby prided himself on the discomfiture we had caused as a mark of our power and prestige. It was like a child that had upset a china vase and chuckled at the thought of all the splinters and broken bits it had had the power to scatter on the floor. The case is one exactly in point in regard to the question of intervention. People in England applauded (some did at least) the withdrawal from the Berlin Memorandum as an act of non-intervention, whereas it was in truth an act of the gravest intervention. Lord Beaconsfield in his speech on the 17th committed himself in a still more glaring and arrogant manner to the same blunder. He enumerated one after the other every one of the blunders we had committed and the confusion and disagreement they had caused as so many proofs that we had all along been playing the most considerable part of any of the Great Powers! It is this which makes people abroad hate us as well as despise us. We are in everybody's way yet not so as to either damage enemies or benefit friends. Like some huge ironclad rudderless and with her engine fires out we are an object of scorn to the enemy's fleet, but drifting hither and thither on the tide, one of terror and dismay to the ships we should convoy.

So much for intervention.[1]

The 'important individual' alluded to in the above letter was the Queen's private secretary, Sir Henry Ponsonby, who wrote on 16 January 1878 from Osborne almost as much on the Queen's behalf as on his own, answering a letter from Morier[2] similar to the one to Jowett:

I may ask questions. I don't ask the Queen questions for her views are clear, distinct and unmistakable. Not war if the Colossus [Russia]

[1] Cf. Jowett's reply, 16 Feb. 1878, Jowett papers, Balliol College, printed in Abbott and Campbell, *Life and Letters of Benjamin Jowett*, iii. 92–4.
[2] Original in R.A. H. 18/87 dated Jan. 1878. Pages from the beginning and end of this letter are reproduced opposite.

3

I accept your modified condolences as to being out of the world of politics. The exasperating part of being in a place like this at a great crisis like the present is the being outside all authentic information as to what is going on and the impossibility therefore of forming any sound opinion on matters which one feels so keenly about that they haunt you day and night & leave you no rest. I must confess that, since the 'Times' announcement which only reached us two days ago that H M Gov.t was going to approach the Emperor of Russia with the view of bringing about peace negotiations and the outrageously humiliating leading article with which the Times accompanied this announcement, I have had

Letter to Sir Henry Ponsonby, January 1878 (page 3 and last page)

preach peace at any price
and all the while doing a
roaring business across
the counter in contraband
of war!

Pray accept for yourself
& Mrs Ponsonby our best
wishes for the new Year
and believe me
  Very truly

  R B D Morier

will cave in, but war if he won't. I understand her perfectly. I understand also Gladstone perfectly—and I understand the *paix à outrance* of Bright. But what do you want? The Crimean heroes, soldiers and taxpayers have no desire to repeat that game which didn't gain much for them. Without allies we should not be able to do so much now as we did then. But never mind if honour calls this way. But does she? I can't hear her. I can't imagine it possible that honour could call upon us to fight for the wretched Turks. Honour ought to have told us that when we declared neutrality we should have been strictly and severely neutral and not have encouraged the poor wretches to think that we were going to support them. Now of course we are in an awkward predicament in consequence of being supposed (not unnaturally) by all the world to back up the Turk. You say you don't go by what cabinets think—no more do I, for I don't know what they do think. But I am convinced they can't act against the will of the people and I think the people of this country are determined not to be lugged into an unrighteous war. Your portrait of the Apoplectic Quaker doing a roaring business while preaching peace is severe—and I don't think we have done much in the contraband way—like our Yankee cousins have—but why is the Apoplectic Quaker to run down to the other end of the street and mix himself up in a quarrel in which he has no concern, or rather in which his supposed interests clash with his duty and feeling as a Quaker because his neighbours cry out 'Yah! why don't you fight'. I say supposed interests because I cannot see what real interest has been menaced as yet. The passage of the Straits will of course not be quite so pleasant for us but can we in justice fight for it if Europe thinks otherwise . . .

To this Morier, in his turn writing as much for the Queen as for Sir Henry, replied on 28 January with a plea for the shaking off of *idées fixes* and for clear thinking:

I confess that this difficulty you find in locating me in any of the existing categories of British political Philistines is peculiarly agreeable to my feelings.

Let me formulate my *credo*:

They are to be held accursed who from a blind and unnatural hatred of Russians desire to lead us into an *unrighteous* war. I use the cant phrase.

They likewise are to be held accursed who out of a blind and unreasoning love of Bulgarians and Russians and a blind and unreasoning hatred of Turks would fetter and paralyze our action in safeguarding our position as regards Russia, should such safeguarding require co-operation with Turks.

Yet more accursed than either of the two former are those who neither loving Russians nor hating Turks cry out peace, peace as the one obese deity to which everything that makes a nation and not a mere fortuitous concourse of living atoms is to be sacrificed.

But my choicest cursing apparatus, for which I should have to search the hiddenmost recesses of the Vatican, is reserved for those who like the writer of the 'Times' article of 29th December, say in one breath that we have interests in *Turkey* which (*sub auditur* at the cost of any number of Turkish lives) must be safeguarded and that therefore Turkey must *place herself entirely in our hands*, and yet proclaim that after she had done so we are under no circumstances to do more than act as letter carrier between the belligerents, or *payer de notre personne*.

I think these four categories exhaust the mob of British writers and talkers and snorters such as I make them out in the columns of the 'Times', 'Daily News' and 'Pall Mall' and in the reports of the inane public meetings which fill to putrescence the columns of the daily papers. It is pleasant to me therefore that you cannot catalogue me among any of these.

Morier continued his letter with an attempt to suggest the policy Britain *should* adopt now that Russia was victorious and about to 'carry out her mission of destroying the Ottoman Empire and substituting a Slave Colossus in its stead'.

It is absurd [he continued] to abuse her for this policy—she has a perfect right to it—it is very certainly the same policy we should have if we were in her shoes though we would carry it out more honestly and with less prevarication.

The question then arises:

1. Is the letting Russia reel out the thread of her destiny to its last fathom a course advantageous to Great Britain.

2. If it is not are we in a position to supply the intervening force required to prevent it . . . [Four paragraphs follow in which Morier gives what he imagines would be the answers of the four groups from whom he dissociated himself.] *My* answer is that it is not advantageous to Great Britain to let Russia bring the war to a close in the manner most conducive to the fulfilment of her destiny and as if she and Turkey were the only European and Asiatic Powers concerned in the matter.

You will see that I have used general terms—'what is advantageous to Great Britain' and not the term 'British interests'. I have done so because more harm has been done by the use of the latter term than can well be imagined. I hate the cant of Humanitarianism and the like but there is such a thing as the cant of cynicism and the way in which we have prided ourselves on looking only to our material interest as if this were the noblest thing a nation could do and as if the welfare of the whole Universe depended on our interest rather than [on] anybody else's coming safe out of the fire is a pitiable instance of the latter kind of cant.

Now when I say what is *advantageous* to Great Britain I mean to include not only her material interests but all that affects her *moral* position as a Great Power, that is: as an international individual with a great position, a magnificent tradition, great Rights and therefore great *Duties*.

Morier then took several pages to make it plain that in framing his answer he recognized that Britain had not adopted the policy he advocated (see above, pp. 55-7) of enforcing reform upon Turkey, but adopted what he called (using a prize-fighting metaphor) a bottle-holding attitude. He then continued:

Having, as before stated, committed ourselves to the role of bottleholder, not having, when there was yet time, changed our position from what it was after the Crimean War, I maintain that we were bound in *honour* to prevent a dismemberment of Turkey, such as is generally supposed the three Emperors have in view. I will carry out the simile of the bottleholder. We were as bottleholder not necessarily bound to fight for her, whilst a fair fight was going on. Now she is beaten we can admit the fact and tell her it is time she should give in and hand over the stakes—but what we cannot allow is that whilst she is lying helpless and prostrate on the ground her adversary should spring at her throat, trample upon her and take her watch and purse *besides the stakes* . . . As regards Armenia and the Dardanelles even the 'Times' writer agrees that there are British interests that must be protected in Turkey! But the British philistine will say how was this settlement to be effected except by war—and we have no army, and that this would be an *unrighteous* war. This brings me to the rude fallacy which has pervaded our policy all through viz. that having (*omnium consensu*) interests inseparably wrapped up in Turkish soil these interests could be defended separately from the proprietors of the soil. From this rude fallacy have flowed all the impossible schemes so largely circulated of occupation of Turkish soil independently of Turkish consent and without a declaration of war against Russia! A policy best described as *belligerent neutrality*.

I maintain then that it was the duty of statesmanship to make up its mind that, amongst many evils to choose from, the least was to hold steadily in view the possibility of an eventual co-operation with Turkey as the only force powerful enough to prevent the consummation of that absolute and unconditional victory of Russia which I have described as disadvantageous to Great Britain.

Well I maintain that if, say when the siege of Plevna was still going on but when we knew that it must fall, we had let Russia know quite distinctly, and without [the] *arrière pensée* of getting out of the meaning of our spoken words, that we would not hinder her from obtaining a favourable peace commensurate with the size of her victories after the fate of Plevna, but would recommend Turkey to propose it, but that in the event of her claiming more than such a peace we would assist Turkey in resisting her, we should have been masters of the situation . . . [This was to have been done] by confidential communications of the firmest and most conciliatory kind to Russia . . . [exacting from her an engagement not to take more than certain maxima terms which Morier defines and making it clear that the alternative was war with Britain]. I am convinced Russia would not have hesitated as to the alternative. She knows as well as you and I, that Bismarck wanted her to be *saignée à blanc*—that a glorious and advantageous peace *now* would mean her coming out of the struggle with an intact army 100 per cent better than when she began and an enormous European position . . . [But even if Russia had been ready to take Britain on as well as Turkey] it is my opinion that we were bound to take the risk.

If the British Lion is sick to death with fatty degeneration of the heart, better to die of apoplexy than be slowly kicked to death by home and foreign jackanapes. But I refuse to believe that he is sick to death. He has so glorious a part yet to play in the world that I will not believe that he has lost the capacity of playing it. But my hopes are not great, a democracy tempered by a plutocracy does not furnish the 'climate of opinion' favourable to heroic deeds, and a great empire cannot continue a great empire unless the heroic spirit is evocable. Read the vth scene in the ivth act of the first part of Henry vith. Unless at the great crisis of our history the England of the Present can meet the England of the Past in the temper of Young John when arguing with his father in that scene, the beginning of the end is not far off. From somewhere in the nation when the day of humiliation is drawing nigh the cry must come

> Here on my knee I beg mortality
> Rather than life preserved with infamy.

Unless it does we belong to the past and have no share or inheritance in the future. For my part I am old fashioned enough to maintain that life is not worth living either for a state or an individual unless the national or the individual honour, as the case may be, be kept intact.

This letter met with no little success at Windsor. 'The Queen rejoiced', so Ponsonby wrote, 'that you were not a Russo-phil— and when I went next day into the Equerries' Room I found those ardent warriors complaining at the loss of their morning's ride because they had to make two copies of your letter. "But", as they observed, "it is a capital letter, for it is clear that he wants to fight." "Wants to fight whom", I enquired in a broad-brimmed tone, "Why those damned Russians of course." And they went on with their copying.'[1]

Morier was well aware of how little he in fact knew either of events or ideas and sought enlightenment in a long paper argument with Sir Louis Mallet. To him he wrote on 12 January:

I wish at such a crisis as this that you would have pity on my helpless solitude and give me a few hints of what is really going on. I should much like an exchange of ideas, the more so as I have a sort of instinct we should not agree and that the present would be a crucial test which would exactly establish the point of bifurcation between our views. I think I can almost say for certain that you are heart and soul in the *peace* party: and that you would unhesitatingly, if you were a free man, cast your lot with the peace demonstrators and make telling speeches denouncing war in every form and on any pretext. Now my state of mind is one of the most undivided and unmitigated loathing for the war party and the peace party . . . That the great crisis we are going through should present itself to the mind of the adult population of Great Britain simply as a pretext for making party capital and for a *prise de bec* between rival political clubs is degrading and humiliating.

He recited again his belief in Russia's right to an advantageous peace and described the utmost which this might legitimately include: autonomy north of the Balkans, guarantees of good government south, the cession of Kars and Batum and some further rectification of Russia's Asiatic frontier, the opening of the Straits to all equally. 'The peace I would not submit to and would resist even by a declaration of war is the peace I believe the three Emperors have or have had in view, viz. a partition of the Turkish Empire amongst the European

[1] From Ponsonby, 4 Feb. 1878.

Powers.' If Britain were not prepared to declare war to stop it, she had only the alternatives of acceding and taking her share or of protesting with her 'hands crossed' and sinking down to the position of a third-rate Power. It was this that Morier could not bear: 'to me life is just worth living as it forms part of a great and glorious national life.' It was here that he thought he differed from his friend: 'You are a Quietist and like Dutch scenery with the prospect of life on the bank of a canal and the growth of endless tulips.'

More seriously, Morier believed the difference was not a matter of temperament, but a matter of conviction and a difference about the implications for foreign policy of their common acceptance of economic liberalism. The doctrines of the Manchester School should not mean the abnegation of force, but force used, in his favourite phrase, as fighting *in posse* to prevent fighting *in esse*. 'The moment we showed that we had a policy, a fair and equitable policy and *le courage de notre opinion* you would see that allies would spring up around us . . . We are isolated and alone because no human being all this time has been able to make out what we would be at. Let us once more be a living force in Europe.' He described Britain as she appeared to him:

A buttonholed gibusocratic[1] upper class lisping curses at Russia and revelling in an artificial frenzy for the Turk: a bedevilled People's William[2] lower class ranting about Bulgarians and humanity, and a middle class imaged by my old friend the obese Quaker singing psalms through a carbuncled apoplectic nose and moved by the Holy Ghost on the first day of the week to preach peace at any price, whilst during the remaining six he drives a roaring trade across his counter in contraband of war—that is the British Trinity as it appears at present on the International Board.

Mallet's reasons, given on 26 January, for opposing war in the existing circumstances were three: that Britain's commitments, political and commercial, had outstripped her resources; that she was likely to choose the wrong side; that it would imperil the great political experiment on which she had embarked—that of making a free country out of feudal England.

In this particular war [Mallet continued] I have absolutely failed

---

[1] A coined word of which the first element is the French for an opera-hat.
[2] i.e. bedevilled by Gladstone.

to see any possible pretext on which, without the deepest national disgrace, we could have aided Turkey. The arguments in favour of it have been urged with a cynical effrontery which has surpassed anything in our lives said or done in England, and have revealed a moral depravity in certain classes which is absolutely revolting. I need only refer to the 'Pall Mall' and the 'Telegraph' as the organs of these classes. If one could believe that these writers represented any large amount of sentiment and opinion, I should despair of my country.

... When once we had decided that Turkey could not be upheld, we should have held our tongues. If after all the real interests of England, so far as they are identical with those of civilisation, had been endangered, we should have found plenty of allies to assist us in vindicating them, and I believe, Russia among them, if we made it possible for her to act with us. Our interests are not opposed either in Europe or in Asia.

You say I am a Quietist and love Dutch scenery and tulips. This is true in one aspect of my character, but I believe the passionate side of my nature is by far the stronger of the two, only I require some great cause to kindle the sacred fire. If to be a humanitarian is to place the interests of humanity above those of one's country where these interests conflict, I certainly am a humanitarian. I am a French Protestant by blood, and should be unworthy of my fathers if I were not ready to shake the dust off my feet and leave my country on one side, if it trampled down great principles of human freedom in the pursuit of selfish aims. I love my country, not because I happen to have been born a cockney, which seems to me the stupidest form of patriotism, but because, on the whole, she seems to me to have done more for the human race so far than any other with whose history I am acquainted, and because I see the possibility of achievements far higher and nobler than any which she has yet to record ...

... It puzzles me how you, an economist and a Liberal, can fail to see that the kind of way in which Europe has hitherto been governed, in which the people have been the mere tools and victims of governments and governing classes, is absolutely incompatible with democracy and free trade, and that the choice lies between two courses in deciding on the future foreign policy of England.

Mallet then outlined these: the first, 'a return to a system of foreign alliances, territorial extension, and the further subjugation of inferior races', would throw the material and moral condition of the British people back where it was fifty years before, and 'there can be no greatness or security to any people, unless they rest on the *material well-being* of the population'. The second course was 'to cast in our lot broadly and heartily with the interests of the people, by which I mean the working millions of the human race, beginning with our own. It is upon them that the real cost of wars invariably falls'. If England cast her lot in with them she would avoid wars of honour and prestige. England could not at one and the same time seek to extend 'free institutions, equal civil and religious rights, and above all and before all, as the foundation, free trade' and thereby to hold 'together the national unit called England' and to 'become a civilised country' *and also* become a great military empire holding down subject races by force:

> I believe it is . . . to the confusion [between the two courses] that the vacillation, inconsistency, and feebleness of our recent foreign policy is in a great degree to be attributed.
>
> . . . I cannot understand your saying that 'flatulent humanitarianism' has prevented us from asserting ourselves so as to secure an honourable peace. This is to turn history and fact upside down. It has been the taint of the old traditions about Turkey, and stupid jealousy and hatred of Russia, which is the cause of this. Short of aiding Turkey, directly or indirectly, which I do not suppose you would have advised, it was impossible to take up a hostile attitude to Russia.
>
> . . . I see in you what, in a different form, is so conspicuous in Lytton, and still more in our Anglo-Indian statesmen, a habit of making your opinion on your own purview of facts and principles and policy, with little or no reference to the actual conditions and forces of English life. Your picture of the spectacle we present to the world is well painted, and not pleasing, but it is better than that which we presented during the American rebellion and the great French war, when (i.e. in the former) clergy in full canonicals marched through Manchester at the head of the recruiting sergeants, and poor rates were four times as high as before the war.

Mallet concluded by hoping that Morier might find in his letter 'materials for deciding whether there need really be any point of bifurcation in the general current' of their views. He believed the difference between them occurred only because they were speculating on different sets of facts. 'I think that you would agree with me that, with all our difficulties, there is still a magnificent field for a great foreign policy . . . Even honour and prestige are not excluded from my political vocabulary, but, as they are now commonly used, these words mean little more than the honour of the buccaneer and the prestige of the pothouse.'

Morier's reply of 22 February was an interim one; for he wished Mallet to return his first letter so that he might keep constantly in mind the arguments which Mallet was answering as he himself wrote. Meanwhile he made certain points. First, Mallet's position was both more realistic and more generous than that of Cobden. He had searched in vain through Cobden's writings for much that he had heard Mallet quote as established Cobdenic doctrine. The disciple, as had happened before, had surpassed his master.

You were filled [he continued] with a great enthusiasm and a personal admiration and love for Cobden. You were constantly with him at one of the most important periods of his life,[1] and must have, over and over again, discussed the great questions on which your own mind had long been working, and respecting which your own faith has since become definitively fixed. There must have been the keenest sympathy between you, and the intercourse must have been as great a delight to him as it was to you ... But in such intercourse, it is absurd to assign to the disciple a passive part. What the disciple afterwards gives out as the faith of the master is really a joint product of two minds, and their two individualities.

... You are a Cobdenite *pur sang*. But you have had opportunities, which Cobden never had, of acquainting yourself with the administrative requirements of our Imperial system, and of late years especially you have directly participated in the government of that portion of our Empire [i.e. India] which is so *Imperial* as to have monopolised the Imperial title. In matters imperial, therefore, you have the immense advantage of speaking as an expert.

I, on the other hand, am, and always have been, an Imperialist, but certainly not of that class [in a phrase from Mallet's letter] 'who habitually sneer at Cobden'. I do not believe that Cobden has a heartier admirer than I, either as regards the work actually done by him, or the objects of that higher creed which I do not believe to be so much Cobden's as that of yourself and a few of his choicest disciples. It is in the method of applying the creed that I take it our difference will be found to consist.

An argument between Mallet and himself, Morier therefore

[1] Mallet served under the Board of Trade (1847-72) where he was concerned with commercial treaties and especially the negotiation of the Cobden treaty.

claimed, would be one between 'a Cobdenite exceptionally acquainted with the imperial mechanism and an imperialist exceptionally influenced by Cobdenic ideas'. He defended himself, in the second place, against the charge of making his opinion on his own purview of the facts 'with little or no reference to the actual conditions and forces of English life' by arguing that 'the general principles which should determine international intercourse, and, therefore, the *modus vivendi* of mankind generally' should not be derived 'from the actual, that is, the momentary conditions and forces of English life. I confess I am not ready to assign this absolute preponderance to the national over the international, to the particular over the general point of view.' He admitted that if Mallet simply meant he was ignorant of daily details, this was true, but refused to allow that it was a disadvantage. 'I am, I believe, better able to catch the general outlines of the political *silhouette*, and note general tendencies and currents. When in England I never enter a political coterie . . . which does not assert that it, and it only, knows the conditions and forces of English life. At a distance I can better judge which represents the main current, and which the eddies and backwater.' A third point Morier made was that he was more aware than Mallet, because he lived outside England, of

that international 'climate of opinion' which belongs to the thoughtful portion of civilized mankind as such, and on which you have hitherto laid so great a weight. Now . . . it is a fact well worth taking notice of that from the very commencement of this Oriental question, this general European liberal public opinion has been all through diametrically opposed to English liberal public opinion. Does not this at least prove that there are two sides to the question?

Morier next went on to contest Mallet's two assumptions that to be an economist and liberal made Morier *ipso facto* also a democrat and that democracy and free trade were correlative terms or, at least, stood in some sort of natural affinity with each other.

I look upon democracy as the deadliest enemy of the *liberal* habit of mind and as the born antagonist of economic principles. I perfectly admit that democracy is the current down which we are all drifting, and that to resist it is beyond the power of any of us. But the *really living democracy* of the future is a *socialist* democracy; the breath of its nostrils, the quickening impulse which gives to it its force and vital power of onward progress is hatred of economic principles; for the end it strives to compass is the benefiting of the masses at the expense of the individual, the levelling downwards by the extinction of all higher forms, in a word the pulling down of the altar of liberty to substitute in its place the shrine of equality.

Morier believed that although the current was irresistible, liberal ideas might yet modify the most dangerous results of drifting with it. By reforming the land laws and local government he believed it might be possible to associate the right to vote with service, instead of property, and to bring the notion of the obligation of public service as low down as it could reach in the ranks of society. As for the connection of free trade with democracy, it was true that cheap bread and cheap clothes were good for the masses, but he doubted whether the masses ever recognized what was good for them. Free trade was 'the child of the thoughtful few . . . and therefore of the very class which democracy dooms to impotence. It was by the merest accident that the doctrine became associated in England with the passions of the masses, and, as soon as the corn laws fell, that association ceased . . . Since Cobden first unfurled the banner of free trade, democracy has stalked with giant strides over the face of the earth, and free trade has receded *pari passu* . . .'

'That England', Morier wrote in a concluding paragraph, 'not only is but has been for centuries the freest country which the political genius of mankind has ever succeeded in establishing on a firm and lasting foundation is a cardinal point of my political faith. That the tendency of the day is not towards freedom but towards equality is equally my firm conviction, so also that the two are diametrically opposed to each other.' In a postscript he looked forward to the kind of letter he expected to write when Mallet had returned his original manuscript to him.

My contention will be that it is impossible to give up war *in posse* as the motive force of all international and diplomatic action. That the idea of *moral influence* as a substantive force separable from an ultimate appeal, if necessary, to physical force is the root fallacy which has led to the present deplorable impotence of England. That this fallacy must be rooted out before any step can be taken in the right direction. That the teaching of Cobden has been, in a great measure, the cause of this fallacy getting the hold it has on the best portion of the liberal party. That being an enthusiastic supporter of Cobden's premisses, viz., that the material no less than the moral and intellectual interests of the human race are '*solidaires*', one and indivisible, I consider that I am logical and he is illogical in the deductions we make from those premisses respecting the international duties practically incumbent on Great Britain as the most important and the most powerful representative of those principles. That the withdrawal of Great Britain as the great peace power from active international life and the enthronement in Great Britain of that devil's trinity, non-intervention, moral influence, and British interests, has been the cause of more fighting and bloodshed in Europe during the last 20 years than any other *single* cause, and has, therefore *pro tanto*, been the most direful sinning against the living principle of the Cobdenic creed.

Morier's definitive reply[1] was written in very different circumstances and turned out to be shorter and less critical of actual policy than he had expected. When he wrote it, Britain had in fact done what Morier had wished and in the Anglo-Russian agreement of 31 May 1878 had obtained both Russia's acceptance of the limited terms to be exacted from Turkey and her agreement to their being adopted by the European Powers assembled in congress and embodied in a European treaty. The British conventions with Turkey and Austria of 4 and 6 June completed the protective system which Salisbury designed to build round the decaying Turkish empire.

In his reply Morier began by redefining the aim of the argument.

I desire to bring out clearly the views we respectively hold in the abstract as to the part which is to be assigned to the force 'War' in the intercourse between civilized nations. It seems to me of the greatest importance that a clear idea should be formed on this subject and a clear *general principle* be ascertained and fixed quite irrespectively of any *casus belli*. The literature of the day is filled with rhapsodies about the horrors of war or the glories of war, but I have as yet not been fortunate enough to come across any attempt to treat the matter objectively and to assign to war its true position as one of the political forces which determine the *modus vivendi* of man-

[1] An undated copy (belonging probably to the beginning of June); taken from Lady Wemyss's draft of her continuation of the *Memoirs*.

kind... All civilized nations repudiate conquest and aggression and therefore, so far as words go, we have come to a kind of negative agreement on the subject, but as regards anything positive the *consentiens vox* does not exist.

He believed on this point he should have 'to give up association with Cobdenism'. He could not be a peace-at-any-price man any more than he believed Mallet could be.

In the Oriental question, the great central international drama of our time, the Cobdenic creed would have imposed on Great Britain complete and absolute non-intervention. The *utmost* it would have allowed would have been a *friendly endeavour* to safeguard special British interests—but if the endeavour had failed, we should still have been bound to do nothing, as under no circumstances could we oppose Russia by force without national disgrace. As regards the general settlement of the question complete passivity was the role imposed.

Mallet had, however, avoided the pitfall

into which those fell who proclaimed that we should have gone into Congress unarmed and opposed the moral force of an eloquent rhetoric to the armed legions of our co-assessors. This is a beautiful role for a St Augustine or a St Boniface and admirably adapted for an historical painting, but a St Boniface with military estimates by the million and yet nothing better than a crozier in his hand is an absurd conception. Dignified silence however seems the Cobdenic deportment you recommend and there I entirely agree with you.

Morier then defined the point to which his imperialist beliefs led him to progress from this ground which they had in common. This was that there *was* a moment for active intervention. In the eastern question as it had stood in the spring he had believed that this 'would arrive whenever the danger of a military occupation of Constantinople appeared upon the war horizon'.

On 13 June Mallet, who owing to the uncertainties of the post had not received Morier's letter, wrote that he was still waiting for it but doubted whether he would be converted; since he suspected that Morier approved of the British attitude after Salisbury's accession to the Foreign Office. With a further letter from Morier of 18 June—he had already received Mallet's of 13 June—the controversy died away. It closed then with Morier summing up what he looked for in the future.

You ask what is the future I look for. I answer the giving life and reality to the *new* ideas (which I will briefly summarize as the international solidarity of the civilized races of this microcosmic planet and their guardianship of the non-civilized races) by means of the *old* machinery.

The root fallacy of Cobden's teaching is contained in the motto, from a speech of Washington's, to one of his essays 'Minimum of political intercourse between countries, maximum of commercial intercourse', or words to that effect, and this is the idea that all the rag tag and bobtail of the Rylands[1] stamp of Manchester men have got hold of and which has had so terribly deleterious an effect on the whole of our foreign policy during the last forty years . . . The idea of any progress being possible in the laws, habits and customs which regulate international intercourse by quietly ignoring the political representatives i.e. the Sovereigns and Governments of the national units whom our object is to internationalize seems to me simply silly and the idea that this political intercourse can be supplanted by the automatic process of commerce whose supreme law is self-interest appears to me silliness intensified with lunacy.

The only force for influencing action was 'the moral force based on the physical force of each [national] unit—to keep this force unimpaired and use it in the direction of human progress seems to me the vocation of the statesman—and I am not prepared to hand over the glorious business of statesmanship to private enterprize and companies with limited liabilities'. Morier conformed to Mallet's expectation in approving at least those consequences of Salisbury's advent that he could see.

An instrument which had for years ceased to exist is once more present among the forces which govern Europe capable of doing almost infinite good. With it in his hand a statesman capable of wielding it might have prevented more than half the evils which have afflicted Europe during the last ten years. What use will be made of it I do not pretend to say. But *without this instrument* i.e. without the command of the physical energy of the British Empire to back up its moral decisions, we are not only a useless member of the European family but with our loud talk and humanitarian

---

[1] Peter Rylands (1820–87), a notable pacifist, liberal, later unionist, M.P., 1868–74, 1878–87.

swagger egging on nations into horrible bloodshed and leaving them stuck fast in their enterprizes without stirring a finger to assist them, a most dangerous and harmful member is what I am ready to defend against all comers.

John Morley, another friend of Mallet, subsequently printed part of this correspondence in the *Fortnightly Review*, which he edited, but the argument between the two friends had lost its impetus. When Mallet avoided the subject in later letters, Morier protested against its being tabooed and insisted once again on their common faith in 'Cobdenic internationalism'.

My starting point was an anathema of Jingoism and Chauvinism and . . . my second anathema only was directed against the violent pro-Russian peace at any price Gladstonites. I have not identified you with the latter, why identify me with the former? What I want you to keep in mind is that our programmes as far as they are parallel are absolutely identical—that the Cobdenic internationalism which forms two thirds of my programme was derived directly from you— that I am certainly the only living Dipl[omatic] Representative who honestly and conscientiously strives to realise the programme and that therefore to turn your back on me is to turn your back on the only pupil you have succeeded in bringing out in a position sooner or later to do good work in the Cobdenic vineyard.

Finally Morier summed up yet again their point of difference. 'Where I differ . . . is that I say for England to do good work of the *international* kind in the world she must keep up and maintain her material power, aye, and her *prestige* and that for us to assume the shovel hat and the brown coat of the Quaker is to doom Europe and civilization to the horrible sterilities of unsatisfied chauvinism.'[1] Mallet in reply insisted that the true root of power and prestige was 'a carefully husbanded wealth created by a sound domestic policy',[2] but dropped the subject.

In two letters to Jowett, Morier completed his judgement of Derby's policy in the eastern question and referred to other causes of despondency in the spring of 1878. He wrote that he believed it to be his duty to keep on registering to Jowett the blunders of foreign policy

as we go along. Two astounding ones lie before me and here, as on so many previous occasions, I am quite unable to discover that they have struck the public or that anyone in England has perceived or

[1] To Mallet, 14 Jan. 1879.   [2] From Mallet, 20 Jan. 1879.

commented upon them. Yet to anyone who knows anything of diplomatic craft . . . they stand out like the pillars of Stonehenge on Salisbury Plain.

1. In the Parliamentary papers published in the Times of the 8th is a memorandum by Colonel Wellesley containing the programme of Russia in regard to the war as it stood in July [1877]. The words recorded are those of the Emperor and they are at H.I.M.'s request communicated officially to H.M.'s Government. In this memorandum the Emperor says two things—first . . . that he has no intention of making *any conquests*, secondly he says that he means to annex the territory lost by Russia in 1856 [i.e. Bessarabia], . . . that he intends to make a conquest of the very gravest and most important kind.

. . . Well what was the way in which this communication was received? H.M. Government *expressed their satisfaction at the Emperor's disclaimer of any extensive ideas of annexation*!! i.e. by implication acquiesced in the moderate proposal of Russia repossessing herself by conquest and in the way of annexation of the territory which would place her once more in the position of a Danubian Power, the exclusion from which is all that is now left to us of the fruits of the Crimean War.

If ever at any period of the 'question' there was a moment when a bold and decisive protest ought to have been put in it was then. As it is, as honourable men, we are precluded from raising objections now . . . But how, may I ask, can we expect Europe to help us to protect *our* interests when Europe learns the sort of way we treat *her* interests in our confidential communications with the Czar?

Morier deplored the habit of thinking of British interests as if they were distinct from those of other states and the folly of not recognizing that to keep Russia away from the Danube mouths was both a British and a European interest and as much one as the other.

And [he went on to ask] what value must people think we place upon treaties wrung from our enemies by the blood of our gallant soldiers and the 100 millions we paid in taxes when on learning that the victorious Czar only intends to tear up this last shred of the treaties[1] left to us by the cowardice of Gladstone and Granville in 1871[2] all we do is to express our satisfaction at his moderation!

[1] The allusion is to the Peace of Paris, 1856.
[2] The allusion is to their acquiescence in the Russian repudiation of the clause of the treaty of 1856 neutralizing the Black Sea.

And all this is printed in thousands of copies and no one rises up in Parliament or elsewhere to demand satisfaction.

2. The second blunder I wish to register is the declaration just given that we send up the Fleet to Constantinople to protect the lives and property of British subjects. First it is a lie and a false pretence and therefore a kind of diplomatic instrument we should never have recourse to, because though we do lie much oftener than people fancy, we are very bad hands at it and our lies are always clumsy. But apart [from] the lie the absurdity of the plea is that it gives Gortchakoff exactly what he wanted, a perfectly sound diplomatic reason for entering Constantinople . . . We had a perfectly sound diplomatic reason for going up and it was used in the original orders to the Admiral viz. *to keep open the waterway*. We knew that a peace was in the process of negotiating [of San Stefano, between Russia and Turkey] which Russia refused to give us the conditions of. But we knew one of the conditions was an arrangement to close the waterway and therefore we had a right to establish a *status quo* which should render such a treaty of peace *de facto* null and void until we and others had been consulted . . . It would have been a thousand times better and more honourable to have given the right reason, and not go in with a humanitarian lie in our mouths.

If you ask me how I account for all these blunders I will tell you how I account for the worst. Lord Derby is *stupid* and he is a coward . . .[1]

Morier, aware that this strong language was unforgivable without some explanation, especially because of his and his wife's friendship with Lady Derby, returned to the subject in his next letter to Jowett.[2]

By cowardice I mean rather what I can only express in German by the phrase *Mangel an Selbstständigkeit* [i.e. lack of self-reliance]. He is morally and intellectually incapable of shaping out an opinion of his own—and his mental attitude is a deprecatory one to the opinion of others. The intellectual cause is the exclusively critical nature of his mind. He is totally incapable intellectually of any kind of generous impulse or of that enthusiasm which presupposes a certain capacity for being dazzled or at least of enjoying the brightness of things . . . The moral cause has a curious history of its own. I *think* at least I can discern in much of his ways and character the traces of a most unhappy youth and here I feel strong sympathy for him . . .

[1] To Jowett, 17 Feb., continued 22 Feb. 1878.
[2] To Jowett, 1 Mar. 1878.

As regards the stupidity I do not of course mean to say that he is not a man of great culture and considerable intellectual power[1] of a peculiar kind but that he is stupid in reference to his craft. If I remember right each craft according to Aristotle has its own ἀρετή; there is the ἀρετή of the shoemaker and the ἀρετή of the thinker and the ἀρετή of the statesman—and, according as the craftsman altogether fails in mastering this ἀρετή I opine he is to be accounted stupid. It is this kind of stupidity I mean when I talk of Lord Derby as stupid. His craft is that of a Foreign Minister and in regard to it I should place him amongst the people who are (I forget alas the Aristotelian phrase) naturally incapable of acquiring the ἀρετή of their craft.

In the several pages which followed Morier detailed the reasons for this incapacity. He was arrogant towards foreigners with all the *outrecuidance insulaire* of the Englishman who divided the world into Englishmen and the rest, and he neither could nor would weigh his words with any regard for the impression they were likely to produce abroad. He addressed himself always to the British public and to the British public only. He had often given offence abroad for this reason. But Morier went further and insisted that it was not even to the British public as a whole that Derby addressed himself but rather to the special Lancashire public. 'The great territorial Lord and the head of the great historical family in the par excellence great manufacturing county of the United Kingdom, it is strange to see how he has become identified with and his modes of thought shaped by the specifically Lancashire climate of opinion.'

In the spring of 1878 Morier had one of his recurrent attacks of gout, he lost money—his own and trust money as his father's executor—by the failure of a bank, and he suffered a personal loss when H.M. Frigate *Euridice* with Captain Hart and all hands went down in a storm at sea. This letter to Jowett had opened sadly:

I never felt more absolutely lonely in the world than I do at present and it is a very different thing this feeling lonely at fifty one and at twenty one. At twenty one one feels lonely but one fancies there are innumerable friends around one if one could only get at them—and one believes that somehow one will get at them—that

[1] He took a first from Trinity College, Cambridge. The details of his childhood are set out by D. Schreuder in *Gladstone and Kruger* (1969), p. 308.

one has only to work on and that people will get to see that you are *the* man, that you see things more perfectly, appreciate the beautiful and the good more keenly than others and that they will rally round you. There is only a wall between you and them. Some day Joshua's trumpets will bray and the wall will fall down. At fifty one one knows there is nothing the other side of the wall—that one is lonely because one has not known how to influence other people—cared too much about loving and being loved—hated too heartily, cared too little about being hated—lived too much with one's abstract ideals, snubbed too much other people's concrete realities. In a word settled down to be an old man without the capacity of throwing off the dreams of his youth, yet fully knowing them to be dreams and the shadows of dreams. But this self-contemplating mood is folly.

So the letter went on to bemoan the fever for war with Russia that possessed England at the end of February 1878 and to develop the discussion of Derby's character already quoted.

It is fitting to conclude this chapter with Morier's idea of the ultimate solution of the eastern question.

The great desideratum [he wrote to Lord Odo Russell on 14 June 1878][1] is to find some nucleus round which the heterogeneous political units about to be constructed out of European Turkey may gather with a fair chance of their ultimately coalescing into some kind of Confederation. To attempt at present to *octroyer* a Confederation would I conceive be utterly hopeless and absurd. But I do not see why Europe should not impose certain *collective* duties on the totality of the units the performance of which would lead up to an ultimate Confederation and for which she should herself find the necessary machinery. Now why should England not suggest the union of all the States, or quasi States, south of the Danube, into a Customs Union on the model of the Zollverein, the legitimate progenitor of the German Empire? . . . A union of this kind would necessarily in its inception at least, require to be worked by a European commission, and the tariff, one of fiscal duties pure and simple and of absolute free trade in other respects, would be imposed by Europe—the collectors in the principal ports be European (civilized, unbribable Europeans I mean, not Russians or Turks or Austrians) appointed by the commission. The zollverein thus composed might enter into some kind of commercial alliance with Roumania north of the Danube . . .

It was a dream remote from Balkan realities.

[1] F.O. 918/55.

5

ASSESSMENT

ROBERT MORIER's gift for vivid reporting was outstanding during his period at Lisbon. When he had not much to report he made trivialities amusing if not revealing. He made much of the story of the cardinal's hat (see above, pp. 113–14) and even more of an instance of cheating the Lisbon octroi by the editor of a national newspaper (the *Progresso*) and former cabinet minister. The man had been discovered smuggling sausages in a hamper, purporting to contain oranges, and had subsequently in his newspaper accused the customs authorities of victimizing him for political reasons. The *Commercio*, a hostile newspaper, had taken up the cause of the customs officers. Lisbon was divided between the two parties and rival factions had come to blows in the streets. In the end the real victims were the customs officers who were fined. The government confirmed the sentence. Morier concluded, after drawing attention to the feeling in Lisbon, that 'the reappearance of this kind of political and journalistic rowdy-ism with a tendency to descend into the street (an old complaint in Portugal, but which had been effectually put down under the firm administration of Senhor Fontes) is itself a sign of the Government's having got into weak and nerveless hands'.[1] The temptation to which this gift for anecdotal reporting exposed him was to claim to have unearthed the explanation of mysteries, to have found out the inside story. For example, the reason, he wrote, why Senhor Aguiar refused office in the Sampaio administration was that he believed the government was going to play a dishonest part over the Lorenço

---

[1] To Derby, no. 28 confidential, 11 May 1877, F.O. 63/1062. The phrase 'descend into the street' was a gallicism. 'Descendre dans la rue' is a French phrase still current and describes ambiguously going into the street to participate in insurrection or merely to see what is going on.

Marques treaty and he did not wish to compromise his personal character.[1]

Morier's gift for identifying himself with a particular minister at the court to which he was accredited, though it gave him great initial advantages, proved at Lisbon to be a weakness in the end. The energy which he put into the effort of sympathy at their first meeting gave him the personal friendship of João de Corvo in Lisbon as it was to give him that of Nikolai de Giers in St. Petersburg. (There is corroborative evidence of this in Corvo's papers preserved in Portugal.[2]) No minister with whom Morier subsequently had relations in Portugal ever, in his view and perhaps in consequence, equalled Corvo in strength of purpose, frankness, and straightforward readiness to co-operate with Britain. Later he was constantly to measure all that afterwards happened in Russia by the assurance which Nikolai de Giers gave him that he would always deal with him with all his cards on the table in return for equal frankness from him. There is a close parallel between the 'franc-parler dont nous nous sommes mutuellement engagés de faire usage dans nos rapports officiels et particuliers' of which Morier spoke to Corvo[3] and 'my contract with Giers' of which he afterwards wrote,[4] 'namely always to put the Russian case absolutely fairly and without bias before my employers' in return for which de Giers on his part 'has never once deceived me'; though he might not tell the whole truth, 'he has never led me into error'.

Morier was a good representative of his country in his ability to present British policy in the large and liberal terms of the day. Questioned by Corvo and King Luis about the matters at issue between Britain and Russia, when there seemed in April 1878, on the advent of Salisbury to the Foreign Office and the consequent increase in the firmness of British policy, a chance of the long-anticipated Anglo-Russian war, Morier replied that what was at issue was international morality and the sanctity of treaties.

[1] To Granville, no. 74 most confidential, 29 Mar. 1880, F.O. 63/1093.
[2] See F. Latour da Veiga Pinto, *de Portugal et le Congo au xixe siècle* (Paris, 1972), pp. 36, 124, 128, 133, 135–7.
[3] To Corvo, 20 Oct. 1876, enclosure in no. 49 consular to Derby, 20 Oct. 1876, F.O. 84/1447.
[4] To Goschen, 2 June 1888.

The great issues at stake between ourselves and Russia [he reported himself as saying] were not British interests merely, nor even European interests merely, but the elementary conditions of civilization, the cause of Law versus Anarchy, of Right versus Wrong, of the sacredness of treaties versus a cynical apathy for international obligation; in a word that the key of the position we were defending on the diplomatic battlefield was the Declaration of 1871. I then gave His Majesty an analysis of Lord Beaconsfield's speech [in the House of Lords on the previous Monday], showing that, from the very first lifting of the curtain in this eventful drama, Her Majesty's Government had never ceased to remind Russia of her international duties and to warn her that she was breaking one by one her most solemn pledges to Europe . . .

Morier then added a doctrine that was more peculiarly his own:

The great difficulty . . . with which we had had to contend and with which we were yet contending, in making our meaning clear arose, paradoxical as it might sound, from an excess of simplicity in the point at issue. Diplomatic language was a delicate instrument, well suited to highly finished work and to express the subtlest shades of meaning, but for this very reason totally unfit to do so simple a thing as the calling a spade a spade. Nor was this difficulty confined to diplomatic language, for even in everyday life there were sometimes very simple intimations which it was extremely difficult to convey to others. For instance a clergyman could without the slightest risk of giving offence enunciate Sunday after Sunday to his congregation the simple proposition 'thou shalt not steal'.[1] But to convey this intimation *in concreto* to a person with whom you live on visiting terms and who is in the habit of dining at your house, presents obstacles almost insurmountable. Now this was precisely the kind of difficulty under which we laboured. International good manners on the one hand, the rules of procedure logically required by public and international law, on the other, stood in the present instance in fatal antagonism.

Morier then returned to a more conventional view.

A Congress had been summoned to settle the Eastern Question. International good manners required that Russia should be invited to it as an honoured guest with the same forms of courtesy as the other signatories of the Treaty of 1856. Indications had not been wanting to show that she had ambitioned even more than this and

[1] The Anglican Communion Service as then read entailed the reading in full of the Ten Commandments.

had aspired to the Presidency. But however this might be, she at least claimed, and, in virtue of the invitation she had received, she had the right to do so, to assume her place at the Congress on precisely the same terms and with the same liberty of action as the other Powers parties to the Treaty of Paris. In common with those others therefore she reserved to herself 'la pleine liberté de ses appréciations et de son action'. But what aspect did the question assume when viewed from the standing ground not of international good breeding but of international law and in the light of the Declaration of 1871? Why simply this, that instead of having a right to claim a voice... in the Congress she was in reality a prisoner at the bar, or, to put the case in a milder form, a petitioner suing for a Bill of Indemnity. In 1871 she had been guilty of the offence of withdrawing by a unilateral act from a solemn European Treaty. Europe had condoned the offence and returned a verdict of 'not guilty' but upon the express condition in writing that she was 'not to do it again'. But she had done it again and that in a far more aggravated form and before the ink of her written engagement was dry.

Morier went on to show that if Europe allowed Russia to take her place at the Congress on an equal footing with the other Powers, she

would declare herself for the future impotent to assert the elementary conditions on which the intercourse of civilized communities depended. It was the infinite merit of Her Majesty's Government that, alone and single-handed, they had prevented Europe from drifting into this humiliating position... by simply insisting upon the elementary condition that Europe, not Russia, should occupy the judgment seat... I thought that Great Britain might fairly claim the merit of having caused this revival of [European] life. She had given back to Europe the sense of her solidarity, and had pointed out the old paths as the only ones which it was safe to follow. It was high time this stand should be made, for during the last ten years the sense of international duties and obligations had been dying out at an alarming rate. I deeply regretted that, as far as theorists at least were concerned, many of our public men and a great part of our public press had been amongst the worst offenders. It was a commonplace amongst these to regard treaties as interesting from the antiquarian point of view and as a kind of historical *bric-à-brac* valuable to collectors, but devoid of all practical value or living interest either to the present or future generation. I believed that the recent action of Her Majesty's Government would mark the turning of the tide and that from to-day we might look with a better hope into the future.[1]

It is, of course, difficult to guess the effect of this long harangue, and one has no means of knowing whether Corvo was appreciative or only amused. It was not by any means the first or only one of its kind. In a striking phrase, for example, Morier had earlier described Russia as a Power to be opposed since she '*revendiquait comme Droit l'absence du Droit*, thus importing into politics that strange doctrine of *nihilism* which was sapping at the roots of her social existence'.[2] It is difficult to believe Corvo was bored.

Morier had a talent for writing dispatches which proved the high *personal* influence which he was able to exercise on the government to which he was accredited. He told for example the story of the fishing dispute between Portugal and Spain in October 1877. The Spanish fishers who fished in Portuguese waters at the mouth of the river Guadiana used nets of a small mesh prohibited by Portuguese law to the Portuguese fishermen. When this led to contention, the Spanish agreed to the appointment of a joint commission to inquire into the rights of the matter, but prejudiced the issue by sending a Spanish gunboat under whose protection the Spanish fishermen continued their illegal acts with impunity. The failure of the Portuguese fishermen to protest would thus enable the Spanish to present their claims to the joint commission with a chance of success, which otherwise they might not have had. In the end the gunboat and the Spanish fishing galleons were withdrawn and the incident closed. It had failed to provide the pretext for the invasion which the Spanish prime minister, Antonio Cánovas del Castille, was thought by the Portuguese to be planning after the Cuban insurrection was finally suppressed in 1878. Cánovas was said to have cast himself for the role of Iberian Cavour or Bismarck.

The incident was entirely unimportant though it had all the appearance of seriousness. In Portugal, both King and government, however, consulted Morier. It is this fact that lingers after the rest has been dismissed as insignificant. Morier's dis-

[1] To Salisbury, no. 34 most confidential, 13 Apr. 1878, F.O. 63/1075.
[2] To Derby, no. 28 confidential, 31 Mar. 1878, F.O. 63/1075.

patch of 13 October 1877[1] opens: 'As I was driving this afternoon from my house at Cintra to Cascaes to pay my respects to Their Majesties . . . I was met by Senhor Barros e Cunha . . . who stopped my carriage to say that he was on his way to me with an important message from the King.' The minster of public works, the 'alter ego'[2] of de Ávila, communicated to Morier the events at the mouth of the Guadiana up to the arrival of the Spanish gunboat. The story was subsequently elaborated by the King. Morier later described himself as called in 'somewhat after the fashion of a family physician to give my advice'. In this later summary he wrote that he had warned them 'that it would be unwise to give to the matter an undue and international importance by even the appearance of consultation with a foreign Power,' and said, 'I refused to deal with the question in my official capacity but consented in my private capacity and academically to give my diagnosis of the case.'[3] 'This proposal being eagerly accepted', Morier said in his report of 13 October, he proceeded to impress on both King and ministers that

the utmost degree of calm and moderation was the policy clearly indicated to Portugal for the wantonness of the Spanish aggression would appear in its strongest relief if viewed against the background of perfect self-possession and a calm insistence on undoubted rights. Portugal had many friends. No one knew this better than Spain. The more completely Spain, therefore, was induced to place herself in the wrong, the stronger would be the influence brought to bear upon her by the verdict of this international jury.

The King assured Morier that he would be reasonable, but at the same time repeated that there had been an overt act of aggression on the part of the Spanish government and insisted upon the extreme gravity of the situation if this were not repudiated. It had been decided that a strong remonstrance should be made at Madrid.[1] But Count Valbom, the Portuguese ambassador, declined to carry out his instructions and the Portuguese government was apparently either unable or unwilling to enforce their decisions. So the whole situation

[1] To Derby, unnumbered, 13 Oct. 1877, F.O. 63/1063.
[2] To Derby, no. 85, 16 Oct. 1877, F.O. 63/1063.
[3] To Derby, no. 41 most confidential, 25 May 1878, F.O. 63/1075.

suddenly changed and, to quote the later retrospective dispatch of 1878, the new 'danger lay not in an excess but in a want of firmness'; and Morier found himself unable to preach fortitude as he had before preached moderation; for, whereas a sermon on moderation might pass unnoticed, one on fortitude might always afterwards appear 'as an act of interference on the part of Her Majesty's Representative'. A long dispatch of 1877 describes the further consultations with Morier by Barros e Cunha, the King, and the minister of marine. A passage sums up Morier's position.

When . . . I reflected that, at a particularly busy time, a particularly busy Minister had been twice, in three days, sent to me by the King from Cascaes to Cintra—a journey of 18 miles over heavy roads, and that again, by His Majesty's command he had come to me on his way to the Cabinet Council, I could not but come to the conclusion that it was my opinion, if not my advice, on the various phases of the conflict that was desired, and not merely the keeping me 'au courant' of what was going on.[1]

The dispatch also shows that Morier had in fact advised, though under reserves, that no time should be lost in lodging a formal protest in Madrid.

Morier's personal part in the episode was again thrust into prominence by its sequel. When asked for his opinion, he had rightly insisted on having positive evidence that the Spaniards had been guilty of a breach of international law and, after infinite trouble, had obtained from Barros e Cunha a telegram from the governor of Villa Real containing the exact text of the letter written by the captain of the gunboat, in which the Spaniard related how he had, in Portuguese waters, given chase to a Portuguese fishing-boat, and warned the governor that on the next occasion he would, in obedience to his instructions, use force. Morier asked for a copy of this document, but was told that he was 'welcome to the original which consequently remained in [his] possession'. A few months later the Fontes–Corvo ministry was in power and the Duke of Tetuan was appointed Spanish representative at Lisbon. Corvo praised to Morier the conciliatory attitude of the new representative, talked of the incident as if it had been entirely mismanged by his predecessors, and asserted that the Spanish government had

[1] To Derby, no. 89 confidential, 20 Oct. 1877, F.O. 63/1063.

been quite in the right and that Portugal had nothing of which to complain. Morier was taken aback and sent him the Spanish captain's letter. Corvo, Morier reported,

was completely upset by the sight of this document which he told me had made his blood boil within him. There could be no doubt of its genuineness and having had a further search made through the archives of all the ministries, a copy of the paper had at last been found in the Colonial Office.

The story [Morier concluded] requires no comment. A new Minister comes into office inheriting from his predecessor a very ugly quarrel with a limitrophe State. The whole quarrel turns, as upon a pivot, on one particular document of which there is no trace either in the Foreign Office or in the Home Office, the only two Offices concerned in the dispute. A chance conversation with a foreign Representative reveals the fact of this document being in the archives of a foreign Legation and to make the matter complete it is addressed to the Minister of Public Works and the only existing copy is found after much search in the Colonial Office.[1]

It is a story which well illustrates Morier's failings as a diplomat. Two things are obvious to a later reader of his dispatches as they were obvious to his superiors in the Foreign Office at the time. The King and the court wished to take a firm line with Spain. The majority of the King's council of ministers wished to conciliate her. The court party drew Morier in, hoping to use his advice as a means of pressure on the opposition in the council. Morier did exactly what was wanted and lent himself to a scheme that enabled the King and court party to overrule the council. Morier's critical sense was lulled by the flattery, and, unreflecting, he failed in penetration. It was obvious, secondly, that although Morier had given his advice as a personal opinion he *had* given it. If Spain had chosen to resent the Portuguese protest, his part must have been revealed to her. The Foreign Office must then either have disowned Morier or have accepted the association and stood by Portugal in what might, for all they knew, have been a weak case. Either alternative would have been bad for Morier. He was, however, lucky in that nothing came of the affair. Far from taking pride in it, he ought to have seen that he was undermining trust in himself at the Foreign Office. This want of trust is in turn the

[1] To Derby, no. 41 most confidential, 25 May 1878, F.O. 63/1075.

explanation why his good qualities were less appreciated than they might have been.

The incident looked all the worse to the Foreign Office because it was not the first mistake of which Morier had been guilty. He began by insisting that he should be allowed 'to kiss hands' on his appointment although an audience of the Queen on appointment was an honour reserved for ambassadors. The Foreign Office gracefully gave way then.[1] But Morier's remonstrance, in 1876, soon after he arrived, against an anti-British article in a Portuguese newspaper[2] had provoked an unusually tart minute from Tenterden: 'This is rather a ridiculous affair and I should have thought that Mr. Morier would have been wiser not to make a serious representation about it... These exchanges of repartee are not at all likely to improve the feeling towards England.' He noticed, what Morier might well have missed, that the answering newspaper article which Morier prided himself on having procured had in its own way scored at his expense. Derby, moreover, who could usually be relied on to support Morier, agreed this time with Tenterden, saying that Morier's language should be approved 'with a caution that newspapers were best left to answer newspapers and scarcely deserve the notice of Her Majesty's Legation'.[3]

Nor did Morier seem to see that to say there was a 'state of chronic feud'[4] between the Portuguese Foreign Office and the British Legation, caused by slipshod Portuguese ways of doing business, was, if true, likely to rouse little confidence in his own proclaimed intention of creating better relations between Britain and Portugal, and if untrue, likely to increase the official mistrust of his habit of exaggerating. By the autumn of 1876 he was beginning to make the mistakes, already noticed, in relation to the Goa treaty. He prepared a long memorandum as a start of the negotiation and sent it home for approval before submitting it to the Portuguese.[5] Before the approval was sent to him, he telegraphed that he had submitted the British counter-proposals to the Portuguese proposals of

[1] Memorandum by Sir Henry Ponsonby, R.A. L 14/9 and 10.
[2] See above, p. 26.
[3] Minutes on Morier to Derby, no. 143 most confidential, 20 Oct. 1876, F.O. 63/1035.
[4] To Salisbury, no. 41 most confidential, 25 May 1878, F.O. 63/1075.
[5] To Derby, no. 60 commercial, 27 Nov. 1876, F.O. 63/1081.

ASSESSMENT

January 1876, thus formally opening the negotiation. T. V. Lister might well minute that 'he was lost'.¹ In February of the new year his mistake about the wine duties became plain.² It is also clear that Morier's pressure on the Foreign Office was in itself a tactical mistake. Lister wrote to Mallet, 'I have been away and I have somewhat lost the thread of the Portuguese Negotiations . . . As I understand the case, its present position is this [which he describes] . . . We also feared that matters were getting muddled by over much telegraphing', and he was moved to conclude his letter with a reminder that 'almost all Plenipotentiaries would sooner sign the worst Treaty imaginable than none at all'.³ The negotiation of 1877 failed, but Morier still had the ear of both Derby and Salisbury. Both appreciated his vigour and imagination. On Morier's long historical account of the negotiations of 1877 Lister wrote 'very interesting'. One suspects sarcasm. But, if so, Derby did not suspect it; for he wrote 'Yes a good despatch'. In 1878 on Morier's account of the sequel to the 'great sardine controversy'—it does indeed make wonderful reading—Salisbury minuted in his characteristic red ink 'Worth reading'.

The 'scrapes' however continued. In 1878 when the Goa negotiations were reopened, Morier's communications home and to the Portuguese were too long, their tone was hectoring, and the air of urgency given to the negotiation was inappropriate. Lister wrote, 'Mr Morier's note to Sr Corvo is not a commendable production'. A little later he minuted that the negotiation had 'an awkward appearance' and he did not see how to make it 'graceful'.⁴ This cannot be put down to Lister's prejudice; for Salisbury concurred in condemning Morier's tone to Corvo. Of a note of the same time protesting against Portuguese arms going to the Zulus he wrote, 'It is a very odd note to approve: but I suppose we must. There is no harm in Morier writing in that tone to us: it amuses us: but it must puzzle Senor Corvo.'⁵ On top of this came Morier's mistake

¹ To Derby, telegram, recorded in no. 63, 1 Dec. 1876, F.O. 63/1081.
² See above, p. 30. From Derby, no. 8 commercial, 4 May 1877, corrects Morier, F.O. 63/1082.   ³ Lister to Mallet, 25 Jan. 1877, F.O. 63/1082.
⁴ Minutes attached to Morier to Salisbury, no. 46 commercial, 28 Sept. 1878, F.O. 63/1083.
⁵ Minute by Salisbury on the back of Morier to Salisbury, no. 43 slave-trade, confidential, 3 Oct. 1878, F.O. 84/1504.

in committing his government by his draft article 5, on the railway, in the Lorenço Marques treaty. In 1879 Morier scored successes with the ratification of the Goa treaty, his unorthodox procedure in creating the Stafford House Committee, and the signature of the Lorenço Marques treaty. But the note of mutual irritation is again there at the end of the year. Salisbury himself had grown tired of Morier pedantically using the 'Slave Trade' classification for the African side of his work. He minuted that dispatches on the Lorenço Marques treaty, the Congo negotiation, and the Nyasaland settlements should be numbered in sequence with Morier's political dispatches. Morier, who could not know that the instruction came from Salisbury, personally, demurred and there was a sharp rejoinder from the latter.[1]

Morier's position with the next foreign secretary, Lord Granville, rapidly deteriorated. He made three tactical mistakes in 1880, quite apart from any there may have been in the substance of his work. First, he came away on leave, having extorted permission by a proposal to go and return in less than three weeks, by an insistent demand for consultation on grounds that, mysteriously, could not be explained by telegraph, and by a threat that he would 'take no responsibility' for the consequences if permission were refused. He added, for good measure, a breach of the rules by leaving a mere third secretary in charge.[2] His second mistake was to put himself in the wrong by communicating, over the Lorenço Marques treaty, directly with the Colonial Office (by a private letter to R. G. Herbert) behind the back of the Foreign Office.[3] Finally came the disagreeable controversy, as Tenterden described it, between Morier and Saurin in which both appealed to Granville as has been described.[4] Nor did Morier improve his position by then asking for a K.C.M.G. 'It would be difficult', Morier wrote to Granville on 17 October 1880, 'to overestimate the advantages which I would derive at this particular juncture from a K.C.M.G.'

[1] See the docket on Morier to Salisbury, no. 60, 23 Dec. 1879, F.O. 63/1084.
[2] To Granville, telegram, 11 June 1880, and subsequent minutes, F.O. 63/1094.
[3] See correspondence between Herbert and Pauncefote, Herbert and Morier, and Kimberley and Herbert in Sept. 1880, F.O. 63/1092.
[4] See above, p. 11; minute by Tenterden, who decides both are in the wrong, on Morier to Granville, no. 138, 11 Nov. 1880, F.O. 63/1094.

ASSESSMENT

for himself and C.M.G.s for two consular service men who came under him.[1]

Morier's principal failing as a diplomat was a dangerous propensity to consider he had been let down—either by his own government or by the government to which he was accredited. It is typical that, after the failure of the Goa negotiations in 1877, Mallet should write, 'I hear from Morier that . . . he has drawn the very erroneous inference that Lord Salisbury distrusted his discretion in communicating with the Portuguese Government.' He goes on to say the reverse is true and that Salisbury highly appreciated his services.[2] Morier further believed the instruction of 25 October 1878 'to commence and conduct *pari passu*' the negotiation of the Lorenço Marques treaty with the Goa treaty was silently repudiated by his own government without his ever having been forewarned or even properly told. Again, he believed that Braamcamp had not honoured the engagement he had taken on 28 March 1880.

Having engaged that the [Lorenço Marques] treaty should in the current session be submitted to the Cortes, [he], of set purpose and without any warning given, determined that the session should close without the Cortes having been afforded the opportunity, which the Government could alone give them, of voting either for or against the treaty. He intended to lay the treaty on the table and argue that that was sufficient to fulfil his promise.

It will be recalled how Morier went to the ultimate limit in pressure and succeeded in gaining the prolongation of the Cortes on the very day it was to have dispersed, in order that it might consider and vote upon the treaty, only to be let down, as he believed, by his own government which, after the treaty had passed the Chamber of Deputies, consented to its withdrawal from the Chamber of Peers. He believed, indeed, that he was being let down all the time. Earlier he considered he had been misunderstood by the home government over the point at issue in the articles of the Lorenço Marques treaty concerned with a twelve-year term for the treaty, the home government suddenly stepping in with a profession of readiness to agree to a ninety-nine-year term when the question at issue was between

[1] To Granville, private, 17 Oct. 1880, F.O. 63/1094.
[2] Mallet to Lister, 12 Nov. 1877, F.O. 63/1082.

perpetuity and accepting the Portuguese proposal for a long-enough term in which to pay off the capital. He again believed he had ground for complaint when the British government assented to the withdrawal of the Lorenço Marques treaty from the Chamber of Peers on the representations of the Portuguese envoy in London. Morier's plea was that, the fresh rising in the Transvaal and the defeat at Majuba Hill having rendered the future uncertain, its ratification should be suspended. 'I must presume', Morier wrote to Granville, 'that the decision of Her Majesty's Government has been solely based on the representations made to them by Senhor d'Antas. These representations must have been the same as those which he made to me . . . I cannot of course complain that Your Lordship should have accepted these representations in preference to mine.' But he went on to explain 'how entirely my views differ from those of His Excellency' and that 'I am now in a position to state in the most emphatic manner that not one of the pleas of the Portuguese minister holds good.'[1] No. 86 of 6 April 1881 was an earlier and similar dispatch of self-justification. He argued that the rising of 1881 could not have occurred had the road, that would have preceded the Lorenço Marques railway, been built, since its existence would have offset the Boers' capacity to hold the passes from Natal which had just given them success. He continued:

I most sincerely beg your Lordship not to ascribe my recalling these facts to a vainglorious desire to prove that I was right, when others, who had had less opportunities of studying the subject than I had, were wrong, but solely to the two following reasons: first to show that the wearisome urgency with which I fear I have importuned H.M. Government in regard to the treaty at times when it was clear that they felt no interest in the matter, was not owing to professional vanity, but to the deep conviction that the matter was one of the greatest national importance . . . Secondly, because having been right then gives me some claim to be listened to now.[2]

He went on then to plead that the new circumstances meant that it was more than ever necessary for Britain to have article 4 with its security for the passage of British troops through Portuguese territory to the Transvaal, and that the only way

---

[1] To Granville, no. 129, 21 May 1881, F.O. 63/1132.
[2] To Granville, no. 86, 6 Apr. 1881, F.O. 63/1131.

ASSESSMENT

to prevent Portugal claiming its modification would be to retain a strip of British territory all along the Portuguese frontier so that it would still be Britain and not the Transvaal who was neighbour of the Portuguese. The plea went unnoticed; d'Antas made his representation; and Morier received instructions to drop the whole thing.

The difficulty would seem to be that Morier did not remember that when he complained of being let down, it was nearly always because he had wrung decisions from others which represented, in fact, something more than they had wished to give. This was true of Braamcamp's engagement to get the treaty through the Cortes, and again when Morier contrived its passage through the Chamber of Deputies. He believed that d'Antas represented the danger of allowing the treaty to go through so effectively to Lord Granville because he was the tool of General Fontes. As was described above (p. 17), this was the period when a ministry under Sampaio, from Fontes's party, was in power without Fontes. D'Antas had been briefly foreign minister, but had resigned and returned as envoy to London. While Morier urged upon Granville a policy of inducing Sampaio to push the Lorenço Marques treaty through the Chamber of Peers—so completing the parliamentary formalities necessary for ratification—D'Antas pleaded with Granville for postponement until 1882 and prevailed. Morier, in resenting this, ignored both the possibility that Sampaio's alleged assurances might have been extorted by his own vigorous approval and that the Portuguese might have had a case that had nothing to do with a petty desire to get the better of him (Morier) that he ascribed to Fontes. Morier was, in fact, open to the charge of having bullied the Portuguese government. He knew this and indeed complained of it to Ponsonby.

From a victim I have been changed to a kind of diplomatic bully. The first thing the Prince of Wales said when I [he was in London on leave before his transfer to Madrid] saw him was 'Why do you so bully those poor Portuguese?' Then amongst all the foreign brethren of my craft in London I find the same legend prevailing. On all sides I am told 'Pourquoi avez-vous fait maigrir ce pauvre d'Antas comme cela, vous le tuerez etc.'

Morier called this a legend and put it down to Fontes, who, he asserted, had spread a myth that he and Corvo had signed the

Lorenço Marques treaty not on 30 May, but on 1 June, after the Corvo ministry resigned; that he as prime minister knew nothing about it and that it was an invalid piece of trickery, the result of Morier's hold on Corvo.[1] Morier failed to remember that he himself had boasted to Salisbury of having 'got my friends to sign my second treaty three quarters of an hour *after* they had resigned'.[2] He failed to recognize that there was anyhow enough foundation, in the kind of pressure he exercised, for the charge of bullying to be just.

This raises the question whether his removal to Madrid at this date was a deliberate effort on Granville's part to clear the air at Lisbon. It would not be out of character for Granville to sacrifice a positive gain, such as the Lorenço Marques treaty was, for the sake of a comfortable relationship—especially if he could argue that the Lorenço Marques treaty and the Congo treaty would only be postponed and gained in the end without so much dust being raised. The telegrams instructing Morier to drop the treaty and offering him Madrid were sent one after the other. Morier did not accept or refuse until he had seen Granville and satisfied himself. He was easily satisfied. 'The first five minutes with Lord Granville, however, set my mind completely at rest on this matter', Morier wrote to Ponsonby. 'He left the choice absolutely in my hands and did not wish to influence me in the slightest way. After giving due consideration to the case I decided on public grounds it was better I should leave Lisbon, though on private grounds I would have much preferred to stay.'[3] He had written a month earlier[4] to Lady Derby, immediately after the meeting with Granville, that it was entirely satisfactory, but was then constrained to end with a lingering doubt.

Lord G. left no doubt on my mind that he had offered me Madrid solely as an advancement to take or to leave and that it was not a case of being kicked upstairs. After my talk with Lord Derby and yourself I had no doubt left on my mind that the right course for me professionally (however odious on private grounds) was to accept, and to do so with the fewest possible phrases. If I felt I could trust

[1] To Ponsonby, 1 July 1881.
[2] To Salisbury, private, 29 June 1879, F.O. 63/1091.
[3] To Ponsonby, 1 July 1881. It is the last paragraph of an extremely long letter justifying himself on the Lorenço Marques treaty.
[4] 2 June 1881.

ASSESSMENT

Lord G . . . I should feel quite happy so far . . . But I have got it into my head that he is false, and I find many other people think so too.

Lord Granville's courtesy no doubt precluded him from a forthright answer 'yes' or 'no' to Morier's question whether his being removed from Lisbon was a mark of official disapproval, and the suspicion remained. The German ambassador in London reported to Bismarck that he would have been promoted to Madrid even if Granville had not been dissatisfied with his conduct over the ratification of the Delagoa Bay treaty.[1] There is no evidence either way in the Granville papers. In the Queen's papers[2] are two shreds of evidence to suggest that any convenience in moving Morier at least coincided with promotion in the ordinary way. Already in 1877 when a vacancy occurred in Madrid the Queen, in inquiring who was to fill it, asked Derby, 'Would not Mr. Morier do very well there?' In 1881 Morier at least still had enough of Granville's confidence for him to suggest his replacing Lord Dufferin in St. Petersburg. 'Mr. Morier is the cleverest [of the possible men] and thought by some people very agreeable—but he is vain, sensitive and not without temper.' When Morier returned from London to Lisbon for two more months, he appealed for a demonstration of confidence in himself. He proposed a question in Parliament about the Goa treaty, which could be answered by the publication of a dispatch on the subject and by a reference 'to the ability and tact he had displayed' in its negotiation 'under exceptionally difficult circumstances' and by some indication of the profit which would accrue to both British India and Goa from it. He also again suggested a knighthood[3] since this would disarm anyone who wished to put it about that he had been kicked upstairs. He asked in vain. The knighthood did not come until 1882 and no question was asked in Parliament.

[1] Münster to Bismarck, no. 88, 21 May 1881, GFM 10/180.
[2] The Queen to Derby, 28 Sept. 1877, R.A. B 28/110; Granville to the Queen, 20 Apr. 1881, R.A. B 28/91.
[3] To Sir Louis Mallet, 2 Aug. 1881.

6

MADRID, OCTOBER 1881 TO JANUARY 1885

MORIER was slow to discuss in his reports the complicated internal politics of Spain. Even in May 1882 when he made his first tentative effort to write about them, he did not feel himself competent to do so, 'without a larger experience than any I have as yet been able to store up'.[1] Spanish internal struggles, it will be remembered, had provided the pretext for the Franco-Prussian war. In 1870 the candidacy of Leopold of Hohenzollern-Sigmaringen for the Spanish throne had been withdrawn and Amadeo of Savoy had been chosen instead. He had ruled until February 1873, when the Spaniards set up a Republic. The Republic in its turn failed, and the Bourbon line had been restored in the person of Alfonso XII. He was still ruling in 1881 and Spain was still under the relatively conservative constitution of 1876. His consort was his second wife, Maria Cristina, daughter of Archduke Charles Ferdinand of Austria. The King was popular and was, Morier thought, 'doing right well'.[2] He was looked upon as 'the stablest thing in this unstable country and the symbol of order'. In 1883 he toured his kingdom and the strength of his hold on it was made plain. 'The spontaneous ovations with which he was greeted everywhere (Catalonia excepted) revealed this as by a magnetic touch. It was not known or realised before.'

Morier did not perceive the method upon which the political system in Spain worked. He had nothing to say, that is, of the system of *turnismo* inaugurated by Antonio Cánovas del Castille. By this system each faction's legitimate claim to political power, and to the financial advantages which went with it,

---

[1] To Granville, no. 33 commercial, confidential, 5 May 1882, F.O. 72/1635.
[2] To Ponsonby, 28 Aug. 1883.

was satisfied in turn and the King's prerogative of dissolution, judiciously exercised, could bring about elections, which if carefully controlled would ensure the accession to power at a well-chosen moment of the faction whose turn it was next. Morier's reports on the prolonged ministerial crises of October 1882 to January 1883 and of November 1883 to January 1884 are interesting because they describe the symptoms of this system. As a good British liberal he laments the control of elections—they were, like the Portuguese, made in the Ministry of the Interior—and the absence of a two-party system. 'The apparent incapacity of any Spanish political patronage to keep up a healthy permanent hatred for the opposition' was 'perhaps the most unhealthy feature of present Spanish politics'.[1] In January 1883 he welcomed the *rassemblement* of the Left under Moret y Prendergast and the Duke de la Torre, and the new party, the Dynastic Left so-called, as the beginning of an authentic Opposition.[2] He deplored the violence of the political battle and the emptiness of the struggle of the factions. 'The only analogy' to them he can think of 'are the faction fights in the Byzantine hippodrome' where red fought blue and black fought white for the mere joy in battle and for no real issues.[3] Morier was apt to assume that the British parliamentary system, or the current nineteenth-century stereotype of it, was the only right method. He never penetrated to the principle which enabled the Spanish method to work and which in a country with a restricted political class provided a sort of underlying stability by the piecemeal reconstruction of administrations behind a screen of apparently meaningless battles.

The army, rather than *turnismo*, provided the substance of Morier's analysis of internal conditions. The army, which has been described as Spain's only 'secular internal institution', had, he believed, the fate of the country in its power. It had given Alfonso his throne and, if it remained united, could keep him on it. But Morier considered it was rotten to the core and was as untrustworthy as the office-hunting politicians. He might have added 'for the same reason'. The army, to

---

[1] To Granville, no. 11, 22 Jan. 1883, F.O. 72/1644.
[2] To Granville, no. 165 confidential, 29 Nov. 1882, F.O. 72/1618; no. 7, 10 Jan. 1883 and no. 10, 20 Jan. 1883, F.O. 72/1644.
[3] To Granville, no. 10, 18 Jan. 1884, F.O. 72/1678.

summarize the views of a modern writer, was a bureaucratic institution in a country plagued by *empleomania* (the rage for office), providing careers for a middle class with few openings in industry and commerce.[1] What Morier in fact reported were particular signs of 'corruption'; he did not guess at the general reason for the army's character.

The case of the army [he wrote] is a very peculiar one and one so far as I can see that admits of no remedy. It consists of 80,000 men—600 generals and 26,000 officers. This state of affairs has resulted from the late civil wars and perpetually recurring *pronunciamientos*. Every successful *pronunciamiento* resulted in all the sergeants being made officers. Every *raccommodement* between the contending parties was made on the invariable basis that all the grades of the beaten army should be recognized by the victorious representatives of the Spanish Government *pro tem* and incorporated with the Spanish army so that a *pronunciamiento* became a sort of recognized mode of pushing on promotion.[2]

Morier was fortunate in that political stability was maintained during his time in Madrid; for Cánovas, the dominant figure until he died in 1897, achieved the remarkable feat of keeping the army out of politics and loyal to the King. But Morier could not foresee that he would not after all have to report the fall of a regime. The rapid succession of administrations kept his sense of insecurity alive. Three ministries, one after the other, held office during his three years in Madrid: a coalition ministry, a liberal-free-trade one, and a conservative one. But these distinctions were nominal; they were all really 'place-hunting coalitions'.[3]

When Morier arrived in Madrid in October 1881, the government had been, since 8 February, in the hands of the coalition or fusionist group supported from the Centre. It was headed by Práxedes Mateo Sagasta, whom Morier reported to be 'an entirely unscrupulous politician',[4] yet one in whom 'the great bulk of the liberal party, then certainly in the ascendant',[5] reposed confidence. Morier failed to recognize that Sagasta was, like Cánovas, a key figure in the Spanish system of

[1] C. A. M. Hennessy, *The Federal Republic in Spain* (Oxford, 1962), pp. 3, 8.
[2] To Ponsonby, 28 Aug. 1883.
[3] To Granville, no. 132, 30 Oct. 1882, F.O. 72/1618.
[4] To Granville, no. 33 commercial, confidential, 5 May 1882, F.O. 72/1635.
[5] To Granville, no. 32 commercial, 5 May 1882, F.O. 72/1635.

turnismo. The King had brought Sagasta into power by dismissing Cánovas, who had ruled the country since his own accession to the throne. Cánovas was still in possession of a parliamentary majority. The King could not have set up Sagasta had he not set up beside him, as minister of war, General Martinez de Campos, the man to whom he owed his throne. Campos had just returned from suppressing insurrection in Cuba. He was a liberal but of the conservative kind; his presence gave to the ministry its coalition character and was the second element of strength in it. The government and the parliamentary majority which supported it contained men from the pronouncedly liberal and free-trade administration of 1869 and men in sympathy with the conservative and 'strongly protectionist' government which, after the several changes of regime, had eventually succeeded in 1875.[1] The third element of strength in the government was Juan Francisco Camacho of the Left, the moderate free-trade minister of finance. He was notable for 'his knowledge, both theoretical and practical, of economic matters . . . singlemindedness and integrity of character . . . immense powers of work and capacity for mastering detail'. He was a party man, but less a politician competing for office than a man wedded to the accomplishment of a single policy: the restoration of the finances of Spain and the development of her productive powers. He had elaborated a programme of measures, all the parts of which were interdependent, and he was for the first two years of Morier's time in Madrid engaged in carrying it through.[2] Among these measures was the gradual reform of the tariff in the direction of free trade. It was unfortunate that his increasing of the taxes had provoked opposition which took the form of general resistance to their payment.[3] Alonzo Martinez, the minister of justice, was 'a strong man and a politician before all things' and represented 'the Centre, but with a strong leaning to the Right'.[4] At the Foreign Office was the Marquis de la Vega de Armijo. He was to enjoy further periods in office from June 1888 to July 1890 and December 1892 to April 1893. De Armijo

[1] To Granville, no. 30 commercial, 25 Apr. 1882, F.O. 72/1634.
[2] To Granville, no. 13 commercial, confidential, 7 Mar. 1882, F.O. 72/1634.
[3] To Granville, no. 32 commercial, 5 May 1882, F.O. 72/1635.
[4] To Granville, no. 132, 30 Oct. 1882, F.O. 72/1618.

represented a pro-German policy and wished for a German alliance. He was much concerned with Spanish interests in Morocco and sought to draw near to Italy and Germany as a means of protecting them against France.[1] After a prolonged crisis lasting from the autumn of 1882, the administration was remodelled in January 1883 and Pelago Cuesta succeeded Camacho.

Next autumn, in October 1883, the Sagasta administration fell. Their successors were liberal free-traders and accordingly much praised by Morier. Posada Herrera was president of the council; at the Ministry of the Interior was Segismundo Moret y Prendergast, 'descended from an old English stock, the *preux chevalier* that other Spaniards would wish the world to fancy that they are',[2] 'well known in England as a distinguished member of the Cobden Club' and 'notorious' as an orator at public meetings convened by the Spanish Free Trade League. At the Foreign Office was 'a statesman and not a politician', Ruiz Gomez, 'described by friends and enemies, by the one in the way of praise, by the others in the way of blame, as an English politician'; he was an 'earnest free trader . . . the declared enemy of phrases and rhetoric', an economist through and through, who sought 'to influence his countrymen by logical arguments laboriously deduced from the widest and most accurate statistical studies', by pamphlets, by speeches in the Senate and before the public.[3] He was well-disposed to France and repudiated his predecessor's pro-German policy.

Much influence on the fate of this administration was exercised by C. Martos, who was not in fact a member of it, but the owner and editor of the newspaper *El Progreso* and recognized leader of the Republicans.[4] But on 19 January 1884 this ministry was brought down in its turn and Cánovas del Castille and the conservatives, with José Elduayen, the Marquis del Pazo de la Mercedi, as foreign minister, returned to power and remained in office until November 1885.

Morier was baffled and alienated by Spanish politics and

[1] Federico Curato, *La questione marocchina e gli accordi italo-spagnoli* (2 vols., Milan, 1961, 1965), *passim*; see especially i. 104–5, but the book is principally concerned with the period 1887–91.
[2] To Granville, no. 132, 30 Oct. 1882, F.O. 72/1618.
[3] To Granville, no. 67 commercial, 1 Nov. 1883, F.O. 72/1663.
[4] To Granville, no. 165 confidential, 29 Nov. 1882, F.O. 72/1618.

did not find his interest and sympathies engaged as they had been in Portugal. Nor, though the Spanish mission had meant promotion, were the material conditions of his life improved. There were troubles again with the Legation house,[1] but the house itself was less worth troubling about. The members of the Legation were always too few when there was a rush of business. Edmund Fane bore the brunt of the work deputizing, organizing and when necessary, copying secretary of Legation; Henry Fitzroy Langley was second secretary until he was appointed to Buenos Aires in 1884; Maurice de Bunsen was third secretary until he was moved up. Arthur Hardinge then arrived as the junior man. With Bunsen and Hardinge, Morier had two able men with notable careers before them, but this was only in the last year of his mission. Morier had also attached to the Legation a chaplain and a translator, while William Macpherson was a stand-by, as consul in Madrid and Clerk and Assistant to the Legation.

Morier did not go to Spain with the sense that a new phase of his life was beginning, nor with the ambition to stretch his abilities by new tasks, nor with the hope of using a fresh chance to prove them equal to the highest achievements, 'I am not going to be such a fool', he wrote to Sir Charles Dilke, 'in making my new start, to continue on the old lines. For five years I have thrown my soul into self-conceived projects ... At Madrid ... my ambition will be to reach the minimum of inter-communication on which relations can be kept alive.'[2] The post, in short, was the low ground between the peaks of his career. He described working with the Spanish, who seemed to corrupt his energy, as a 'daily martyrdom'.[3] He contrasted the ways in which Portuguese affairs, on one hand, had laid hold on him and filled him with the ambition to make his mark on international relations with, on the other hand, the concentration of his endeavours in Madrid to level himself down to what he described as 'Foreign Office notions of international intercourse'[4]—meaning routine without the excitement of bringing off a coup. He thought he had cured himself of

[1] From Granville, no. 15, 13 Feb. 1882, F.O. 72/1616.
[2] To Sir Charles Dilke, private and confidential, 26 Aug. 1881.
[3] To Lady Derby, 8 Feb. 1883.
[4] To Lady Derby, 16 June 1883.

caring about foreign questions for their own sake.¹ He fancied himself an impassive instrument of the Foreign Office. Yet even at Madrid Morier was to be given a chance to negotiate yet another treaty—a commercial one—and the desire to succeed was to prove irresistible.

He was, however, concerned in only one political negotiation and this came early in his period there; by his last year his political dispatches had dwindled away to a mere handful. The political negotiation related to Morocco. The territorial integrity of this sultanate, which both Britain and Spain were determined to preserve against French infringement, was their principal common concern. The representatives of thirteen states had recently met at Madrid and by the Convention of Madrid, 3 July 1880, agreed on 'the forms regulating the relationship of his subjects to the Sultan and bound themselves to maintain the integrity of his Empire'. Great Britain had, in 1881, 'the principal European influence' in Morocco. The French, however, always had a strong interest in mitigating the deficiencies of the Sultan's weak rule, because disorders might affect their own security in Algiers. At the same time their trade and influence were penetrating, hand in hand, the Sultan's ports along the coast.² In the autumn of 1881 an agreement was effected between the French consul at Mogador and a local chief which opened the coast south of Agadir to French trade. The agreement was suspect since any arrangement of that sort between a local authority and the representative of a Great Power was bound to undermine the Sultan's authority, which the Powers were pledged to maintain. The movement of French troops towards Figuiz in November 1881 caused an appeal from Spain for a combined protest to France. Morier, with characteristically exaggerated vigour, forwarded what he called a Spanish overture for 'joint action by sending warships to Tangier and temporarily occupying part of Morocco'.³ Granville, with equally characteristic phlegm, invited the Marquis de Casa La Iglesia, the Spanish minister in London, to visit him at Walmer and told him that he valued a good understanding with Spain over Morocco, but that any

¹ To Lady Derby, 7 July 1883.
² Granville to Gladstone, 7 Oct. 1881, A. Ramm (ed.), *The Political Correspondence of Mr. Gladstone and Lord Granville* (Oxford, 1962), i. 301; cf. F.O. 99/217.
³ To Granville, no. 214 confidential, 26 Nov. 1881, F.O. 72/1596.

premature appearance of suspicion or any joint action by Britain and Spain would only hasten a decision on the part of the French, who must be perfectly aware of the complications they might create by any attempt on Morocco.[1] The incident was closed by Granville's procuring through Lord Lyons, the British ambassador in Paris, a renewal by France of old disclaimers of aggressive intentions. Léon Gambetta, then president of the council, categorically stated that France 'is quite resolved not to touch Morocco'.[2] This was passed on to Spain whose foreign minister professed himself satisfied.[3] A provocative speech in the French Senate by Charles de Freycinet, who had succeeded Gambetta, produced a renewal of hints from Madrid about Britain and Spain 'taking possession of a port or other favourable position as a means of resisting or counteracting French aggression'. Granville abruptly threw cold water on the suggestion and affirmed that he did not think 'a policy of aggression or encroachment was to be apprehended from M. de Freycinet'.[4] The Spanish foreign minister now bemoaned British unreliability, feared Spain might be left in the lurch by the one Power equally interested in maintaining the *status quo*, and ended, according to Morier's report, with a request for some formal agreement about the steps the two governments should take in the event of French aggression. Morier's vigour had again brought an unfortunate decisiveness into the exchanges. But he was perfectly correct—as he reports his reply— in drawing a distinction between possible eventual aspirations of France to extend her Algerian empire to the Atlantic coast and her immediate and harmless aim of restoring peace across her Algerian frontier. He advised against provocative warnings on speculative contingencies. He added a colourfully worded argument, with a characteristic load of metaphors, about the unwisdom of action 'when the Egyptian question was in a state of acute inflammation', and the risk 'of adding another burning question to the general volcano of north African politics'.[5] There the question again rested until the French actually

[1] From Granville, no. 142 confidential, 7 Dec. 1881, F.O. 72/1594.
[2] To Lyons, no. 1199, 10 Dec., F.O. 27/2487, and from Lyons, telegram, no. 97, 14 Dec. 1881, F.O. 27/2498.
[3] To Granville, no. 2, 7 Jan. 1882, F.O. 72/1617.
[4] From Granville, no. 60 confidential, 15 May 1882, F.O. 72/1616.
[5] To Granville, no. 48 confidential, 27 May 1882, F.O. 72/1617.

occupied Figuiz.¹ By now it was August and Britain was taking the military measures involved in the occupation of Egypt. There was, therefore, no Spanish or British response to the French move in Morocco.

So ended Morier's political work in Madrid. Much the most important part of his activity there was commercial. The adoption of free trade by Britain had put her at a disadvantage in her commercial relations with Portugal and Spain. Since she no longer had protective duties, she could no longer negotiate with these protectionist countries a reciprocal reduction of duties. She could only buy a reduction of *their* duties by sacrificing duties which *she* levied for revenue purposes. Moreover, reductions of duty by Portugal or Spain made in favour of France, or any other country, could not be claimed by Britain since she had no most-favoured-nation treaty with either of them.² She was thus the only European Power excluded from the advantages to be derived from the revised Spanish tariff of 1877. Indeed, she was powerless even to prevent any discrimination that Portugal or Spain chose to make against her goods. Portugal, in fact, had imposed a supplementary duty of 1 per cent, which only Britain paid, and this had been doubled in 1880.³ It was only when Portugal and Spain pressed for a reduction of Britain's fiscal duties on wine that she had a position from which to bargain. The basic duty Britain levied was 1s. a gallon on wine with up to 26° alcoholic content. This being assumed to be the normal alcoholic content, wines with more paid an additional 1s. 6d. per gallon spirit duty, since they were assumed to contain 15° of extra introduced spirit.⁴ They thus paid the extra 1s. 6d. duty, even if only of 27° alcoholic content. It was for a reduction of duty at this level that Portugal and Spain pressed because of their export of reinforced wines, such as sherry. It was appreciated that a possible way to reduce it was by introducing a scale of duties to supersede the two fixed rates.

[1] To Granville, telegram, 28 Aug. 1882, F.O. 72/1617.
[2] Memorandum by Sir John Walsham on commercial relations with Spain, 18 Nov. 1881, F.O. 72/1613; copy in the Morier papers.
[3] To Granville, 26 May 1881, enclosing a report by consul Brackenbury, F.O. 63/1107.
[4] Memorandum by Sir John Walsham on commercial relations with Spain, 18 Nov. 1881, F.O. 72/1613; copy in the Morier papers.

The advent of the Liberals in Britain in 1880 had brought a revival of interest in commercial questions. The Liberals wanted to remove the last restrictions on trade and especially to improve the relationship with France, and, if possible, to restore something like the Cobden treaty instead of the temporary arrangement negotiated in 1873, which then governed Anglo-French trade relations. These negotiations would affect the duties levied on wines according to the scale of alcoholic content and would affect, therefore, Portugal and Spain as well as France.[1]

In 1880 Portugal and Spain attempted to gain a reduction of Britain's wine duties, but they failed. They tried again in 1881. Sackville West, Morier's predecessor at Madrid, was then told that Britain, on her side, sought lower duties on cotton, woollen, iron, and steel goods imported into Portugal and Spain, and offered, in exchange, to propose to Parliament, in the budget of 1882, a new scale of wine duties: 1s. a gallon on wine of up to 28° alcoholic content; 1s. 6d. a gallon on wine of between 28° and 36°; and wines between 37° and 42° to pay an additional 3d. a degree a gallon.[2] On 2 April 1881 these proposals had been made by Sackville West to the Spanish government.[3] On 18 May they had been rejected by Spain, who insisted that the limit for the 1s. duty should be extended to wines of 33° alcoholic content. She offered in return to levy on British goods only the duties of the so-called conventual tariff, i.e. those paid by the countries who had commercial treaties with Spain containing a most-favoured-nation clause.[4] These terms were unacceptable to Britain and by July 1881 it was clear that negotiations on this basis could not proceed.[5] They were brought to an end by an exchange of notes.

A new turn was given to events by the signature on 19 December 1881 of a commercial treaty between Portugal and France and on 6 February 1882 of a similar treaty between

[1] To Granville, 13 June 1880.
[2] West to Granville, no. 34 commercial, confidential, 5 Mar. 1881; Granville to West, no. 28 commercial, 10 Mar. 1881, F.O. 72/1613.
[3] West to Granville, no. 49 commercial, confidential, 2 Apr. 1881, F.O. 72/1613.
[4] De la Vega de Armijo to West, enclosures in West to Granville, no. 67 commercial, 21 May 1881, F.O. 72/1613.
[5] West to de la Vega de Armijo, 28 June, enclosure in West to Granville, no. 79 commercial, 28 June 1881; West to Granville, no. 87 commercial, 8 July 1881, F.O. 72/1613.

Spain and France, both providing for a reciprocal lowering of duties. Britain was now prepared to be satisfied with the negotiation of a commercial treaty with Portugal which, by giving her most-favoured-nation treatment, would extend to her the benefit of Portugal's new treaty with France. In return Britain would adjust her wine duties.[1] A convention was concluded in these terms by C. L. Wyke (who replaced Morier at Lisbon) on 22 May 1882 and ratified by the Cortes on 3 June.[2] One can well imagine the effect of this success upon the competitive and ambitious Morier.

Soon after his arrival in Madrid in October 1881 he had already unofficially sounded the Spanish ministers about a renewal of Sackville West's negotiations. It was agreed to discuss the wine question *de novo* and to disregard the notes exchanged in 1881 between West and de Armijo.[3] After some doubt in London whether talks should take place there or in Madrid, Morier was instructed on 1 April to open negotiations and to proceed on lines he had himself proposed.[4] Sir Charles Dilke, then parliamentary under-secretary, supervised the negotiation. He was also in charge of the negotiations with France; for he made these commercial subjects his special responsibility. Many of Morier's dispatches, and all the important drafts of dispatches to Morier, bear signs of having also been read by Gladstone, who, as long as he was chancellor of the exchequer as well as prime minister, had a special concern, because any alteration of the wine duties would affect his budget. When H. C. E. Childers replaced Gladstone as chancellor, he took a share in supervising the negotiation. Many of the documents were seen by Joseph Chamberlain. Lord Kimberley, as colonial secretary, was drawn in by the question of smuggling tobacco into Spain through Gibraltar. Charles Kennedy, as head of the Commercial Department in the Foreign Office, was the permanent official in charge.

[1] From Granville, telegram, 16 Jan. 1882, F.O. 72/1634.
[2] Granville to Wyke, no. 26 commercial, 2 May 1882; Wyke to Granville, no. 41 commercial, 23 May 1882; the treaty was supplementary to the Anglo-Portuguese treaty of 1842; Granville to Morier, telegram, 25 May 1882, F.O. 72/1620.
[3] From Granville, telegram and no. 6 commercial, 16 Jan. 1882; to Granville, no. 11 commercial, 22 Feb. 1882, F.O. 72/1634.
[4] From Granville, no. 22 commercial, 3 Mar., and no. 32 commercial, 1 Apr. 1882, F.O. 72/1634; see also Dilke's minute giving instructions for the latter to be drafted, F.O. 72/1620.

The basis of the new negotiation was obvious. Morier was told by Granville to gain complete most-favoured-nation treatment for Britain, so that she would enjoy at once the benefits of the new Franco-Spanish tariff. He was also told that Britain was ready to revise her scale of wine duties for wines with more than 26° of alcoholic content, perhaps in the budget of 1883. The instructions were so cast as to make most-favoured-nation treatment point one of an eight-point plan.[1] An intricate negotiation demanding much technical knowledge that would have to be taken calmly and slowly was thus in view.

On 25 April, Morier proposed something quite different and asked for an alteration of his instructions. The tone of his dispatch is such as to make the present-day reader think he was exercising a gift for cutting through verbiage and for discovering a better policy than that of the Foreign Office. At the time it was only irritating; for something like his suggestion had already been proposed, as Dilke noted on the dispatch. Indeed, the point that Morier had now taken was an obvious one: Britain was to enjoy the revised duties at once, but her counter-concession, the revision of her wine duties, was not to come in until after the budget of 1883. Morier, therefore, proposed that instead of embarking upon detailed negotiations for a complicated treaty, Britain and Spain should each undertake simply to do spontaneously by separate pieces of legislation (or as Morier wrote by 'municipal legislation') what was necessary: Spain to give Britain most-favoured-nation treatment; Britain to reform her wine duties by extending the 1s. duty to wines of 28° alcoholic content. But Morier now slipped in from the side a completely new element—an additional counter-concession. Spain had long complained of the smuggling of tobacco from Gibraltar to the mainland, where its retail sale was a government monopoly. Morier, with characteristic thoroughness, had visited Gibraltar in March to inquire

[1] The remaining points were: 2. The reduction of Spanish duties on British imports (the details of what Britain would consider satisfactory for cottons, paper, and metals were given); 3. The reduction of Spanish export duties on wines and mineral ores imported by Britain; 4. Security against Spanish surcharges on fixed customs duties; 5. Readjustment of the Spanish classification of goods and system of levying duties; 6. Provision for the assimilation of the treatment of British shipping and navigation to that of Spanish nationals; 7. The revision of the regulations about vessels arriving at Spanish ports from foreign ones; 8. Examination of Spanish consuls' fees.

into this. He now proposed that Britain should also undertake to establish at Gibraltar such custom-house regulations as would effectively stop this smuggling. He had in his no. 29 commercial of the previous day (24 April) with great exactness and at inordinate length indicated what these should be.[1]

Morier's reason for suggesting, now, this simplified form of transaction rather than the intricate one, which the month before he had wished to negotiate, was an alleged need for haste. The Spanish ministry had just introduced a bill into the Cortes which, he believed, would make it legally impossible for the Spanish government to grant most-favoured-nation treatment to countries like Britain with whom Spain had no commercial treaty. It was important, therefore, for Britain to get what she wanted before the bill became law.

This, at least, was Morier's inference from a complicated bill. Its purpose was to revive and modify a part, suspended since 1875, of the liberal free-trade law of 1869. This had aimed at ending by 1882 all import and export duties, except the proportion of them estimated as levied for revenue purposes. In practice no duty would have exceeded 15 per cent. The new bill substituted a phased reduction of Spanish duties. In detail it provided that:

1. All duties between 15 per cent and 20 per cent should be reduced in 1882 to 15 per cent.
2. All duties above 20 per cent should be reduced to 15 per cent in three stages, in 1882, 1885, and 1888.
3. The government should be empowered to open negotiations for new treaties of commerce granting reduced duties only to those nations who would lower their actual tariffs for the benefit of the products and manufactures of Spain (Britain with virtually no tariff would thus be excluded).
4. The reduced duties should not apply to the goods of the countries who had no treaties with Spain (again Britain would be excluded).
5. The government should retain the power to impose surcharges on the imports and manufactures of nations which discriminated against the products and commerce of Spain.[2]

[1] To Granville, no. 29 commercial, 24 Apr. 1882, and no. 30 commercial, 25 Apr. 1882, F.O. 72/1634.
[2] To Granville, no. 30 commercial, 25 Apr. 1882, F.O. 72/1634.

Morier pointed out that if the third and fourth provisions of the bill became law, the government would not be legally able to grant most-favoured-nation treatment to Britain. He summed up in his vigorous style:

> Thus, on the very threshold of the new negotiation, there would once more be re-established the double *non possumus* by which the former negotiation was arrested, only, in a far more aggravated form, for, before, the Spanish *non possumus* was merely the *non possumus* of the executive Government for the time being, now it will be a *non possumus* on the point of becoming the law of the land.

In order to get what Britain wanted before the bill became law, he proposed that he should be empowered 'to ask for it in return for a valuable consideration'—that is the suppression of smuggling at Gibraltar.[1] The government at home, hesitating to give Morier at once what he wanted, was assailed with a spate of telegrams and dispatches. He urged first the necessity of putting the negotiations on to a firm basis quickly, since the opposition, provoked by Camacho's financial measures, had considerably weakened the government's support in the Chamber of Deputies and he anticipated 'one of those unexpected crises which so frequently occur in Spain' and the possible fall of the administration.[2] Dilke seems to have been ready enough, but could not persuade Kimberley to make any promise about the Gibraltar smuggling 'without further enquiry'. Gladstone and Granville were appealed to and finally a meeting took place at which Kimberley was won over.[3] On 10 May Morier was accordingly authorized to *sound* Camacho *informally* on the scheme he had proposed on 25 April.[4] Morier had feared that the French tariff under the new Franco-Spanish treaty would come into operation and damage Britain's trade before he could begin to negotiate for its extension to her. By this telegram the fear was for the moment dispelled. The treaty was passed by the Spanish Cortes late on

---

[1] To Granville, no. 30 commercial, 25 Apr. 1882, F.O. 72/1634.
[2] To Granville, no. 32 commercial and no. 33 commercial, confidential, 5 May (received 8 May) 1882, F.O. 72/1635.
[3] See minute by Kimberley on draft of Granville to Morier, no. 37 commercial, 6 Apr., and several minutes on Morier to Granville, no. 29 commercial, 24 Apr. 1882, F.O. 72/1634.
[4] From Granville, telegram, 10 May 1882, F.O. 72/1635.

8 May and its tariff was to come into operation on 15 May.[1] But he was still not satisfied; sounding was not enough and he continued his pressure on the home government.[2] Somewhat aided by a speech from Sagasta to the Spanish Cortes and simultaneous pressure from the Association of Chambers of Commerce in London, he got what he wanted. On 13 May he was instructed to make a *formal* proposal to Spain in the terms of his dispatch of 25 April.[3] But meanwhile a split in the cabinet (with Sagasta thinking the French treaty had taken the reform of the tariff far enough and Camacho willing to go further) made the fall of the administration more and more likely.[4] Nevertheless, on 15 May 1882 Morier put the new British proposal to de Armijo and Camacho, who withheld their reply for the time being.[5] Morier kept up his pressure on London. On 27 May he telegraphed for authority to submit a draft instrument. He was encouraged when an unfavourable amendment to the free-trade bill failed; but the bill was withdrawn to be reintroduced with the last phase in the lowering of duties postponed.[6] Two daysl ater Camacho emerged victorious from the ministerial crisis.

Morier now telegraphed that it was essential that his proposals should be taken into consideration in their entirety by the government before the bill was reintroduced in the Cortes, and he proposed to submit a draft in accordance with his proposals, almost at once, unless told not to do so. His course was approved.[7] But he tried in vain to induce Sagasta, de Armijo, and Camacho to modify the bill so as to allow the government to admit Britain, at least provisionally, to most-

---

[1] To Granville, no. 34 commercial, 9 May 1882, F.O. 72/1621, and telegram, 9 May 1882, F.O. 72/1635.

[2] To Granville, nos. 35 and 36 commercial, 9 May 1882, and nos. 37 and 38 commercial, 10 May 1882; all of these four dispatches were 'extenders' of telegrams, all in F.O. 72/1635; see also memorial from Associated Chambers of Commerce, 1 May, and attached minutes, 7–10 May, ibid.

[3] From Granville, no. 54 commercial, and telegram, 13 May 1882, both F.O. 72/1635.

[4] To Granville, no. 43 commercial, 17 May 1882, F.O. 72/1635.

[5] To Granville, telegram and no. 47 commercial, most confidential, 23 May 1882, F.O. 72/1635.

[6] To Granville, telegram, 27 May, and no. 52 commercial, 29 May 1882, F.O. 72/1635.

[7] To Granville, telegram, 29 May, no. 51, 27 May, no. 52 commercial, 29 May 1882, all in F.O. 72/1635.

favoured-nation treatment without a commercial treaty.[1] The bill, without this change, was reintroduced into the Cortes on 1 June 1882.[2] This Morier alleged was done without a previous warning to him and without a reply having been given to his formal proposals to Camacho. It appeared that it was to be clandestinely hustled through the Cortes to defeat his proposals in advance. By 5 June he knew that there was 'not the slightest hope of our obtaining most-favoured-nation treatment otherwise than as part of a Treaty in which we shall have conceded to Spain such modification of the alcoholic scale as she may deem sufficient'.[3] He had made an eleventh-hour effort after the debate on the bill had already begun, by paying a call, together with Sagasta, upon Camacho and de Armijo in the meeting-house of the Cortes, to induce them to modify the fourth clause of the bill with the purpose of restoring to the government liberty in regard to negotiations with those states who had no commercial treaties with Spain, since he had learned that Moret was going to propose such an amendment.[4] His attempt failed and the bill was voted law on 9 June and received the royal sanction in July 1882. Morier's first negotiation had miscarried. The Spanish were not to prove as amenable to the force of his pressure as the Portuguese had been.

The whole negotiation shows Morier's worst failings without the merit of the really constructive ideas behind his Portuguese policy. He had made himself look foolish by overdoing his pressure for haste. He could not have given his communications home a more portentous urgency, if the Spanish commercial negotiation had been the single, overriding preoccupation of Parliament and Cabinet. Their inordinate length provoked from Gladstone, when Morier wrote 'I analysed in great detail to Senor Camacho', the pencilled comment, 'unhappy Senor Camacho!'[5] He had, moreover, missed, in the urgency of his wish to pull off a success, a quite simple point which Dilke saw, that if the passage of the free-trade law prevented the

[1] To Granville, telegram, 3 June 1882, F.O. 72/1635.
[2] To Granville, no. 58 commercial and confidential, 1 June 1882, F.O. 72/1635.
[3] To Granville, telegrams, 5 June 1882, F.O. 72/1635.
[4] To Granville, nos. 59, 62, 64, 65 all commercial, 3, 5, and 6 June 1882, F.O. 72/1635.
[5] On Morier to Granville, no. 47 commercial, most confidential, 23 May 1882, F.O. 72/1635.

Spanish government from granting Britain, out of hand, most-favoured-nation treatment because she had no commercial treaty, then all she needed to do was to try to negotiate such a treaty. As Dilke minuted and Granville agreed, 'If a mere bare Treaty is all that is needed to satisfy the law a mere most-favoured-nation treaty would do'[1]—that is, a single-clause treaty providing that British goods should be admitted to Spain on the same terms as those of the most-favoured nation. Worse still, Morier had got himself into a position where he could again believe himself let down. The truth seems to be that his own exuberant wish for success had led him to interpret de Armijo's and Camacho's language to him as more encouraging than they had meant it to sound. He was, therefore, taken aback when they put the law through and made plain their determination to continue to discriminate against British goods. He wrote home that their action was 'eminently unfriendly and discourteous . . . for not one of [the three, prime minister, foreign minister, or finance minister] had said a word to induce the belief that they rejected the proposals, but rather the contrary'.[2] This sense of having been deceived was still not the worst for Morier. Beyond that, he got himself wrong with his own government and received a rebuke for going beyond his instructions.[3] He had *pledged* his government on both the wine duties and Gibraltar smuggling, when his instructions were to hold out the *prospect* of a change in the wine duties and a mere *consideration* by the British government of measures to stop the Gibraltar smuggling. His instructions on that point had been formally confirmed after a cabinet meeting on 31 May. Morier, convinced that he had only done what he was told to do, defended himself. It was clear, however, that he had offered to *commit* his government when, as Gladstone minuted, 'It is certainly impossible to give any pledge.' Dilke wrote on the back of Morier's defence that he certainly had overstepped his

---

[1] On Morier to Granville, no. 57 commercial, 31 May 1882, F.O. 72/1635.

[2] To Granville, no. 58 commercial, confidential, 1 June 1882; no. 64 commercial, 5 June 1882, F.O. 72/1635.

[3] From Granville, no. 75 commercial, 10 June 1882; the draft of the actual words of rebuke is in Granville's hand; there are two versions, the second and final one milder than the first; see also Dilke's minute on the back of Morier to Granville, no. 64 commercial, 5 June 1882; see also from Granville, telegrams, 30 and 31 May; all in F.O. 72/1635.

instructions, but that since the negotiation had failed it was not worth pursuing the matter.¹ Morier had, however, also fallen into an argument with the Spanish minister of finance, who complained that he had broken a promise made to him not to refer, in the public notes which wound up the negotiation, to an informal conversation they had had on 15 May. This was too much for Dilke, who referred to Granville with the comment, 'Morier is getting into trouble again.' Granville consoled him by pointing out that Morier had been granted leave and would soon be in London.² Still more serious than all this was that Morier had got his bearings completely wrong. He saw everything as it affected himself and his own success, so that he never asked himself how much his own government really wanted any settlement with Spain. He would have found this difficult to answer because, though those concerned—Dilke, Granville, and Gladstone—were agreed, they were agreed on two opinions that were not easily reconciled: one that they did not wish to settle wine duties with Spain until they had used their wine duties to bargain with France to induce her to lower her protectionist barrier against British manufactures;³ and two, to adopt Morier's words, which Dilke pointed out were unfortunately true, that British trade with Spain would now 'be subjected to a differential treatment of such portentous proportions that its annihilation, unless some prompt remedy can be found, must . . . be regarded a matter of certainty'.⁴ But the very fact that it was not easy to be clear about his government's objective would have given a wiser diplomat pause for thought before he rushed in with such urgency to get an agreement.

By the summer of 1882 the negotiations of 1882 had failed, as by the summer of 1881 the earlier ones had failed. The position then was that the Spanish wished to begin negotiations for a treaty proper as soon as possible, intending to strike a

¹ To Granville, no. 84 commercial, 4 July 1882, with Dilke's minute on the back, F.O. 72/1636. Gladstone's minute is dated 19 June and is attached to Morier to Granville, telegram, 15 June, F.O. 72/1635.
² To Granville, nos. 78, 79, and 80, all commercial, 25 June 1882, and the several minutes attached, F.O. 72/1635.
³ Gladstone's minute of 19 June already quoted continued: 'I think neither Ld. G[ranville] nor I am anxious for a treaty with Spain unless there is one with France', see Morier to Granville, telegram, 15 June, F.O. 72/1635.
⁴ To Granville, no. 66 commercial, 8 June 1882, F.O. 72/1635.

bargain. Britain stood by her refusal to pledge herself to alter her alcoholic scale in the budget of 1883 and was not likely to do so unless financial circumstances admitted. This was the stumbling-block.[1] The negotiations were wound up by a formal note from Morier to de Armijo who replied on 3 June—a reply deemed thoroughly unsatisfactory.[2] On 6 July Morier left Madrid for England and did not return until August. In London he was calmed down and brought back to confidence in his superiors by Dilke. Granville was now near the end of the parliamentary session and in the midst of the Egyptian imbroglio. Morier believed that the explanation of the failure was pressure from the Catalan defenders of strong protectionist industrial interests. The Catalonians were opposed to both the French and the British treaties. But the British treaty, Morier said, had been 'the Jonah by the sacrifice of whom' the ratification of the French treaty had been gained from the Cortes.[3]

In the autumn of 1882 the situation again changed, when Spain did for a number of countries what she had refused to do for Britain and granted them most-favoured-nation treatment provisionally, despite the law of July 1882. They were thus admitted to the low tariff of the French treaty, from which Britain remained excluded. Treaties of Commerce with Germany, Denmark, Greece, Italy, Holland, Portugal, Russia, Sweden–Norway, Switzerland, and Turkey, which expired in October, were by a mere act of the executive, 'without the interference of the Cortes', to be continued in force after they had lapsed, to avoid placing those countries in the position of having no commercial treaties with Spain. Legally—by the law of July 1882—those countries were not eligible for most-favoured-nation treatment—unless fresh treaties had been negotiated before the existing ones expired or fresh legislation passed. The government's decision simply overrode the legal fact and was in glaring contrast to Spain's taking her stand on the same legal fact when she refused most-favoured-nation

[1] To Granville, telegram and no. 72 commercial, 15 June 1882, F.O. 72/1635.
[2] To Granville, telegram and no. 76 commercial, 24 June, no. 78 commercial, 25 June, no. 79 commercial, confidential, 25 June 1882, F.O. 72/1635.
[3] To Dilke, private, 18 Oct. 1882, F.O. 72/1636; to Granville, no. 7 commercial, 12 Feb. 1883, F.O. 72/1662.

treatment to Britain. Nevertheless, Morier did not believe it was taken in a spirit hostile to Britain.[1] He thought that it was de Armijo's 'fantastic' dream of an alliance with Germany which explained what had been done. Morier wrote an enormously long argument to explain that the whole comedy had been played for the sake of Germany and for her sake alone.[2] It led subsequently to complicated proceedings in the Cortes in order to legalize what the government had done.[3] Meanwhile Morier counselled doing nothing and waiting for a Spanish initiative which he believed was bound to come.[4]

This policy brought its reward, though not in the expected shape. King Alfonso proposed to make a tour of the European capitals, Vienna, Berlin, Brussels, London, and Paris. Morier was instructed[5] that a visit to London could not take place that year in view of difficulties being made by the Queen. He was obliged to resort to a stratagem in order to convey this information to the Spaniards; since no formal overture had been made, he feared that it would be made at the last moment and then the Spaniards would suffer from injured pride at an unexpected refusal. So profiting from Alfonso's illness, Morier was able to speak to the under-secretary and to let out the information as from himself in what was made to appear a casual conversation. It was this conversation that had the surprising result of drawing from de Armijo a few days later the formulation of the Spanish wish 'to establish close relations with the United Kingdom'. There was no point, de Armijo said, on which the foreign policy of the two countries clashed. In Morocco it was identical—this was the dominant question of de Armijo's foreign policy—and the two governments were acting most harmoniously together. He could not believe that England would look jealously on a close and intimate alliance between Spain and Portugal. 'On the contrary, he believed that if there chanced to be menacing combinations against the Peninsula from across the Pyrenees, England might be glad of the

[1] To Granville, no. 123 commercial, most confidential, 26 Sept. 1882, F.O. 72/1636.
[2] To Granville, no. 137 commercial, secret and confidential, 28 Oct. 1882, F.O. 72/1636.
[3] To Granville, no. 6 commercial, 6 Feb. 1883, F.O. 72/1636.
[4] To Dilke, private, 18 Oct. 1882, F.O. 72/1636.
[5] From Granville, private, 5 June 1883.

influence of Spain to combine the common Peninsula forces in resistance to the common Peninsula danger.'

In the conversation, which lasted more than two hours, the Spanish overture was prefaced by a statement that France was bidding high for a Spanish alliance and offering 'des concessions immenses', and that Spain was cultivating Germany; and it was followed by an assurance that if Morier would show patience and understanding, he would see de Armijo achieve the commercial treaty which England wanted so that—as Morier recorded his speech—'the settlement of the matter should form the portal through which the two Governments should enter into a period of close and cordial relations'.[1] Morier responded with warm generalities. He was correct in replying that it was not the policy of Great Britain to seek out or enter into political alliances, but that it was of the essence of her policy to cultivate friendships. He made a mistake, however, in yet seizing upon de Armijo's talk as if it were a serious overture from which 'a diplomatic success' might be harvested. His line of thought followed a pattern that had been set at Lisbon and was to be three times repeated at St. Petersburg.

As it turned out the King's tour was not an unqualified success. The visit to Paris was almost given up owing to incidents at Badajoz. When it did take place, it was a disaster. The King, having accepted in Berlin the colonelcy of an Uhlan regiment, was hissed in Paris. At the last moment he had insisted on his wish to go to Paris first, and it was President Grévy who was responsible for his ending his tour, instead of beginning it, in Paris. Morier credits himself with having given the advice that the King should go to Paris first. The consequence of the visit to Paris taking place after the visit to Germany, he wrote, was that it was 'a huge mistake'.[2]

The incident was nevertheless turned to good account. A personal message from the Queen, conveyed through Lady Ely to Morier and by Morier to the King, expressed Her Majesty's concern at what had happened during the King's visit to Paris and her admiration for His Majesty's noble

---

[1] To Granville, private and confidential, 27 June 1883; cf. to Granville, no. 110 confidential, 3 July 1883, F.O. 72/1635, which contains the quoted phrase.

[2] To Granville, private, Biarritz, 29 Sept. 1883.

bearing and tact and forbearance throughout.[1] It left Morier with little doubt 'that nothing that has occurred since the late events has given the Spanish King and Queen anything like the pleasure and confidence which they have derived from the personal approval of the one great Constitutional Sovereign of the world'.[2] A private message from Granville expressed his regret in well-chosen terms and ended: 'But for the King, his reception at Paris has been a Godsend. No military or diplomatic victory, could so suddenly have given him such a position as he now holds both in Europe and at home.'[3] A copy of this was left by Morier with de Armijo.[4]

It was over this matter that Morier made one of the first of a fresh series of mistakes. It drew upon him a rebuke, through Ponsonby, from Queen Victoria. She had used Lady Ely in order to avoid involving the Spanish Foreign Office or Anglo-French relations. But what should Morier do but, in his vanity, report to Granville the elaborate stratagem he had used? This had meant asking de Armijo to arrange that the King should chance to be present at a function of the Queen to which Mrs. Morier had been invited and that Morier, accompanying his wife, should be able unobtrusively to deliver the message. Queen Victoria was quick to notice that in bringing in de Armijo, he had done the precise opposite of what she wished. Ponsonby, on the Queen's instructions, pointed it out. Morier was much ruffled by the humiliation of being guilty of a 'gross professional blunder'.[5]

In November 1883, Granville and Morier seized the opportunity offered by the accession of a new Spanish government, pledged to the establishment of free trade (see above, p. 164).[6] They urged the reopening of negotiations on Britain's terms, but by a Spanish initiative.[7] Circumstances were

[1] From Lady Ely, 4 Oct. 1883, and to the Queen, 11 Oct. 1883.
[2] To Granville, private, 11 Oct. 1883.
[3] From Granville, private, 3 Oct. 1883.
[4] To Armijo, 10 Oct. 1883.
[5] From Ponsonby, 20 Oct. 1883; to Ponsonby, 25 Oct. 1883; from Ponsonby 2 Nov. 1883, all in the Morier papers; Morier to Granville, 11 and 18 Oct. 1883 and mem. by Ponsonby, 30 Oct., 1883, R.A. I 54/103–7.
[6] To Granville, no. 67 commercial, 1 Nov. 1883; from Granville, telegram, 31 Oct. 1883, quoted in Morier to Granville, no. 70 commercial, 3 Nov. 1883, F.O. 72/1663.
[7] To Granville, no. 71 commercial, secret, 3 Nov. 1883, F.O. 72/1663.

altogether more favourable; for, since the publication of a British parliamentary Blue Book on the negotiations of 1882,[1] which had been translated and analysed by the Spanish Free Trade League, and the declaration of 1882 in the House of Commons, the whole question of the wine duties had been 'brought down out of the clouds on to the solid earth, examined on all sides and handled, with the result that a complete *consensus* of opinion' had been obtained that a graduated scale with some alleviation of duty in the middle part of it was the object to be striven for.[2]

Accordingly, on 8 November 1883, Morier telegraphed:

Spanish Government accept, as basis of a negotiation for a Treaty of Commerce the proposals of Her Majesty's Government contained in the Memorandum communicated to Spanish Government on 28th March 1881, providing shilling duty be extended [not from 26° to 28° but from 26° to 30°]. They propose immediate nomination of an Anglo-Spanish Commission to determine how far existing Convention Tariff [that is the tariff under the Franco-Spanish treaty] . . . can be modified in sense desired by Her Majesty's Government. Until such Commission has finished its labours they accept *modus vivendi* proposed last year, provided equally that the shilling duty be extended to 30 degrees. Spain to grant [most-favoured-nation treatment] at once to Great Britain. Great Britain to grant at once extension of shilling duty to 30 degrees. With regard to *modus vivendi*, both Governments to act municipally, but to be bound to maintain this arrangement until conclusion of negotiations for definitive treaty. Immediate decision necessary as Bill to obtain powers must be presented to Cortes first week in December . . . I write at length by post but even now earnestly urge general acceptance of these proposals, as indispensable to a scheme, which if successful, will place Spain foremost among the free-trade nations of the Continent.[3]

The cabinet agreed[4] on 10 November 1883 to Morier's being instructed that Her Majesty's Government 'will consent that Spain shall immediately concede most-favoured-nation treatment to this country, and that Her Majesty's Government

[1] *Parliamentary Papers* (1882), lxxxi. 289.
[2] To Granville, no. 68 commercial, 2 Nov. 1883, F.O. 72/1663.
[3] To Granville, telegram and no. 72 commercial, no. 73 commercial, secret, 8 Nov. 1883, F.O. 72/1663.
[4] From Granville, telegram drafted by T. H. Sanderson, his private secretary, 10 Nov. 1883, F.O. 72/1663.

should propose to raise the 1*s*. limit to 30 degrees, and also examine what further steps can be taken to suppress the Gibraltar smuggling'. A reminder was added that the wine duties could only be altered (a) by Parliament and (b) in March 1884 when it would consider the next budget. Morier was left discretion whether or not to try to gain the rest of the eight points of the instructions of 1 April 1882.[1] Within less than three weeks, on 1 December 1883, and a little more than a month after the advent of the new ministry, Morier had secured the signature of a protocol embodying in seven articles the terms described as follows:

The Governments of Great Britain and Spain being desirous to put an end to the unsatisfactory state of the commercial relations between the two countries, the Undersigned have come to the following agreement:

1. The two Governments engage at once to open negotiations for a Commercial Treaty which shall include a Consular Convention and a Treaty of Navigation, and shall be concluded with the least possible delay.

2. The two Governments, with a view to increasing their trade by respectively widening the markets for each other's produce, engage: Spanish Government to make, within the limits compatible with their financial requirements, with due regard to present state of Spanish industry, and with the sanction of the Cortes, such modification in their Conventional Tariff as, after enquiry, shall be found necessary to meet legitimate requirements of British trade; Her Majesty's Government to apply to Parliament for sanction to modify wine duties scale so as to meet legitimate requirements of Spanish trade.

3. Should the modifications proposed by the Spanish Government after enquiry above mentioned, be such as to satisfy Her Majesty's Government with regard to the Spanish Customs Tariff on British goods, Her Majesty's Government engage to apply to Parliament for sanction to extend present 1*s*. limit from 26 to 30 degrees, and above 30 degrees to modify the present scale to such an extent as, for the purposes of the Treaty, they may deem possible and convenient.

4. The two Governments engage at once to name a Mixed Commission for the purpose of the investigation provided in paragraph 2. Such Commission shall thoroughly investigate values and all the conditions which go to make up prices, and also take cognizance of

[1] From Granville, no. 99 commercial and telegram, 12 Nov. 1883, F.O. 72/1663.

any hindrances which militate against that perfect liberty and free movement of trade and commerce [*sic*] which are so desirable in the interests of both countries. The Commission will be ready to hear interested parties, whether Spanish or British.

5. With the further view of removing, as quickly as possible, the grave prejudices resulting to the trade of both countries from the differential system in force towards British goods, the two Governments agree on the following *modus vivendi* which shall remain in force until such time as the Treaty shall have been signed:

> The Spanish Government at once to apply to the Cortes for power to admit British goods according to the second column of present Spanish Tariff [i.e. most-favoured-nation treatment].
>
> The British Government on their side, to apply for sanction to extend 1*s*. scale from 26 to 30 degrees. These reciprocal concessions to take place simultaneously. [This last sentence was subsequently omitted.]

6. This arrangement to remain in force pending conclusion of definitive Treaty of Commerce, with liberty, however, should unforeseen circumstances interrupt the negotiations, of termination in 1887.

7. The two Governments further engage, that so long as *modus vivendi* remains in force, they will accord each other most-favoured-nation treatment in regard to all matters appertaining to trade and navigation.[1]

There was some further negotiation, because London insisted on improvements in the wording and successfully induced Spain to agree to omit the sentence in article 5 about simultaneity, but tried and failed to substitute the date 1892 for 1887 in article 6. Yet the final stage was remarkably quick and smooth, partly because the Spanish wished to forestall the opposition of Catalonia by presenting that province with a *fait accompli*. The Spanish government was also rendered anxious by the agitation over the bad state of the Spanish army and the consequences which were expected to flow from the Crown Prince of Germany's visit late in 1883. The main reason was Morier's activity. Nearly all the work was done by Morier and his chancery rather than the Spanish civil servants.

Señor Ruiz Gomez [wrote Morier], altogether unused to diplo-

---

[1] See draft received in London on 1 Dec., having been sent home in Morier to Granville, no. 88 commercial, 27 Nov.; the text telegraphed on 28 Nov. 1883, F.O. 72/1663.

matic work, ignorant even of the forms of business, and with his time and thoughts altogether engrossed by the internal crisis and the visit of the Crown Prince of Germany, could only give me a few minutes conversation at odd times of the day and night . . . To render yet more abnormal this abnormal state of things, His Excellency, having as yet but an imperfect knowledge of the *personnel* of his Ministry, did not dare, in view of the absolute secrecy required, to trust anyone at the Chancery of State with the knowledge of the negotiation.[1]

The protocol of 1 December was accompanied by a declaration (actually signed on 12 December, though it bore the same date). This satisfied the Spanish wish for the security they had sought to obtain by originally inserting the provision for 'simultaneity'. Spain declared her confidence in the British Parliament's agreeing to the extension of the 1*s*. duty, but said that, nevertheless, the extension of most-favoured-nation treatment to Britain could only take effect under a law which would stipulate that the concession would operate when Parliament's agreement had been gained. Britain explained the reason why the Spanish bill would have to pass the Cortes before the date at which her government proposed the budget to Parliament in order for the wine duty alteration to take effect that session.[2]

The Mixed Commission was made up pretty well according to Morier's recommendations.[3] It was agreed that Charles Kennedy, the head of the Commercial Department of the Foreign Office, because of his standing in the Foreign Office hierarchy and capacity, therefore, to lead the Commission and to inject business-like habits into the proceedings, should head the British delegation. William Macpherson was to act as the second member, because of his knowledge of Spanish customs regulations and the confidence shown in him by the Madrid customs officials. Sir John Walsham, who possessed a knowledge of Spanish trade, Spanish official ways, and the Spanish language, was the third member. For Spain were named Don Raffaele Prieto, a man of independent position and a retired

[1] To Granville, no. 96 commercial, secret, 2 Dec. 1883, F.O. 72/1664.
[2] Final text in F.O. 72/1664; published in the *London Gazette*, 10 Dec. 1883; for the declaration, see Morier to Granville, nos. 97 and 98 commercial, 2 Dec. 1883, F.O. 72/1664.
[3] To Granville, no. 94 commercial, 30 Nov. 1883, F.O. 72/1663.

official, Bonifacio Ruiz de Velasco, also politically independent and a former official, and in addition a former merchant, and finally Julian Castedo, head of a department in the Spanish customs.

The intention was that the Commission should meet in January 1884, but it had to be postponed as the protocol had not, by that date, been sanctioned by the Cortes. Indeed, although the protocol's signature had prevented the immediate fall of the ministry, it was still not sanctioned before Morier left Madrid. Thus the British budgets of 1884 and 1885 were both missed and no Anglo-Spanish commercial treaty was negotiated during his mission.

It had originally been intended that the protocol should go before the Cortes when it met on 15 December 1883, but it was not presented until 12 January 1884.[1] Morier knew that the conservatives would not vote against the protocol, since on 19 December he had been given an assurance confidentially by Cánovas, their leader, to that effect. But on 19 January the Ruiz Gomez government fell and Cánovas himself came into power. He intended to dissolve the Cortes. When it reassembled at the end of June, he intended it should sit only for one month to pass the estimates and to debate the speech from the throne and that it should not meet again until December 1884. This, then, would be the earliest date at which the Cortes could vote on the bill to sanction the protocol and declaration. Meanwhile Cánovas refused to commit himself to any attitude to it.[2] Morier, who had intended to go to London to consult the Foreign Office about the lines of negotiation for the commercial treaty and the work of the Commission, went all the same on 24 January 1884, but with blank prospects before him. The picture was apparently the same as it had three times been in Lisbon: quick success up to a point, and slow disillusionment as the success failed to be confirmed by the Cortes. But there was a deeper bitterness. Morier had been enormously pleased with his success. 'I have, so far as I am concerned', he wrote to Lady Derby,[3] 'obtained a very considerable victory here,

---

[1] To Granville, telegram and no. 4 commercial, 10 Jan. 1884, telegram and no. 8 commercial, 12 Jan. 1884, F.O. 72/1695.
[2] To Granville, no. 12 commercial, confidential, 21 Jan. 1884, F.O. 72/1695.
[3] 22 Dec. 1883.

and signed a protocol after three weeks' negotiation which I venture to say no-one in Spain would have believed signable, if at all, under a six months' negotiation.' He had, as has been shown, been fully supported at home. But then, it appeared that the government were not going to support him in pressing for quick ratification. 'Now the deed is done, it almost appears to me as if they were not pleased with it.' He went home to find out where he stood. He hoped to stay at Knowsley with the Derbys but was disappointed in this too; for it transpired that they intended to return to London soon after the New Year. He had thought he might get over from Knowsley to Hawarden and see Gladstone and talk with him as well as with Derby.[1] But he was obliged to be content with discussions—not in themselves rewarding—at the Foreign Office. They were based on a memorandum which he submitted on 31 January 1884.[2] It was agreed, as Morier here suggested, that at all costs there should be no reopening of negotiations, but the protocol be maintained and an effort made to get it passed by the Cortes, the meeting of the Mixed Commission being postponed if necessary. Morier was desperate that the protocol should not 'die an unnatural death'. By 2 April it became known that the Cortes was to be dissolved and elections to take place for a new Cortes to meet already in May.[3] But Morier's remonstrances when he learned that the government did not intend to put the protocol before the Cortes, when he was obliged to listen to the ministers' talk of 'complete neutrality', and to hear them admit that a Cortes 'elected by themselves' would regard this neutrality as a mandate not to pass it—these remonstrances were met with bland reiterations of goodwill, and there the matter virtually rested. On 1 April Morier again left Madrid and was in London until the end of July, not returning to Madrid until 16 August. The Spanish foreign minister replied to a note presented to him on 29 March

[1] To Lady Derby, 22 Dec. 1883.
[2] Copy in F.O. 72/1695; cf. also a minute by Charles Kennedy, 1 Feb. 1884, and draft of instructions drawn up after the discussion, no. 18 commercial from Granville, 20 Feb. 1884, F.O. 72/1695.
[3] Maurice de Bunsen to Granville, no. 51, 2 Apr. 1884, F.O. 72/1678. Elections in fact took place on 27 Apr. and brought back a house with more than three-quarters committed to supporting the ministry in power; nos. 54, 56, 30 Apr., 10 May 1884, F.O. 72/1678.

1884, complaining about the failure to ratify the protocol, with an attack on its substance.[1]

Morier learnt[2] in the first week of December 1884 of his nomination to the embassy at St. Petersburg. It was the end of three months' tension and misery. Lord Odo Russell, by then Lord Ampthill, had died in August 1884. The ambition of Morier's heart had long been the embassy at Berlin, but he well knew that he could not have it, 'with advantage to the public service,' as long as Bismarck was in power. Lord Ampthill's death was a bitter personal blow because of their friendship, but, from this last point of view too, he had died too soon. 'It had always been my hope that he would have remained at Berlin till Bismarck shut up, and that I should succeed him whenever he got Paris. Now a vacancy is made which when filled up will probably shut off ambassadorial promotion for some years to come.'[3] Morier knew he could not hope to be chosen, but he hoped at least that in the general post Vienna might fall to him. Through Lady Derby he urged his claim, reminding Lord Derby of his work in Vienna in 1865–7 and his wife's popularity there. 'I can honestly say,' he wrote, 'that I feel myself better fitted than any other possible candidate', and he advanced his knowledge of the country and the Emperor's goodwill towards him as reasons.[3] Meanwhile in London there was much discussion between Granville and Gladstone and canvassing of candidates at court. By mid-September the choice had fallen upon Sir Edward Malet. By 25 November Morier had heard that he had been passed over. He intended to resign from the service and was suffering agonies of humiliation. This he worked off in a long confidential letter addressed to Derby 'through a friend of mine in London begging him to post it as soon as the nominations to the Embassies were published in the papers ... It was intended, at a moment when I thought I was leaving the career, to put out what I believed to be a fair account of what I had done during the important section of it which embraced my work as Minister'. It was a justification elicited 'by the prospect of

---

[1] To Granville, no. 41 commercial, confidential, 20 Mar. 1884, no. 43 commercial, 24 Mar. 1884, no. 46 commercial, 1 Apr. 1884, F.O. 72/1696.

[2] To Lady Derby, 6 Dec. 1884.

[3] To Lady Derby, 6 Sept. 1884.

being turned out of the career as a dangerous and untrustworthy servant'. It was to be a silent witness to testify to the truth and confound in the long run those who misrepresented him. It was also, since he owed his position at Lisbon and Madrid to Derby, to be an account of his stewardship. 'But naturally,' Morier continued in subsequently writing to Lady Derby, 'I did not wish this to reach his hands till the matter was decided and the blow struck, as he might have thought it had been written for the purpose of averting it.' But then it proved unnecessary and this 'terrible and almost unbearable load' was removed from Morier's mind. The offer of St. Petersburg arrived and Morier believed that he owed his embassy entirely and wholly to Lord and Lady Derby.[1] He did not know that he had been considered for it in 1881.[2] Nor did he know that the Queen had urged his appointment— so much so that she was subsequently to blame herself for it.[3]

Morier left Madrid as he had left Lisbon with the knowledge that he had failed in the object he had set himself—again a treaty—and the conviction that his failure was due to his government's having let him down.

I would have got the whole thing settled in 24 hours [he wrote to Ponsonby], if those blessed Cherubim in Downing Street had only given me what I asked for, an ultimatum, instead of a rupture, but it was they who wanted to get out of the engagement [the protocol of 1883]. This was told me confidentially and I had to cut my cloth accordingly and this with God's assistance I shall never forgive them . . . all because that idol of yours the G.O.M. (new reading Gory Old Man) and his jackal Mr. Childers, choose to hate Commercial Treaties and regard them as heretical.[4]

There is, however, another side to the story. There was, it will be recalled, very little political work for Morier at Madrid. He was harassed with a series of unimportant technical questions that yet demanded the same care as if they had been supremely important. There was the question of the Zamora

[1] To Lady Derby, 6 Dec. 1884.   [2] See above, p. 159.
[3] See R.A. A 78/37 and Ponsonby to the Queen, 'he feels convinced that Sir R. Morier would never have got this promotion but for your Majesty', ibid., B 33/40; the Queen's Journal under 26 Aug. and 29 Nov. 1884; the Queen to the Crown Princess, 'it was I who had him appointed', 24 Mar. 1886, ibid. Add. MS. U 32/426.
[4] To Ponsonby, 8 June 1885; G.O.M. is of course Gladstone.

waterworks, of the empty grain-bags that British merchants entered on the ships' manifests as ships' stores instead of merchandise, of reciprocal requirements in relation to joint stock companies, and a more dangerous question about Cuban refugees. As at Lisbon, Morier took flight from this dullness in anecdote and the over-dramatization of such incidents as did occur. He told at great length the story of Alba Salcedo, appointed ambassador to China after practising an elaborate hoax on the Shereef of Wazan. A considerable amount of money passed into Salcedo's hands on the Shereef's assumption that he was being admitted into a conspiracy with the Spanish government to buy part of Morocco.[1] As for dramatization, phrases such as 'the very remarkable secret history',[2] 'the secret history of what has been going on',[3] 'I will send you the authentic facts . . . that never see the light of publicity'[4]—these are typical of the overheated atmosphere which Morier so quickly generated.

In Lisbon Morier had found an outlet for the opinions on the large questions of the day that accumulated in his head in his long letters to his friends on the eastern question. While he was in Madrid, the Egyptian question and the partition of Africa were the large questions from which he felt isolated, but which he longed to treat. Whereas he had had something to say about the Balkans, he had, however, nothing of his own to contribute on Egypt. All he could do was to take pains to analyse the Spanish comments on what was going on in Alexandria and Constantinople and on the British occupation when that happened. He did so with his usual drama referring to 'the wilful and persistent misrepresentation of the action of Her Majesty's Government, the base motives assigned to the acts of our public servants, civil and military, and the coarse invective daily heaped upon us'.[5] Nor had he anything to say on Africa until, at the very end of 1884, something at last came his way. One is reminded of the communication made to him at Lisbon by M. Glinka and it is again difficult to tell how much importance to attach to Morier's dispatch. But the

---

[1] To Granville, no. 38 confidential, 15 Mar. 1884, F.O. 72/1678.
[2] To Granville, no. 94 commercial, 30 Nov. 1883, F.O. 72/1663.
[3] To Granville, no. 137 commercial, 18 Oct. 1882, F.O. 72/1636.
[4] To Granville, no. 7, 10 Jan. 1883, F.O. 72/1664.
[5] To Granville, no. 126, 20 Oct. 1882, F.O. 72/1618.

indication of Bismarck's motives it contains was certainly one part of the truth. The dispatch[1] begins characteristically: 'I have obtained information from a most confidential but entirely reliable source.' It went on to ascribe to Bismarck, not speculatively but as based on authentic information, the intention of using the West Africa Conference, in session in Berlin from November 1883 to February 1884, 'to break up the alliance between France and England and then to draw France into the net of his policy'. The French were to be 'bribed' by the offer of 'spoils' from 'the far scattered English colonial Empire'. This was the kernel of what Morier had to communicate. It anticipated the conclusions of the first modern historical analysis of the motives for Bismarck's bid for colonies.[2] Two further paragraphs illustrate Morier's characteristic standpoint and manner:

The Congo Conference which, if it really meant what it pretends to mean, would be the first step in a new civilizing direction, of international goodwill and co-operation, of commercial liberty and free trade, has no such meaning, but it is the first step in a well-matured plan of the Chancellor's for carrying out the idea which has never left him, of establishing European peace on a co-operation of despoilment between Germany and France . . .

The Congo Conference has for its object to show the identity of German and French interests and to bring out the antagonism between the new sprung German commercial ambition and your [i.e. the British, he is quoting his informant] old established commercial position all over the globe.

On the credit side also was Morier's skill in advising the Crown Prince during his visit to Madrid in 1883. He succeeded in keeping him off political subjects and earned praise from the Queen.[3]

There were real grounds for Foreign Office irritation with Morier during the first phase of the commercial negotiations, because he went beyond his instructions. The complaint against him had not been pressed. But he continued careless and in 1884 found himself in breach of official regulations by

[1] To Granville, no. 134 secret, 24 Nov. 1884, F.O. 72/1679.
[2] A. J. P. Taylor, *Germany's First Bid for Colonies, 1884–1885* (1938).
[3] See exchanges between Ponsonby and the Queen, 10 Dec. 1883, R.A. Add. MS. A 12/179.

going on leave before Fane, who had been away from Madrid, returned to take charge. Morier presented the second secretary, de Bunsen, as his chargé d'affaires to the Spanish foreign minister, and the Foreign Office drew his attention to his breach of regulations.[1] The protocol of December 1883 was carelessly drafted—phrases such as 'trade and commerce' contrasting with the excellent first paragraph and first and seventh stipulations which were 'well put'.[2] Again and again the readers of his dispatches marked Morier's odd phrases and, once at least, Gladstone did so. His distinctive pencil marks crossed through the unnecessary 'al' in his phrase 'transcendental importance'.[3] By some fluke he once wrote of the Spanish ministry that it was 'as much in earnest in the determination to bring about a Free Trade result in the *wildest* acceptation of the term, as we are ourselves'. He was at once taken up. I think it is Childers's pencil that wrote here, 'I suppose he means *widest*, but the mistake is not unnatural in him.'[4] Just before Morier signed the protocol of 1 December, Childers found his telegrams 'so confused and inconsistent that we may find ourselves in a serious scrape'. He strongly advised that someone should be sent at once to Madrid to 'help Morier (and to keep him out of scrapes)'.[5] It is clear from the other minutes and correspondence that this was no new idea and that sending J. A. Crowe, who acted as commercial attaché in Paris and Berlin, had already been discussed. Crowe was the only commercial attaché then appointed by Britain and had his hands full with the French negotiations.

Morier had not named Crowe as a possible member of the proposed mixed commission for the Spanish negotiation; for his mind had ranged far ahead of the success, which he then thought already his, to a scheme to supplement it by a negotiation with Portugal, and he designed Crowe to conduct this.[4]

One must conclude that Morier's final failure in Madrid happened because he had repeated on a larger scale the mistake

[1] From Granville, draft, 2 Feb. 1884, F.O. 72/1677.
[2] From Granville, telegram, 29 Nov. 1883, F.O. 72/1663.
[3] To Granville, no. 73 commercial, secret, 8 Nov. 1883, F.O. 72/1663.
[4] To Granville, no. 94 commercial, 30 Nov. 1883, F.O. 72/1663.
[5] Minute by Childers, 22 Nov. 1883, following draft of Granville to Morier, no. 114 commercial, 26 Nov. 1883, F.O. 72/1663.

he had made in Lisbon and once already in Madrid, of pushing men further than they wished to go. This time he had, by presenting the situation as an 'emergency,' over-persuaded both his own government and the Spanish into signing a protocol and declaration that neither positively wanted. The short three weeks of the negotiation were not due to efficiency, but to Morier's disastrous method of rushing men to a conclusion lest their real interest, in not giving him exactly what he wanted, should come to the surface. One would need to quote *in toto* the series of telegrams from April to May 1882 and again of November 1883 to prove the mounting urgency with which Morier presented what he wanted both to his own government and to the Spanish. The series would also show how, in the end, he rushed both into doing what the Spanish Cortes at least was not prepared to ratify, though his own government would have gladly accepted most-favoured-nation treatment had Morier really been able to get it for British trade, without pledging his government to do anything more than express intentions which it remained for Parliament to fulfil. The opening of one telegram may stand for all, 'Immediately endeavoured, though it was late at night to find His Excellency . . .' Morier had received authority by telegraph to go ahead with the negotiation of the protocol. He rushed at once to the Spanish Foreign Office. Needless to say there was no one there. Disappointed, he left a message that 'he had a pressing communication to make and would call again next morning'.[1] He had gained nothing and would have made a better beginning had he acted more slowly. But he might then have had to hear views which differed from his own and could not have been overridden.

The truth behind Morier's failure at Madrid was partly that it followed upon a loss of confidence in his abilities that his experiences at Lisbon caused. The natural resilience of an exuberant nature meant that he tried desperately to obtain a success of some kind in order to redress the disappointment there. Morier was a man made on too big a scale, physically as well as mentally, to take a check. But he was without the supreme excellence of abilities to match the scale on which he

[1] To Granville, no. 79 commercial, secret, recording this telegram, 13 Nov. 1883, F.O. 72/1663.

was made. He never had the penetration to match his fertility of mind; nor the reasoning power to match his imaginative power; or perhaps it was simply that he never had the calmness of temperament to enable him to control and deploy the abilities, the intelligence and imagination, that he had to the best advantage.

7

ST. PETERSBURG, 1885 TO 1893

Leningrad, or St. Petersburg as it then was called, was a city with a low skyline following the silhouette of stone buildings. The fortress, the Admiralty, the palaces, the ministries, embassies, and private mansions were aligned along the curve of the Neva. Within the curve the city was chequered with paved squares and cut by the fine vistas of the wide 'prospekts'. It had a cold grandeur and much formality. Morier arrived there on 6 November 1885. The winter was not unpleasant, but late in the spring the melting of the ice brought tension, the settled discomfort of fog and damp, and what was to prove an annual bout of feverish illness. Morier came to think of it as a city dominated by its river which he grew to dislike and fear. Russia outside the city, even after he acquired a country property and had travelled in the Crimea, remained to him a mystery. When he understood it at all he did so as one understands something one has read about and not directly experienced. Portugal, and even Spain, he had known more intimately. His work in Russia was intellectual. It was human only in so far as he saw Russia through the minds of those who governed her.

He began his new work with the same warm eagerness and surrender to whatever it should demand of him as he had shown in Lisbon in 1876. The differences were that he had learnt that he could not expect to make what he believed to be right policy prevail by the mere power of his own eloquence, and that he would work with old acquaintances however new the surroundings. He could not expect in Russia any progressive movement to which his liberal sympathies might attach themselves. The reforming period associated with Loris-Melikov was over. Alexander II on the eve of his assassination (1/14 March 1881) had given his assent to Loris-Melikov's proposed reforms which

Morier mistakenly thought amounted to a parliamentary constitution. Alexander III had summoned a conference of ministers and high officials to consider them, but in the end had proclaimed his intention to maintain the old autocracy. Eight years later, in 1889, Morier had occasion to report that the constitutional movement had evaporated and was not likely to be revived.[1] Nor was Morier confronted with an externally aggressive power, such as Russia had been under Nicholas I, boldly pushing towards Constantinople and India. The superficial passivity of Russia at the beginning of Alexander III's reign and throughout Morier's period was remarkable as well as baffling. Morier explained it by the Tsar's imperfect control over the impulses behind Russian policy. St. Petersburg represented western or German impulses: peaceful, fair-minded, and co-operative. Moscow represented eastern impulses: assertive, acquisitive, and masterful.[2] These impulses played upon a Tsar who practised the general virtues of integrity, loyalty, courage, and moderation rather than the special virtues belonging to kingship and authority. He had much intelligent good sense, but he had neither the military virtues of a good general nor the civil virtues of a good statesman. He had an autocrat's pride of race without an autocrat's appreciation and understanding of power.[3] He lived in the shadow of assassination and in the consciousness of the impending social catastrophe to which Nihilist plots, Jewish pogroms, and the agitation of the literate proletariat seemed to point.[4] Railways and industries were already breaking up the old social immobility as if in preparation for the catastrophe.

Morier's view of the conflicting impulses playing upon the Tsar was a common one and finds its parallel in Russians' comments on their own government. He was more out of the way in his information on the personalities of the government. The Tsar's surroundings, outside the family circle, were

[1] To Salisbury, no. 140 very secret, 25 Apr. 1889, F.O. 65/1361.

[2] To Rosebery, no. 149, 19 Apr. 1886, F.O. 65/1258; to Salisbury, no. 314 confidential, 8 Sept. 1886, F.O. 65/1261; to Salisbury, no. 197 secret, 30 May 1888, F.O. 65/1330.

[3] This account is culled from detached comments on Alexander III scattered through Morier's private letters and dispatches throughout his period at St. Petersburg.

[4] To Salisbury, private, 19 Nov. 1885; no. 384c secret and confidential, 11 Nov. 1885, F.O. 65/1218.

circumscribed by the court headed by Prince Vorontsov-Dachkov—a great aristocrat but one free from Muscovite leanings. Beyond the court the Tsar relied on the Council of the Empire, a body of the greatest dignity, including Grand Dukes and elder statesmen, ministers, and, indeed, anyone whom the Tsar chose to summon. Its advice was rarely asked for, but solemnly given when required. Its debates could be highly important because it was the theatre where eastern and western impulses clashed. For day-to-day advice the Tsar looked to the committee of ministers which, after the reorganization of 1891, was a body of fifteen men, sometimes said to resemble a western cabinet. So long as the collegiate system prevailed in the ministries and so long as there was no parliament, the resemblance was slight. Indeed, Morier found it difficult to describe the relationship between ministers and crown convincingly. The ministers showed a devotion to the Tsar that it was difficult for western minds to accept.[1] A man might be dismissed, but a request to be allowed to retire was an act of disloyalty that the Tsar, who liked old servants and old habits, refused to consider and much resented when he was asked to do so. A western European was inclined to infer servility from this combination of devotion and life-long commitment.[2] Morier rightly insisted that it was a wrong inference: 'a high and intelligent sense of public duty' led ministers to shape policies of their own which they hoped in the long run to bring to fruition by however tortuous a course of alternate submission and pressure.[3] Loris-Melikov had been replaced as minister of the interior by Ignatiev who in turn was dismissed in 1882 in order to bring Count Dmitri Tolstoy to power (died 1889). Tolstoy was the leading spirit of the administration of which he was in a sense the head.[1] He was conservative, an aristocrat reluctant to destroy aristocratic institutions yet with much independence. He tempered the policy of russification of the Baltic provinces in the interest of the Lutheran, German-speaking barons against the Russian Orthodox peasants.[4] He was a promoter of peasant self-improvement, showed great

---

[1] To Salisbury, no. 355, 25 Oct. 1888, F.O. 65/1333.
[2] To Rosebery, private, 15 July 1886.
[3] To Salisbury, no. 389, 28 Nov. 1887, F.O. 65/1299.
[4] Hardinge to Salisbury, no. 10 confidential, 12 Jan. 1888, F.O. 65/1329.

confidence in the schools and universities as agents of social stability—he had been minister for education—yet he realized their disturbing potentialities and sought to limit access to the great state schools, established in all the country towns and theoretically open to all. He carried through the reform of local government, intended to promote public spirit among the gentry and the activity of the elected councils, or *zemstva*, in the teeth of the opposition of the Council of the Empire, where Muscovite influences had caused the measure to be twice rejected. Morier did not observe that these reforms cut down the openings for the peasants and increased the power of the gentry over them.[1]

General Vanovski at the Ministry of War embarked upon a far-reaching scheme for the reorganization of the Russian army, the fruits of which could only be harvested after some years. In October 1888 Morier reviewed the military attaché's reports and concluded that he had shown

the steady and systematic manner in which by continuous accretions year by year, 'hastelessly but restlessly'[2] the immense military forces of Russia are being welded into a standing army more than double the size of any other European army, with untold masses of reserves in the background . . . The number of men actually with the colours this year [1888] is 930,000; in two years times the number will normally be over a million.[3]

In the last months of Morier's period at St. Petersburg—after the appointment of Count Witte (1892)—the Ministry of Finance exercised the dominant influence in the government. The contrast was complete between the time when the primacy of foreign policy had been recognized by the bestowal of the title 'chancellor' upon Prince Gorchakov and the years of Count Witte's financial imperialism. In Morier's day a half-way stage was marked by a rough equality between foreign and financial policy. N. Ch. Bunge was a conventional but successful minister of finance from 1881 to 1886. He was succeeded by I. A. Vyshnegradski, who began to raise the status of the Ministry of Finance. The latter was associated with a series of great loans,

---

[1] To Salisbury, no. 33, 5 Feb. 1889, F.O. 65/1360.
[2] He translates a German phrase, 'ohne Hast und ohne Rast', but 'ohne Rast' means 'without a rest', 'ceaselessly', not 'restlessly'.
[3] To Salisbury, no. 364 confidential, 31 Oct. 1888, F.O. 65/1332.

raised in the European money market, and with a number of debt conversions. He used the proceeds for railway building and other projects for which private capital was unavailable or insufficient. He had begun life as a schoolmaster, had made a vast fortune in trade and, owing to the efforts of Mikhail Katkov and K. P. Pobiedonostsev, had been rapidly pushed up in the Russian bureaucracy until he became a member of the Council of the Empire and, at last, minister of finance. His appointment was regarded as a triumph for the Moscow party. His protectionist and reactionary proclivities, however, proved less important than his experience in railway building. Morier described him as 'a man of power, clearness and energy . . . and almost boundless ambition'.[1] He turned out to be a powerful ally of de Giers and supporter of his policy of peace.

Nikolai de Giers was foreign minister from 1882 to 1895. He had many qualities which Morier admired. Morier believed him to be without ambition, thoroughly reliable, true, sincere, and conciliatory. Meeting him at a continental watering-place, then just inside Bohemia, in the summer of 1885, Morier had come 'to the intuitive conviction that here was a man I could trust and that if I trusted him he would trust me'. They agreed to forewarn each other of difficulties and to smooth the path of negotiations between themselves by frankness. They talked there, at Franzensbad, for two hours in an hotel room. Morier looked back afterwards upon de Giers's loyalty and conciliatoriness and believed them unbroken. With de Giers were associated Baron Jomini as second in command and—after his death in 1888—A. Vlangally who, in turn, was succeeded by N. Chichkine. Morier also had to deal with I. A. Zinoviev and N. Kapnist, heads successively of the Asiatic Department in the Foreign Office. Morier described Baron Jomini as the *enfant terrible* of the Foreign Office, the licensed critic whose calculated indiscretions were always useful pointers, if properly interpreted.[2] In 1885 he was 71 years old and a man whose wisdom and knowledge were a steadying rather than an active influence. He was the son of 'a Swiss strategist and military historian', had served Nesselrode and been Gorchakov's 'most important

[1] To Salisbury, no. 24 confidential, 21 Jan. 1887, F.O. 65/1295; but see also below, pp. 318–19.
[2] To Rosebery, private, 26 Apr. 1886.

factotum'. 'Soaked in the world of western diplomacy, of Russia, he knew little or nothing.' He was already virtually replaced by Vlangally. This man was much more stubborn and Russian, both in his sympathies and in his antipathies, than de Giers, but was loyal to his chief and at no time seems to have represented a really conflicting trend.[1] De Giers and Jomini were both Protestants; Vlangally alone was of the Orthodox faith.[2]

Ivan Alekseievich Zinoviev had been Russian representative in Bucharest until July 1876 when he was transferred to Teheran. He became head of the Asiatic Department of the Foreign Office in 1884 and was 'the real workman' in the Afghan negotiations. 'A very able man, who thoroughly understands the work,' wrote Morier, 'but I have been quite unable to fathom him.' The puzzle arose because he was at one and the same time nationalist and a trusted subordinate. Morier was only able to explain him by arguing that he deceived de Giers and was working for the military party underhand.[3]

In 1891 Zinoviev was appointed to Stockholm and Count Kapnist ruled the Asiatic Department in his stead. At the same time Vlangally was appointed to Rome and Chichkine took his place as deputy foreign minister. Morier at first thought Kapnist the abler of the two, but came to like and respect Chichkine, when he realized what a formidable antagonist in negotiation his knowledge made him. They were both, in Morier's phrase, more chauvinist than de Giers, who had, however, placed them where they were as the 'stays and supports of his old age'. Morier reported that de Giers's mental powers were declining in 1892 and 'the note of senility beginning to pronounce itself'.[4] He was disabled by illness for most of that year, but had recovered by 1893.

These were all men who might be said to represent the western, peaceful current of social and economic development in Russia. The committee of ministers also contained representatives of the Muscovite, Orthodox current. The Procurator-General of the Holy Synod, K. P. Pobiedonostsev, was

---

[1] To Salisbury, no. 148 secret, 18 Apr. 1888, F.O. 65/1329.
[2] To Rosebery, private, 26 Apr. 1886.
[3] To Iddesleigh, private, 12 Aug. 1886.
[4] To Salisbury, no. 27 confidential, 27 Jan. 1892, F.O. 65/1435.

prominent among these and was said to have great influence with the Tsar. Morier once said he was 'in some ways the most important of the Russian ministers'.[1] His reputation for Muscovite fanaticism was derived from the force with which he upheld the political influence of the Church. He believed that Orthodoxy and Tsarism must stand together in the great battle against the Revolution. For him parliamentary government was the 'great lie of our time'. He was a man of sincerity, high character, and great cultivation of mind. Morier reported his friendship with Dean Stanley and his command of Anglican theology and English literature to illustrate the breadth of his sympathies.[2] Count Delianov, the minister for public instruction, appears sometimes to have sided with Pobiedonostsev.

The principal Muscovite pressure came from the army and the bureaucracy and, to some extent, from the universities of St. Petersburg, Moscow, and Kiev. Morier reported that in the army Muscovite ideas were formulated into policy and sometimes into action. The ideas themselves sprang up and found support in the universities and bureaucracy. The first leader of the Panslavs, Ivan Aksakov, had been a country gentleman of exceptional personality, but he had been supported by the professors of St. Petersburg and Moscow universities. His newspaper had been the principal vehicle for spreading his ideas. Something of his idealism still lingered and there were still those who talked of Russia as the servant of the Slavs, their liberator and protector. But the followers of Mikhail Katkov[3] (1818–87) were more important in the Muscovite party during Morier's period. Katkov had been a student and then (1843–50) professor of philosophy at Moscow university. He was from 1850 to 1887 editor of the *Moscow Gazette* which he made the principal organ of Panslavism. It enjoyed, as those newspapers which avoided any allusion to domestic affairs normally did, almost complete immunity from the censorship. He was the protagonist of an imperialist, nationalist, and assertive policy of Russia for the Russians, standing shoulder to shoulder with France against Germany. The mysterious and enormous sums of money of which the party was able to dispose, in order to

[1] To Salisbury, no. 439, 17 Dec. 1886, F.O. 65/1263.
[2] To Salisbury, no. 313 very confidential, 12 Sept. 1887, F.O. 65/1298.
[3] To Salisbury, no. 270, 5 Aug. 1887, F.O. 65/1298.

provoke Panslavist solidarity among soldiers and civilians, came from a limited number of very wealthy merchants of Moscow who, being possessed of great wealth and living simply in an old-fashioned way, had no use for their money and no enthusiasm beyond a blind will that Russia should reassert herself as the Russia of the past. Katkov had levied fabulous sums from them.[1] General Obruchev, Chief of the General Staff, was the leading Panslav among the generals.

Morier's colleagues in St. Petersburg constituted a small and close-knit group in which the German element predominated.[2] General von Schweinitz was the doyen of the corps. He had represented Germany at St. Petersburg since 1876 and was to remain there until 1893. His relations with Morier were never warm. Count Wolkenstein, the Austrian ambassador, was from the first on much closer terms with him. By November 1886 he and Morier were on 'very friendly and confidential terms'.[3] The French ambassador, General Appert, who was well liked by the Tsar as an army man and an Orleanist without any of the 'republicanism' which the Tsar hated, was recalled in 1886. There was for some time only a French chargé d'affaires in St. Petersburg because the Tsar refused to accept the man the French wished to nominate in his place; so the Russian ambassador in Paris made a diplomatic retreat to Cannes. In November 1886 the Tsar accepted a diplomat *de carrière*, Count de Laboulaye, who had been Morier's colleague at Lisbon (see above, p. 22). Mohrenheim returned to Paris from Cannes and relations were restored to normal. Morier, who first reported that Laboulaye was an 'amiable man of considerable culture',[4] came later to think less highly of him and unfortunately, at the time when Russia and France were so significantly drawing together in the months before the Franco-Russian *entente*, habitually dismissed him as a man of no influence. 'Un bien pauvre Sire' he called him, and wrote: 'that the French Gov[ernmen]t could have sent such a Representative to St.

[1] To Salisbury, no. 145 secret, 18 Apr. 1888, F.O. 65/1329.
[2] As evidence of this Morier describes 'the complete paralysis of all political life' caused in the court and government by the death of the Emperor William I in the spring of 1888, Morier to Salisbury, no. 102, 21 Mar. 1888, F.O. 65/1329, and no. 162, 2 May 1888, F.O. 65/1330.
[3] To Iddesleigh, no. 401 secret, 13 Nov. 1886, F.O. 65/1262.
[4] To Iddesleigh, no. 392, 4 Nov. 1886, F.O. 65/1262.

P[eters]b[ur]g at such a crisis, is an appalling proof of the political decadence of France. Society had been prepared to receive them with open arms—but in a week's time they were condemned as *petits bourgeois*, incapable of even giving an eatable dinner.'[1] The Italian, Count Greppi, was treated as a nonentity by the Russians and Morier was often at pains to pass on information to him. The sharpening up of Italian foreign policy, which the advent of Francesco Crispi marked, entailed the replacement of Count Greppi by Baron Morochetti in January 1888.

The business of the St. Petersburg embassy was heavy and Morier was obliged to ask for extra assistance. Yet apart from the negotiations over the Russo-Afghan frontier and later the Russo-Afghan-Chinese frontier, which were anyhow mostly the concern of experts on the spot, there was no single negotiation to compare with the African negotiations carried on with Germany and France, the Egyptian and Bulgarian negotiations at Constantinople, or even the Mediterranean and Balkan negotiations carried on in Rome and Vienna. There were long periods in 1888 and in 1889 when the political dispatches shrank to half the quantity coming from other embassies. A minor reason why the post was an onerous one was that official entertaining was long and exacting. A more important reason was the detail in which the contents of the press were reported. From other capitals there were parliamentary proceedings to report. There were none to report from St. Petersburg, but reporting the contents of the eight leading St. Petersburg newspapers[2] more than made up for this. Because the press was controlled, newspaper articles were an important indication of the direction in which the government sought to guide public opinion. Because the autocracy was open to the pressure of public opinion in foreign policy, newspaper articles indicated the way in which government policy might develop. Moreover, it was in the newspapers that laws, proclamations, regulations, and the Russian equivalent of budget and annual estimates

[1] To Salisbury, private, 10 Mar. 1887, Morier papers; Salisbury papers, A/73, fo. 15.
[2] See memorandum by Col. Herbert, Jan. 1887, F.O. 65/1295. *Isvestia, Novoe Vremia, St. Petersburg Gazette, Moscow Gazette, Svet, Russkaia Gazeta, Novosti, Grazhdanin.* In addition there were the *Herold* (printed in German) and the *Journal de St. Petersburg* (printed in French) for foreigners.

were published. A command of the Russian language was still a rare accomplishment, which Morier himself did not possess, nor was he able to use, he said, 'outsiders, newspaper correspondents and the like' as was done in other embassies.[1] The mere work of summarizing the contents of the daily press represented, therefore, an amount of labour for the embassy staff to which the précis themselves scarcely did justice.

The watching of Russian military and naval developments was essential and difficult and was another reason why the post was arduous. Morier exercised a general supervision over Lieutenant-Colonel I. Herbert's journeys and conclusions. Herbert succeeded Colonel Trench as military attaché in 1886. A naval attaché Morier had asked for but failed to acquire.[2] The main reason, however, why work was so heavy was that Morier lent himself to a number of activities which were not diplomatic in character. He argued at great length with Salisbury on policy; he cultivated his connections with Germany —he regularly saw Roggenbach at Cologne on his way from England to Russia—and continued to build up his indictment of Bismarck until the climax came in the Bazaine incident which put him entirely on the defensive; finally he promoted the opening up of Siberia. All this entailed a stupendous amount of penmanship by himself and deciphering (his handwriting was almost impossible to read as it got smaller towards the end of a long letter) and copying by the secretaries.

The formal business, which at one time amounted to no more than attending de Giers's weekly receptions and reporting his conversation with the foreign minister, was not exacting. Morier had, moreover, the services of an outstandingly able group of men. The Hon. T. Grosvenor was an able first secretary, but he died in November 1886. H. N. Dering, A. C. Gosling, and Henry Howard then succeeded in turn to the post. The two most outstanding men were Arthur Hardinge and Charles Eliot. Hardinge, it will be recalled, had been with Morier at Madrid. He had also been précis writer (virtually a private secretary) to Salisbury (1885-6) and was to act again as private secretary to him in 1890-2. He was second secretary at

[1] To Salisbury, no. 97, 8 Mar. 1888, F.O. 65/1330.
[2] To Rosebery, no. 166, 6 May 1886, F.O. 65/1258; to Rosebery, private, 6 May 1886.

St. Petersburg from 1886 to 1889 when E. Thornton replaced him. Charles Eliot was third secretary from 1887 to 1893. F. D. Harford and Arthur Peel acted first as attachés and then as third secretaries, and Walter Ralegh Kerr was an honorary attaché. E. G. F. Law was employed to report on the social, economic, and financial condition of Russia. Morier called him his commercial adviser.[1] His short and able accounts were a channel of information to the British public as well as to the government.[2]

In the Foreign Office, Lord Tenterden had retired from the permanent under-secretaryship (1882) while Morier was in Madrid. Sir Julian Pauncefote reigned in his stead, until he was appointed in 1889 to Washington. Philip Currie and Thomas Sanderson were assistant under-secretaries and Eric Barrington was Salisbury's private secretary. With all of them and with Sir Henry Ponsonby, Morier kept up a continuous flow of private letters. He wrote to colleagues, to Sir Frank Lascelles at Teheran, for example, as well as to Sir William White. He corresponded with Lord Randolph Churchill, when he was chancellor of the exchequer, and with Lord Dufferin, when he was Viceroy of India.

If Morier moved among striking unrealities in Russia he was yet nearer reality than successive foreign secretaries in London. This the Bulgarian and Batum questions showed clearly enough; since they were treated from London as if Alexander II or even indeed Nicholas I were still in power in Russia. The tasks of an ambassador at this date were to negotiate, to inform, and to conciliate. Morier had little to do for the first, much for the second, and most for the third. And he sought as at Lisbon to find some basic proposition from which he could begin. His mind, he wrote, was an

absolute blank about Russian politics. I have never been able to occupy myself seriously with any business excepting that of the post for which I have been responsible. I absorb myself absolutely in the work I cut out for myself in the country where I represent Her Majesty's Government—a bad habit, as this work has invariably been far beyond the range of Downing Street eyes and has

[1] To Salisbury, private, 6 Jan. 1890.
[2] See for example E. G. F. Law, 'The Present Condition of Russia', *Fortnightly Review*, xxxi (1882), 453–67.

consequently resulted in exhausting friction with my commanding officers, leaving me no time to follow what was going on elsewhere. I therefore had no *parti pris* of any kind in regard to Russia and only a vague kind of Russophobia which is the natural inheritance of every living Englishman . . . When in the autumn of 1885 I was preparing to start for my new post, the first *grande politique* post I had occupied . . . I felt the absolute necessity for a pivotal point on which to rest my policy. By pivotal point I refer to my old axiom that *'diplomacy is the art of using the force of war in posse to avoid the calamity of war in esse'*. I was determined, therefore, if possible to get Downing Street to tell me exactly the point at which I was authorized to pull off my coat.[1]

Since the only diplomatic question standing then for settlement between Britain and Russia was that of the relationship between Britain's 'ally' Afghanistan and Russian Turkestan—the so-called Central Asian question—Morier addressed himself to this. He sought to know exactly at what point Britain would call a halt to the advance of Russian power. But his endeavours misfired. The trouble about a preference for *une situation nette*—such as Morier's direct question, would Great Britain fight Russia for Herat, was intended to produce—is that definition excludes as well as includes. In this instance the question prompted—after a tussle—an instruction to the chargé d'affaires at St. Petersburg to warn Russia that a Russian advance into the valley of Herat would justly constitute a *casus belli* between Britain and Russia. The large question of the premisses of policy was ignored. The warning was delivered *à propos de rien* and was met with a well-deserved snub.[2] Meanwhile Morier was no nearer the authoritative definition of basic assumptions which he sought. Yet these inevitably worded themselves in his mind. He formulated at least one: 'If Panslavist dreams attempted to shape themselves into Pan-

[1] To Goschen, 2 June 1888, from which the following account is also taken.

[2] This is Morier's version, recorded in his letter to Goschen (2 June 1888), of an incident reported in Grosvenor to Salisbury, no. 336 confidential, 6 Oct. 1885, F.O. 65/1251. Salisbury's instruction to Grosvenor relates the warning precisely to the successful conclusion by the protocol of 10 Sept. of one phase of the Afghan negotiations (to Grosvenor, no. 336 confidential, 11 Sept. 1885, F.O. 65/1250). It was not, therefore, a warning delivered quite *à propos de rien*. The Russian minister expressed surprise, and when Grosvenor, in pursuit of his instructions, disclaimed all suspicion of Russia's present intentions, he turned the conversation. But there was no particularly marked snub.

slavist action, there were two *casus belli* staring us in the face. Any movement on Constantinople would bring up the British fleet to the rescue. One Cossack pony's head deliberately turned towards Herat would compel me to ask for my passports.' He then turned the image, which he thus held before his mind, the other way up and looked at peace instead of war.

Let us say that a generation or perhaps even less passed by during which we had earnestly co-operated in together keeping the Asian peace, had cultivated close commercial relations and joined the two empires by the railway which according to General Ammenkov would give us a nine days' overland route to India and it would require no prophet to show that the whole attitude of public opinion in regard to Russia's European position would be radically changed.

It was to this act of conciliation that Morier bent his energies. His objectives would be co-operation with Russia in Asia— recognizing 'our joint "cultur" mission'—and co-operation with Russia in Europe in order to keep the Turk alive while there was breath in him, and 'euthanasia for the Turk when his appointed race is run'.[1] So he would remove 'the malformations' from Anglo-Russian as he had sought to remove them from Anglo-Portuguese relations. The disastrous outcome of this approach to his new work was that he came to be thought of—not without justice—by his own government and by the Queen as a better spokesman for Russia in London than ever he was for Britain in St. Petersburg.

[1] To Goschen, 2 June 1888.

8

BULGARIA AND BATUM, 1885 TO 1887

IN the autumn of 1885 Russia and Britain confronted each other over a Turkish question for the third time since the mid century. Lord Salisbury, prime minister and foreign secretary from June 1885 to January 1886, thought Russia meant war. 'We have ... reason to believe', he wrote privately to Morier 'that Giers himself assured a foreign Ambassador at St. Petersburg that if the present [Conservative] Government remained in office after the elections [due in December 1885], the Russian Government would prepare for immediate war. There is no doubt that preparations are going on, as far as we can see, with uninterrupted effort.'[1] He was writing two days before Eastern Rumelia proclaimed its reunion with Bulgaria. After the revolution and the achievement of the Big Bulgaria whose creation Britain and Austria-Hungary had foiled in 1876–8, Salisbury behaved as if he wished to defy Russia to attack Britain. He deliberately prevented a real common front of the six Powers—'la politique comme au congrès de Vienne'[2] —such as would save Russia's face if she aimed at avoiding war with Britain. He wished, indeed, that military preparations might take their toll of Russia's embarrassed resources. Russia was 'really invulnerable to military attack' from Britain, who in fighting her must therefore have the temerity to make an undermining approach. 'We must lead her into all the expense we can in the conviction that with her the limit of taxation has been almost reached, and that only a few steps further must push her into the revolution over which she seems continually

---

[1] From Salisbury, private, 16 Sept. 1885; cf. Lady Gwendolen Cecil, *The Life of Robert Marquis of Salisbury* (1921–31), iii. 231, 249.
[2] *Documents diplomatiques français* (Paris, 1929–62), I. vi. 94.

to be hanging.'[1] Some eight years later Count Witte, by boldly restoring Russia's finances, made Salisbury's plan look less promising, but for nearly six months in 1885–6 it governed the course of Anglo-Russian relations.

The Treaty of Berlin of which Salisbury, as foreign secretary in 1878, had been a chief architect had separated Eastern Rumelia from Bulgaria. The latter under Alexander of Battenberg paid tribute to Turkey, but was otherwise independent; the former, the province south of the Balkans, was governed by a Christian governor under a European-devised and guaranteed statute but was still part of Turkey. Turkey, as sovereign over both, could perfectly well have sent troops into Eastern Rumelia after the revolution of 18 September, and taken possession before sufficient forces had rallied to the defence of united Bulgaria. She, however, had no reason of general policy to intervene. Her sovereignty and her tribute were assured to her when Prince Alexander, having proclaimed himself prince of united Bulgaria, also proclaimed his continued loyalty to his sovereign (21 September). Nor had she any reason of immediate policy to intervene, since Alexander had acted so quickly—he had gone to Philippopolis (now Plovdiv) already on the evening of 18 September—that there was no real disturbance of the peace. The Turkish council of ministers in session all day on the 20th, though it might look merely weak, was wise in its inaction.

The Russian court, despite its close connection with Bulgaria, seems to have been taken by surprise. Alexander III was at Copenhagen with his father-in-law, Christian IX, and did not return to St. Petersburg until 21 October. De Giers was at Marienbad, a watering-place just within Bohemia (now Marianske Lasne in Czechoslovakia). He travelled to Copenhagen, visiting Bismarck on the way[2] (29 September), but only returned to St. Petersburg, again going by way of Bismarck's country residence, on 11 October. General Vanovski and N. Ch. Bunge, like the European ambassadors, including Morier who did not arrive till November, were away and did not hasten to return. The Tsar acted, it was said, under the influence of Aleksandr Nelidov, his ambassador in Constantinople,

---

[1] From Salisbury, private, 16 Sept. 1885.
[2] *Die große Politik der europäischen Kabinette* (Berlin, 1922–7), v. 7 n.

a typical Muscovite champion of an active and ambitious eastern policy, and he was stiffened by his own mistrust of the Bulgarian prince. He publicly dissociated himself from Prince Alexander's action, called home the Russian officers of the Bulgarian army, and instructed Prince Cantacuzene to resign from the Bulgarian Ministry of War and limit himself to his other office of Russian agent and consul-general in Sofia.[1] De Giers in a circular dispatch to the Russian representatives with the Great Powers went no further than to insist that 'the Bulgarian question be kept within the domain of European diplomatic action'.[2] But Russia steadfastly refused to accept the union and, doggedly saying she sought to restore the *status quo ante* September, yet took no active steps to enforce the Treaty of Berlin.

As far as Britain was concerned, Salisbury declined Bismarck's proposal of collective warnings to Serbia, Montenegro, and Greece that they should not disturb the peace; refused his invitation to send the British fleet to the Piraeus, and rejected his overtures for a full-dress European conference which should summon Bulgaria to withdraw from Eastern Rumelia and itself take on the regulation of its future.[3] He proclaimed to the French ambassador Britain's inability to associate herself 'à un écrasement des jeunes races chrétiennes dans les Balkans',[4] and to the Russians insisted 'that any absolute repression of the Bulgarian and Roumeliote populations would be contrary to the traditions of this country' and, moreover, 'impolitic inasmuch as it would be equivalent to an intimation to the populations of both Provinces that when next they make a move of union, they must before taking action come to a preliminary understanding with the Serbian and Greek Govts. as to the seizure of compensation for those countries out of Ottoman territory'.[5] His ultimate object was both to maintain the authority of the Berlin settlement and to accommodate the union to it. Prince Alexander should be accepted as the Christian governor of Rumelia, provided for by the Treaty of Berlin, and some

---

[1] Salisbury to Grosvenor, no. 355, 22 Sept., reporting communication from the Russian chargé d'affaires in London (Boutiniev), F.O. 65/1215.
[2] Salisbury to Grosvenor, no. 350, telegram no. 153, 24 Sept. 1885, F.O. 65/1215.   [3] Cf. from Salisbury, no. 416, 12 Nov. 1885, F.O. 65/1215.
[4] *Documents diplomatiques français*, I. vi. 94.
[5] Salisbury to Grosvenor, no. 462, telegram no. 202, 2 Nov. 1855, F.O. 65/1215.

adjustments made in the statute under which it was governed. The Powers should induce Turkey to accept this personal union. It was thus clear—Salisbury wrote to Morier who had only arrived on 6 November in St. Petersburg—that 'the knot of the difficulty... lay in the difference between the views entertained by the Russian and English governments'.[1]

Morier's purpose, however, was to make the incident play a part in the attempt to improve Anglo-Russian relations to which he had committed himself. Nearly three years after the event he set down his recollections:

I returned to England [after meeting de Giers at Franzensbad in August] and found the F.O. under the conviction that the Philippopolis revolution had been planned by Russian agents and was an unmasking of the Russian batteries. I expressed my conviction that such was not the case... When it was discovered that the Emp[ero]r was acting in perfect good faith in repudiating the action of the Philippopolis revolutionaries and Prince Alexander... we made an unblushing right-about-face and went in for Revolution and Prince Alexander, a G.O.M. [i.e. Gladstonian—an allusion to Gladstone's attitude over the Bulgarian massacres in 1876] Bulgaria.

Such was the situation when I joined my post on the 6th of Nov. 85. I was full of my contract with Giers... I would obey my instructions not only in the letter but the spirit, but not make myself the champion of Prince Alexander or be enthusiastic about infant liberties and such like. I took soundings at the F.O. to discover whether this was a line approved of and I was told it was, but I soon found out this was far from being the case higher up [i.e. with the Queen, see Hardinge to Morier, 24 Nov. 1885]. But I stuck to my guns and loyally carried out my contract with Giers—namely always to put the Russian case absolutely fairly and without bias before my employers.[2]

As long as Salisbury remained in office, despite his unshaken conviction that the knot of the Bulgarian question was a conflict between British and Russian views, Morier had his co-operation in conducting intricate negotiations in St. Petersburg to the greatest advantage possible in the circumstances for Anglo-Russian relations. Salisbury's action Morier thought so in harmony with the eternal logic of things that any momentary friction would be forgotten when its rightness was appreciated.[3]

---

[1] From Salisbury, no. 416, 12 Nov. 1885, F.O. 65/1215.
[2] To Goschen, 2 June 1888.   [3] To Salisbury, private, 14 Dec. 1885.

Meanwhile, to resume the narrative, under Bismarck's pressure all the Powers had agreed to the ambassadors meeting in informal conference at Constantinople (4 October) and to their accepting the appeal—a piece of hollow politeness—of the Sultan 'to intervene in order to bring to an end the troubles which divide one of the provinces of his Empire and in order to re-establish order and prosperity there'.[1] The decisions which they reached were published on 22 November.[2] They were never put into effect. The Turkish commissioner and the European delegates to assist him, who were to deal with the grievances of Eastern Rumelia, were never nominated. The Bulgarians were proving quite capable of managing their own affairs. The conference had just been conventional procedure and had nothing to do with this—the one reality in the situation. Its only value was that it had allowed the Great Powers time to adjust themselves while war and a three-day battle finally vindicated the union. King Milan of Serbia declared war on Prince Alexander on 14 November and was soundly defeated at Slivnitsa on 17–19 November. United Bulgaria proved herself the viable state she claimed to be and was apparently capable herself of imposing peace in the Balkan peninsula. No one could now pretend, wrote Morier in one of his early dispatches, that Prince Alexander was 'the supposed tool of an anarchic and revolutionary faction', nor could anyone expect to undo the union of 'a nation conscious of its strength and determined to fight for its existence'.[3] By 21 December it seemed likely that Russia would give way[4] and by 23 December she had done so. De Staal to Salisbury (in London) and de Giers to Morier admitted frankly that the union, which Slivnitsa showed clearly to be a fact, would have to be maintained.[5] 'It exists *de facto*, its existence must be regularized, and some formula must be found to do this.'[6] 'The issue', Salisbury wrote to Morier, 'from the beginning to the end under various forms has

[1] Declaration of 13 Oct., *Documents diplomatiques français*, I. vi. 5.
[2] *Die große Politik der europäischen Kabinette*, vi. 17.
[3] To Salisbury, no. 405A confidential, 26 Nov. 1885, F.O. 65/1219.
[4] To Salisbury, no. 435 secret, 21 Dec. 1885, no. 436 confidential, 23 Dec. 1885, F.O. 65/1219.
[5] C. L. Smith, *The Embassy of Sir William White at Constantinople* (1957), p. 35.
[6] To Salisbury, no. 436 confidential and telegram no. 77, 23 Dec. 1885, F.O. 65/1219.

been whether we would or would not pledge ourselves against any alteration of the Treaty of Berlin. We have steadfastly declined to do so until some account had been taken of the desires of the inhabitants of the provinces concerned.'[1] A European military commission to assist in the negotiation of peace between Bulgaria and Serbia was now appointed. Like the Constantinople conference its function was to save the face of the 'concert of Europe'. But Salisbury and de Giers, despite Russia's acceptance of the union, remained as much opposed to each other as before.

There were now two subjects of negotiation: Balkan disarmament and Turco-Bulgarian terms of agreement. Russia was alarmed by a considerable Turkish force (said in February 1886 to number 150,000 men) in Macedonia. She took the lead in proposing a collective summons to disarm to be made by the Great Powers to Bulgaria, to Serbia, and to Greece, who in December had come forward with demands for Macedonian territory. Her object was by their disarmament to induce Turkey also to demobilize. Britain accepted the Russian proposal. The joint summons was made, but it was ignored. De Giers next proposed a second collective summons accompanied by a wordy warning that the Powers would declare (1) their readiness to take the side of any attacked Balkan state, (2) their determination to pronounce themselves against the aggressor, and (3) their resolution to prevent changes in the territorial settlement of Berlin. It was this proposal which disclosed anew the essential antagonism of the British and Russian attitudes. If this proposal meant anything at all, it meant, as the earlier one did not, measures of force, say, against Serbia attacking Bulgaria. In theory, as Morier saw, 'we should all be bound to defend her, but in practice the role would necessarily fall to Russia. But if Russia entered Bulgaria, Austria would have to enter Serbia'.[2] The spectre of Austro-Russian war thus stood between Russia and Britain. For although Salisbury wished to encourage Russia's readiness for war and her military preparations, he worked to avoid the actual event of a Russian war, whether against Austria-Hungary or Britain. Salisbury,

---

[1] From Salisbury, private, 2 Dec. 1885; see also Lady Gwendolen Cecil, *Life of Salisbury*, iii. 249.
[2] To Salisbury, no. 21 confidential, 21 Jan. 1886, F.O. 65/1256.

therefore, rejected the Russian proposal, if it meant 'that the antagonism threatened by the Powers against any aggressor [must be] taken as necessarily assuming a material form'.[1]

A proposal of his own, however, crossed with that of de Giers. Both proposals were made on 20 January. Salisbury's, which already had German support, was drafted by him at Hatfield in the morning and telegraphed to Morier at 1.40 p.m.[2] Morier telegraphed de Giers's proposal from St. Petersburg just after midnight.[3] Salisbury, had he done so deliberately, could not have timed his own proposal better to gain de Giers's acquiescence and to neutralize in advance the ill effects of his rejection of the Russian. He proposed a separate summons by each Power to Greece with an uncompromising notification that their navies would prevent a Greek naval attack upon Turkey. De Giers, though taken aback by the decided character of the British proposal, agreed to it without delay.

Morier had exercised all his formidable persuasive powers to induce Salisbury to make some sign of friendship to Russia without pushing her beyond her attitude of reluctant acquiescence in the union. 'Could we not . . . show that we are ready to co-operate with her in doing that which is right? By doing so in however mild a way we should be removing the myth that all we have had in view was to *contrecarrer* her and to say *yes* when she said *no* and *no* when she said *yes*.'[4] He was delighted with Salisbury's action over Greece. 'Your action in regard to Greece', he wrote, 'has produced the very best effect here. It came wholly unexpectedly and at first startled them but the moment they saw its full portée they were overjoyed.'[5] In drawing the moral Morier as usual sought to make a point in favour of his enduring purpose: the improvement of Anglo-Russian relations. 'The fact of this reception will I think convince you', he concluded, 'that my diagnosis has been right' and that Russia's only wish was to get rid of the Bulgarian question and not to use it against Britain.

Action was suspended by the change of government that installed Lord Rosebery in Lord Salisbury's place (6 February

[1] From Salisbury, no. 23A, 22 Jan. 1886, F.O. 65/1254.
[2] From Salisbury, telegram no. 8, F.O. 65/1264.
[3] To Salisbury, telegram no. 5, 12.25 a.m., 21 Jan. 1886, F.O. 65/1264.
[4] To Salisbury, private, 14 Jan. 1886.
[5] To Salisbury, private, 26 Jan. 1886.

1886). A European blockade of the Greek coast—which was only raised after Greek military and naval demobilization, on 5 June—was, however, the outcome of Salisbury's last step. This blockade, since it was executed under Rosebery's supervision, was not quite what Salisbury had intended. Morier was to find some difficulty in adjusting himself to the changed temper of foreign policy after Rosebery took office. He was a young patrician, though Morier, alluding to his liking for racing, had once called him a stable-boy. He had a propensity to dictate to the foreigner, to moralize, and to claim a monopoly of being right. Salisbury's instructions to the ships assembled in Suda Bay, off the island of Crete, under Admiral Sir John Hay had been worded with great ingenuity. Admiral Hay was only to act if a Greek commander was found *in flagrante delicto*, actually attacking a Turkish squadron, and if the commander continued, after being warned that he would be prevented, in his endeavour to sink or disable ships.[1] Rosebery attempted to use the European ships, not to prevent what they were capable of preventing, but to enforce a demand to disarm. This ships alone, by their mere presence, were not capable of doing. The European ships, if Greece defied their summons to disarm, would look as ridiculous as 'the six washing tubs with flags' of 1880—Salisbury's phrase for the naval demonstration of that year to compel Turkey to yield territory to Montenegro. Rosebery at least prevented a ridiculous outcome when he succeeded in inducing the Powers to agree to a naval blockade empowered to seize ships off the Greek coast instead of a mere demonstration.[2] But the course seemed full of hidden dangers. It was not until 2 April that Rosebery was able to announce his completed plans. Meanwhile the Russian ships, at one point leaving Suda Bay for Syra to revictual, caused Rosebery to protest sharply in fear that Russia was deserting.[3] The ships came back and the negotiations were successfully completed, so that a blockade was established along the east coast, the commanders being

[1] Admiralty to Admiral Hay, 26 Jan. 1886, *Parliamentary Papers* (1886), lxxiv. 565.
[2] Proposed 18 Feb., accepted 21 Feb. 1886; from Rosebery, telegram no. 55, F.O. 65/1264; to Rosebery, telegram no. 27, dispatch no. 69A, F.O. 65/1264, 65/1257.
[3] From Rosebery, telegram, 30 Mar. 1886, F.O. 65/1264; to Rosebery, telegram no. 55, dispatch no. 125, 31 Mar. 1886, F.O. 65/1258.

instructed to seize any Greek vessels under weigh. On 26 April a joint note, making the summons to disarm with a week's ultimatum, was presented, the ships sailing up to the Piraeus at the same time. The ultimatum being rejected, the blockade was established. But there was always a risk that Russia would back out.[1] As it was, France refused to take part, and then Greece tried to save her status as an independent state, and to avoid submitting to the ultimatum, by making a declaration to France that she would disarm. But Rosebery stood firm. Greece capitulated. Rosebery had exacted not only decrees demobilizing army and navy, but their communication to the Powers. The blockade was then raised on 5 June 1886.[2] It was a racecourse gamble that succeeded, but Rosebery with his 'blood and iron policy'[3] ran a risk out of all proportion to the danger he sought to neutralize. He had, however, won his success.

Morier, intent on his purpose of improving Anglo-Russian relations and despite his general sympathy with a 'strong' policy, was with good cause critical. His criticism applied with special force to this naval blockade.

What I consider was the mistake [he wrote in 1888]—one for which Lord Rosebery was mainly responsible—was playing the first fiddle, instead of contenting ourselves with a less prominent part, forgetting that we were the only party who had a great extra-European interest not to push matters to extremities with Russia. Moreover, *me judice*, we contributed more than anyone else to put the question in a wrong perspective by maximising it out of all proportion to its relative importance in regard to the other great questions of European politics . . . We made for Russia, as a bull does in a Spanish arena for the red cape of a Matador. We never left an alternative policy in view and deliberately refused to provide a second string to our bow.[4]

Morier could never shake himself free of the memory of a remark Prince Gorchakov (whom he had met at a watering-place, Wildbad, three years running) had made to him in

[1] See from Rosebery, no. 169, 11 May 1886 for Rosebery's great relief that she joined, F.O. 65/1284.
[2] To Rosebery, no. 196, 2 June 1886, F.O. 65/1259, and *Parliamentary Papers* (1886), lxxiv. 657, 665, 676, 693.
[3] Joseph Chamberlain to Rosebery, 6 Oct. 1886, Rosebery papers, box 63.
[4] To Goschen, 2 June 1888.

1875 to the effect that 'one of Russia's main objects in drawing near to us in India was to make her Asiatic politics react on our European politics', so that 'for every act of nagging on our part at Constantinople there would be a corresponding act of nagging' on the Indian frontier.¹ If Russia's policy might thus compel Britain to weigh the eastern Mediterranean against India, then Morier believed Britain should put India first.² He thought in 1886 Rosebery was endangering India *de gaieté de cœur*.

To continue the narrative, the second subject of negotiation on which Rosebery had to shape a policy was the substance of the Turco-Bulgarian agreement. Salisbury's policy had been to leave Turkey and Bulgaria to come to terms by themselves about the necessary changes in the statute under which Eastern Rumelia was governed. He hoped that the Turks and Bulgarians might thus begin to go hand in hand, themselves keep out the Russians and Austrians, hold back the Greeks and Serbs, and so release Europe from the perpetual threat of a Balkan war, leading to war between the Great Powers. Russia here, too, took an opposite line. Her object was that the Turco-Bulgarian agreement should be made under European mediation and its terms be subject to European acceptance. To maintain European 'rights' in this way was to shield the maintenance of her own claim to interfere.

By February, negotiations between Bulgaria and Turkey had reached the point where a draft agreement could be communicated to the Powers.³ It contained provision for (1) Bulgarian military assistance to Turkey in certain eventualities; (2) Prince Alexander's nomination as governor-general of Eastern Rumelia, which was to continue to pay tribute to Turkey and to be governed under a separate statute as provided for in the Treaty of Berlin; (3) the revision of the statute in order to assimilate the institutions of the two provinces; (4) the incorporation in Eastern Rumelia of Rhodope territory restored to Turkey in 1878. Russia objected to the first three of these provisions, but Morier rightly believed that it was evidence of

[1] Ibid.; cf. to Salisbury, private, 1 Sept. 1885, where Morier writes: ' "pour vous ennuyer en Asie" if you seek to *ennuyer* us in Europe'.
[2] To Ponsonby, 15 Dec. 1885; to Salisbury, private, 19 Nov. 1885; to Rosebery, private, 19 Feb. 1886.
[3] Circular telegram from the Porte to its representatives abroad, 2 Feb. 1886.

her wish to come to terms that she had accepted the retrocession of the Rhodope territory as compensation for concessions on her side.[1] Russia based her objections, firstly, upon the sacrifices she had made in executing her age-old policy of the protection of Christians against Moslems and of their liberation. How could she then tolerate the use by Turkey of Christian troops against, say, Christian Macedonians? She based her objections, secondly, upon the rights of the European Powers under the international settlement of Berlin. Their rights were those of approvers and guarantors of the person of the governor-general and of the terms on which he governed. Russia therefore insisted (1) that Alexander be nominated with European sanction for a term of years and that the sanction be renewed should he be renominated for another term, and (2) that the Powers participate in the revision of the statute.

Rosebery agreed to yield to Russia so far as to attempt to induce Turkey to give up the military clauses. Morier had not waited for Rosebery to begin their private correspondence, but had at once written a private letter to him to urge this concession.[2] Rosebery made it, expecting that Russia might then yield on the position of Prince Alexander and the revision of the statute. With what followed next Morier was not in sympathy, for Rosebery sought in his policy to work with Germany. Rosebery did not appreciate the significance of Salisbury's complex attitude to Bismarck. Rosebery had been responsible in the spring of 1885 for reaching agreement with Bismarck's son, Herbert, on the colonial question in the ironically termed 'Peace of Kensington Gardens', and for bringing to an end the colonial quarrel into which Granville had unguardedly fallen. He wished to continue this association when he himself came to the Foreign Office a year later. He now believed Bismarck had agreed to instruct General Schweinitz to join Morier in pressure at St. Petersburg to yield over the proposed position for Prince Alexander and the revision of the statute.[3] He in fact was outwitted by Bismarck who secretly gave Schweinitz latitude so that he might avoid—as he did—making any such representations lest they imperil Russo-German relations. At the same

[1] To Rosebery, no. 64, 17 Feb. 1886, F.O. 65/1257.
[2] To Rosebery, private, 11 Feb. 1886.
[3] From Rosebery, telegrams nos. 50 and 60, 16 and 19 Feb. 1886, F.O. 65/1264.

time he complained to Sir Edward Malet[1] in Berlin that he had been let down: saying that Schweinitz had been instructed to join in British representations and then found that none were being made; so that when he remonstrated he did so alone. Rosebery was sufficiently hoodwinked to see, in Morier's report of his action on his instructions, full confirmation of Bismarck's charge. He administered a sharp rebuke. 'Inform Sir R. Morier', he wrote, 'that I regret that I cannot see in this despatch any sufficient justification for not fully and effectively carrying out the instructions contained in my telegrams of Feb. 16 and 19 and so promised by him in his telegram No. 21 and beg him in future when he sees serious objections to his doing so to communicate them to me by telegraph.'[2]

The incident is important in Morier's career, since for him it was more evidence, a mounting volume, of Bismarck's intention to break him. He had in fact not pressed his representations and had perfectly good reasons for not doing so. These were the knowledge that the two points on which Russia still insisted constituted a minimum to which the Tsar had been reluctantly reduced by negotiations 'des plus serrées et suivies' with Germany and Austria; and that the acceptance of the Rhodope retrocession had been compensation for concessions made in these negotiations. Thus for Morier to have pressed to the bitter end would have meant both isolating Britain from the Powers, with whom she was supposed to be acting, and courting diplomatic defeat.[3] He might in reporting his action on his instructions have said only that he had executed them. He had, however, unwisely volunteered the additional statements that 'he knew from the first that the attempt' to persuade Russia to yield the two points 'was a hopeless one and that it would be only wasting powder and shot to try seriously to move her to further retrograde steps—whilst the endeavour to do so by rousing the latent sullenness of the Emperor might do much mischief'.[4] This had unjustifiably created the impression that he was not executing his instructions. Morier answered also the charge that, if he was going to press *par acquit de conscience* and

[1] Malet to Rosebery, telegram no. 30, 15 Feb. 1886, F.O. 64/1120.
[2] Rosebery's minute on the docket of Morier's no. 75; a copy of the letter, sent on 3 Mar. in this wording, is in R.A. B 37/24a.
[3] To Rosebery, no. 96 secret, most confidential, 11 Mar. 1886, F.O. 65/1257.
[4] To Rosebery, no. 75 most confidential, 24 Feb. 1886, F.O. 65/1257.

not *à outrance*, he should have telegraphed to say so and asked for guidance. He replied that he could only have telegraphed as his reason that he was not being backed up by Germany.[1] This would have led to explanations in Berlin and, as he rightly thought, have put Rosebery in a worse position than ever. The Foreign Office was obliged to repent, Sanderson writing to Rosebery:[2]

I annex to Sir R. Morier's despatch of explanation [no. 96, above] a private letter which he has written to me [of the 11th, just quoted]. I have no doubt that the Germans were anxious not to put themselves forward in the matter, and I think Sir R. Morier shows that he did more in execution of his instructions than his first despatch [no. 75] showed. The matter might perhaps be allowed to drop. T.H.S.

The minute, 'The matter may be dropped. A. R.[osebery] 16.3.86', closed the incident as an Anglo-German one. Soon afterwards Russia abated her objections a shade further, accepting the nomination of Prince Alexander for an undefined period and renouncing European participation in the revision of the statute; though she still insisted on European sanction to the revised statute. On 5 April a protocol, signed at Constantinople, recorded these decisions.[3]

As a personal incident there were consequences, but not in Morier's relationship with Rosebery though the latter had been much provoked.[4] Part of the sharpness of his rebuke had been due to a simultaneous appearance of revolt from Sir William White, chargé d'affaires at Constantinople, who had sent home a long argument against his instructions to remonstrate with the Turkish government on this same subject.[5] Part of the sharpness had been due to his sensitiveness to anything like disregard.

[1] To Sanderson, private, 11 Mar. 1886.
[2] 15 Mar.; the private letter with this note and Rosebery's minute follow Morier's no. 96 in F.O. 65/1257.
[3] W. L. Langer, *European Alliances and Alignments, 1871-90* (New York, 1950), p. 357.
[4] Sir Edward Hamilton, who had been Gladstone's private secretary (1873-4, 1880-5) and was in close touch with both Rosebery and Gladstone in 1886, recorded that Rosebery 'seems to have been almost provoked into recalling Morier', Diary, 4 Mar. 1886, B.M. Add. MS. 44864, p. 31.
[5] From Sanderson, 17 Mar. 1886. C. L. Smith, *The Embassy of Sir William White at Constantinople* (1957), p. 39, does not mention this incident.

But Rosebery had sent for Sanderson and given him an opportunity to defend Morier to him and him to Morier. Of Rosebery, Sanderson wrote to Morier: 'He is, whether young or old, the centre of our foreign policy with the Cabinet at his back and responsible to Parliament . . . But he seems thoroughly good-natured and tolerant, very methodical—works very hard and has got a complete grasp of his subject—and seems to me to be showing remarkable ability.'[1] The serious consequence was the addition of another item to Morier's bill of indictment against Bismarck. Morier's haunting fear of Bismarck's underground workings was becoming an obsession. The appearance of betraying an understanding with Germany and of letting Schweinitz remonstrate alone (which he had not of course actually done) was 'a regular plant' on Bismarck's part 'to oust me out of the saddle'. For Bismarck had carried his false suggestions to the Crown Princess[2] and thence they had reached the Queen (cf. below, pp. 273–5). Morier received through Baron Stockmar a private message from her that she was displeased by his behaviour at St. Petersburg and that 'I shall for ever forfeit her confidence in me unless I change it', that further it had met 'with the strongest disapproval of Mr Gladstone and Lord Rosebery'.[3] On Sanderson's advice[4] Morier did not, at this point, write the apologia that his whole being craved to write, but it was to come.

Morier boasted of one success in the course of these negotiations. After the terms of the agreement between Turkey and Bulgaria had been decided by the Powers and Turkey, Prince Alexander made a formal protest at the modifications which had been introduced by Russia. Russia was anxious that the protest should be ignored and the Powers proceed to signature all the same. Britain held back. Meanwhile, Russian ships had been withdrawn temporarily from the European naval demonstration against Greece, and sent from Smyrna to Syra, apparently (see above, p. 215) for technical naval reasons. Morier saw his chance for what he called an artistic success. By persuading de Giers to send back the ships and Rosebery

[1] From Sanderson, private and confidential, 17 Mar. 1886.
[2] To Sanderson, private, 14 Mar. 1886.
[3] From Stockmar, 18 Mar. 1886; for retrospective account, see to Goschen, 2 June 1888.
[4] From Sanderson, private, 23 Mar. 1886.

to agree to the signature of the protocol, he dispelled a fog of mistrust.

Nothing I could do could make the Russian Gov[ernmen]t in their hearts, believe we were going straight in Bulgaria. Of course they never even hinted this disbelief to me. But a diplomatist's art is to be a thought reader, and my conviction is that they always thought we would go on postponing the prompt settlement . . . to the fancied advantages immediate and prospective of Bulgaria and P[rince] Alexander.

In like manner we most certainly have been doubting whether they were not protecting K. George [of Greece] at the expense of the European Concert.

The instruction to White to sign the Protocol broke up the one delusion; the order to the ships to return to Suda Bay broke up and was intended to break up the other . . . Anyhow the result of the last two days' work has been to establish perfect trust on this side, and Giers' last words when I left him today were: 'Je ne peux pas vous dire la confiance que nous inspire Lord Rosebery.'[1]

Morier prided himself on his own success and criticized Lord Rosebery's policy. This characteristic combination of self-satisfaction and criticism of his superior was, as usual, imprudent, but there was much truth in his view. His criticism was summed up in the third point he made in his letter of 2 June 1888 to Goschen (see above, p. 216). While we still did nothing to disabuse Russia of the notion that Prince Alexander was acting under British advice in going to Philippopolis and had stopped accepting Russia's guidance, we did not calculate the consequences of antagonizing her. Prince Alexander 'was a six shooter of exceptionally good make which we had picked out of their [i.e. Russia's] pocket and pointed at their head'.[2] Yet, as he wrote in the letter to Goschen, we had not looked ahead or thought what we should do 'should the embroglio become such as to require a forcible solution'. The two conditions for accepting such an eventuality if it came—that we had an adequate fleet 'or rather fleets—a fleet for the defence of our commerce and a fleet for the operations of an offensive war'; that we could rely on the support of public opinion, 'that is on a majority of the House of Commons'—were absent.

[1] To Rosebery, private, 2 Apr. 1886.
[2] To Rosebery, private, 19 Feb., by mistake not sent before 11 Mar. 1886.

Scarcely were the anxieties connected with the joint action against Greece finished by the lifting of the blockade, when Russia announced the end of free trade at Batum. Russia had acquired Batum by the Treaty of Berlin, but she had paid for it as she paid for all her gains under that treaty. She was obliged not only to undertake that the port would be used only for commercial—not, that is, naval—purposes, but had also agreed to its being a free port with no customs duties. Since 1878 Batum had grown greatly in importance because it was the terminus of the railway, bringing petroleum and naphtha for export from Baku. A costly customs cordon was drawn round the town so that imports destined for use outside should pay the duties not paid on those for use in the town. There was still much smuggling through Batum to avoid the high protective duties levied elsewhere. Industries within the town were discouraged by the town's not giving them a big enough market and their not being able to tap the market of the whole locality, without having to pay customs at the cordon. To set the cordon further back would increase its cost and still not solve the problem. In short, a free port in a country under a protective tariff system was an anomaly with bad economic effects.

Russia had for some time contemplated altering Batum's status before she did so at the beginning of July 1886. She saw it as a domestic step of administrative convenience and of no international importance. The other signatories of the Berlin Treaty saw it in this light too, and did not protest at Russia's failure to consult them beforehand. The incident is not noticed in the *Documents diplomatiques français* and, according to de Giers, France had indeed gone out of her way to express approval. A British Liberal government, however, was sensitive to any imputation of weakness and specially afraid of seeming to repeat 1871. The Conservatives habitually scoffed at Gladstone's action in 1871 when he condemned in principle the unilateral denunciation of treaties, while 'compounding the felony' of Russia's denunciation of the part of the Treaty of Paris neutralizing the Black Sea. Furthermore, Russia's announcement unfortunately coincided with the elections of June–July 1886, which disabled the cabinet, and it looked therefore like a calculated insult. Rosebery did not accept Morier's telegraphed advice that any action on the Russian announcement should be (1) collective, that is, made by all the Great Powers together, and (2) mild.¹ Morier was here wiser than official opinion for which Edward Hamilton spoke, when he wrote in his diary, 'Russia has exposed herself to a strong rebuke to say the least of it.'²

Rosebery, in his magnificent vindication of the sanctity of treaties on 13 July, made a bad mistake. He overdid his protest and failed to apprehend the meaning of his own language, so that he was quite taken aback by its effects.³ He needed only nine short lines⁴ to summarize a dispatch, four printed pages long. He had yielded to the seduction of words—though Lord Granville caused the worst flourish to be removed, when he wrote 'this is for others to judge' against the words 'we would rather stand alone than be associated in any way with this step'. Rosebery had, moreover, yielded to the temptation to moralize and to claim a monopoly of international morality. His tone was dictatorial and his text insulting. He was wrong completely to disregard the Tsar's distinction between the stipulating part of the 59th article—that clause providing for the purely commercial use of Batum, a commitment to the Great Powers which was to be maintained—and the recording part—that clause which simply registered the voluntary declaration of the Tsar about the customs duties, and was to be withdrawn.⁵ He was wrong to refer to the protocol of 1871 with its condemnation of the unilateral denunciation of treaties. The climax was a passage in which the British government

---

¹ To Rosebery, private telegram, 12 July 1886; from Rosebery, telegram and letter, private, 13 July 1886, explaining why the advice was unacceptable.

² 9 July 1886, B.M. Add. MS. 44864, p. 59.

³ 'It is strange', he minuted, 19 July, on Morier's earlier report of his own spontaneous response to Giers's announcement, 'that M de Giers should have been so stupefied by my despatch'—a stupefaction that he was inclined to put down to the way Morier had communicated it, but he was obliged to confess that Morier's account of this earlier conversation showed that he had used 'very proper language on this occasion', no. 226, 5 July 1886, F.O. 65/1259.

⁴ Rosebery to Gladstone, 9 July 1886, Gladstone papers, B.M. Add. MS. 44289, fo. 52. The dispatch is printed in H. Temperley and L. M. Penson, *Foundations of British Foreign Policy* (1938), pp. 437–41.

⁵ Cf. James Bryce to Rosebery, 9 July 1886, Rosebery papers, box 63. Rosebery had consulted him. He was parliamentary under-secretary and had visited Batum. He took the opposite view and argued that Russia's having declared her intention in an international treaty made her declaration 'in spirit' a contract 'binding on her'. But he admits that she had formulated her intention 'in a purely declaratory and not (so far as language goes) in an obligatory form',

asserted that it was compelled to place on record its view that the Russian action 'constitutes a violation of the Treaty of Berlin, unsanctioned by the signatory Powers, that it tends to make future conventions of the kind difficult, if not impossible; and to cast doubt at least on those already concluded'.

This Morier had regarded 'as the pith of the despatch', had 'carefully prepared the French version beforehand, and translated it slowly and with much solemnity'. He, at least, knew that 'translated into the language of familiar life' it meant 'I regret that in our future transactions I cannot any more accept your paper, but must insist on Bank of England notes', and was not unprepared for the 'something between a suppressed exclamation and a groan' with which it was greeted. At the end of the recital de Giers was trembling and green with anger and fright. He would carry the wound in his heart till he died. Morier, though at first inclined to think the show theatrical, believed it was real enough and due to the wholly unexpected attack 'with buttonless foil' from a Gladstone government—breaking the spell of the dream that anything could be 'tried on', when the Liberals were in power—and sheer fright at the prospect of having to pass on Morier's communication to the Emperor.[1] De Giers, in short, pronounced Rosebery's dispatch 'just such a note as you might have addressed to the Khedive. You sit in judgment upon us, and your verdict is one of condemnation. Do you suppose,' he asked, 'we shall accept this condemnation in silence?'[2] Morier, not unmindful of the virtual rupture in Russo-French relations since the recall of General Appert and Mohrenheim's departure from Paris for a long holiday in Cannes, was genuinely alarmed and expected, when de Giers carried Rosebery's dispatch to the Tsar, some such manifestation of resentment as the recall of de Staal from London.

The incident brought out the particular mixture of shortcoming and talent that made up Morier's personality. He dramatized the protest and dramatized his own part in foiling in advance this expected manifestation of the Tsar's resentment. Yet he did show genuine skill of a high order in neutralizing the harmful effects of Rosebery's arresting protest. De Giers in

---

[1] To Rosebery, private, 25 July 1886.
[2] To Rosebery, no. 253 secret, 21 July 1886, F.O. 65/1260.

fact replied mildly. Rosebery's flame and thunder was exhausted and his tenure of office at an end,[1] so the incident, as a Batum incident, was over. As an incident in Anglo-Russian relations, it was not over; for Morier had got out of it a curious overture from de Giers for an Anglo-Russian *entente*: curious, because de Giers had had no previous intention of making it; it sprang out of an act of sympathy between foreign minister and ambassador in face of a common fear of the disastrous consequences of a disproportionate protest. Morier was sure that it was not meant as a formal communication to the British government.[2] He, therefore, recorded de Giers's words in a memorandum separate from his dispatch and, sending it with his private letter, asked that it might be kept in the archives, but not printed or circulated to the embassies.

Memorandum by Morier[3] (holograph):

Secret St Petersburg, 18 July 1886.

In the conversation reported in my despatch 253 of the 21st instant M. de Giers, referring to the questions impending in Europe on which he deemed it of vital importance that England and Russia should come to an understanding, made a statement of great importance but the circumstances under which it was made gave it so intimate a character that I am averse to recording it an ordinary despatch even of the most confidential nature.

I can report almost textually what he said, as I made a note of it in french as soon as I could after leaving him. I had previously referred to the imperative necessity there was not to get up a *brouille* about Batum at a moment when the point of all absorbing interest to both countries was the establishment of a solid *modus vivendi* in Central Asia. He said:

'Vous avez parlé de l'importance de ne pas nous brouiller sur l'affaire de Batum vu la nécessité que rien ne mette obstacle à l'entente que nous devons établir sur la question de nos relations en Asie. Mais les questions vraiment importantes et qui priment toutes les autres sont celles que nous aurons à envisager de bien plus près, ici en Europe et sur lesquelles une entente entre les deux

---

[1] The government had resigned on 20 July 1886, two days after Morier communicated Rosebery's protest but before his own dispatch arrived in London.

[2] To Rosebery, private and confidential, 24 July 1886, described the circumstances of the overture and enclosed the memorandum quoted below.

[3] A copy is Doc. no. 78 in vol. 1885–6 of the Morier papers. The original is in F.O. 65/1260 endorsed by Sanderson, 'Ld Rosebery wished this to be entered and kept: but not printed or circulated'. It is also marked seen by 'Ld Iddesleigh, Ld Salisbury and the Queen'.

puissances est de la première nécessité. Il y a la question d'Orient que d'ici à *trois* ans, qui sait même, d'ici à *deux* ans l'Europe sera appelée à résoudre. Il y a la question de la France et du retour des Orléans qui peut éclater d'un jour à l'autre.'[1]

I have on more than one occasion referred in my despatches to the persistency with which on various sides the date of three years has come round to me as that at which it seemed established as a foregone conclusion that the crisis in the Oriental Question would declare itself. On the other hand in an important report from Sir William White well-informed opinion in Southern Russia is represented as fixing two years as the date. I was therefore I confess greatly startled at hearing the two dates fall from the very lips of the Foreign Minister especially as I well knew that he himself was resolutely bent on putting off the day as long as possible and as he had repeatedly said and again not later than a few days ago that if there was one Power for which the maintenance of the status quo in Turkey as long as possible was a vital question it was Russia. It at once flashed on me that not very long ago an intimate friend of M. de Giers had told me that he would have served out his time two years hence and have arrived at the date at which he could legally demand his retirement and, the friend added most confidentially, I know quite positively that he is perfectly determined to insist on its being granted. Is it possible that he may *dans son for intérieur* have nursed the hope that some arrangement come to with England, made within the next two years, might after all conjure away this terrible oriental cloud which is depressing and paralysing all the vital forces of Europe? I cannot tell, but more than once before, though he has never said so, but as it were listening between his spoken words, it has struck me that he was wishing to come out with the idea that the only chance of a settlement of the Oriental Question when the Turkish Empire collapsed would be for the two great Empires in the East, England and Russia, to take it in hand.

As regards the question in France I know that it is strongly preoccupying the attention of the Imperial Gov[ernmen]t and there are many rumours about of confidential *pourparlers* going on between others than the recognized official representatives of the two

[1] 'You have spoken of the importance of our not quarrelling about Batum, given the necessity that nothing should stand in the way of the *entente* which we must establish for our relations in Asia. But the really important questions, those which take precedence of all others, are those which face us nearer home, here in Europe and on which an *entente* between the two Powers is essential. There is the Eastern Question which *three* years hence, who knows, *two* years hence Europe will be called on to solve. There is the question of France and the return of the House of Orleans which may burst on us any day.'

countries. But I have no reliable data to go upon. My impression, but it is an impression only, is that the Emperor who abominates the present system in France would probably be in favour of an Orleanist restoration, whereas it is well known that such a restoration is what Germany most abominates and which would probably meet with great hostility from her. Was M. de Giers already discounting the possibility of a grave dissentiment on this question between the bosom friends on the Neva and the Spree? I cannot tell.

I need not say that I made no observation of any kind in regard either to the one or to the other question. The words were spoken in parenthesis and *exempli gratiâ* and H[is] E[xcellency] passed on to the remaining portions of his *plaidoyer*.

This overture had no response from the Foreign Office owing to the succession of Lord Iddesleigh to Lord Rosebery on 3 August. But it led Morier to open an argument about Anglo-Russian relations in September with Lord Salisbury, and the Russians renewed the overture in October, after the Bulgarian question had entered a new phase.

Meanwhile, the struggle for an international balance of power in the Balkan peninsula died down, since united Bulgaria proved itself a viable state, able to defend itself against its neighbours and, with the help of outside factors, against Russia too. If Russia reasserted her influence within Bulgaria, the struggle would be at once renewed. But, meanwhile, because Russian influence was eliminated, an internal balance of forces and constitutional stability were achieved.

Prince Alexander's kinship with Queen Victoria and the respect he paid to the advice of the British representative, Sir Frank Lascelles, meant that his success in making united Bulgaria independent of Russia was tantamount to a British success. His stature, since the victory over the Serbs, had grown. The parliamentary elections in the new Bulgaria and the proceedings of the Parliament, or Sobranje, which followed further increased his reputation.[1] Russia's resentment deepened as Prince Alexander's stock rose. Suddenly, on the night of 20 to 21 August 1886, Prince Alexander was kidnapped by Russophil officers of the Bulgarian army. He was released at the town of Renni, in Russian territory on the Rumanian-Russian border

[1] To Rosebery, no. 209 confidential, 16 June, no. 212, 19 June 1886, F.O. 65/1289; from Rosebery, no. 149a, 26 June, F.O. 65/1254.

on an arm of the Danube near Galatz. He was escorted to Lemberg in Galicia where he met his brother Louis (28 August), and then he returned with him via Bucharest to Sofia (30 August). A Russophil provisional government had been set up under the Metropolitan Bishop Clement. Against this display of Russia's power there was a counter-revolution under Stambulov, so Alexander was able to maintain himself a week longer. His nerve finally giving way, on 7 September he abdicated and found refuge at Windsor. He left a regency of Stambulov, Mutkurov, and Karavelov. Lord Iddesleigh, the new foreign secretary, telegraphed for information on 23 August, but Morier had nothing to tell. A telegram had been received in St. Petersburg announcing the deposition of Prince Alexander and another announcing the provisional government; but nothing else. Morier could not tell anything more than the newspapers during the whole period of the regency, the Kaulbars mission, and the canvassing of various names as candidates to the vacant Bulgarian throne. At last the Bulgarian Parliament elected Ferdinand of Coburg prince in July 1887.

The fall of Prince Alexander had been a personal tragedy and not an international calamity owing to the sluggishness of Turkey, of the Central Powers, and of Britain. 'I have not', wrote Iddesleigh in a postscript to a letter on Central Asia, 'attempted to work on the Bulgarian business.'[1] Russia, therefore, was reticent too, finding this general abstention more to her advantage than the activity to which any movement on her part would have provoked others. Morier was interesting on General Kaulbars's failure and his second secretary of embassy, Arthur Hardinge, interesting on the Russian candidate for the Bulgarian throne.[2] Above all, Morier was interesting on the change that was taking place in the direction and character of Russian Panslavism so that it was becoming a doctrine of Russian national self-assertion. The Kaulbars mission was justified by the Russians on the ground of the terrorism which the Regents' regime was alleged to exercise over the country. It was condemned by the critics of Russia as intended itself to

[1] To Morier, private, 1 Sept. 1886.
[2] Hardinge's memorandum on the Prince of Mingrelia, Nov. 1886, is in F.O. 65/1262.

terrorize the Regents. This interpretation seemed to have some colour of truth when the General induced the Regents to release those responsible for kidnapping Prince Alexander, and two Russian warships arrived at Varna apparently to enforce an ultimatum that he presented to the Regents. But nothing came of these alarms, and on 22 November 1887 Kaulbars was withdrawn together with the Russian consuls in Bulgaria. Diplomatic relations were thus broken off. Russia appeared to have washed her hands of Bulgaria—except that she continued to assert her wish to assist Europe in establishing a 'legal' government there. Morier's task was to enlighten his own government about Kaulbars's intentions, so that it might gauge the significance of his failure. His conclusion was that de Giers had all the time been ignorant of what Kaulbars was doing. Official Russian foreign policy was not, then, implicated in his failure. He believed that General Kaulbars, who as a German Lutheran from the Baltic provinces, a Baltic Baron, was poor and scorned, was a man whose career the Tsar and the military party could break with impunity in a last desperate effort to recover Russia's position in Bulgaria. He was a man appointed to lead a forlorn hope who went expecting not to come back alive.[1]

The Bulgarian Parliament had first elected Prince Waldemar of the Danish Royal House, but he had declined their invitation. During the autumn and well into the New Year the Prince of Mingrelia was the candidate favoured by Russia. He was the ruler of a principality in southern Russia, that had been independent until his great grandfather, in 1803, accepted Russian protection. He was a youngish man, then forty years old, with a reputation for ability and generosity.[2] There was never any inclination to regard him as Russia's *dernier mot*.[3]

Attention was drawn to the Panslavists by the attempt on the life of the Tsar in March 1887, owing to an ignorant confusion of them with the Nihilists. The Russian police had arrested six young men, armed with explosives and knives, waiting in ambush for the Tsar to cross from the Anichkov

---

[1] To Iddesleigh, no. 433 confidential, 6 Dec. 1886, F.O. 65/1263.
[2] Memorandum by A. Hardinge, Nov. 1886, F.O. 65/1262.
[3] To Iddesleigh, no. 11, 14 Jan. 1887, F.O. 65/1295.

palace to the chapel in the fortress of St. Peter and St. Paul, where the service on the anniversary of his father's death was to be held. They were in fact Nihilists, but Panslavists and Nihilists were spoken of indifferently as being responsible for the plot. They were lumped together presumably because both were agitators, but they had nothing more in common. One group of Panslavists saw, in a rigid and intolerant Orthodoxy, the strongest weapon both for the establishment of Russian supremacy in all Orthodox lands and for the purging from Russia of all non-Russian elements. Morier rightly reported, however, that the chief leader of the Panslavs, Mikhail Katkov, the editor of the *Moscow Gazette*, was more moderate and mainly interested in foreign relations.[1] He was not leading a movement away from Germany and towards France, but only urging that Russia should aim at a free hand. Morier constantly drew attention to Katkov's anti-German and anti-English articles. Katkov to him stood for a doctrine of Russia for the Russians in a nationalist, though not an extremist, sense.

After the Batum crisis Morier had been occupied in negotiations about the Russo-Afghan frontier to which the new foreign secretary attached much importance. He was still occupied with these when Prince Alexander abdicated, and was much concerned to see that they continued to dominate Iddesleigh's mind. He received no instructions about Bulgaria[2] and became increasingly anxious. Recurring to his fixed idea of the connection between Europe and Asia in Russia's policy (see above, p. 217), he wrote privately to Iddesleigh on 9 September to try to convince him that the two matters hung together. 'The ultimate success or non-success' in the Afghan negotiations 'will depend, as it has all along depended, on the state of the score

[1] To Salisbury, no. 92, 21 Mar. 1887, F.O. 65/1296.
[2] There is overwhelming evidence that this reserve was deliberate policy, but nothing makes it clearer than a pithy summary of his policy which Salisbury wrote to Cross, at his request, for the Queen. Cross was staying at Balmoral, 'in attendance'. It was written on 2 Oct. 1886, the same date as Salisbury's long letter to Morier, quoted below. 'The present seems to me a moment for reserve, and not for action. We have staked all our hopes on Alexander—and he has been driven away. There is no one to take his place—and the events to be expected in the Balkan peninsula will take time to shape, and are not even foreshadowed yet. In Europe the future is still more uncertain.' The situation might change, 'but I dare not run the risk of a humiliation for England [from Parliament and public opinion forcing her to break off in the middle of some resolute course of action] by counting on such a change until I see the signs of it' (Salisbury papers, D/15-19, fos. 306-8).

in the Bulgarian *Kriegsspiel* . . . In the portentous Siamese twinship with which we have to deal, the Asian twin is subordinate to, and made to subserve the purposes and objects of the European twin—and every phase of the game in Europe will have its *contre-coup* in Asia.'[1]

Five days later Morier took the unusual and irregular course of writing to Salisbury, now prime minister, making their previous correspondence in 1878–80 and 1885 his excuse. He wrote an enormously long review of Anglo-Russian relations since 1870, a strong plea for an *entente* with Russia, and a vigorous condemnation of the whole Bulgarian policy.[2] 'I am sure', his letter began, 'you will not take it amiss if, at so very grave a crisis in the relations between us and a country in which I am the responsible Minister of the Crown, I write with a frankness and unreserve, which under less serious circumstances might seem out of place.' After referring to their previous correspondence and to a review of his own activity which he had drawn up in February 1886 and 'pigeon-holed', he went on to assert that ever since 1871 Britain and Russia had been in a state of cold war, what he called 'crypto-belligerency'. 'It was a *Kriegsspiel* but one in which at any moment the leaden mannikins might change into serried regiments of living combatants.' He summed up the history of 1871–86 as four dramatic moves in a game in which each Russian move had been answered by a British counter-stroke. It is difficult to take the next passage, in which he attempted to characterize Russia, as anything but imaginative nonsense, except that it wonderfully conveyed the incalculability of Russia to western eyes. 'What is Russia?' he asked.

In one sense it is the Tsar . . . In another sense it is a Dual, double headed being, not a double headed eagle like the national emblem, but a double headed Bear like the national beast, and never was a national beast more typical of the national character—a great lolling, awkward gambolling, good natured *bonhomme* of a beast at first sight, an eater of roots and fruits and devoted to honey and sweetmeats— a cunning, ferocious, flesh-tearing beast from another point of view . . . Lastly, in another sense . . . an immense ocean, now violently

---

[1] To Iddesleigh, private, 9 Sept. 1886.
[2] To Salisbury, private, 14 Sept. 1886. The copy in Morier's hand in the Morier papers is dated 15 Sept., the original in the Salisbury papers, 14 Sept.

agitated, now subject to deep and sudden calm, but all the while, whether on the surface still or furious, moving on with an irresistible tide in a very ascertainable direction. A homogeneous body . . . of 100 million souls . . .

He explained his view that British policy had been mistaken in so far as its makers had had exclusively in mind the double-headed Russia, its government, that is, with its conflicting western and Slav members. 'Our true adversary . . . is not exclusively the crafty, intriguing, mendacious diplomacy of the dual headship, but the hundred million unit, who is passionately interested in the game, and has the other unit of the Czar, more unconsciously perhaps than consciously, as its organ and executive.' 'The British, newspaper-reading, Philistine' looked on the Russo-Turkish war of 1877-8 'as a political war of the worst and most criminal kind . . . Now this is an absolutely false view.' It was for the Russian 'a War of Liberation' which 'stirred to its depths not merely the Russian but the whole Slav cosmos'. Yet the Russian found he had nothing to show for the expenditure of '140 millions sterling' and the loss of 'some hundred thousand lives'. Britain, Morier represented the average Russian as arguing, had deprived Russia of all the just fruits of victory and, in imaginative language, he showed the emotion with which this was resented. The philistine Britisher did not appreciate this emotion; since foreign affairs were for him 'a dram to stimulate a languid appetite, a something to enliven the eternal dullness of English middle class business life'. The letter continues in this strain to the conclusion that by imposing her views in the Bulgarian question in 1885-6 Britain had inflicted a humiliation on the Russians 'far greater than we dreamt of, because what was a diplomatic victory for us was felt as a national defeat by them'.

Morier next passed rapidly over the Rosebery interlude. Though Lord Rosebery 'manfully strove to introduce a strain of "Jingo" blood' into Gladstone's government 'he could not in the eyes . . . of the Russians make it other than the war-at-no-price administration which had lowered the Union Jack to Russia at Penjdeh and to Germany on the coast of Africa'. A policy so bold as that inaugurated by Salisbury in 1885-6, one 'so patently announcing to the world that it was the resolute determination of Great Britain to defend India in Europe, by defending Constantinople in Bulgaria', required more understanding and skill for its execution than Rosebery possessed. Morier then detailed at length the reasons why he himself, had he 'been in a position to have an opinion on the subject, would not have selected the policy' that Salisbury had inaugurated. Nor, it having been selected, would he have carried it through to make Prince Alexander so ostentatiously the caretaker at Sofia of British interests, but rather would he have taken pains to have made him the mandatory of a European concert of which Russia was as much part as Britain. Finally, Morier passed to his recommendations for the future, introducing them with the sentence: 'Pray do not take it amiss or consider it presumptuous if, as an old public servant, deeply impressed with the overpowering character of the crisis in which we stand, and almost sick with the responsibility of the post I occupy, I venture frankly to state, for what it is worth, the deliberate opinion I have arrived at. There are it appears to me two alternatives, and only two, open to us'; for he deprecated from the bottom of his heart the continuance of what he called 'the sterile game of buzznagging'.[1] One alternative was to continue the policy of using Bulgaria as an outpost of British influence against Russia. If Russia chose then to answer this challenge by eventually declaring war, Britain could win that war by parading her navy through the Black Sea and asserting her supremacy there and mobilizing the military power of Serbia, Bulgaria, and Rumania, on one side, and, on the other, by landing an Anglo-Turkish army on the east coast of the Black Sea to beat the Russian army in the Caucasus, to take Tiflis, and to cut eastern Russia off from Transcaucasia and Central Asia. The reality in all this fantasy was the relative naval weakness of Russia in the Black Sea. There was even an element of fantasy in the only argument he put forward against it, which was the use Bismarck might make of such a war.

The second alternative he had had in view, he wrote

from the day I arrived here, improbable and quixotic as it may appear . . . [was] an *entente* with Russia if only in the nature of a truce and temporary *modus vivendi* . . . I believe the materials for such an *entente* are at hand. Russia, that is the Emperor, and those

---

[1] A word he explained as American to describe 'not the simple nagging of angry females, but such nagging superlatived by the buzz of a giant mosquito'.

he works with, and is likely to go on working with, desire, quite as keenly as we do, the maintenance of Turkey . . . To co-operate in the maintenance of Turkey would be the basis of the agreement. There remain Bulgaria and Afghanistan. That we cannot by diplomatic means alone build up an anti-Russian Bulgaria, is I think now as clear as noonday. On the other hand Russia can do us endless mischief in Afghanistan. A truce, that is an abstaining from offensive politics at the one extremity and at the other, would be the complement of the arrangement.

The main argument for it was the impossibility of the alternative: of the fantastic war he had described and the existing 'buzznagging' he deplored. The only other argument he advanced was the characteristic one that such an understanding would deprive Bismarck of his role of 'omniscient and omnipotent arbitrator'.

An incidental interest attaches to this plea for understanding with Russia in that Morier used, to write the fair draft, Arthur Hardinge, who from Teheran, where he was British minister (1900–6), was to watch the negotiation of the *entente* with Russia eventually signed in 1907, an *entente* with which his cousin, Charles, was even more closely identified.

Morier also tried, but in vain, to gain an interview with Lord Salisbury, since he had been summoned to London in another connection. When Salisbury told him he would not be in London, Morier offered to go to France. But Salisbury was decisive. 'Your kind proposal . . . does not seem to be hierarchically proper. I think you must see the Foreign Secretary before you see me. I am not going to Royat. I am very apprehensive of the evils which I have seen result from two Ministers, who are at a distance from each other, dealing with the same bit of business. It must produce confusion.'[1] In the end Morier did not go to England until December, and he received a long written reply from Salisbury.[2] It was a convincing argument for a dilatory policy of not forcing the issue.

After an opening phrase or two Salisbury came to the point:

I am much pleased to find that with certain exceptions our studies have led to much the same line of thought. At least we agreed in the answer to be given to the question 'What is Russia'. The philosophy

---

[1] From Salisbury, private, 23 Sept. 1886.
[2] From Salisbury, private, 2 Oct. 1886.

that would be satisfied with the reply—a despotism—would be a shallow one. Most essential is it to bear in mind that we have to deal not with a man, or a Government, but with 'an immense ocean, moving on with an irresistible tide'. The acknowledgment of this fact is the difference between saving knowledge and deadly heresy in framing a Russian policy.

If I venture to differ somewhat from your conclusions, it is because I do not think you apply your dogma with unflinching consistency. You speak at the end of pursuing as your policy 'an *entente*—a modus vivendi, a temporary truce with Russia'—I own this savours to me of what I termed the heresy. You can have an *entente* with a man or a Government: but, no one, except Canute's Courtiers ever tried to have it with a tide. The tide is constantly advancing—not because of the ambition of Courts, or the schemes of Statesmen—but moved by the forces which cause vast, rude populations to overflow their borders. The forces which are pushing outwards the Russian frontiers are mainly two—the religious, and the military—the forces which moved the hosts of Mahomet, and those which moved the hosts of Attila: the attraction of faith and spoil: or if you will, faith and glory. It is far too limited a view to say that Russia's movements are inspired only by the desire to put the cross on the top of St. Sophia. That motive works strongly—and for the present marks out the channel along which the tide must roll. But it is not the only—I doubt if it is the strongest force. Working with it, is the constant appetite for gain and distinction which animates the officers of a vast military organization—which the Czar cannot disregard if he would: for their fidelity is the one sure buttress of his throne. And when the religious dream is satisfied, and S. Sophia is again a Christian Church, the frontier of Russia will not cease to expand. The military appetites will be as imperious as ever: and the frontier must go on expanding, wherever military distinction and advancement is to be obtained. This belief it is which makes me distrust a policy that aims at a Russian *entente*. She can promise nothing with respect to Affghanistan except that she will eat Constantinople first. When it is eaten she must go forward, with all the weight of her augmented mass, in the direction of India.

What then should be the policy of England? I entirely accept your view of the British Philistine, and his martial instincts. He will not fight—really fight—except in self preservation. He will not fight for India. But when the battle gets within distance of the Indian armies, he will give the orders to fight: because he will not have to pay the bill. Taking the matter, therefore, at its worst, our prospect is—no real resistance to Russian advance, till the Russian armies can be seen from Candahar. If some democratic caprice should induce him to fight earlier, so much the better: but let us lay our plans on the least favourable assumption. Russia *must* go to C[onstantino]ple first—the religious tide dictates that condition: and then she will advance eastwards till we meet her in Affghanistan. What should our policy be? It seems to me that we have but one—the Fabian policy. Let her take as long on the road to C[onstantino]ple as we can possibly contrive. We have everything to gain, and nothing to lose by the delay. If we can make it long enough, there are many things that may happen.

1. She may fall out with one of her neighbours.
2. The Nihilists may succeed: and she may break up internally.
3. The Philistine may pluck up heart of grace; and give her a reception when she gets to the borders of the Bosphorus which may keep her quiet for many years.
4. A Turkish leader may arise: who will rally the still vast material forces of Islam against her.
5. Some leader among the 'Nationalities' may arise, who will dispose of a considerable moral force, and may embarrass her for some years—if not permanently.

These chances are none of them improbable: some are even very probable. In proportion as we can delay the ultimate issue, we shall have the advantage of them. In proportion as by any *modus vivendi*, we smooth Russia's way to C[onstantino]ple, we diminish the value of our hopes from these contingencies. I think, therefore, they justify a dilatory diplomacy. Every difficulty we can raise in the shape of an Alexander, or a patriotic Bulgarian, is so much to the good. But there is one condition of this view which I must state—otherwise you would easily find a fatal flaw in it. It would be too dangerous a policy to pursue, if a war between Russia and England were really a matter to be much alarmed at. I should not dare to pursue such a line of conduct in regard to France. But neither of us is likely to hurt the other much. I am no believer in any formidable danger even if Russia gets within sight of Candahar. The various difficulties are so great that she will only incur a huge disaster—a hot Moscow retreat. And short of that contingency, it will be nothing but a naval warfare, varied by a few unsuccessful descents upon the coast—so far as we are concerned. I am not, therefore, discouraged from my Fabian policy by the bare chance that it might issue in a premature explosion. There is one reply to this line of argument which I have heard used, though I think you will hardly deem it tenable. It is that if we are too dilatory and too 'buzznagging', Russia will go to Candahar first, and leave C[onstantino]ple for another time. I do not think the Slav party will let her do that: and I do not think she could do it safely. The attack on Candahar will want all her strength and while she is occupied on it—it will take her several years in any event—the Balkan nationalities will be gaining strength and may bar the way to her when she comes back.

On the whole, therefore, I think our policy may be summed up in the maxim—keep Russia out of C[onstantino]ple as long as you can: and therefore make every step in that direction as slow as you can make it. Of course, such a policy ought not to be made needlessly unpleasant to Russia: and I quite agree with you as to the bad taste and folly of our bragging journalists. But her goodwill is not worth buying by concessions; she is too impersonal, too much of an 'ocean'. The roll of her insincerities is endless if you look upon her as a person.

I have said nothing about the actual value of C[onstantino]ple. I do not rate it very highly except for its legendary influence over the East. I think the possession of it will make every Arab, Kurd, Persian, and Affghan think, more than he did before, that Russia is stronger than England, and holds the winning cards: and that is a strength in itself. Nor have I said anything about Affghan negotiations. I regret the whole policy of demarcation. It sins against the maxim that a tide cannot contract. And I fear its only result will be to make the Affghans begin to sell themselves sooner than they would otherwise have done.

I have spoken very unreservedly—and I hope you will let me add, confidentially. But—while fully admitting the cogency of much of your reasoning—and the attractiveness had it been feasible, of the *entente* policy—I was anxious to let you know why I did not believe in it: and if possible to show, that whether I was right or wrong, the policy I favoured was neither Quixotic, nor aimless.

I wish I had an Arthur Hardinge to lighten for you the task of decyphering this.

In October 1886, Morier, entirely disregarding the cogency of this long and patient argument against any *entente*, reported that Russia had renewed the movement towards an understanding with Britain, which he seemed to have precipitated at the time of the Batum incident. His report[1] opens with a reference to the memorandum of July, recording how de Giers had given him to 'understand that the idea prevailed that it would be absolutely necessary for England and Russia to seek to come to an understanding within the next three, if not two years on the Eastern question'. He then sums up the new proposal. It amounted from the Russian side to an agreement on Bulgaria

[1] To Iddesleigh, private, 13 Oct. 1886.

of three parts: agreement on a candidate for the Bulgarian throne; an undertaking by Russia not to occupy or seek to 'Russianize' (through Russian ministers or army officers) Bulgaria; an undertaking by Britain to observe Russia's right to moral pre-eminence in Bulgaria.

As evidence of the seriousness of this overture Morier could cite certain preliminary feelers which had preceded it and the substance of which he summarized. Two memoranda by Arthur Hardinge (now in Morier's service) dated October 1886, recount that Baron Jomini had said to Hardinge's uncle, Sir Charles Mansfield,[1] that Russia and Britain might put forward the Duke of Edinburgh (Queen Victoria's son and the husband of the Tsar's sister) or his son as a candidate for the Bulgarian throne. Russia wished to know whether, if she made the proposal, it would be met in a friendly spirit; if a snub were to be expected, she would not make it. The maintenance of the closure of the Straits of the Bosphorus and Dardanelles and security on the Afghan frontier were also mentioned and added to the serious air of Jomini's talk. The memoranda are among Morier's letters and there is no sign that they were ever seen by Salisbury or Iddesleigh, nor that they were used by Morier except as evidence for the seriousness of the October overture.

Morier asserted that this overture came direct from de Giers, who had also made it clear to him that Jomini had talked to Hardinge's uncle with his (de Giers's) and the Tsar's knowledge. Morier had, however, to admit that he had deduced only from the most general language that de Giers wanted an agreement to end Anglo-Russian antagonism in the Near East. Yet de Giers had, at least, made a defined and firm proposal for an agreement on a joint candidate for the Bulgarian throne. It is difficult to judge the Russians' intentions, without evidence from the Russian side, but it is perhaps fair to say that Morier was led by his own strong convictions to report the Russians' overture as going somewhat further than they intended, but

---

[1] Sir Charles Edward Mansfield (1828–1907) had been political agent in Rumania, 1876–8. He had married Annie Eliza Howard de Walden, sister to Hardinge's mother. The identification is not certain. Though Morier wrote 'Gen. Mansfield', he also wrote 'Hardinge's nephew' which, since I cannot trace a Mansfield nephew, I have taken as a slip of the pen. Hardinge's memoranda do not name the man to whom Jomini was talking.

that he was not essentially misleading; for he was only putting them further along the road they wished to take.

Whether an agreement on a joint candidate for the Bulgarian throne, far less an agreement on general policy, was at this stage possible is doubtful. Queen Victoria would have opposed it; she was Russophobe; she disliked political ambitions for her sons, and she had failed lamentably in her efforts to secure a more active support from her government for Prince Alexander of Bulgaria[1] and must have learnt from this not to try again with another candidate even if he was also supported by Russia. For Lord Salisbury's government it would have created precisely the commitment that in arguing for a dilatory, fluid policy he had condemned. Further, a general policy of non-intervention would cause events to develop in Bulgaria much more to Britain's advantage than co-operation with Russia to impose a candidate from outside. Bulgaria left to herself would become, as she did become, an effective Balkan state. Two other reasons weighed with Salisbury. First, an Anglo-Russian agreement would give to his policy an anti-German bias which, owing to Germany's influence on Austria-Hungary and Italy, might in turn endanger Britain's position in the Mediterranean. Second, he preferred a different order of events—one in which a specific agreement should grow from a habit of pursuing similar policies rather than precede it.

Though Morier did not know it, an agreement would have proved at this stage, so far as one can judge, equally impossible from Russia's side. Her policy in Bulgaria arose from the pressures upon her from Germany, Austria-Hungary, and France. It was not one that she would lightly abandon just because Britain was ready to agree on an active joint Anglo-Russian policy there. De Giers's overture had another and different explanation. During the regency of Stambulov, Mutkurov, and Karavelov, which lasted until June 1887, Russia affirmed that their position was illegal and unconstitutional. She asserted that it was the duty of Turkey to bring it to an end and for the Great Powers to bring pressure to bear on Turkey to do so. Russia's policy was one of passive protest.

[1] See her correspondence with Lord Granville preserved in the Granville papers, P.R.O. 30/29/42; cf. A. Ramm (ed.), *The Political Correspondence of Mr. Gladstone and Lord Granville*, ii. 83, 85, 89, 94, 95, 99, 100, 102, 111, 282.

Morier, as he had done over the Goa railway in 1876-8, was arguing from a partial point of view without all the evidence available in London. He could not know that Bismarck's pressure upon Russia was now in the direction of restraint.[1] He made a mistake in reporting to his government:

> I am now in a position to state on evidence which is convincing to my mind that the proposals lately made by Prince Bismarck to the Emperor of Russia, but not then accepted by His Majesty from his fear of being led into a trap, were: the acquiescence and connivance of Germany in the occupation by Russia not only of Bulgaria and Eastern Roumelia but *of Roumania* in return for an engagement that Russia would formally and solemnly recognize the sovereignty of Germany over Alsace Lorraine.[2]

Morier was inclined to select from current rumours the one which showed Bismarck in the worst light, and to believe that.

From November 1886 until July 1887 it was not Bulgaria but the possibility of a Franco-German war which governed Russian policy. The Boulangist agitation in France, the German army bill, its failure to pass the Reichstag, and its eventual passage after a general election were behind the speculation about a Franco-German war. The explanation of the soundings of Jomini and de Giers, about an understanding with Britain, is that they were calculated to draw information about British intentions, which they could then use in the debate about the future evolution of Russian policy. Should Russia favour France or Germany? As for France Katkov had presented a memorandum to the Tsar in which he argued that Russia could not afford to see France attacked by Germany and beaten; the Tsar had used encouraging language to de Laboulaye in November and de Giers had told him on 12 January 1887 that Russia had as free a hand if France attacked Germany as contrariwise; at the end of January, Émile Flourens in Paris had made a friendly overture to Mohrenheim. As for Germany, Peter Shuvalov had begun to make the approaches in Berlin which were the prelude to the signature of the Reinsurance

---

[1] See the scanty evidence in *Die große Politik der europäischen Kabinette* on the meeting of the German and Austrian Emperors at Gastein, on Bismarck and Giers at Franzensbad (26 and 27 Aug. 1886) and Berlin (2 to 4 Sept. 1886), v. 55 n. xxx, 57, 58–62.

[2] To Iddesleigh, no. 418 most secret, 26 Nov. 1886, F.O. 65/1263; see below p. 280.

Treaty in June 1887. By January, Germany had offered her abstention in Bulgaria and the Straits, while Russia secured her ascendancy there, in return for Russian abstention in the event of a Franco-German quarrel. Morier boasted of his friendship with Peter Shuvalov, brother of the Russian ambassador in Berlin, but he never penetrated his well-guarded secrets.

Although there was no real chance of agreement from either side, Morier's eloquence had made such an impression on Iddesleigh that when they eventually met in London he was asked formally to reply to two questions, which I give in Morier's words:[1] 'Q. 1. If overtures were now made to Russia for coming to an understanding of a friendly kind on pending differences, in what spirit did I conceive that they would be received? Q. 2. If it were contemplated to make such overtures, what in my opinion, would be the best mode of approaching the question?'

Morier replied while he was still in London. To the first question his answer was hesitant, but he adhered to his view that 'there was a strong desire on the part of the Russian Govt. for a full and friendly exchange of thoughts'. 'The mere change', he wrote, 'from an attitude of crypto-hostility to one of conciliation and of being desirous of an *entente* would be the winning of half the battle.' To the second question, he reminded Iddesleigh, he had made an answer during their talk to the effect that an effort should be made to find out through the Queen's family connections with the Tsar what the best approach would be.

On reconsideration, however . . . I cannot but strongly urge that I should be authorized on my return to St. Petersburg to say words to the effect that the disposition of H.M. Government is certainly not averse to a friendly discussion. This would commit us to nothing but if they have hoped that I might possibly be the bearer of an olive branch, it would show that olive branches were somewhere about. I should not be instructed to offer one, but I might be seen with one in my button-hole.

Morier's other discussions at the Foreign Office concerned the Afghan frontier, and with Salisbury he discussed his relations with the Queen. But he did not carry back to St. Peters-

[1] To Iddesleigh, private and confidential, 26 Duke St. Manchester Sq., 30 Dec. 1886.

BULGARIA AND BATUM, 1885 TO 1887

burg any precise instruction about Anglo-Russian relations, and Iddesleigh had relinquished the Foreign Office by the time he regained his post. Iddesleigh died soon afterwards. Meanwhile, Morier had learned from Peter Shuvalov, with whom, ironically enough, he travelled back in the train from Berlin to St. Petersburg, sufficient to discourage him from pressing forward.

On my road from Berlin to Petersburg, two days and two nights, I had as my companion [wrote Morier][1] Count Pierre Schouvaloff . . . He had driven straight from dining with the Chancellor [Bismarck] to the railway station *plenus veteris Bacchi pinguisque ferinae*.[2] What he had to say therefore was clearly of no small interest, for he must have been in intimate converse with the great man, at the moment the great man was big with the speech he would be delivering whilst we were driving along amid the snowdrifts.

How about the war I asked—war in the West, and war in the East? There will be no war he said. Certainly not in the West. This I can absolutely guarantee to you. No power either in Heaven or Earth can kick France into declaring war, and I will guarantee that Germany does not declare war or seek a pretext for one. Do you mean to tell me, said I, that the two Powers are to go on arming *ad infinitum* and never to fly at each other's throats. I do not speak for the future, he replied, but for the present, for *this year*, I am ready to bet you my entire fortune that there will be *no* war between France and Germany.

From the mode in which he said this, and many later allusions, I am quite convinced that this is the message he is charged to take as a New Year's Gift to the Emperor [version in the Salisbury papers: from Berlin to Petersburgh]. Like myself he was hastening to be present at tomorrow's reception.

But how about the East? There will be no war there either. Russia does not mean to occupy, and even if she did, Austria would not mobilize a man to prevent it, because she knows that Germany would let things be. But Russia does not mean to occupy, and Germany knows this. But he added, significantly, much depends on you, and indeed it is not too much to say that the point of gravitation is now shifted to London. If you encourage Austria in her hostility to us, and she provokes war, then indeed the danger will come thence. I said that the idea of our *encouraging* Austria to provoke Russia was

---

[1] To Salisbury, private, 12 Jan. 1887, copy in the Morier papers; the letter actually received by Salisbury is in the Salisbury papers, letters from Morier, fo. 68.

[2] Virgil, *Aeneid*, 1. 215. Morier substituted *plenus* for *implentur*.

simply absurd. No one wished for peace more than we did, and the idea of England as an *agent provocateur* was too grotesque even for the Charivari [*sic*]. But, I added, the case would be very different indeed, if Russia provoked Austria. I came straight from London where I had felt the pulse of public opinion, if not in the daily press sense of the term, in that of men of light and leading, of different shades of opinion, who were unanimous in thinking that if Austria were wantonly attacked, England could not leave her to her fate, nor allow of so important a member of the European community's being extinguished. As far as that goes, he observed, there are other Powers also, who could not allow Austria to be crushed out, but that would not prevent [us] if we were provoked to it, from fighting her enough to get what we want.

The only thing he went on to say that required to be done was to clear the Bulgarian question out of the way. He was very eloquent about the mountain that had been made out of this molehill. He had his own solution he said but it was of that simple kind which would be certain to secure its rejection. It was clearly impossible to get a Prince *now*. What Russia proposed would be rejected by Bulgaria and her friends, what Bulgaria and her friends proposed would be rejected by Russia. A *provisorium* was wanted. And if the present regents and Gov[ernmen]t were to take to themselves in equal parts members of the Russian party, a mixed Provisorium could be found which might *vivoter* till such time as a Prince would be invented. I said the idea seemed an excellent one, and I hoped he would air it. He said that its coming from him would be certain to damn it, and added, and so it would be if it came from England.

In January 1887 Salisbury took over the Foreign Office and until 1892 held the two offices of foreign secretary and prime minister concurrently. He effectively checked Morier's movement towards an Anglo-Russian agreement. In a private letter[1] which begins with an echo of the assumption I quoted at the beginning of the chapter, he wrote of Bismarck's wearing out Russian strength. 'In all Russia's three wars [in the nineteenth century], she has been in desperate straits for the sinews of war at the end.' He went on next to enlighten Morier about the Italian overtures of 7 and 17 January which were to lead to the first Mediterranean Agreement between Italy and Britain on 12 February, to which Austria-Hungary acceded on 24 March.[2] Morier was never to know in full of these, but it seems he could

---

[1] 19 Jan. 1887; not traced in the Salisbury papers.
[2] C. J. Lowe, *Salisbury and the Mediterranean, 1886–1896* (1965), p. 13.

have done so had he grasped the importance at this date of what Salisbury was telling him and replied with an inquiry then or at a later time. Salisbury wrote:

But it seems to me to be our strong interest, now, that Russia should not attack Austria: and therefore we must lose no opportunity of putting forward in the fairest light we can the probability that Austria will not stand alone. I do not, of course, want to send any direct message to M. de Giers: I should be sorry that anything were said to show undue distrust of Russia. But you should lose no opportunity of representing the importance attached to the Austrian alliance by public opinion here—as was shown by the general assent [with] which my observations to that effect at the Guildhall were received. It may be well to draw the conversation on [to] the peculiar characteristics of English opinion—how it passes with great rapidity out of a condition of apparent langour and indifference into a condition of violent excitement which carries every party and government before it. No better instance of that state of mind can be found than the changes which took place during the years 1876-78. The rapidity with which the sight of armed men moving across the frontier of one of the allies of England turned the fierce philanthropic fever into an Imperialist fever equally violent, conveyed a valuable lesson—that it is never safe to trust in the apparent apathy of the English people. Nor will Austria want other allies. Italy, which might naturally have been looked upon as her enemy is, on the contrary, very deeply preoccupied with the menace which any disturbance of European peace in the South East of Europe might carry with it to Italian interests on the shores of the Mediterranean: and she has made overtures to us very unusual in the earnestness and emphasis with which they are pressed. Again if Russia trusts to Turkey she makes a great mistake. Projects for a Confederation of the Balkan States are in the air on one side and the other: but any evidence, appreciable to the popular eye, that Russia was combining with Turkey, would ensure, as nothing else could, the union of all the Christian races on the side of independence.

I have run over these topics, well known to you, partly because you have encouraged me to err rather on the side of diffuseness and explicitness than on the other—and also because I wished to insist on the point, that I am suggesting to you *not* a message—but a *tone* of conversation. These views should not be 'vues' but 'entrevues'.

Kalnoky I hear holds to his statements. There is no doubt he would fall if he abandoned them.

P.S. Of course I do not mean by the above to suggest that your tone to Russia should be more hostile: or that you should give the impression either that we mean to raise difficulties for them in Bulgaria, or that we mean to encourage Austria to do so. Our interest is in a peaceful issue. I am only anxious that Russia should not believe too readily that that issue is to be reached by bullying Austria. My impression is that the chances are in favour of Austria resisting: and very much in favour of her not being left alone if she does.

Morier's reports from St. Petersburg now become very thin, except on the Afghan frontier question to which attention was fully directed from January 1887 and continued to be directed until the signature of the Reinsurance Treaty in June 1887 between Russia and Germany. There was a small flurry in March, when there were rumours of a Russian expedition to Varna,[1] and some further stir was caused by the attempt on the Tsar's life later in the year—to which allusion has already been made. 'It was the deep conviction of every Russian that as regards the oriental question', wrote Morier, 'he has time on his side and can afford to wait.'[2] A little later he added in a private letter:[3]

There are no grounds as I have endeavoured to show for expecting any immediate action on the part of Russia, but the big fact we have to deal with is the essentially *nervous* character of the 100 million Russian unit, and the result of the late events in Bulgaria, results undoubtedly reckoned upon by the Moscow dynamiters, cannot but be to excite this neurility to a maximum. An hysterical mammoth is not a comfortable tenant in the European aquarium.

Salisbury was not disturbed. 'The uncanny calm still continues', he wrote on 30 March.[4] To this Morier replied on 7 April:[5] 'Things remain in *status quo* and I have nothing to say worth saying. It would be very delightful if we could hope to continue indefinitely in this cataleptic state, but I suppose even the sleeping Frenchman in Soho will wake some day.'

In Bulgaria the Regents strengthened their position, succeeded in raising a loan, and showed that they could hold their own despite talk of Turkish action to turn them out in favour

---

[1] To Salisbury, no. 73 confidential, 9 Mar. 1887, F.O. 65/1295.
[2] To Salisbury, no. 57 confidential, 23 Feb. 1887, F.O. 65/1295.
[3] To Salisbury, private, 10 Mar. 1887, Morier papers; Salisbury papers, A/73, fo. 14.
[4] To Morier, private, Morier papers; not traced in the Salisbury papers.
[5] To Salisbury, private, Morier papers; Salisbury papers, A/73, fo. 26.

of a temporary governor appointed with European sanction. In July, the Bulgarian Parliament elected Ferdinand of Coburg Prince of Bulgaria. Morier wrote privately[1] from Orienbaum, on 6 July 1887, the day before the election:

I regret that I have no information to send worth confiding to a private letter, but at the present time important and interesting as are the issues being decided at Constantinople and Tirnovo, St. Petersburgh is the last place in the world where it is possible for a diplomatist to collect news. Everybody is living a hundred miles from everybody. Giers is 150 miles in the heart of Finland. Schweinitz 20 miles off. Wolkenstein away. Chakir [the Turkish ambassador] buried in the islands. The minor Gods all gone to their respective hearths.

Nor was his public dispatch reporting a conversation with de Giers on 13 July, a week later, any more informative.

It was just at this date that the Bulgarian question prompted the third Russian overture—if overture is the right word—for an Anglo-Russian agreement. The signature of the agreement with Britain over the Afghan frontier, described in the next chapter, created a favourable atmosphere. Russia had, however, just signed the Reinsurance Treaty with Germany, so that the explanation of the 'overture' is probably again that Russia was rather seeking information than making firm advances for an *entente*.

At the end of July, Morier and de Giers had a long conversation in which they agreed on the interest Britain and Russia had in the preservation of both France and Austria as viable units in the European balance of power.[2] Then on 17 August, Morier had a second conversation with de Giers, the gist of which he telegraphed home in a telegram so long that it took two and a half pages of writing when deciphered. In his private letter of 27 July Morier had stressed that de Giers was anxious that he should not be thought to be making a formal overture: he made an appeal. He pleaded that Britain should cease to work against Russian policy in Bulgaria. The plea about Bulgaria was accompanied by charges[3] against Nicholas

---
[1] Morier papers; Salisbury papers, A/73, fo. 56.
[2] To Salisbury, no. 260 confidential and no. 261 most confidential, 26 July 1887, F.O. 65/1297; to Salisbury, private, 27 July 1887.
[3] Morier characteristically believed these originated with Bismarck.

O'Connor, now British representative at Sofia, which was why Morier put it into a private letter. The telegram of 17 August, and the dispatch which amplified it, described how de Giers had deduced, from Salisbury's recent speech at the Mansion House and his friendly reference there to the agreement on the Afghan frontier, the possibility of a general Anglo-Russian *entente* and a specific agreement for a common policy in Bulgaria to replace Ferdinand of Coburg by a Regent jointly chosen by Britain and Russia.[1] On 24 August,[2] a week later, de Giers returned to the subject and explained that he had meant in the conversation of 17 August to put the stress upon the general advantage of better Anglo-Russian relations, not upon Bulgaria.

In the general bursting of the waters [i.e. in a Franco-German war], which might any day occur in Europe, Russia and England were the Powers least desirous of change and most interested in the maintenance of peace, and therefore, most naturally called upon to exercise a calming influence . . . The true policy of the two countries was to draw near to one another as the representatives of a conservative international policy, opposed to the disruptive forces that were everywhere at work . . .

Salisbury's reply was decisive:

Your telegram No. 61. I do not think we can safely draw closer to Russia on the subject of Bulgaria. We are agreed as to policy of having a Regent: but we should not agree as to choice of that Regent. At present our attitude must be negative. Italy wishes to head a movement for Prince Ferdinand, Russia is strong the other way: Porte leans to Russia. Austria, Italy, England are pressing Porte to be quiet and are giving the same advice to Italy.[3]

Salisbury's reference in the last sentence to the Mediterranean Agreement with Austria and Italy Morier failed again to notice as significant. One would think Salisbury's reply was plain, but Morier was too reluctant to give up the hope of making an *entente* with Russia to trust it and he telegraphed for further instructions.[4] He would have done better to have asked for

[1] To Salisbury, telegram no. 61 and dispatch no. 287 secret, 17 Aug. 1887, F.O. 65/1298; cf. minute by T. V. Lister in F.O. 65/1300.
[2] To Salisbury, nos. 293 confidential and 294, 24 Aug. 1887, F.O. 65/1298.
[3] From Salisbury, telegram no. 112, 10 p.m., 19 Aug. 1887, F.O. 65/1300. The draft is in Salisbury's own hand.
[4] To Salisbury, telegram no. 62, 22 Aug. 1887, F.O. 65/1300.

elucidation of the reference to Italy. As it was his request prompted only the explanation: 'In speaking to the Russian Minister for Foreign Affairs your best course will be to insist on the difficulty any English Minister would have in formally sanctioning opposition to the expressed wish of the population, especially if there was any danger of that opposition taking a material form. Use friendly but cautious language.'[1]

One factor in Salisbury's firm attitude may well have been the alarming German response to his own independent suggestion, made on 2 August in conversation with Count Hatzfeldt, German ambassador in London, that it would be to Britain's advantage to come to an agreement with Russia over eastern Europe, if necessary at the expense of the Ottoman Empire.[2] This was interpreted by Hatzfeldt as 'a serious change of front' in England—serious enough for a summons to his friend Friedrich von Holstein to come to London to talk over the general situation. The Germans urged the danger of an Anglo-Russian *rapprochement* throwing Italy into the arms of France and compelling Austria-Hungary to reach agreement with Russia at any price.[3] By 24 August Salisbury had assured Bismarck's son, Herbert, that the idea of a closer understanding with Russia would 'remain in abeyance'.[4]

In St. Petersburg Morier executed his instructions on 24 August. In their conversation on that day, already mentioned, Morier drew de Giers away from his idea of a general Anglo-Russian agreement and made quite clear that it stood no chance. He brought the conversation back to Bulgaria and told de Giers that Russia was like the aunt giving to the boy going back to school a guinea with strict instructions not to change it. Russia had given Bulgaria her liberty with strict instructions not to use it. He then spoke of the English tradition of respecting the wishes of the population, and the third Russian 'overture' ended in a haze of platitudes.[5]

It is curious in all this story how near Morier came to

[1] From Salisbury, telegram no. 113, 22 Aug. 1887, F.O. 65/1300. The draft is in Salisbury's own hand.
[2] *Die große Politik der europäischen Kabinette*, vi. 335–7.
[3] M. Rich, *Friedrich von Holstein* (1965), i. 212–13 referring to the Holstein papers.
[4] *Die große Politik der europäischen Kabinette*, vi. 175–7, 345–9.
[5] To Salisbury, nos. 293 and 294, 24 Aug. 1887, F.O. 65/1298.

knowledge of the two realities in international relations in 1887: the Russo-German Reinsurance Treaty and the Anglo-Italian-Austrian Mediterranean Agreements. Yet he never divined their existence and continued to be obsessed by his misplaced wish to reverse British relations with Russia and to overthrow Bismarck. Just before the talks began in St. Petersburg—the talks which were followed up by Paul Shuvalov in conferences with Bismarck on 11 and 18 May and then by the Reinsurance Treaty itself—Morier had a long conversation with his brother, Peter.[1] He had just returned from Berlin. He told Morier that Bismarck adhered to alliance with Russia as the sheet-anchor of his policy and that as it was perfectly certain that the Tsar whatever might be said or written, equally regarded this alliance as securing the maintenance of peace, which His Majesty so ardently desired, peace was certain. 'Then much to my surprise,' Morier's account continues, 'he burst forth in a violent attack on Giers.' After recounting this Morier ends:

Now taking into consideration that this onslaught, which was very unexpected ... coincides with Peter's visit to Berlin where his presence was synchronous with Schweinitz's, and with the presence of Paul at St. Petersburgh,[2] I think it gives one cause for reflexion, the more if you call to mind this curious coincidence that, as reported by me in a public despatch, Schweinitz the dear and bosom friend of Giers, indulged in just such an onslaught last December at the very time that Peter and Paul were both engaged in the great temptation scene in which Bismarck offered the Czar all the kingdoms of the East for his countenance and passivity in regard to the Republic of the West. I do not think therefore that I am far wrong in surmising that the plaint these friends and confederates have against Giers is that he did not sufficiently back them up and an interjection of Peter in his onslaught to the effect that any day Giers might be found at the head of the French party confirms this.

But I think there is yet more behind. Last December Peter very positively stated that if Giers went he most sincerely hoped his brother Paul would not accept his succession. In order to see which way the land lay I observed that if Giers went now I did not envy the man who would have to step into his shoes. To this Peter replied

[1] To Salisbury, private, 21 Apr. 1887, Morier papers; Salisbury papers, A/73, fo. 29.
[2] Where he had an audience of the Tsar together with de Giers on 23 Apr. and the new treaty *à deux* with Germany was discussed.

he did not see this in the least. It was true that there was the horrible muddle of Bulgaria, which had to be got out of, but barring this he thought that a new Minister of Foreign Affairs would have an easy time of it. The union of Germany and Russia would be the rock on which his policy would be necessarily founded and as it would guarantee the peace of the world it would bring back those still waters which Europe so yearned for.

Morier drew from this the wrong inference—that de Giers was likely to be dismissed—and missed the significance of the tightening of Russo-German relations which Shuvalov had made so plain.

As for the Mediterranean Agreements, Salisbury, it will be recalled, had first referred to them in clinching his argument against a *rapprochement* with Russia over Bulgaria. Later, when Morier saw Salisbury in London in January 1888, that is after the Second Mediterranean Agreement of December 1887, Salisbury told him: 'There is of course no present question of our formal adhesion to the Triple Alliance, but you must always remember that we entirely sympathise with the policy of the Central Powers and that you must act accordingly.'[1] Later he wrote: 'It is necessary to insist that our policy is identical with that of the Central Powers. England and Germany and to a great extent Austria are "satisfied" Powers. France and Russia are "hungry" Powers. Italy, it is true, is eminently a hungry Power but the objects of her appetite are no great matter to us.'[2] Had Morier shown an awareness of the significance of what he was told, the Mediterranean Agreements might have been communicated to him, but they never were.

[1] So Morier recalled his words in writing to him afterwards, to Salisbury, second letter, most secret, 25 Jan. 1888, Morier papers; Salisbury papers, A/73, fo. 125.
[2] From Salisbury, private, 1 Feb. 1888, Morier papers; not traced in the Salisbury papers.

9

CENTRAL ASIA, 1885 TO 1887

It is difficult in modern conditions to realize the work involved in fixing the comparatively short frontier (375 miles) from the Hari-Rud river to the Oxus river between Russian Turkestan and Afghan Turkestan. Movement was on foot or on horseback and the country was much as it was in the days of Sohrab and Rustum. The land was grainless, waterless waste, though parts became excellent pasture with the melting of the snows. It was cut, roughly south to north, by three main rivers along whose banks there was cultivated or cultivatable ground. The population was nomadic with occasional new settlements of farmers. Only among the farmers could the western notion of a frontier, as a line of white pillars separating what was permanently and exclusively one nation's from what was that of another, be made intelligible. The nomads expected to have rights in pastures that might shift and change with the seasons.

War or peace depended upon the successful fixing of the frontier: war or peace in Europe, because Britain acted for the Amir of Afghanistan whose defence against Russia meant for her the safety of India; war or peace among the Turkoman tribes, since the frontier had to be acceptable to the local population. The frontier was thus determined, on one hand, by the strategic needs of Russia and Britain as the military advisers of their governments understood them and, on the other hand, by local knowledge—of watersheds, wells, and pasturage rights, of which side valleys of the main rivers were cultivated and which were not, of what constituted good land for what purposes—and this in an area where landmarks were apt to disappear with the changing seasons, a ferry or river-crossing to be there one year and gone the next, river-courses to change, and innumerable places to have the same name.

It had at first been thought that a kind of no-man's-land might be preserved between Russian and Afghan territory. This had become impossible when the Russians took the fair-town of Merv, established encampments with garrisons south and east of it, and asserted their authority over a growing number of tribes. In 1869 Russia and Britain had agreed that they would each abstain from influencing the tribes on the Afghan and Russian steppes respectively. This policy of abstention failed when it proved impossible to observe the line between the Russian and Afghan steppes, laid down in general terms in 1873 as running eastwards until it reached the river Oxus and then running along it. There were two reasons for this. The structure of government in the Russian-contolled province of Bokhara was military and the soldiers inevitably probed their way forward. But in the second place the line of the river was a choice made in ignorance; the four provinces Shignan, Roshan, Wakhan, and Darwaz, over which Afghanistan exercised a loose control, straddled across it.[1]

In 1884 the Russian and British governments agreed that a joint commission should mark the western end of this frontier in detail on the ground. The British commissioner, Major-General Sir Peter Lumsden, arrived with his escort of soldiers and military surveyors. The Russian commissioner constantly postponed his arrival, while the Russian troops as constantly advanced their encampments. He should have arrived in November 1884. He had still not come when the Russians crossed into Afghan territory (14 February 1885) or rather into territory which the Viceroy of India recognized as Afghan.[2]

Lumsden with his escort was encamped on this frontier at its western end and, with approval from London, he encouraged the Afghans to resist any further Russian advance.[3] Meanwhile Granville protested in St. Petersburg and Gladstone in the House of Commons announced an Anglo-Russian agreement that neither Russians nor Afghans would advance further (13 March).[4] Gladstone was premature, but was deliberately

[1] See G. J. Alder, *British India's Northern Frontier 1865–95* (1963), pp. 165–99.
[2] Sir Ronald Thomson (Teheran) to Granville, telegram no. 28, 2 Mar. 1885, forwarding Lumsden's telegram of 14 Feb., F.O. 65/1237.
[3] Granville to Thomson, telegram no. 21, to send on telegram no. 4 to Lumsden, 3 Mar. 1885, F.O. 65/1236.
[4] *Hans. Parl. Deb.* ccxcv. 1204, 1244–7, 1427, 1439–44.

forcing Russia's hand. Sir Edward Thornton, who was still ambassador in St. Petersburg, could now inquire of de Giers whether his assurances in fact constituted an agreement such as Gladstone had described. He replied that Russia accepted Gladstone's declaration, with the reservation that her restraint depended on there being no disturbances at Penjdeh. Thus was made what was later referred to as the agreement of 16/17 March.[1] Nevertheless, on 30 March a battle did occur between a small force of Russians and 200 Afghans, under the eyes of the British officers and men and 400 Indian troops, at Penjdeh in the valley of the river Kushk. Morier's later view was that the clash would never have happened had Lumsden kept his escort in line with the Afghan troops, and he suspected that Lumsden wanted it to happen, expecting the Russians to be defeated. It is a characteristic judgement, but difficult to substantiate.

In the crisis that followed Britain accused Russia of breaking the agreement of 16/17 March. The navy had already occupied Port Hamilton with the object of a descent on Vladivostock in the event of an Anglo-Russian war[2] and, in the last week of April, Parliament voted a credit of £11,000,000 for the possibility of war in both the Sudan and Afghanistan. But in fact, the battle had broken the tension of the last six months and made negotiation possible. These negotiations between the two governments produced decisions to shelve the dangerous question between Russia and Afghanistan of military responsibility; to submit to arbitration the question 'of honour' between Britain and Russia about the breaking of the agreement of 16/17 March; to bring the Russian frontier to the Pass of Zulficar (the word means snow beauty—a west–east pass in a north–south range of hills) at its western end and so to recognize Russia's title to the territory over which she had advanced between November 1884 and 30 March 1885. A protocol and a convention were to record these decisions. Arbitration on the frontier itself was most carefully

---

[1] Granville to Thornton, telegram no. 24, 14 Mar., and reply, telegram no. 8, 16 Mar. 1885, F.O. 65/1237.

[2] See memorandum by Northbrook in Northbrook to Granville, 28 July 1885, P.R.O. 30/29/22A. Northbrook was First Lord of the Admiralty; see also A. Ramm (ed.), *The Political Correspondence of Mr. Gladstone and Lord Granville*, ii. 362–3 and notes.

avoided;[1] only the one question—whether Russia had broken the March agreement, a question which turned on the interpretation of documents—was to go to arbitration. This was easily dropped when, with the lapse of time, interest in laying the blame evaporated.

Meanwhile, the government in Britain changed. It was for the new foreign secretary, Lord Salisbury, to execute the decisions of May 1885. Arbitration was abandoned, no convention was signed, but a protocol on 10 September 1885, signed in London, recorded the agreement about the frontier. A new attempt was then made to mark this out on the spot. Sir West Ridgeway and Major Durand with Captain A. F. Barrow, Captain A. F. de Laessoe, and a civilian, E. H. S. Clarke, were joined by Paul Lessar, Colonel Kuhlberg, and P. Guedeonow for the Russians. This new commission assembled at the Zulficar Pass on 10 November 1885 and erected there the first frontier post on 12 November. It has been said that the Russians surrendered at Zulficar in order to be free to strike a blow in Bulgaria.[2] It is true the Russians might have obtained more, but they had the essential head of the pass. Moreover, their policy was less coherent than such co-ordination would imply and they would seem to have been taken by surprise and, as has been shown above, to have disliked what had happened, when Eastern Rumelia proclaimed reunion with Bulgaria.

The fixing of the frontier at Zulficar by the protocol of 10 September, signed within a fortnight of Morier's first meeting with de Giers, meant that Central Asia, as it was called in the geographical idiom of the day, was nearer the forefront of his mind than the Bulgarian question. It was on this Central Asian question that his first conversation—when his receptiveness was most acute—with de Giers at Franzensbad (in August 1885 before he actually took up his post) had turned. There were two points of interest, Morier reported. First, the Emperor of Austria, writing to de Giers, had expressed his pleasure that, Zulficar being settled, good relations might be re-established

---

[1] R. L. Greaves, *Persia and the Defence of India* (1959), p. 77 is too concise here. See also de Staal (Russian ambassador in London) to Granville, 1 May, and reply, 4 May 1885, F.O. 65/1242; Granville to Thornton, no. 176, 8 May, F.O. 65/1242.
[2] Cf. Mrs. Greaves's account, op. cit., p. 77.

between Britain and Russia. Second, de Giers had concluded their conversation, 'speaking as if he were making a confidence' by insisting on the importance of the signature of the protocol.[1] Morier also recorded some of de Giers's general reflections. He had observed that 'when England and Russia were united the peace of Asia was secured, when we were divided, there was seething everywhere, every Oriental deeming that our dissensions were his opportunities. To be on good terms with England was therefore a matter of real interest to Russia in Asia.'[2]

Morier recorded far more of his own side of their two hours' conversation.[3] He had enlarged on the difficulty of maintaining good relations, if Russia threatened Herat. His lecture on this subject took ten pages to record, and had its characteristic passages. 'The British lion, like all other respectable carnivora,' he wrote, 'had his *chorde sensible*, that *chorde* was his bone, that bone was India. Try to touch it and the whole energies of the Empire throughout the entire globe, mother country and colonies will be united in its defence ... Herat was not the bone, but it was within the sacred precincts of the bone.'[2] Thus it was the Central Asian question that Morier believed to be the touchstone of Anglo-Russian relations. This belief remained with him.

In correspondence with Sir Henry Ponsonby he was driven to sound the depths of his thought about British relations with Russia, since he was in distress at the position they had brought him into with the Queen. Referring to Penjdeh, he wrote:

We are only just out of a very ugly quarrel in which bad blood has been engendered on both sides. The incident is, for the time being, closed. But the most delicate of operations, that of the delimitation of the Affghan frontier, is going on and will have to go on for many months to come;—apparently the promise given by Giers at Franzensbad that everything would be done to let this work be begun and concluded smoothly, is being kept. But until it is done and until our defensive works on the Indian frontier are [?completed] which will not be for another two years and a half, we live on a volcano. Is it not my very first duty to establish during the

---

[1] To Salisbury, private, 31 Aug. 1885.
[2] To Salisbury, private, 1 Sept. 1885; Morier uses the phrase 'chorde [i.e. corde] sensible' several times over the years in his letters and always in this spelling.
[3] To Goschen, 2 June 1888.

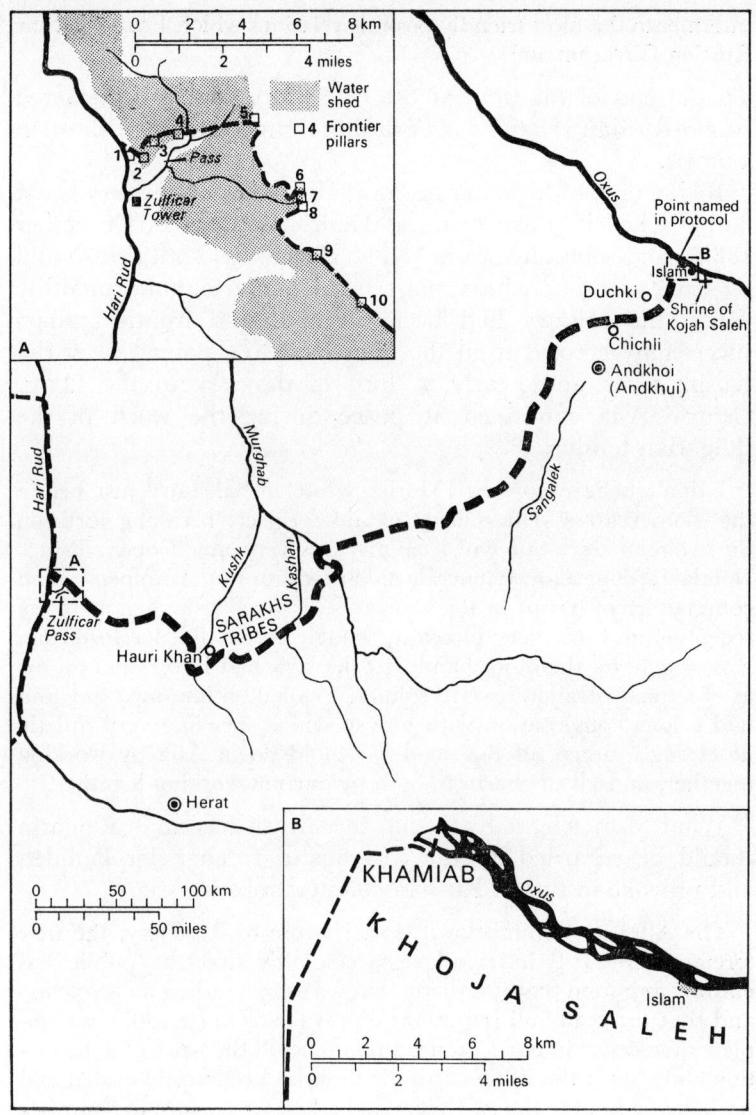

MAP 4. The Russo-Afghan Frontier

intermezzo the most friendly possible relations which I can with the Russian Government?[1]

To the end of his time at St. Petersburg Morier considered Anglo-Russian relations in Asia more important than those in Europe.

By the date of his letter to Ponsonby the frontier commission had reached its third camp at Hauri Khan (6–15 December 1885), and soon afterwards, on 26 December, both British and Russians went into winter quarters. All had so far gone smoothly —half the country had been surveyed and frontier pillars successfully erected from the Hari-Rud to a point east of the Kushk river and nearly a third of the way to the Oxus. Central Asia continued at peace during the worst of the Bulgarian tension.

I don't believe a word [Morier wrote to Salisbury just before the Conservatives left office][2] of any projects breaking forth on the Affghan side, but will keep my eyes very much open. Prince Doudakoff-Korsakov [General, aide-de-camp to the Emperor, and commander of troops in the Caucasus, and a Panslav] came to my reception and was very pleasant, though not confidence inspiring. Rosenbach, on the other hand, left the very best impression on me as of a quiet, straightforward soldier. I called on him next day and had a long conversation with him in which speaking very quietly he strongly urged all the good we could do in Asia by working together, and all the harm to both by our not working together.

What Morier feared was that the British success in Bulgaria should be regarded by the Russians as revenge for Penjdeh and provoke in turn a Russian counterstroke in Asia.

The Affghan Commission [Morier wrote to Rosebery, the new foreign secretary][3] has worked so smoothly that the public has entirely forgotten that it is there, that we were treading on a volcano and that the really all important object for us to strive for is complete quiescence in our European relations till the work of delimitation and with it the Emir's attitude to us is satisfactorily settled and we have tided over the two years and a half we require to complete our defensive system in north west India.

The 'complete victory' in Bulgaria was 'excellent and delightful

[1] To Ponsonby, 15 Dec. 1885.
[2] To Salisbury, private, 26 Jan. 1886.
[3] Private and confidential, 19 Feb., not sent by mistake before 11 Mar. 1886.

from the artistic side of diplomacy but heartbreaking [to one] who was conscious the whole time of the recoil out in Asia. It is *there* we have become neighbours and it is, in my humble opinion, our relations *there* which should mainly occupy our attention and to which we should subordinate our policy in Europe.'

Meanwhile, the Afghan delimitation had in fact run into difficulties. Points of disagreement in the interpretation of the general line laid down by the protocol of 10 September had already emerged in December. In April 1886 the commission was directed to continue despite disagreement and to defer the disputed points.

Up to Christmas [Morier wrote some years later] everything had gone without a hitch and with a clear determination to bring the matter to an end rapidly and smoothly. When the Commissioners met after the Christmas interim the whole scene had changed. Every possible difficulty was raised and chicanery was clearly the *mot d'ordre* from headquarters. The period coincided exactly with the accentuation of our respectively hostile attitudes at the conference on the Bosphorus.[1]

Morier's recollection, however, was at fault, since the demarcation was still going smoothly when the conference adjourned on 25 November. The new dispute coincided, in fact, with the deadlock in Bulgaria before the negotiations for pressure on Greece to disarm (20 January) and for the European sanction to the Turco-Bulgarian agreement began.

The dispute was at first about the stretch of frontier between the rivers Murghab and Oxus. The protocol of 10 September 1885 laid down that the frontier from the Murghab should 'follow a line [i.e. run northwards] to the west of the valley of Sangalak [a north–south valley] and leaving Andkhoi to the east reach Khojah Saleh on the Oxus'.[2] The principle, furthermore, was to be observed that the land cultivated by the Turkoman subjects of Russia, and their pasturages, would be left to Russia, while the land cultivated by the subjects of Afghanistan, and their pasturages, would be left to Afghanistan. The Russian commissioners claimed that the river valley named in

[1] To Goschen, 2 June 1888; see above, p. 256.
[2] *Parliamentary Papers* (1887), lxiii. 618.

the protocol was what *they* called the Shirin Tagao: a north–south valley further to the east. According to their claim the bulge in favour of Afghanistan made by the northern trend was to be deflected eastwards to take in a little more Afghan territory for Russia. The Russians also claimed that the principle about the pasturages should be interpreted as relating to the state of possession in 1875[1] at the time of the Russian occupation of Merv.

Meanwhile, the actual work of demarcation was postponed until February 1886. Very shortly after it was resumed the Russians, on 13 March, revived these claims, and a decision on them was now inescapable since the area to which they related was about to be surveyed and assigned. In addition they now disputed the point at which the frontier was to reach the Oxus. The identity of Khoja Saleh was uncertain and the Russians were able, therefore, to deny the Afghan claim to the district of Khamiab and hold fast to a line further south than that claimed by Ridgeway for the Afghans.

On 17 March 1886 it was mistakenly thought in St. Petersburg —Morier took his information from de Giers—that proceedings were brought to a standstill in order to allow this last question to be referred to the two governments.[2] The truth was that Ridgeway had been told to continue the settlement of the frontier as far as possible towards the Oxus, and then, after careful examination on the spot with his Russian colleague, to endeavour to arrange the question of Khoja Saleh without referring it to the two governments.[3] Similar instructions did not go to the Russian commissioner until 15 April, but they did go and enabled work to be resumed. On 25 April 1886 deadlock had been reached for the third time, and Ridgeway proposed that both the Russian and the British lines should be marked out with pillars on the spot and the choice between them settled in London or St. Petersburg. Three weeks later, 14 May, he was, however, able to report a provisional settlement, the marking of the frontier as far as Duchki, and the

---

[1] Protocol 4, 26 Dec. 1885, and Sir W. Ridgeway to Salisbury, telegram, 10 Dec. 1885, ibid., pp. 640 ff.

[2] To Rosebery, telegram, 17 Mar. 1886; Ridgeway to Rosebery, 5 June 1886; Ridgeway to Rosebery, telegram, 19 Mar. 1886, F.O. 65/1284.

[3] Rosebery to Ridgeway, 26 Mar. 1886, F.O. 65/1284.

proceeding of the commission to the disputed Khamiab area.[1] On 2 June 1886 the commission began their examination of the Khamiab question. An exchange was now proposed, the Russians admitting the Afghan claim to Khamiab and asking for compensation. It was quite clear that there was no place, Khoja Saleh, which fulfilled all the conditions of the protocol and that the muddle had arisen because it was a whole district and not the name of a village.

The Russian compensation was to be found in Sarakhs territory. In agreeing to the protocol of 10 September 1885 the Russians had mistakenly given up territory cultivated by the Sarakhs, who were Turkomans accepting Russian sovereignty. It was supposed that they were confined to the valleys of the Kushk and Kashan (south–north rivers), but in fact they had extended their cultivation into the side valleys of these rivers. The two governments had fixed the points where the frontier was to cross these rivers, so as to allow the Russian Sarakhs to keep their cultivated territory in these valleys. When the commissioners arrived on the spot, they carried out the protocol to the letter and the Sarakhs were driven out of side valleys lying to the south of the line of the crossing of the rivers and so accordingly falling to Afghanistan. When the commissioners reached the Oxus, they found that the literal execution of the protocol of 10 September would now have the reverse effect and be to the advantage of the Russians; the Afghans would lose the district of Khamiab; and pasturage and wells enjoyed in common by the Uzbeg Turkomans, who acknowledged no allegiance, would have to be divided, some going to Afghanistan and some to Russia and thus dividing the Uzbeg Turkomans too, or else depriving them of rights in one or other territory. The Russians proposed that the Sarakhs should be restored in the Kushk–Kashan area and the frontier redrawn, and in exchange the Afghans and the Uzbeg Turkomans might have the whole of the Khamiab area. The Russian commissioner, who had been instructed[2] not to give up Khamiab, would not take upon himself the responsibility of effecting this exchange,

---

[1] To Rosebery, 7 Apr. 1886; to Rosebery, telegram 15 Apr. 1886; Ridgeway to Rosebery, 12 Apr. 1886, and telegrams nos. 675, 683, 25 Apr., 14 May 1886, F.O. 65/1285 and 1286.
[2] Ridgeway to Rosebery, telegram, 17 June 1886, F.O. 65/1287.

when it came to the point, so that by the time Rosebery had fallen and Iddesleigh was at the Foreign Office, the commission had broken up and the question of the frontier from the Kushk to the Oxus was before the two governments.

It was at this point, in the summer of 1886, that the Central Asian question first became Morier's responsibility. On 17 July the Russian commissioner referred the Khoja Saleh question home.[1] On 6 August Iddesleigh instructed Morier to open negotiations with de Giers[2] with the object of reaching agreement as soon as possible on identical instructions to their two commissioners. Behind this formal instruction lay a clear objective. 'What we want', wrote Sanderson privately, 'is to get the Russians to say that the frontier being settled as far as Duchki, the remaining bit should be settled between the two Governments. We should then withdraw our commissioner.'[3] Currie wrote in much the same sense on 12 August, adding that the wish was that the boundary east of Khoja Saleh should 'stand over'. Iddesleigh already on the 4th had written, 'it is an object with us to settle the residue of the matter by direct negotiation, and to change the venue from the Oxus to the Thames or Neva.' Morier opened discussions with de Giers on 8 August 1886 and continued them with Zinoviev on the 11th. By 25 August it was agreed that the commission should separate and the line from Duchki to the Oxus be negotiated between the two governments, the *status quo* being maintained meanwhile. The next phase of discussion was to decide whether these negotiations should take place at St. Petersburg or London. This was not settled in favour of St. Petersburg until Ridgeway and his staff made their way there, arriving in April 1887, during the Easter holidays. Discussions were then opened but soon languished, and Ridgeway was recalled to London. He returned to St. Petersburg on 22 July 1887, completed the negotiations, and signed a protocol. Why were these negotiations so slow? Why was so little left to Morier and, indeed, why were they at one point taken back to London?

---

[1] Ridgeway to Rosebery, 18 July 1886, F.O. 65/1288.
[2] From Iddesleigh, telegrams no. 153 and 156, 6 and 7 Aug. 1886, F.O. 65/1289.
[3] Sanderson to Morier, private, 18 Aug. 1886.

The government of India was the source of the wish to get the commissioners away. As Morier dramatically put it, since the Russians had become hostile, 'our commissioners were virtually hostages in the Russian hands'.[1] It was thought, too, that the retention of Khamiab by Afghanistan, whether or not at the price of surrender on the Kushk and Kashan rivers, would be easier to settle with the Russians in St. Petersburg than on the spot, where their presence and the ease with which they gained the co-operation of the Turkomans seemed to prompt new claims. But Ridgeway listed four possibilities of which the surrender of Khamiab and arbitration were second and fourth; the retention of Khamiab in return for compensation was the third; and the first was to repudiate the letter of the 1873 agreement, and to insist on most of this part of the Oxus valley for Afghanistan without any price being paid to the Russians.

Salisbury and Iddesleigh were not concerned with these various possibilities, but like the government of India were more anxious to suspend the negotiation completely than to conclude it. Iddesleigh, however, was not sufficiently firm in writing to Morier about this and merely cautioned him against appearing to surrender. 'Please be very careful', he wrote,[2] 'not to give the Russians any points in the game and above all to limit yourself to discussing how the negotiations are to be conducted', and to defer the substance; 'it is most inexpedient to mix up the two questions of *modus operandi* and the work to be accomplished.' Given Morier's anxiety for a success, it was not enough to trust that he would read between the lines of this letter and understand that his government did not want a settlement; it should have been expressly said. Salisbury, after he became foreign secretary, was quite candid:

> I think our business for the moment is to mark time. I do not like the idea of settling the Affghan boundary at St. Petersburg. In fact, I am not very keen for settling the point that remains in dispute at all—at least just now. What the Ameer expects is far beyond what any settlement will give him: and he will consider us to blame if the agreement falls short of his expectations. His resentment is certain—and may be violent. On the other hand, the chances of

---

[1] To Salisbury, private telegram, 12 Feb. 1887.
[2] To Morier, private, 17 Aug. 1886.

a Russian invasion being produced by the unsettled bit of the line seem remote. It is not the place the Russians will care to invade—because it leads nowhere. If they invade at all it will be somewhere where they are not blocked by the Hindu Kush.[1]

'I regret the whole policy of demarcation', he had written earlier.[2] He wished to keep open the possibility of extending British influence among the Turkomans—of inducing them to look to Britain rather than to Russia, and he believed a definite frontier would set a barrier to that policy.

Thus the dispersal of the commission, the refusal to discuss the substance of an agreement, and the dragging discussion of the place of the negotiations were the consequence of the gradual re-establishment after the fall of the Liberals, of the more subtle Fabian policy that Salisbury favoured in Anglo-Russian relations.

Now with this Morier was entirely out of sympathy. It was quite clear that from August 1886 to February 1887 he was pulling against his government. He began wrong, by leaping to the task,[3] when Iddesleigh's instruction first arrived. It came three days before de Giers was due to leave St. Petersburg to meet Bismarck at Franzensbad.

Everything depended [Morier, dramatizing after the event, wrote][4] on my obtaining the assurance from him that he would vigorously support our demand for the break up of the Commission and the resumption of the negotiation at St. Petersburg or London. The moment was a peculiarly favourable one in one sense. It was just *after* the Batum incident, the evil impressions of which Giers was naturally anxious to soften down, and it was *before* the last Bulgarian trouble. Accordingly Giers took up the matter with the greatest energy and vigour. He caused a report to be at once made to him on the subject, had a conference with the departments, at one o'clock in the morning, on the day of his departure, and obtained the Emperor's full consent to the matter being settled in a friendly manner on the basis of the transfer of the negotiation to Europe.

Morier, it is clear, made two further mistakes. First, he was

[1] From Salisbury, private, 3 Feb. 1887.
[2] See above, p. 238.
[3] As if there were something really to construct and not merely a negotiation to be tidily broken off.
[4] To Salisbury, private, 9 Feb. 1887, Morier papers; Salisbury papers, A/73, fo. 4.

wrong to allude to the substance of a compromise line in the conversation of 8 August with de Giers. For this he was rebuked by the mild Iddesleigh: 'I was a little sorry that you should have been the first to talk of "compromise"; one comes on the word rather abruptly in the telegram.'[1] Iddesleigh repeated his rebuke on the 17th: 'We are rather in trouble over the discussion of compromise which appears to us premature.' Secondly, Morier was wrong to adopt such a formal method of procedure as the note of 25 August to record the Russian agreement to the dispersal of the commission. It was not agreeable to the Foreign Office and again Morier was rebuked: 'The form of the Note rather took us by surprise, and our impression is that it might have been more clearly worded.'[2] Morier was then summoned home. But the Bulgarian question—the more important cause of the summons—growing quiet again, his first secretary dying, and then de Staal's going to St. Petersburg being likely to coincide with Morier's sojourn in London, and finally the Foreign Office not liking Morier's reason (see below, pp. 277–8) for himself asking for a personal interview—all these things delayed his going to London. He was at last there from 20 December 1886 to 9 January 1887. While there he was briefed at the India Office and Foreign Office and had some discussion with Ridgeway; for it was quite clear that Russia and Morier wanted the negotiation to be in St. Petersburg and not London.

It would appear to have been Morier who got the negotiation to St. Petersburg and, in the end, found a way to defeat Salisbury's preference for delay. He took up Salisbury's plea of 3 February 1887 for postponement and argued against it. His arguments were four: first, that it would be good in itself to clear away a source of trouble and of the nagging policy he so much deplored: second, that its being cleared away would strengthen de Giers against the military party, which constantly exposed him to 'the endless wear and tear' of argument on this question; third, that British good faith and especially his whole personal credit were pledged to its being cleared up. He had gained the insertion of a clause in the note arranging for the *status quo* to be preserved until demarcation

[1] From Iddesleigh, private, 12 Aug. 1886.
[2] From Iddesleigh, private, 1 Sept. 1886.

was resumed. If it was not resumed, the *status quo* being favourable to the Amir, this would bear the appearance of a ruse. His fourth argument was that a settlement was better made in St. Petersburg where he and Ridgeway would be in direct contact with de Giers, who always had access to the Emperor, and would be able to co-operate to defeat the military party. It was better to defeat them than merely to be out of their way with Lessar and de Staal in London.[1]

Salisbury gave way, not on the first, second, or fourth, but solely on the third ground. 'Lord Salisbury has given way about the boundary', wrote Currie.[2] Salisbury himself wrote: 'The best argument in favour of proceeding with the Affghan demarcation at St. Petersburg is that apparently the Russian Gov[ernmen]t will impute to us bad faith for taking a different course—and especially that your whole personal credit with them will be injured. Otherwise, I should have preferred postponing the matter indefinitely.'[3] Cross at the India Office shared Salisbury's reluctance to reach a settlement and feared Morier's wish for a diplomatic success. When Morier appealed to him to support negotiation in St. Petersburg, he sent Morier's letter to Salisbury explaining that he would agree, but adding: 'This is a curious and somewhat irregular piece of Diplomacy . . . it is difficult to say my chief objection is that you are in St. Petersburg.'[4]

After a promising beginning when Ridgeway arrived in April, negotiations languished because the Russian military party disliked demarcation as much as Salisbury, and wished to keep the frontier undefined, so as to retain the opportunity for unlimited political influence with the Turkoman tribes. The Russians, already when Salisbury gave way and agreed to the resumption of negotiations, widened the whole matter by insisting on the reopening of the thirty miles of frontier between Chichli and Duchki. There were then three matters at issue: (1) this thirty miles; (2) the thirty-four miles of frontier between Duchki and the Oxus; and (3) the stopping-place on the Oxus river, now disputed between Islam, fourteen miles

[1] To Salisbury, private, 9 Feb. 1887, Morier papers; Salisbury papers, A/73, fos. 6–7.
[2] From Currie, 16 Feb. 1887.
[3] From Salisbury, private, 16 Feb. 1887.
[4] Salisbury papers, E/box of letters from R. A. Cross, no. 114.

higher up than the mistaken point named in the protocol, and the so-called shrine of Khoja Saleh, twenty-one miles higher up. Ridgeway's instructions were to refuse to yield on the first, 'except where it might be right to make allowances for minor errors of surveying, or where some moderate concessions would facilitate a favourable settlement in regard to Khamiab'. He was to point out to the Russians that the frontier from Duchki to the Oxus was governed by the intention of the agreement of 1873, which the protocol of 10 September 1885 sought only to fulfil, and that it intended to leave the Amir all he then had and that this included Khamiab. On the Oxus itself he was to seek a reasonable compromise.[1] Of all the possibilities he had listed, the solution of retaining Khamiab, and giving back to the Russian Sarakhs the cultivated land of which they had been deprived by the joint commission, most commended itself to the British government. The attempt in fact was being made to settle the question according to its merits and to resume where the work had been broken off. Zinoviev was appointed to negotiate with Ridgeway and they examined the points at issue in the light of the evidence. No difficulty was found in inducing Zinoviev to accept the compromise of Khamiab in exchange for restorations of territory to the Russian Sarakhs. The negotiations were then held up by the Russians' extortionate demands on behalf of the Sarakhs.

Moreover, by now Morier had come round to appreciate Salisbury's Fabian tactics and he sought to 'hang up' a settlement. On 11 May 1887 Salisbury had taken up once again his theme of the danger of settling. This was after the first conference and his fear that Zinoviev was going to insist on having Khamiab or breaking up the whole negotiation. The Amir will probably quarrel with us if we do not secure Khamiab for him. It seems to me that under these circumstances a speedy decision is the last thing for which we ought to wish. We must not let the Russians break off and repudiate the line that has been already drawn: but short of that we had better delay as long as we can a conclusion that must be unwelcome and discreditable to us, and which is likely enough to bring us into trouble with the Amir. Time may give us a chance of getting out of this dilemma, but I see no chance of that kind now.[2]

[1] *Parliamentary Papers* (1888), lxxvii. 732.
[2] From Salisbury, private, 11 May 1887.

A week later Morier was urged to allow the negotiation 'to continue a semi-animate existence until some acceptable compromise is discovered'.[1] If this were not enough, Currie echoed his chief, 'Lord Salisbury's idea is not to hurry the frontier negotiations, but to let them traîner a bit'.[2]

Morier understood that 'if we cannot come to an arrangement satisfactory to ourselves you would prefer a provisional state of non settlement to an acute rupture, and, as this, I am convinced, is Giers' own view, I shall work if all else fails in this direction.' But in this sentence the conditional clauses were the important elements. It was his determination to get a satisfactory settlement which led Morier to intervene when a favourable opportunity came and to try after all to get a conclusion.

Such an opportunity offered itself when the Emperor cut across the policy of the military party, summoned Ridgeway to an audience on 13 May, and urged his wish for a settlement. At the same time rumours ran that the Russians intended to repeat the tactics of Penjdeh and, while negotiations hung fire, to take possession of Khamiab. On 18 May Morier intervened with a bold warning that public opinion would never allow a British minister to submit to a repetition of Penjdeh. It was intended as 'a friendly warning from an exceptionally friendly ambassador who had established personal relations which enabled him to speak out boldly and frankly . . . without . . . giving offence'.[3] Ridgeway described this as an important conversation with 'Giers which no doubt considerably influenced negotiations'. The Tsar returning to St. Petersburg called for a report and the result was a decided change, for Zinoviev considerably reduced the Russian demand for compensation (31 May).

Negotiations were now being speeded to an end quite against the British government's wishes. It recalled Ridgeway and summoned him to attend a meeting of the cabinet, at which the whole policy was reviewed.

The calling of the negotiations back to London was thus

[1] From Salisbury, private, 18 May 1887.
[2] Currie to Morier, private, 18 May 1887.
[3] To Salisbury, private, 19 May 1887, Morier papers; Salisbury papers, A/73, fo. 46.

because Morier had again got out of step with his government, but the cabinet finally settled for a change of policy, and Ridgeway returned with a fresh offer of compromise on the compensation to be offered to the Russian Sarakhs in the Kushk area. This failing, the negotiators tried again at the Khamiab or Oxus end. By July both the compensation in the Kushk area and the point where the frontier was to meet the Oxus, so as to leave Khamiab to the Afghans, had been settled and only the line behind Duchki remained to be drawn[1]—by a fair decision about the distribution of the wells. At that point Morier intervened once again (15 July) and took the difficulties to de Giers. They were settled on the 16th. The protocol was drafted on the 17th and signed on 22 July 1887. The great problem of the legal position of the provinces of Shignan, Roshan, Wakhan, and Darwaz, which straddled the Oxus further east and were claimed by Afghanistan, still remained open. But Morier had gained his success, despite his government rather than in fulfilment of its policy.

[1] Details are clearly given in Ridgeway's report, 15 Aug. 1887, *Parliamentary Papers* (1888), lxxvii. 751.

10

MORIER AND BISMARCK

MORIER had watched in the sixties with interest and sympathy the development of Prussian policy as a policy of what he called German reconstruction. His exposition,[1] published anonymously, of the Schleswig-Holstein question was a statement of the German case for the information of a British public largely Danish in its sympathies. His article, also anonymous, in the *North British Review* of March 1869 reviewed three books, a collection of diplomatic documents edited by Karl Ægidi, and two others by H. Schulze and A. Schmidt respectively, and commented on the remarkable national revival represented by the foundation of the North German Confederation.[2] After 1870 he was still sympathetic to what he hoped might be a strong, liberal, and united Germany. His reports to Lord Granville on opinion in Alsace-Lorraine were not perhaps in step with the intentions of the new Germany, but he was, in 1871, still devoted to the 'one idea . . . the Anglo-German alliance'.[3] Yet even while he was chargé d'affaires at Darmstadt (in 1867), Bismarck accused him to Lord Augustus Loftus, then British ambassador in Berlin, of being 'at the head of an active anti-Prussian propaganda in Southern Germany'.[4] Morier subsequently learnt that this charge was based on anonymous letters sent to Berlin by the Prussian representative in Darmstadt.[5]

The new Germany was, in ideas, still deeply divided. The

[1] *The Dano-German Conflict and Lord Russell's Despatch of September 1862* (1863)—an anonymous pamphlet.
[2] 'Reconstruction in Germany', *North British Review*, li (1869), 253.
[3] Wemyss, Memoirs, i. 393.
[4] To Lord Salisbury, 1 June 1887, Morier papers; Salisbury papers, letters from Morier, fo. 74; cf. pp. 6–7 above. Morier named Lord Napier by mistake in his letter to Salisbury.
[5] Wemyss, ii. 98–103.

liberals, who had withstood Bismarck over the army bill in Prussia, capitulated when he emerged as the organizer of victory over Austria and the creator of the North German Confederation. The constitutions of 1867 and 1871 marked a defeat for liberal principles of parliamentary government. The party of Bismarck's supporters was essentially a Prussian party, neither liberal nor conservative, as contemporaries understood those terms. The spearhead of this party was the National Liberal *Fraktion* in the Reichstag. Liberals to the left of them were not reconciled to Bismarck. Then, outside the politics of the Reichstag were other potential opponents of Bismarck: those who were clearly identified with classical liberalism and looked to the circle round the Crown Prince and Princess for inspiration. It will be recalled that it was to this circle that Morier belonged and that his first serious clash with Bismarck occurred in 1875 (above, p. 7). Indeed from 1875 men of liberal opinion grew increasingly hostile to Bismarck. They disliked the tilt away from the west in foreign policy, represented by the Austro-German alliance of 1879; they could not accept the departure from political liberalism marked by the anti-socialist law of 1878, nor that from economic liberalism marked by the tariff of 1879. Yet they did not necessarily wish to adopt the position of the Left Liberals in the Reichstag. Many avoided the conventional party organizations of the day altogether. Bismarck knew where he was with the formal parties. The Crown Prince's circle and its unidentifiable following he feared, because he could not fight them openly. He harried them, therefore, through the press and eventually, in, for example, the Geffcken case, in the courts. Morier had his share of this harassment.

It took the form of a cloud of suspicion, created by the talk of agents, not specifically instructed and therefore easily disavowed, and paragraphs in newspapers whose authors could not be traced. This, at least, was Morier's belief; for, at Madrid, he had been acquainted with one of Bismarck's agents 'continuously employed in Spain for eighteen months' before the Franco-Prussian War, and from him he had learnt that it was Bismarck's practice to leave his agents to do, or say, what they thought he would like them to do or say, and 'then suddenly not only to disavow them but to send them about their business to ponder in poverty and disgrace on the mutability of human affairs'.[1]

Another of Bismarck's practices was to insert a tendentious paragraph in some obscure provincial newspaper which the national papers then copied, so providing occasion for a controversy that implanted a suspicion in the public mind without anyone being able to trace it to its source. Morier described this practice to the King of Portugal already in 1876.[2] He believed himself to have been the victim of it when an unimportant German newspaper described him as a well-known enemy of Germany and stated as an authenticated fact that he had been the instigator of the Spanish government's defiance of Bismarck at the time—1885—of the Jolo incident in the Caroline Islands.[3] A fortnight later the *Norddeutsche Allgemeine Zeitung* reproduced the paragraph. The accusation was quite patently false, since, after the breakdown of the commercial negotiations at Madrid, Morier was only transacting the most formal business with the Spanish government. The accusation, Morier's imagination showed him, could only have had the purpose of preventing his appointment to St. Petersburg, then under discussion. Yet at the time he had seemed unaffected by it. He called at the Foreign Office in Berlin, and saw Count Herbert Bismarck and Count Hatzfeldt, on his way to St. Petersburg. 'Nothing could be more prévenant than the former so that', he wrote at the time, 'I think I shall make my start at St. Petersburg in good *form* at least as regards the Chancellor and his family.'[4] It was a delusion. When he arrived at St. Petersburg, he found 'confirmed to the letter what de Staal had previously warned me of in London, viz. that means had been taken to represent me in the worst possible colours as the deadly enemy of Russia, a *mauvais coucheur* of the worst description and the most cantankerous and quarrelsome of men'.[5]

While Morier put himself wrong with Bismarck by his

[1] To Derby, 20 Sept. 1876.
[2] To Derby, 20 Oct. 1876, and above, p. 25.
[3] To Grant Duff, 31 Dec. 1888: 'when Bismarck attempted to force his ships into the Karolinas [which belonged to Spain] and had to go and hold on to the Pope's petticoats, for safety'. The incident was settled under papal mediation. See also Morier to Ponsonby, 6 Feb. 1889, R.A. I 57/16.
[4] To Salisbury, private, 4 Nov. 1885.
[5] To Salisbury, private, 1 June 1887, Morier papers; Salisbury papers, letters from Morier, fo. 74.

identification of himself with the Crown Prince's circle, he put himself equally wrong with the Queen by his efforts to improve Anglo-Russian relations. He had barely been a fortnight at St. Petersburg—he arrived on 6 November—when the Queen asked Salisbury, in allusion to Morier's weak defence of Prince Alexander, whether he did not think Morier 'very luke-warm in the right cause' and agree that he only repeated Russian views. Salisbury professed himself surprised because Morier had been keen, in talking to him in October, against redividing the Big Bulgaria that Prince Alexander seemed so successfully to have stabilized.[1] But the Queen's conviction that Morier was failing to present the British point of view only grew stronger. When she agreed to make him G.C.M.G., among the honours awarded on the resignation of the government, she did so in a spirit of precaution. Salisbury had written that it might depend on Morier's 'hearty goodwill whether the Czar behaved tolerably to Prince Alexander or not'. It was as 'a matter of prudence' that he recommended that he should submit Morier's name to her, and as a matter of prudence the Queen accepted it.[2] To her new foreign secretary, Lord Rosebery, she wrote almost once a week with fresh information against him; for she was anxious lest a Gladstone government should not be firm enough against Russia. On 11 February she repeated a story that de Giers had said he could not believe Morier 'as he *flattered them too much*!!'[3] On 23 February, after asking Ponsonby's views on a number of telegrams from Morier which she thought showed he was 'most dangerous',[4] she telegraphed to Rosebery: '... Sir R. Morier is in the hands of Russia and very dangerous.' A letter expanding the telegram gave an unidentified source for her view and enclosed an extract from a letter to support it. On 27 February she wrote: 'The impression at the Foreign Office at Berlin is that Sir R. Morier wishes for *an ideal* Alliance between England and Russia at the expence of the P[rin]ce of Bulgaria.'[5] On 3 March she approves of the rebuke to Morier

---

[1] The Queen to Salisbury, draft telegram, and Salisbury's reply, both 19 Nov. 1885, R.A. H 28/78 and 79.
[2] Salisbury to the Queen, 3 Feb. 1886, R.A. C 37/229.
[3] See the Queen to Rosebery, Rosebery papers, box 51, and some extracts in translation from letters from a German informant to her in box 90.
[4] The Queen to Ponsonby, 23 Feb. 1886, R.A. L 15/76.
[5] This information seems to have come from the Crown Princess; see her letter

that Rosebery had administered 'and would like to see Sir R. Morier's face when he gets it'. 'He really needed a check for he is quite bent on a policy of his own.'[1] By now Rosebery, nettled that the Queen could think it possible that he was not in control of his own policy, had been brought entirely to take her view. 'The Empire can afford to have only one policy at a time and Your Majesty would have had to choose between the two essentially different policies pursued by Sir R. Morier and [myself]... Sir R. Morier's despatches are expositions of Russian, not British policy: witness his telegrams of last night in which he refers to various despatches to vindicate Russian consistency.'[2] On 6 March the Queen sent further information; this time that Morier was supplying misleading information to *The Times*' correspondent in St. Petersburg, and suggested that he should hint privately at transfer to another post. Rosebery wisely demurred at a further rebuke, but took her literally about a transfer.[3] On 7 March she then withdrew this suggestion and confessed that what she heard was only rumour, but even then added, 'but these rumours have constantly come true'.[1] Meanwhile, Ponsonby had tried to pacify the Queen by again sending her Morier's letter to him of January 1878 (see above, p. 125) with its insistence on British support for Turkey against Russia.

Through Geffcken, of whom the Crown Princess later wrote, 'so indiscreet and such a chatterbox... always quoting one person to another',[4] Morier had heard that the Queen was dissatisfied, and, still smarting under Rosebery's rebuke, he wrote to the Crown Princess. She, in turn, sent Morier's letter to the Queen, pointing out that he was being calumniated. The Queen thereupon replied to the Crown Princess that these calumnies 'were all nonsense. It is his own Tels. and despatches wh. shewed such a *Neigung* [leaning] towards Russia—and the words which he has repeatedly dropped about Constantinople which alarm us... I want no inquiries etc. only warnings and it is his own words which have made me anxious and

to the Queen, 25 Feb., received 27 Feb, and the Queen's reply, 27 Feb. 1886, R.A. Add. MS. U 32/424.

[1] Rosebery papers, box 51.
[2] Rosebery to the Queen, 4 Mar. 1886, R.A. B 37/29.
[3] Rosebery papers, box 51, and Rosebery to the Queen, 6 Mar. 1886, R.A. B 37/31.
[4] See R.A. H 18/87.

his overweening vanity.'[1] She did not return Morier's letter until 31 March, when she returned it together with one from Ernst von Stockmar which the Crown Princess had also enclosed. Morier had to be content with a mild reply from the Crown Princess. The Queen, however, held her peace for nearly a month.

On 3 April she took up her tune again. 'The Queen thinks Sir R. Morier's Telegrams and Despatches are worse and worse and shew more and more that he is quite Russian.' On 9 April she had again 'some very *confidential* but she believes *entirely reliable* news to communicate to Lord Rosebery . . .', from which it appeared that 'he [Morier] is working in a sly underhand way for an Anglo-Russian alliance'. She then quotes in French Morier's language to de Giers as reported to her by this unknown informant. In her own papers a copy of this letter to Rosebery represents the whole passage by a row of dots; so that what she goes on to call 'monstrous' and 'too true' has been omitted. 'The Queen', she continued, 'thinks such a man so dangerous and evidently so full of his own ideas of petty *"rancune"* that she thinks we ought to get him away *as soon as possible*.'[2] At bottom the common sense of the Queen revolted against Morier's elaborate professionalism. She summed up, for instance, the complicated diagnosis behind his recommendation of a *modus vivendi* with Russia (above, pp. 232-5): 'Sir R. Morier . . . thinks England should let Russia have her own way in the Balkan Peninsula, so as to save India!!' But it is also undeniably true that someone, other than the Crown Princess, was passing information to the Queen, behind Morier's back, and it is at least plausible that her unknown informant was, in turn, supplied from the Bismarcks, who derived their information from the German embassy in St. Petersburg. On 30 July the unknown informant wrote to the Queen in German that Morier had not presented the stiff note about Batum, but a much milder version, to the Russian government. This was too unlikely and too easily shown up for the Queen to believe and she appears to have done nothing with it, though she preserved a copy of part of the letter among her

[1] The Queen to the Crown Princess, 24 Mar. 1886, R.A. Add. MS. U 32/426.
[2] The Queen to Rosebery, copy, 9 Apr. 1886, R.A. H 29/150. The two letters to Rosebery of 3 and 9 Apr. are in original in the Rosebery papers, box 51.

papers.¹ The tone of the communication marks it as from the same source as her other information; for it speaks of Morier's exaggerated friendship for Russia and his readiness to gain good relations with her by the sacrifice of Bulgaria. The Bismarcks, profiting from Rosebery's dislike of Morier had, in fact, come into the open. Hatzfeldt, on instructions, made a formal complaint to him of Morier's hostility to Germany, and he seemed only to welcome it.²

By August Salisbury was again prime minister. He had only been in office a couple of days when the Queen sent him some papers—now no longer recoverable—about Morier that caused him to comment, when returning them, on the strangeness of the story and to add: 'If there is no mistake, Sir R. Morier is the reverse of an honest man.'³ A fortnight later (20–1 August) Prince Alexander had been kidnapped. The Queen, in setting down for Salisbury her sense of outrage, was inclined to blame 'that dishonest Morier (who MUST NOT remain)'. 'Sir R. Morier', she wrote, 'has *tacitly encouraged* the bad and wicked feeling of the Emperor against his cousin and one could read between the lines in all his letters. He is *not safe there*. He should be given leave of absence at once.'⁴

Meanwhile Herbert Bismarck saw Malet in Berlin and said that Bülow had reported from St. Petersburg that 'Morier spoke of the Prince in terms more contemptuous than even the Russians used.' Malet refused to believe this, and renewed his assurances of British support to Prince Alexander. But 'in some consternation', he reported the incident in a private letter to Iddesleigh, 'for his eye alone', asking that his name should not be revealed. He commented: 'It is an open secret that Prince Bismarck greatly dislikes Morier and would not hesitate to undermine him when he gets the chance.'⁵ Iddesleigh at once telegraphed to Morier that he should take steps to neutralize the false reports being circulated of his language.

Morier was deeply distressed and felt himself the victim of a malicious persecution. He wrote to Iddesleigh:

---

[1] R.A. H 29/194.   [2] Hatzfeldt to Bismarck, 26 Apr. 1886, GFM 10/200.
[3] Salisbury to the Queen, 6 Aug. 1886, R.A. A 65/1a. Salisbury had communicated the papers to Iddesleigh, the new foreign secretary.
[4] The Queen to Salisbury, 23 Aug. 1886, R.A. H 30/15.
[5] Malet to Iddesleigh, private, 4 Sept. 1886, Iddesleigh papers, B.M. Add. MS. 50042, fo. 179.

I dislike more than I can say introducing personal matters into public business but the knowledge I have that in the highest quarters my action since I have been Ambassador at St. Petersburg has been disapproved, and that I am distrusted is ... too important a factor, seeing what my public position is, to be ignored ... My line of action has been entirely misunderstood because it has been misrepresented by outsiders, and I ought to have an opportunity of explaining my conduct.[1]

By now (8 September) the Queen had in fact received yet another instalment of Morier's misdeeds—this time from the Crown Princess to whom she had written the week before, 'Morier must be got away'.[2] The Crown Princess reported that 'Morier is much pleased now and went about saying the P[rin]ce was a liar, and the British Govt. should never have supported him. The Russians were astonished at his language and think him very odd.'[3] Salisbury replied by striking a note of sanity, distinguishing between the particular reports from secret sources and the general drift of Morier's own telegrams and dispatches which, however pro-Russian, were still not dishonourable. 'All our information as to Sir R. Morier's misconduct with respect to Prince Alexander', he telegraphed, 'appears to come through Prince Bismarck.' The Queen thereupon stoutly denied that her information came from Prince Bismarck, but dropped her demand for Morier's recall, saying she would be content if he were only called home and *told how to act*. This she most earnestly urged,[4] and Iddesleigh did in fact summon Morier home. He had suggested it on 1 September and now telegraphed more peremptorily. But Morier did not go. Instead he wrote, as always preoccupied with his own personality, as if he was being asked to come to London to give advice and not to receive it. He said that 'one of the several very important matters I wish to seize you with *viva voce* has reference to the desperately delicate question of my *locus standi* with the Queen.' He asserted that it was essential that he should find out something from Lord Salisbury before he could talk about this and

---

[1] To Iddesleigh, private, 9 Sept. 1886.
[2] The Queen to the Crown Princess, 28 Aug. 1886, R.A. Add. MS. U 32/438.
[3] The Queen to Salisbury, telegram, 8 Sept. 1886, R.A. H 30/192.
[4] Salisbury to the Queen, telegram, and her reply, both 9 Sept. 1886, R.A. H 30/194 and 195.

so proposed delaying his visit.¹ The mild Iddesleigh had already written, 'I don't know that there is any special reason for your coming home immediately.' Yet he added a postscript: 'Sept. 28. I think you ought to come home without further delay. It is important that I should see you.'² Morier still did not go, finding reasons in the death of his first secretary and the likely journey of de Staal—the Russian ambassador in London—to St. Petersburg at the same time (see above, p. 265).

Meanwhile, the gossiping Geffcken had again been at work. He let Morier know that reports were circulating of his general malfeasance at St. Petersburg together with renewed assertions that the Queen disapproved of his whole line of action since he had been there. Much to Morier's embarrassment, Geffcken appears also to have 'interviewed' several people in London on Morier's behalf and found out that 'the Ministers', as distinct from the Queen, 'were not dissatisfied'.³ It may be Geffcken's activity that explains young Eyre Crowe's knowledge of the reports about Morier.⁴ In any event, they seem to have been more than was needed to make an overwrought Morier protest his innocence in much detail to Iddesleigh in a long letter that more than did duty for the oral explanation he might have made in London. He believed, rightly, that it was being asserted that he was hostile to Prince Alexander and an obviously forged telegram, alleged to have been sent by the Queen to the Tsar, was cited as evidence. An article in *The Times* on 6 September asserted, wrongly, that Morier had failed to warn Russia, as he had been instructed to do, that Britain was prepared to offer her support to keep Prince Alexander on the throne. It was easy to disprove the assertion about his hostility to Prince Alexander, and he believed he could also show that it originated in Berlin. He traced it back to a misrepresentation of a remark of his own to Vlangally (deputizing for de Giers), relayed by

---

¹ Morier to Iddesleigh, most secret, 28 Sept. 1886.
² Iddesleigh to Morier, 27 Sept. 1887.
³ The Crown Princess to the Queen, 20 Dec. 1886, reporting Morier's account of this incident to her, R.A. H 32/133.
⁴ Eyre Crowe, then 22 and in his second year as a junior clerk in the Foreign Office, had also heard that Bismarck deliberately made Morier believe that reports were circulating, so that when Morier's remonstrances in turn came back to him, he would have cause to complain. 'It is no secret how he [Bismarck] hates him [Morier]', Eyre Crowe wrote to his father, J. A. Crowe, 7, 8 Sept. and 4 Nov. 1886, letters in the possession of his daughter.

him to von Bülow and by von Bülow to Berlin. The article in *The Times*, he said, belonged to a series which had certain features that proved it to have been written by someone in close touch with the German Foreign Office.[1]

By now Prince Alexander had finally abdicated and the Queen, after Salisbury's telegram of 9 September, had abandoned those of her accusations which were based on information supplied by her secret informant. But her indictment of Morier's conduct, based on the general policy he advocated, was formidable enough. Then suddenly the whole situation was made more serious by the appearance of allies for Morier in the cabinet. Lord Randolph Churchill, the chancellor of the exchequer, was, like Morier, arguing with Lord Salisbury in favour of an Anglo-Russian understanding and, when the matter was brought to the cabinet, was supported by Lord George Hamilton, First Lord of the Admiralty, and W. E. Smith at the War Office.[2] The Queen could only presume that those in the cabinet who were ready to abandon Britain's traditional policy were so, because 'they did not understand'.

The very fact of Egypt being in our power—would become useless if Constantinople were in the hands of Russia. And it is dreadful to think that this idea (as well as smaller and more personal motives) have guided and influenced Sir R. Morier all the time he has been at St. Petersburg.... The Queen hopes Lord Salisbury will put his foot down and not allow 2 young men comparatively ignorant and inexperienced in these affairs to pretend to oppose what older, wiser heads understand and know is the only true policy for this country.[3]

Iddesleigh agreed that 'the new lights in foreign policy were dazzling rather than guiding', but would not let the Queen cherish any illusion that Morier was to be recalled.[4] She continued, however, to press for this and to the Crown Princess continued to lament the 'irreparable harm' Morier had done in not making it clear to the Russians that Britain wished to keep Alexander on the Bulgarian throne. Of Morier, she said the Crown Princess had been 'very fond of him', the Prince Consort 'rather liked him', 'the 2 Stockmars—Father and Son

---
[1] To Iddesleigh, most secret and confidential, private, 17 Sept. 1886.
[2] Salisbury to the Queen, 7 Sept. 1886, G. E. Buckle (ed.), *Letters of Queen Victoria*, 3rd ser., i. 201–2.
[3] The Queen to Salisbury, 17 Sept. 1886, R.A. H 31/30.
[4] Iddesleigh to the Queen, 18 Sept. 1886, R.A. H 31/34.

liked him, but I—never could bear him, tho' I tried to overcome my repugnance. We seldom agreed—and he clearly dislikes me.'¹ In November as cabinet and Parliament reassembled and London came to life again, it was clear that Morier was in worse odour than ever.² Then, on 3 November he telegraphed to say he had heard that Bismarck was urging upon Russia the military occupation of Bulgaria but that the Tsar, fearing a trap, hesitated to respond. Within the week Herbert Bismarck called on Malet and Hatzfeldt spoke to Salisbury formally to deny the truth of this information.³ When Pauncefote let him know that the Bismarcks had got hold of this telegram, he replied that Bismarck might have pretended to have it in the hope of finding out its contents, and on 26 November he confirmed the information (see above p. 241). What mattered in all this was its effect on Morier. 'Every one of my steps is dogged and watched', he wrote.⁴ This conviction was intensified by a message from Salisbury that he should be cautious in his language because of the spies with which he was surrounded. Morier, now beyond a cool appraisal of the facts in relation to his obsession, replied that no caution 'would avail against the invention of deliberate falsehoods such as Bismarck's fertile brain has indulged in with respect to myself for the last 25 years'.⁵

He did, however, at last make arrangements to go to London and, on the way there, he saw the Crown Princess in Berlin. She wrote the same evening to report to the Queen what he had said. Much of it was the reverse of what the Queen wished to hear and very little of it calculated to improve his position with her. 'He said he had tried hard', wrote the Crown Princess, 'to get on with Russians and had succeeded wonderfully. Then he spoke of Bulgaria, said AS IT WAS OF NO SORT of *importance* to ENGLAND or to GERMANY, what did it matter what became of it!! It was *India* and Central Asia that mattered to England and all else was insignificant—always, this fatal mistake!!!'⁶

[1] The Queen to Salisbury, telegram, 13 Oct. 1886, R.A. H 31/36; to the Crown Princess, 18 and 25 Sept. and 18 Oct. 1886, R.A. Add. MS. U 32/441, 443, and 447.
[2] F. H. Villiers to Rosebery, 19 Nov. 1886, Rosebery papers, box 63; the Queen to the Crown Princess, 8 Nov. 1886, R.A. Add. MS. U 32/449.
[3] Malet to H. Bismarck, 10 Nov. 1886; H. Bismarck to Hatzfeldt, no. 955, 11 Nov. 1886; Hatzfeldt to H. Bismarck, no. 561, 16 Nov. 1886, GFM 10/200.
[4] To Pauncefote, 2 Dec. 1886.   [5] To Salisbury, 2 Dec. 1886.
[6] The Crown Princess to the Queen, 20 Dec. 1886, R.A. H 32/133.

It is hardly surprising after this that, when he arrived in London, the Queen refused him an audience and deputed Ponsonby to interview him on her behalf. Morier complained that he was unable to disabuse the Queen of the suspicions which he believed, but Ponsonby denied, Bismarck had found means to implant in her mind. To a modern reader of Ponsonby's record of their conversation it is clear that, if there was deliberate intention in Berlin and the purpose was to make an excitable man desperate, the Bismarcks had wonderfully succeeded. Morier continued, in face of Ponsonby's passivity, to beg to be told where he had gone wrong and ended the conversation by committing yet another mistake. He had not made himself, he said, 'the champion of Prince Alexander at St. Petersburg, because he believed to have done so would have been detrimental to Prince Alexander's interests'.[1]

Ponsonby's minute of their conversation the Queen sent to Salisbury, who had meanwhile received a letter from Morier written in 'a very excited tone'.[2] 'I cannot but presume', Morier had written, 'that the object aimed at' [by his calumniators] 'is to induce me to resign. But that is a course which after 33 years of not dishonourable service I do not think I could in fairness to myself adopt. I think I should have a right to demand dismissal with a public record of the reasons for such dismissal.'[3] Morier was hopelessly far from understanding the situation. Writing later of this December, he said the calumnies against him had been kept 'as mysteries carefully veiled' from him, when he had 'implored in high places to let me be confronted with my accusers or at least their accusations'.[4] Yet his every word in explanation was but more self-accusation of the capital crime of working for an understanding with Russia and depreciating the importance of supporting Prince Alexander.

Even Salisbury failed to make Morier understand. He returned to St. Petersburg in January 1887, and again saw the

[1] Minute by Ponsonby of their conversation, 22 Dec. 1886, R.A. Z 280/1; Ponsonby to the Queen, 20 Dec. 1886, demurring at seeing Morier without the Queen's permission and on the difficulty of referring to information which had reached the Queen confidentially, with the Queen's pencil note, '. . . the Queen won't see him', R.A. Add. MS. A 12/1318.
[2] Salisbury to the Queen, 26 Dec. 1886, R.A. C 38/84.
[3] To Salisbury, 22 Dec. 1886.
[4] To Salisbury, 7 Apr. 1887, Morier papers; Salisbury papers, A/73, fo. 27^v.

Crown Princess on his way through Berlin (10 January). His exuberant optimism welling up, and quite mistakenly thinking he had made things plain in London, he misread all the signs.

I had a *very satisfactory* interview with the Crown Princess [he wrote to Salisbury]. She was exceedingly friendly . . . I confess I am more than ever at a loss to understand the cause of *tantae coelestinae irae*. I said I had every ground for believing that I had been the subject of very hideous calumnies, and I appealed to her old friendship to tell me what they were, that I might refute them. She said there was nothing of the kind, and that nothing had ever been reported to her except the general *consensus* of the Russians that I was an Ambassador after their own heart . . .[1]

It is so difficult to believe that Morier could have failed to hear the irony, or to have realized that this was the gravamen of the charges against him, that one begins to doubt whether it was so, until one reads the Crown Princess's own account of the same interview.[2]

Yesterday [she begins] our fat friend arrived and I saw him for an hour! He was looking ill and changed . . . much depressed and dejected . . . he said he wished to *explain* his views and notions and hear from me—*what* lies and calumnies had been told about him, so that he might refute them! I then said I had heard no calumnies nor anything said with the intent and object to injure him—but that the *general impression* everywhere was that he was more Russian than the Russians and certainly than his Government or his Sovereign— . . . that it was known he belonged to a school who saw no harm in Turkey falling into Russian hands . . . Then came a very long explanation which was very intricate.

Morier in fact launched into a full defence of the policy of reaching an understanding with Russia on all oriental questions; since Britain was not prepared to fight her on her Indian frontier. It is clear that despite herself, the Crown Princess appreciated the intellectual verve and courage behind Morier's disquisition. Indeed, she acknowledged that he was both 'profound' and 'far-seeing'. It is equally clear, however, that she saw that this very explanation made matters worse, unless he was prepared to drop the very policy he was advocating. 'I still think', she wrote, 'he has *surchargé* his sympathy for Russia

[1] To Salisbury, 12 Jan. 1887, Morier papers; Salisbury papers, letters from Morier, fos. 68–73.
[2] The Crown Princess to the Queen, Berlin, 11 Jan. 1887, R.A. H 34/9.

very much and that it has been a great mistake.' Morier, on the contrary, left her with no intention at all of abandoning his search for an agreement with Russia and certainly no understanding that she meant him to do so.

He seems to have satisfied himself that he had vindicated his conduct, and he went back to St. Petersburg intending to go on as before. In London and Windsor he had been treated with patience and charity, but was clearly expected to turn over a new leaf. Within a month the flow of information about his misbehaviour began again. The Crown Princess wrote in February 1887 of his having resumed his language about leaving the Balkan peninsula to Russia. Salisbury found it incredible. 'Sir Robert Morier', he wrote to the Queen,[1] 'remains a puzzle. Lord Salisbury cannot imagine that after all that has passed, he should tell the Russian Minister that England will in the end accept the policy which he is instructed by the English Government to oppose'.

Morier, on his side, began again to give vent to his sense of persecution. 'Schweinitz goes away on leave,' he wrote to Salisbury in April, 'and Bülow will reign in his stead, and we may be on the look out for a fresh flight of *canards* as regards my humble person . . . I have come on the *spoor* of a very hideous calumny as regards myself of which he was the author.'[2] Relying, indeed, on a report from Bülow—it was confirmed in Vienna—Bismarck had caused another formal complaint to be made to Salisbury about Morier.[3] Referring to the arrest of Schnaebele in Alsace, which was then creating tension between France and Germany, he had said to Wolkenstein that it was worse than anything that had happened since the abduction of the duc d'Enghien by Napoleon.[4] Salisbury told Morier without revealing his source, and he responded with disproportionate alarm. He telegraphed: 'The latest accusation is as false as the calumnies which have preceded it. I hope sincerely for Your Lordship's protection against systematic espionage whose

---

[1] Salisbury to the Queen, 16 Feb. 1887, R.A. I 55/66.
[2] To Salisbury, 7 Apr. 1887, Morier papers; Salisbury papers, A/73, fo. 27ᵛ; from Ponsonby, 20 Apr. 1887.
[3] Bülow to Bismarck, no. 149, 26 Apr. 1887; Herbert Bismarck to chargé d'affaires in London, no. 401, 1 May 1887; chargé d'affaires in London to Prince Bismarck, no. 168, 4 May 1887, GFM 10/200.
[4] From Salisbury, 11 May 1887; from Arthur Hardinge, 25 May 1887.

object is to render my position here untenable and which appears to be very derogatory to [an] Ambassador of the Queen.'[1] A postscript to a private letter on the Afghan question, written to Salisbury on the same day, enlarged on his sense of injustice. 'I am quite aware', he concluded, 'of the stupendousness of the Bismarckian Minotaur but I nevertheless think the British Ambassador is too august a virgin to be thrust into his maw.'[2] Salisbury grew impatient. This remark, he wrote, 'seems to imply a motive on my part, which certainly was not the one which led me to communicate to you the allegations I had heard as to the language used by you in conversation'. He added that the complaints which had reached him could 'not be attributed to personal malignity as they came from sources absolutely distinct'.[3] Morier replied with equal impatience. 'You have entirely misunderstood what I meant to express by saying that I thought a British Ambassador was too great a victim for the Bismarck Minotaur. I never dreamt for one moment of implying that there was or could be any other motive on your part in repeating to me the slanders of which I had been the object than that of warning me against false friends.' He then somewhat tiresomely reviewed his relationship with Bismarck since his Darmstadt days.[4]

It was not unnatural that Salisbury should return to the idea of bringing Morier away from St. Petersburg. 'If Rome were vacant Sir Robert Morier might be induced to go there', he wrote to the Queen, 'and his place be supplied by Lord Vivian.' Rome, he thought, might be *made* vacant if Sir John Lumley was persuaded to retire by the offer of a peerage. 'He was an old man and childless', so that the peerage would die with him. Salisbury asked whether the Queen would agree and proposed, if she did, to find out whether the scheme was practicable.[5] The suggestion was informally made to Morier by Currie and refused.[6] Morier did not see that, in view of Salisbury's Mediterranean policy, the transfer was not a step

[1] To Salisbury, 19 May 1887, Morier papers; Salisbury papers, A/73, fo. 43.
[2] To Salisbury, 19 May 1887, Morier papers; Salisbury papers, A/73, fo. 48ᵛ.
[3] From Salisbury, 25 May 1887.
[4] To Salisbury, secret and private, 1 June 1887, Morier papers; Salisbury papers, letters from Morier, fos. 74–9.
[5] Salisbury to the Queen, 4 June 1887, R.A. A 65/25.
[6] From Currie, 11 June 1887.

down. Lord Dufferin, who was then Viceroy of India and had been at St. Petersburg in 1879–81, was to be content with Rome in 1888. But Morier had his *idée fixe* about the importance of an Anglo-Russian *entente* and his wife and daughter liked the life of St. Petersburg.[1] Meanwhile, Salisbury, nevertheless, gained the Queen's approval for Morier's transfer to Rome when Sir John Lumley should retire.[2]

In August 1887 Morier yielded to another wave of nervous excitement. He had turned to Schweinitz during the launching of a Russian warship, of which they were both spectators, to remark on the neatness with which the operation had been performed. He complained to Salisbury that gossip had transformed their innocent exchange into a long and serious conversation in which he was overheard to say, in regard to the growing Russian naval strength, 'cela donne à penser', and Schweinitz to have replied, 'ils jettent leur dernier sou dans la Néva'.[3] It is difficult to see why the relaying of this should have seemed sinister except to someone who was looking for hidden meanings.

Salisbury returned to the remedy. Morier was made G.C.B., and Ponsonby, who received the order at the same time, made it pleasantly plain that he was restored to favour at court. 'The Broad Belly band is, I think, always becoming and even necessary for an Ambassador . . .'[4] More important, Salisbury, in terms that were both flattering and remarkably frank, informed him that he was to be moved to Rome.[5] It is an almost painful experience to a modern reader of Morier's reply to see him once again miss the significance of Salisbury's remarks—this time an exposition of the change in the balance of British foreign policy. Salisbury wrote that relations with Italy were likely to become more and more important, while those with Russia would be of a negative kind. Morier devoted all his energy to disputing this last phrase, which he obtusely treated as a forecast instead of the virtual statement of intentions that it was. Morier unfortunately made it plain that he regarded the transfer as a condemnation of his work in Russia.[6] His

---

[1] The Crown Princess to the Queen, 11 Jan. 1887, R.A. H 34/9.
[2] Salisbury to the Queen, 17 July 1887, R.A. A 66/14.
[3] To Salisbury, no. 294, 24 Aug. 1887, F.O. 65/1298.
[4] From Ponsonby, 16 Oct. 1887.   [5] From Salisbury, 15 Sept. 1887.
[6] To Salisbury, 2 Oct. 1887, Morier papers; Salisbury papers, letters from Morier fo. 84.

misfortunes continued; for in the next month Dufferin wrote that he wished to bring his term as Viceroy to an early close, and Salisbury was able to ascertain, through Lord Cross, the secretary of state for India, that he would be available for Rome.[1] The alternative possibility of a move to Vienna—Sir A. Paget being transferred from there to Berlin—was also closed to him, for it turned out that Lady Paget's having offended the Crown Princess had made Berlin impossible for them.[2] On top of all this, Morier produced one more instance of his nervous susceptibility. This led Salisbury to think that perhaps, after all, he would be better left at St. Petersburg, where nothing much of importance would in future be transacted. After the signature of the second Mediterranean Agreement in December, Vienna and Rome would both be more important than St. Petersburg in Anglo-German relations—the concern that was to the fore just then. But the clinching argument was that Francesco Crispi, the Italian prime minister since July 1887, had returned from a visit to Friedrichsruhe entirely under Bismarck's spell and was now rapidly strengthening his control over Italian foreign policy. Salisbury wisely decided that the impetuous Morier and the fiery Sicilian, a worshipper of Bismarck, were an impossible combination.[3] On 6 December 1887 he wrote abruptly, retransferring Morier back to St. Petersburg without telling him the reason.[4] The very next day, 7 December, Bismarck instructed Hatzfeldt to represent to Salisbury that Morier now made no secret at St. Petersburg of his hostility to Germany and was openly, even ostentatiously, intriguing against her. It was a plea for his withdrawal. Salisbury replied firmly. Alluding to incidents in Samoa and Zanzibar, he reminded Hatzfeldt that twice already British agents had been recalled at Germany's request. Besides, Morier on his part complained of the systematic hostility of his German colleague who deliberately tried to disparage him in the sight of his own government. Finally he

[1] Cross to Salisbury, Dec. 1887, Salisbury papers, E/R. A. Cross box.
[2] Eyre Crowe to his father, 8 Oct. 1887, in the possession of his daughter.
[3] The Queen to the Crown Princess, 26 Jan. 1888: 'Ld Salisbury wisely, I think, feared *his* being *with Crispi*—where with the character of the last named, he might be *very* dangerous and far more so than he can *now* be at St. Petersburg', R.A. Add. MS. U 32/496.
[4] From Salisbury, 6 Dec., Morier papers; to Salisbury, 15 Dec. 1886, Salisbury papers, letters from Morier, fo. 88.

asked for facts. On 19 December Bismarck returned to the charge, arguing that Morier's presence at St. Petersburg was damaging British, not German, interests and shortly afterwards obtained Austrian co-operation in pressure on London.[1]

The Bismarcks may have wished to get rid of Morier because the improvement in Anglo-Russian relations that he sought would have made more difficult the maintenance of German-Russian intimacy. It was, however, also clear to them that his nervous susceptibility, his loss of favour with the Queen (of which Rosebery had told them) and his reputation for an unguarded tongue made him an easy victim for an effortless campaign of insinuations.

By 1887 such a campaign had advantages that had nothing to do with Morier personally. It was the year of the second war scare against France. Bismarck had stepped up the struggle against the opposition liberals with a number of objectives in view. The Reichstag had rejected the army bill and been dissolved in the hope that general elections, fought under the shadow of the war scare, would produce a Reichstag willing to pass the army bill and with a pliant majority on Bismarck's side for the time when the old Emperor should die and the Crown Prince come to the throne. The *Kartel* of Conservatives, Left Conservatives, and National Liberals was organized in support of Bismarck against the liberal supporters of the Crown Prince and the Left Liberals as well as against the Centre Party. The election campaign was 'of unprecedented and incredible passion'.[2] The devilry of the Bismarcks lay in their exploitation of Morier's weaknesses to enable them to use the Crown Princess in their battle to destroy the political party of her husband. When the Crown Prince actually reigned, as the Emperor Frederick III from 9 March to 15 June 1888, the battle died down. It was revived with a different objective after his death. Its purpose was then to destroy, not only the liberal and English influence in Germany, but the reputation of the Empress Frederick herself. In this too Morier was to be a tool of the Bismarcks.

[1] Bismarck to Hatzfeldt, telegram, 7 Dec. 1887; Hatzfeldt to Bismarck, no. 420 ganz vertraulich, 14 Dec. 1887; Bismarck to Hatzfeldt, no. 1054, 19 Dec. 1887; German ambassador in Vienna to Bismarck, no. 524 ganz vertraulich, 18 Dec. 1887, GFM 10/200.
[2] From Roggenbach, 23 Feb. 1887.

Yet another ingredient in the evil brew was inadvertently supplied by the Prince of Wales, who chose this year to quarrel with his nephew, William. In May 1888 he had gone to Berlin for the marriage of the Empress Frederick's second son, his younger nephew Prince Henry, to Princess Irene of Hesse on 22 May. He had already been there for the funeral of William I and he was to go yet again for that of the Emperor Frederick; each visit provided fresh fuel to feed the flames of the quarrel. Some of it was supplied by remarks of Herbert Bismarck.

Now, the Prince of Wales had for some time constituted himself Morier's champion. Morier had made a point of being in Lisbon, though he did not formally take up his post there until some months later, when the Prince of Wales arrived on his way home from his tour of India in 1876. Morier had sailed home with him on board the *Serapis* and a friendship had been struck up between the young prince and the older, genial, and immensely talkative Morier. The Prince of Wales had taken up Morier's cause in 1884, writing to Lord Granville and to the Queen to urge his appointment to Berlin after the death of Lord Ampthill.[1] He had taken up his cause in 1886, though he would not interfere directly between Morier and the Queen. He had, however, invited Morier to Sandringham, when the Queen had refused to see him. When the Prince championed his cause in 1888, the disastrous Bazaine incident was the outcome.

Marshal Bazaine was among the flotsam and jetsam from the wreckage of the Napoleonic regime in France and he was washed ashore in Madrid. He had surrendered Metz, it will be recalled, and its army to the Germans on 29 October 1870. He had been subsequently returned by his captors to France, been tried in 1873 for treason by a military court, at Trianon, found guilty, and imprisoned in the Île Sainte-Marguerite opposite Cannes, where 'the man in the iron mask' had preceded him. He had escaped and finally found refuge in Madrid.

In 1883 when Morier was minister in Madrid, Bazaine came to him 'in a ragged and unshaven condition pitiable to behold'. His object was to beg Morier 'to endeavour to get him a pension as a Knight of the Bath', a decoration he had received for

---

[1] The Prince of Wales to the Queen, 28 Aug. 1884, R.A. I 54/54, the Prince of Wales to Granville and reply, 17 Sept. 1884, P.R.O. 30/29/47.

his part in the joint Anglo-French expedition, which took the fortress of Kinburn during the Crimean War. Morier's account continued:

> I pointed out to him how impossible it would be for a man in his position to become the pensioner of Her Majesty's Government but as the man deeply moved my pity I acceded to his request (he said he was starving) to assist him in selling some sketches of the Crimean War which had been made on the spot and contained portraits of Lord Raglan and other English officers. I got I remember 10 or 15 pounds for them and made up the sum to £50 out of my own pocket and gave it to him.[1]

Such was Morier's account, written five years after the event. He preserved among his papers letters which bear out the substance of these recollections, but show him to have attempted to do much more, without, for reasons that will become plain, telling one whether he was successful or not. They show too that the request for help was made by letter and not in person, or not only in person. A letter from Bazaine to himself of 2 June 1883 referred to the Kinburn expedition, enclosed a letter of 18 October 1855 from General Spencer, who commanded the English brigade, and appealed to Morier to obtain for him from the English minister of war 'un secours que Son Excellence pourra, une fois donné, prélever sur les fonds secrets du Ministère'. He signed himself, by way of reminder, 'chevalier du Bain'. A letter from Morier to Lord Hartington, then secretary of state for war, 5 June 1883, summarized and enclosed this, 'the strangest letter that has ever come into my hands', and expressed the hope that he might be authorized to place a sum in Bazaine's hands. A second letter from Bazaine, also of 2 June, sent a carton of scraps about the Crimean War—'V. E. gardera ce qui lui plaira, et me donnera le prix qu'elle jugera convenable'—and a third letter of 4 June forwarded a letter from General Burgoyne to Bazaine. A postscript of 6 June to Morier's letter to Hartington described these additional letters. A letter from Morier to Lord Granville, then secretary of state for foreign affairs, enclosed his letter to Hartington and described the whole incident. Bazaine, he wrote,

has been residing in Madrid for a long time past but he goes nowhere

---

[1] To Dr. Hinzpeter, private and confidential, Neuwied, 5 Oct. 1888, Morier papers, Bazaine correspondence, 1888-9, no. 28.

and I am not personally acquainted with him . . . I do not believe
he is the unmitigated scoundrel they try to make him out . . . I have
returned him his album of scraps, selecting an insignificant photo-
graph and sending a small sum such as I could afford in payment
thereof and I have acknowledged the receipt of his three letters but
I have not told him that I have sent on the one destined for Ld
Hartington. Should a moderate sum, say £300 or £400 be allotted
to him out of the secret service fund and I be authorized to draw
for it, I would propose putting the sum in an envelope with General
Spencer's letter. He would then give a receipt for the envelope
described as returning this letter and there would be no trace of the
allotment in the records.

Morier added, 'it would be as you may fancy most painful to
me to have to tell him his appeal had been in vain.' Nothing
more exists for June 1883 except Bazaine's letter thanking
Morier for a letter of 9 June, asking a question about a sketch
of a Crimean War review.

An occasion when Bazaine did come in person to Morier and
Morier paid over the sum ostensibly gained by the sale of ten
sketches during his visit to London, which had followed the
June correspondence, seems to belong to November 1883 or
later. There is a brief note from Bazaine, dated 19 November:
'Que votre bienveillance est touchante.' There is a longer letter
of 6 March 1884: 'Comment répondre à la gracieuse lettre de
V. E. J'en suis vivement touché', continuing with further
thanks without a sign of what had prompted it. Morier was
himself uncertain when the incident of the visit happened,
since he began by writing 1884, and later substituted 1883, in
his account to Hinzpeter.[1]

Bazaine also had a similarly carefully concealed connection
with Berlin; so carefully concealed that one cannot now tell
when it began. But by the eighties he was in receipt of a regular
pension from Prince Frederick Charles, who had commanded
the Prussian army that had succeeded in shutting Bazaine up in
Metz in August 1870. This pension was paid over by Major von
Deines, then German military attaché in Madrid. The pension
ended when Prince Frederick Charles died in 1885.[2] Von Deines

---

[1] To Hinzpeter, private and confidential, Neuwied, 5 Oct. 1888.
[2] J. A. Crowe to Lord Salisbury, 7 Jan. 1889, R.A. Z 280/22. Salisbury communicated Crowe's letter to the Queen who then asked the Crown Princess for

felt sorry for the Marshal, living in poverty and deserted by everyone including his wife, and he listened to his talk about his various campaigns, finding his recollections clear and good. By dint of questions and answers over several interviews, he satisfied himself about the consistency of one astonishing story. What astonished him about this story was the element chance played in it. When a commander could see nothing of enemy movements, chance had put into his hand a crucial piece of information of which he alone could see the significance and make use. The moral von Deines had drawn from the story was that one side in a campaign could never tell when it was putting information into the hands of the other, and the introduction of the telegraph had only increased the danger.[1]

Von Deines wrote a dispatch on this subject and used Bazaine's story to illustrate his point.[2] Bazaine was speaking of the situation on 15 August 1870: his army was on the right bank of the Moselle with its back to Metz. The Germans had spread a cavalry screen in front of him, made up from part of Frederick Charles's army. This prevented his seeing what was really happening and he did not know that Frederick Charles with the rest of his army was crossing from the right to the left bank of the Moselle behind him. The first news, said Bazaine, of the German movement on his left he had received by telegram from the English representative at Darmstadt. 'Je ne savais rien de vos mouvements jusqu'à ce que l'Ambassadeur d'Angleterre, Mr Morier, m'a fait savoir que les Allemands étaient près de Mars-la-Tour. J'ai reçu ce télégramme par Londres le 16 au matin.' The battle of Vionville had followed on 16 August, 'the most bloody of the whole war, costing 16,000 men to the German army'.[3]

confirmation. She replied that she knew that Prince Frederick Charles had told the Emperor Frederick that Bazaine had asked for money and she thought it likely that Frederick Charles had given it, Crown Princess to the Queen, 14 Jan. 1889, R.A. Z 280/27.

[1] Sir Keith Fraser, British military attaché in Vienna, to Ponsonby, 20 Jan. 1889, R.A. Z 280/36. By this date von Deines was a colleague of Fraser in Vienna.
[2] Von Deines to Berlin, 2 Apr. 1886. This dispatch later appeared in the newspapers. It was summarized and quoted in a letter from Hinzpeter to the Emperor William who had been his pupil, Hinzpeter to Morier, Bielefeld, 10 Nov. 1888. Von Deines believed the French intelligence service in London had got hold of Morier's telegrams, Deines to Bismarck, 12 Nov. 1888, GFM 10/200.
[3] Morier to Hinzpeter, private and confidential, Neuwied, 5 Oct. 1888.

Now Morier had in fact sent two telegrams home from Darmstadt before 16 August 1870.[1] The deciphers read:

Darmstadt, July 28, 1870
Confidential. The Head Quarters of Crown Prince of Prussia will be at Mannheim tomorrow. Those of Prince Frederick Charles at Mayence.

Darmstadt, July 30, 1870
Most Confidential. The King of Prussia takes up his Head Quarters at Mayence on Tuesday: it is supposed that a general advance will immediately follow. The Army of Steinmetz is to the right of that of Prince Frederick Charles protecting Treves. Crown Prince tonight at Speiers.

These telegrams were repeated to Lord Lyons in Paris.

Three other facts are sure. First, Bazaine denied in a letter to Morier in, to quote the letter, 'la manière la plus absolue cette conversation apocryphil' and sanctioned the publication of his denial. Second, von Deines stuck to his story. Third, Morier in 1870 could only have used the public telegraph lines out of Darmstadt, so that it could be established that these perfectly proper telegrams were the only ones that he sent, that he could not have sent anything direct to Bazaine, and all that could have happened was that the French deciphered the telegrams when they were repeated to Lord Lyons, and passed on the deciphers to Bazaine. He may have been able, because of knowledge he already had, to draw inferences from them which no one could have foreseen. The problem of reconciling Bazaine's denial with von Deines's evidence—he could produce a witness in Prince von Solms to corroborate him—remains.

Now in March 1888 Herbert Bismarck thought it right to communicate a garbled version of von Deines's dispatch to Malet. I quote his account to Salisbury.[2]

He said that during the French War when the German army was before Metz the Crown Prince's division was secretly detached and moved towards Sedan—that Bazaine got wind of this and made a sortie which resulted in a battle in which the Germans, by reason

---

[1] From Sir T. H. Sanderson, telegram, 15 Jan. 1889, Morier papers, Bazaine correspondence, 1888–9, no. 71; see also Barrington to Salisbury, 14 Jan. 1889, Salisbury papers, A/73, fo. 250.

[2] Malet to Salisbury, private and secret, 14 Apr. 1888, Salisbury papers, A/61, fo. 244.

of the diminution of their forces, were nearly defeated and that it was touch and go whether the whole result of the war might not have been changed.

I believe the name of the battle was Noiseville [1 September 1870].

Count Bismarck went on to say that General Bazaine a few years ago told the German military *attaché* at Madrid that he had received the news of the detachment of the Crown Prince's army 'from his friend Morier the English Minister at Darmstadt' who had got it from Princess Alice.[1]

It will be observed that Herbert Bismarck had substituted the Crown Prince for Prince Frederick Charles and transferred the whole incident to a later phase of the war when Bazaine, already shut up in Metz, made a sortie, from which the battle of Noiseville had resulted.

Malet noted that some parts of this story were simply impossible and decided to ignore it. On 9 March, just after this, the Crown Prince became the Emperor Frederick, and his English wife Empress, and the quarrels between the Bismarcks, father and son, on one side and the new court on the other became the talk of the hour. The Queen, who was then staying in Florence, was drawn in by the Battenberg marriage question.[2] She set about clearing the air of what she was determined to regard as 'nonsense', and stirred Salisbury to action. He wrote privately to Malet to inquire, among other things, what was the ground for Prince Bismarck's hatred of Morier. Malet replied on 14 April by citing as the reason the Bazaine story in the impossible version in which he had received it, with its point directed against the then Crown Prince and its matter accounting for Herbert's malice, since he had been wounded at Noiseville. The implication was that Morier had got his information from the Crown Princess (via her sister) who had it from the Crown Prince, who, like a traitor intended it to be passed by way of England to the French. Malet added the story 'seemed to me so incredible that I did not believe it and did not like to report it to you or at all commit it to paper'. Salisbury did nothing.

[1] Queen Victoria's second daughter, married to the Grand Duke of Hesse-Darmstadt.
[2] The Empress Frederick defied the Bismarcks in supporting her daughter's wish to marry Alexander of Battenberg, the former Prince of Bulgaria.

It was now May 1888 and the Prince of Wales arrived in Berlin for the marriage of his younger nephew. Among the mischievous tales which Herbert Bismarck told him was that of Morier's 'betrayal' of the German movements to Bazaine. The Prince at once took up his role of Morier's champion. He wrote to Malet, who repeated what Herbert Bismarck had told him, without mentioning that he had by now reported the story to Salisbury. Herbert had now looked up von Deines's dispatch, and the story he told to the Prince was in the correct Vionville version and not the impossible Noiseville one. He had failed to get anywhere by false insinuations and must now trust Deines's actual words.

The Prince bided his time, but during July, when Morier was on leave in England, he invited him to Sandringham (10 July) and told him 'as an old friend of thirty years' standing' what Malet had communicated. The expostulations of the excitable Morier can be imagined. Observing 'that I had for years been made the victim of the most hideous and malignant lies without my having ever succeeded in getting face to face either with the lies themselves, of which only dim shadows were ever held out to me as warnings, or with my accusers', Morier said he was 'grateful to be enabled for the first time to make direct acquaintance with both'.[1] Then the Prince of Wales, insisting that Morier should have the story direct from Malet, who was also on leave in London, invited the two to Marlborough House (23 July 1888), and taking the initiative in the conversation, induced Malet to repeat the story. Afterwards he told Salisbury, through Morier, what he had done. To the Queen, he was hot for action: 'Lord Palmerston would never have permitted such insults.' He had, indeed, effectively made it impossible to do what Salisbury in April had decided to do: to kill the gossip by silence.

Morier, though 'extremely angry', wisely checked his impulse of 'calling directly on Count Herbert Bismarck to furnish me with the evidence on which his libel was founded or to retract and apologize'. He decided he could not act without the

[1] Morier's memorandum for the Queen, 25 July 1888, Morier papers, Bazaine correspondence, 1888-9, no. 2; copy enclosed in Morier to Salisbury, 26 July 1888, Salisbury papers, A/73, fos. 86-7, and Morier papers, Bazaine correspondence, 1888-9, no. 5; copy enclosed in the Prince of Wales to the Queen, 31 July 1888, R.A. Z 280/3; see also Salisbury to the Queen, 31 July 1888, R.A. Z 280/4.

Queen's and his government's direction. After taking a day for consideration, he asked the Prince of Wales to lay the matter before the Queen and begged his permission to discuss it with Salisbury.[1] At the same time, he wrote to Bazaine asking for a repudiation, but required the British counsul in Madrid—the same William Macpherson on whose knowledge of all things Spanish he had relied in the commercial negotiations of 1882–4—not to deliver the letter until he had had time to speak to Lord Salisbury.[2] The Queen's reply was cool though sensible. She had already told the Prince that Morier must find out the truth and then Salisbury could act. She also mentioned that Morier did not stand well in the Foreign Office.[3] The Prince stormed that he did not see what Morier had still to find out nor how the Queen could expect to be served properly if her ambassadors were not defended.[4]

On 26 July Morier warned Salisbury of the disagreeable matter he would have to raise when he came, that weekend, to Hatfield—he had been invited already by Lady Salisbury. He enclosed a memorandum written for the Queen. Salisbury's line was clear: if Morier wished to discuss it, it must be 'entirely outside of and independent of H.M.G.'[5]

The next phase of the affair is one of conflict between Morier and Salisbury. The outcome of the discussion at Hatfield (27–8 July) was that Salisbury both adhered to his own decision, to take no official action, and disapproved of Morier's 'taking the matter into [his own] hands'. Morier wanted his duel with Herbert Bismarck, albeit a verbal one. He felt himself placed 'in the most abominable fix I was ever in in my life' and asked permission to consult George Goschen, a 'less prejudiced friend' than the Prince of Wales.[6] Goschen, born of a German mother, a member of Gladstone's cabinet of 1868–74, ambassador at

---

[1] To the Prince of Wales, 25 July 1888, Morier papers, Bazaine correspondence, 1888–9, no. 1.
[2] To Bazaine, 25 July, Morier papers, Bazaine correspondence, 1888–9, no. 3.
[3] From the Prince of Wales, 4 Aug. 1888, Morier papers, Bazaine correspondence, 1888–9, no. 12.
[4] The Prince of Wales to the Queen, 4 Aug. 1888, R.A. Z 280/8.
[5] From Lord Salisbury, 27 July 1888; Salisbury to the Queen, 31 July 1888, R.A. Z 280/4.
[6] To Salisbury, 3 Aug. 1888, Morier papers, Bazaine correspondence, 1888–9, no. 9; Salisbury papers, A/73, fo. 190.

Constantinople in 1880 and now chancellor of the exchequer, was a good adviser. Salisbury could not refuse. Morier, who was to meet Goschen that evening (3 August) in any event, took the opportunity to talk to him at once.[1] He advised restraint, but to no avail.

Meanwhile, Macpherson had delivered Morier's letter to Bazaine, who promised an immediate reply. Silence followed. This was doubly unfortunate: for Morier began to lose his nerve, and Macpherson had sown suspicion by writing that though Bazaine at once stated 'that he had never said what was therein imputed to him, the Marshal did not look quite comfortable, and by his manner and even by his explanations [made] it apparent to me that, though he may not have said what is imputed to him he had said *something* about you'.[2] 'A fear therefore seized me', Morier wrote to the Prince of Wales, 'that by some vile intrigue, perhaps for money, they [the Germans] have made Bazaine say something which he is afraid to confess.'[3] That same evening (8 August) Bazaine's full denial mercifully arrived.[4]

The difficulty between Morier and Salisbury remained. Salisbury 'was unwilling to quarrel with the Bismarcks and thereby change the policy of the Government'.[5] He wished, moreover, to bring to an end both the quarrel of the Prince of Wales with William II and the acrimony of the Bismarcks against the Empress Frederick. He could not remonstrate about another and smaller matter. Morier, never able to see beyond his own personality, wished to clear his honour. A third factor was the lapse of time. It was March when Herbert Bismarck originally spoke to Malet. A remonstrance after so long would have an exaggerated significance, unless explained by mentioning the Prince of Wales. To bring in his name was to inflate the whole affair to the proportions of an international incident. Morier continued to argue with Salisbury from August to

---

[1] From Salisbury, 4 Aug. 1888, Morier papers, Bazaine correspondence, 1888–9, no. 10.
[2] From Macpherson, 4 Aug. 1888, Morier papers, Bazaine correspondence, 1888–9, no. 11.
[3] To the Prince of Wales, 8 Aug. 1888, Bazaine correspondence, 1888–9, no. 13.
[4] From Bazaine, 8 Aug. 1888, Bazaine correspondence, 1888–9, no. 14; see also Salisbury papers, A/73, fos. 193–8.
[5] Ponsonby to the Queen, 4 Aug. 1888, R.A. Z 280/7.

October.[1] These were just the months when it became more than ever desirable to avoid a remonstrance, for fresh trouble had arisen between the Empress Frederick and the new German regime—over the late Emperor's personal papers; in September came the furore over Professor Geffcken's publication of extracts from the Emperor Frederick's diary, kept during the Franco-Prussian War; in October came the furore created by the publication of Sir Morell Mackenzie's *The Fatal Illness of Frederick the Noble*. The result of the argument by then was deadlock: 'Lord Salisbury does not think it advisable to bring the Foreign Office into the controversy while Sir Robert Morier hesitates to demand explanations direct from Count Bismarck without the support of his Government.'[2] It was not until November that Count Bismarck was after all confronted.

In August, Salisbury had been prepared to instruct Malet to go to Count Herbert Bismarck

and say that he had repeated to me, as he was desired to do, the story concerning you [Morier]: that I had not disclosed the matter to any one: but that I had accidentally the means of investigating it—and especially the essential part of it which depended upon the testimony of Marshal Bazaine: that Bazaine energetically and in the most positive language denied ever having told anybody that he had received information from you in Metz: and that, therefore, it is quite evident to me that your name has got mixed up with the story through some unaccountable misapprehension. Malet might then proceed to point out that, as the matter must necessarily be kept private, the English foreign minister was the only person by whom such a matter could be received; and that I hoped, therefore, he would receive my assurance that the story was wholly without foundation so far as you are concerned, and would dismiss it from his memory.[3]

By October Salisbury had agreed to modify the instruction, so that the egoistical Morier should at least have some place in Malet's remarks to Count Bismarck, even if the latter were not

[1] To Salisbury, 10 Aug. 1888, Morier papers, Bazaine correspondence, 1888–9, no. 15, Salisbury papers, A/73, fo. 193; from Salisbury, 16 Aug. 1888, Baz. corr. no. 16; to Salisbury, 25 Aug. 1888, Baz. corr. no. 17, Salisbury papers, A/73, fo. 199; from Salisbury, 3 Sept. 1888, Baz. corr. no. 19; to Salisbury, 25 Sept. 1888, Baz. corr. no. 21, Salisbury papers, A/73, fo. 209; to Salisbury, 8 Oct. 1888, Baz. corr. no. 30; from Salisbury, 10 Oct. 1888, Baz. corr. no. 32. A précis of all this was made by Ponsonby for the Queen and sent to her on 14 Oct., R.A. Z 280/10–11. [2] Ponsonby to the Queen, 14 Oct. 1888, R.A. Z 280/10.
[3] From Salisbury, 16 Aug. 1888.

to be confronted with him. Malet was to say that Salisbury had not disclosed the story, and then to continue by saying that Morier had accidentally discovered it and had written to Bazaine and procured Bazaine's denial. Copies of the letters between Morier and Bazaine were to be enclosed for communication.[1] Malet was accordingly instructed in this way, and on his return to Berlin he at once (7 November 1888) made the desired communication to Herbert Bismarck.[2] Exactly what Salisbury feared happened: for Count Bismarck proposed further inquiries, the result of which was to bring out the corroboration of Prince Solms, Austrian vice-consul at Madrid and a man of evil reputation.[3] With this Morier could not deal; since Bazaine had died in October 1888.

The effects of the remonstrance and ensuing inquiry were, at first, healthy. When the actual texts of von Deines's report of 2 April 1886 and his later report of 12 November 1888 were used, the correct battle, Vionville, was confirmed, Princess Alice's name was altogether dropped and the Empress Eugenie's substituted—she was known to have had contact at this date with the battle-front—and it was shown that von Deines's theme was 'military telegraphy' and his mention of Morier incidental. For Salisbury there was never any question of Morier's having been indiscreet, even had it been possible for him to have sent anything but the two telegrams he actually did send; so that there remained only the problem of reconciling Bazaine's denial with Deines's corroborated story. Salisbury solved this by guessing that Bazaine had been told something by somebody which 'evolved' in his mind into something else (because of knowledge he had already), which led him to speak as he had done to von Deines, but that when confronted with what he had said, he denied it because it was in fact unfounded, and because in the fluid situation of 12 to 16 August 1870 it was impossible to pin down any one movement of his own or of the Germans

---

[1] From Salisbury, 10 Oct. 1888.
[2] From Malet, 9 Nov. 1888, Morier papers, Bazaine correspondence, 1888–9, no. 42; cf. Malet to Salisbury, 8 Nov. 1888, Salisbury papers, A/61, fos. 381–4; cf. also Bismarck to von Deines, 7 Nov. 1888, GFM 10/200.
[3] Von Deines to Bismarck, 12 Nov. 1888 and Solms to Bismarck, telegram, 3 Dec. 1888, GFM 10/200; this was Count, not Prince, Solms and the German minister at Madrid; Malet to Salisbury, 24 Nov. 1888, Salisbury papers, A/61, fo. 405.

to which it could have applied.¹ The truth to this point had now also been made plain to Morier. In desperate need to unburden himself to more sympathetic ears than those he found in London, he had written all he so far knew to Hinzpeter. Hinzpeter, who was then on good terms with both the Bismarcks and the Emperor William, had thought the best he could do for Morier was to gain William II's intervention. The latter's first response was by telegram: 'weiss von der ganzen Geschichte kein Wort. Sie sieht mir aber sehr nach einer hoax aus'— 'I don't know anything of the story. It looks to me like a hoax.' It was followed by inquiry. So the facts came out and were relayed by Hinzpeter to Morier.² The final word on this part of the subject may best be left with Lord Salisbury. The story, he wrote, as early as September, was no more 'than a commérage: half accidental, half malicious, like most of the calumnies that float about the world . . .' Morier had greatly exaggerated the importance of the incident to himself. An attempt to induce Herbert Bismarck to apologize would infinitely multiply its injurious effect.³

The subject itself, however, cannot be left. Morier now felt he was battering his head against a wall in London as well as in Berlin. He was like a sick man who stubbornly resisted every cure. In Berlin someone was also desperate. On 28 September that indiscreet gossip Professor Heinrich Geffcken was arraigned before the Imperial Court at Leipzig for high treason. He was released on 5 January 1889, the Bismarcks' attempt to make a case against him and the Empress Frederick of treasonable connections with England in 1870 having rudely failed. In the middle of this desperate throw, on 16 December 1888, the *Kölnische Zeitung* published the Bazaine story. This was the beginning of the Bazaine incident, linking Morier with the Geffcken case in a paper commonly supposed to be in the pay of Bismarck.

Under a headline to the effect that Morier knew too much, the newspaper's Berlin correspondent began by recalling his name to its readers as a man often in the public eye and not

---

[1] From Salisbury, 16 Aug. 1888.
[2] From Dr. Hinzpeter, 5 and 10 Nov. 1888, Bazaine correspondence, 1888-9, nos. 40 and 43.
[3] From Salisbury, 3 Sept. 1888, Bazaine correspondence, 1888-9, no. 19.

always to his advantage. He had once been thought of as a successor to Lord Ampthill, British ambassador in Berlin, but had made improper use of his position, so the correspondent insinuated, among the intimates of the Emperor Frederick and had been sent to St. Petersburg instead. The disclosures which might be expected from the Geffcken investigation would throw light upon the part Morier played in giving Bazaine the first news in 1870 of the passage by the German army of the Moselle.

Morier now at last had opportunity to bring on the crisis he desired. He wrote at once to Herbert Bismarck. He said he would have scorned to notice the article in the *Kölnische Zeitung*, had he not 'chanced' to hear of the Bazaine accusation in July. He continued in a characteristic passage: 'Nor did I insult you by crediting you with a cynicism so abnormal as to suppose that a man honoured with the friendship of the late Emperor Frederick could have been so unnaturally base as to use that confidence to betray him and his army to the enemy.' He confronted Bismarck with his exchange of letters with Bazaine and asked him to cause an immediate contradiction to be inserted in the *Norddeutsche Allgemeine Zeitung* 'of the foul and infamous libel and calumny'.[1] He drafted a communiqué for *The Times* which it published on 21 December.[2] This summarized the accusation as Morier heard of it in July, described Bazaine's denial, and ended by saying that an official contradiction was expected. Ponsonby had already denied the story on Morier's behalf in a letter to the editor of the *Pall Mall Gazette* over the initial 'P', which it then published on 20 December.[3]

At the same time Morier telegraphed to Salisbury: 'In view of what has passed in the Bazaine business, I think I may ask Your Lordship in common justice to myself to insist on a categorical refutation in the *Norddeutsche Allgemeine Zeitung* of the charges brought against me in Sunday's Cologne paper.'[4] He

---

[1] To Herbert Bismarck, 19 Dec. 1888, Bazaine correspondence, 1888-9, no. 46 and GFM 10/200; cf. to Goschen, 3 Jan. 1889, Bazaine correspondence, no. 66, where Morier describes the letter to Bismarck as an 'automatic act, the blow instantly following the insult'.

[2] Bazaine correspondence, no. 47 and R.A. Z 280/15.

[3] From W. T. Stead, 20 Dec. 1888; from Ponsonby, 20 Dec. 1888; Bazaine correspondence, nos. 48 and 54.

[4] To Salisbury, 20 Dec. 1888, Bazaine correspondence, no. 52; Salisbury papers, A/73, fo. 234.

told Ponsonby, for the Queen, that anything less than such a refutation would 'leave me at Bismarck's mercy and disgrace us in the eyes of Europe'.[1] On the following day he telegraphed again, telling Salisbury of his letter to Herbert Bismarck and appealing to him to back up this step by an official demand in the same sense.[2] Malet (who had sent Morier at once a copy of the Cologne paper) and Ponsonby were also told and also made privy to Morier's renewed distress and excitement.[3]

Herbert Bismarck's reply was impertinent: 'I have had the honour to receive Your Excellency's letter of the 19th instant and I regret that neither its content nor its tone enables me to comply with your surprising demand and to step out of the limits imposed upon me by my official position in regard to the German press.'[4] Malet, who had discreetly referred to the article in conversation with Herbert Bismarck, was also given a dose of Bismarckian effrontery. Herbert Bismarck had said 'that the matter must come out sooner or later as no special secrecy had been preserved with regard to it and that it appeared certain that Bazaine had made the statement attributed to him —that corroborative evidence of this was now at hand'.[5] Salisbury telegraphed: 'Until German Govt. themselves bring the charge against you publicly I cannot call upon them officially to withdraw it.'[6] But on 30 December Morier communicated his correspondence with Bismarck to Buckle, the editor of *The Times*, for publication, and a little later to the editor of the *Daily Telegraph*.[7]

This was the beginning of an extraordinary press controversy, crossing all the European frontiers, which lasted for more than a week. The *Kölnische Zeitung* answered *The Times* by publishing (2 January) von Deines's two reports (2 April 1886 and 12

---

[1] To Ponsonby, 20 Dec. 1888, R.A. Z 280/16.
[2] To Salisbury, 21 Dec. 1888, Bazaine correspondence, no. 53; Salisbury papers, A/73, fo. 235.
[3] To Ponsonby, 20 Dec. 1888; to Malet, 21 Dec. 1888, Bazaine correspondence, nos. 51 and 52, and R.A. Z 280/16.
[4] From Herbert Bismarck, 25 Dec. 1888, Bazaine correspondence, no. 60; Salisbury papers, A/73, fos. 246–9.
[5] Malet to Morier, 21 Dec. 1888, Bazaine correspondence, no. 55, and Malet, to Salisbury, 18 and 22 Dec. 1888, Salisbury papers, A/61, fos. 413–20.
[6] From Salisbury, 22 Dec. 1888, Bazaine correspondence, no. 57.
[7] To G. E. Buckle, 30 Dec. 1888, Bazaine correspondence, no. 62; see also cuttings from the *Daily Telegraph* in R.A. Z 280/20.

November 1888). On 4 January *The Times* reproduced these. Provincial and metropolitan papers in Germany, France, Italy, Austria, Britain, and even the United States made their several interpretations of the affair and passed judgement on Morier and the Bismarcks. The *Kölnische Zeitung* and the *Post* described Bazaine's denial as a forgery, but the German liberal press, the *Vossische* on the Left, Eugen Richter's *Freisinnige Zeitung* in the middle, and the *National* for the Right Liberals, believed Morier had cleared himself, deplored the attitude of the Bismarcks, and coupled their observations with rejoicings over the release of Professor Geffcken. While the strength of Morier's language was sometimes deprecated, the consensus of opinion by the end of the clamour was against the Bismarcks and their methods. In England an article in the *Contemporary Review*, on the theme of astonishment that opposition to the Bismarcks could ever have been thought treason against the German state, summed up the verdict against them.[1]

Letters of congratulation poured in upon Morier. There is awareness in nearly all of them of the violence of Morier's reactions and an expressed or covert wish that he should say no more. A passage in a letter from Jowett may stand for all: 'I hope that you will not make it a personal quarrel with Herbert Bismarck ... May I say to you a thing which it rather pains me to say because it may pain you to hear it? The weak point of your diplomatic life has been that you have got the reputation of making things uncomfortable.'[2] Malet had a long interview with Prince Bismarck which vindicated Morier in all his fears. The chancellor really had taken Morier seriously. 'For years', he complained to Malet, 'Sir R. Morier has been working against me: he has been in constant communication with a faction which has aimed at upsetting the existing Government ... It is a habit with me to stand by friends and to be hostile to my enemies without counting the cost.' Hatzfeldt later told Salisbury what was true, that it was the father who was respon-

---

[1] Anon. (attributed to W. T. Stead by the *Wellesley Index of Victorian Periodicals*), 'The Bismarck Dynasty', *Contemporary Review*, Feb. 1889, pp. 157–78. The Queen inquired who the author was from Sir Theodore Martin, who told her it was Stead, the Queen to Martin, 7 Feb. 1889, R.A. Y 172/90, and Martin to the Queen, 30 Jan. and 3 Feb., R.A. Z 280/44 and 50.

[2] From Jowett, 7 Jan. 1889, Jowett papers at Balliol College, printed in Abbott and Campbell, *Life and Letters of Benjamin Jowett*, iii. 225.

sible for the rudeness of the son's reply to Morier.[1] The German Foreign Office filed separately three volumes of correspondence and one of press cuttings relating to Morier from the complaint to Rosebery in April 1886 to the Bazaine incident—proof of the seriousness with which this 'comedian' as Herbert Bismarck called him, was taken.

The Queen, first through Ponsonby and then direct, telegraphed to Salisbury that a formal and official expression of confidence in 'her ambassador' was now long overdue.[2] On the evening of 30 January a dispatch drafted on the 24th went off to Malet.[3] Salisbury referred to eight dispatches from Malet, sending home articles from the *Kölnische Zeitung*, running between 17 December and 22 January. He disclaimed any intention of meeting their various accusations, since Morier's character was far above the possible suspicion of being guilty, but since references to the Bazaine story involved rather a charge against the direction of British foreign policy than against Morier's honour, this had been investigated, and it had been shown that 'no reports respecting the movements of German troops were addressed by Sir R. Morier to his Government in the month of August of that year'. This communication formally made to the German government ended the incident. No amount of pressure from the Queen would, however, induce Lord Salisbury to publish it.

As an incident it is scarcely worth recounting at such length. It is certainly not worth the five large volumes of 1,500 press cuttings, supplied by three different press agencies in Germany, England, and France, and one of correspondence preserved by Morier. The Bismarcks come out of the story badly. The historian must record the unedifying sordidness of the fag-end of the Bismarckian regime and the Bazaine incident fits there. W. H. Smith, one of Salisbury's colleagues in the cabinet who had his close confidence, commented on the whole affair, that it did not show a friendly disposition on the part of the Germans. 'Perhaps that may be due to the fact that we on our part have

---

[1] Malet to Salisbury, private, 19 Jan., and Salisbury to the Queen, 25 Jan. 1889, R.A. Z 280/34 and 40; see also telegrams which prove it exchanged between Herbert Bismarck and Bismarck, 23 Dec. 1888, GFM 10/200.

[2] Salisbury to the Queen and the Queen to Salisbury, 19 Jan. 1889, R.A. Z 280/32 and 33.

[3] No. 26, 24 Jan. 1889, sent by Sanderson privately to Morier with a covering letter from himself, 30 Jan. 1889, Bazaine correspondence, nos. 82 and 84.

not evinced any desire for an alliance with Germany.'[1] Smith was writing six days before a famous German overture to Britain for an alliance made on 15 January 1889.[2] His comment gives to the affair the most dignified interpretation it can bear, and even so it scarcely speaks well for German methods.

Lord Salisbury comes well out of the story. Having once decided to take the line of killing gossip by silence, he was both steady and patient. Though he ended (26 December) by saying 'it is no use arguing with Morier', he had argued with him for three months and tolerated language from him so exaggerated that Goschen, a sympathetic intermediary, wrote to Morier that one phrase in his last letter to his chief 'he would not stand if he were Salisbury'. Morier comes out of the 'adventure', to use Ponsonby's word, unscathed in reputation. His good qualities and his failings were perhaps more widely known than before, but they were not altered. Eric Barrington's minute puts the man-of-the-world attitude that Morier was incapable of adopting: 'On the story [i.e. such a story as the Bazaine one] being repeated to you privately you first treat it with contempt and eventually give the best possible proofs of its inaccuracy to the narrator. You can neither convince him against his will, prevent his telling the story to others, or force him to deny it in his own newspaper. All this would be obvious to any one but Morier.'[3] The incident, however, was none the less a turning-point in Morier's career. The expenditure of nervous energy in arguing all round the compass for more than six months with all his colleagues, friends, and superiors, as well as the distress caused by the accusations and the gossip itself, took their toll of his physical health. He was never quite the same man again. The feud with the Bismarcks was over. While it lasted it had given Morier a sense of purpose and direction. This was now gone, or rather was henceforth to be found exclusively in his economic interests. The fruit of his interest in the opening up of new fields to British commercial enterprise was the Siberian project discussed in the next chapter.

[1] W. H. Smith to Lord Cross, 9 Jan. 1889, Cross papers, B.M. Add. MS. 51260, fo. 62. For the whole incident see F. B. M. Hollyday, 'Bismarck, Herbert and the Morier Affair, 1888–1889', *Central European History*, 1 (1968), 56–79.

[2] *Die große Politik der europäischen Kabinette*, iv. 400–4.

[3] Eric Barrington to Salisbury, 26 Dec. 1888, with Salisbury's note that it was no use arguing with Morier', Salisbury papers, A/73, fo. 242.

11

SIBERIA

During the nineties the scope of diplomacy was widened as the scope of politics was widened. To say that either was popularized would be going too far. Yet in international relations it was no longer exclusively the courts and cabinets that made the moves; nor was the prize of victory merely ascendancy in the European power constellation. It is fitting that this chapter should open by recording one symptom of the changed tone that Rosebery's advent to the Foreign Office, in 1892, marked. On one hand, he asked that his correspondence with the representatives in foreign capitals should record not only negotiations which were sometimes 'stilted and sterile, and even when successful and brilliant, often of evanescent interest except to the specialist, but what is neither strictly diplomatic nor political, the inner life of the court and the city'. On the other hand, he required that this should be recorded by weekly letters written direct to him personally by the secretary of embassy or legation. He would thus have broken down that strict hierarchy of persons upon which the order of values that placed politics above trade depended. It is interesting that Morier, however highly he estimated the importance of commercial matters, protested and that Rosebery's plan failed at St. Petersburg, as long, at least, as Morier was ambassador.

An extract from Rosebery's circular of August 1892, as an unpublished and characteristic document, follows.

... the inner life ... of the court and the city. To learn this, vividly and adequately expressed, is ... to breathe, or at any rate to understand, the atmosphere in which the reports are written. For this reason the despatches of the Venetian Ambassadors, and to a lesser degree, those of the French diplomatic agents of the time of Louis XIV and Louis XV, form the best materials for history. During the last decade, however, ... I strongly suspect that our diplomatic correspondence would be found to lack that particular quality which salts social facts for the benefit of posterity.

But if this be the historical advantage of the proposal I wish to make, the present purpose is not less important.

It is in these days necessary, or at least expedient, that the Foreign Secretary should know everything—every part of his trade. Of course, he will not know everything; firstly, because the scope is too wide; secondly, because there is much that is too obscure; thirdly, because human capacity is not sufficiently receptive. But let him attempt to know everything. There is scarcely any gossip so trivial, which has any bearing on the life of a nation of importance, that the Foreign Secretary should not have the opportunity of knowing it. But I take it, if an English Foreign Minister were to talk to a German Foreign Minister, he would be surprised to find how much more the latter knew of every detail of London life than himself, and *a fortiori* of the life of every other capital. This should not be ... The Indian Foreign Office seems to understand this, and uses nets with a very small mesh. Our mesh is heroic, and a good deal that is not heroic but important slips through it.

But there is another point. I hold that the Foreign Secretary should have the means of knowing not merely everything, but everybody, connected with his business, and that he cannot be too well acquainted with the personality of the staff of which he is the head. In my short experience I have always been anxious to give the younger men a chance of distinguishing themselves, so that they might not feel themselves chained to a dull hopeless tramway of promotion by mere seniority. I think that the enlargement of diplomatic correspondence which I suggest would have that effect. The Foreign Minister would learn more about the promising Secretaries and subordinates than he can at present, for he would be brought into direct relations with them, and could form some judgement of their capacity from their letters.[1]

It is a proof of the need which Rosebery had apprehended that Morier's Siberian venture can be followed without reference at all to the official telegrams and dispatches. To understand it one must go back three centuries. Russia's conquest of Siberia was gradually effected between 1579 and

---

[1] A printed copy of Rosebery's circular, dated Foreign Office, Aug. 1892, was enclosed in Rosebery's private and confidential letter of 12 Sept. 1892 to Morier, which stated baldly his intention of having letters from the secretaries of embassy or legation.

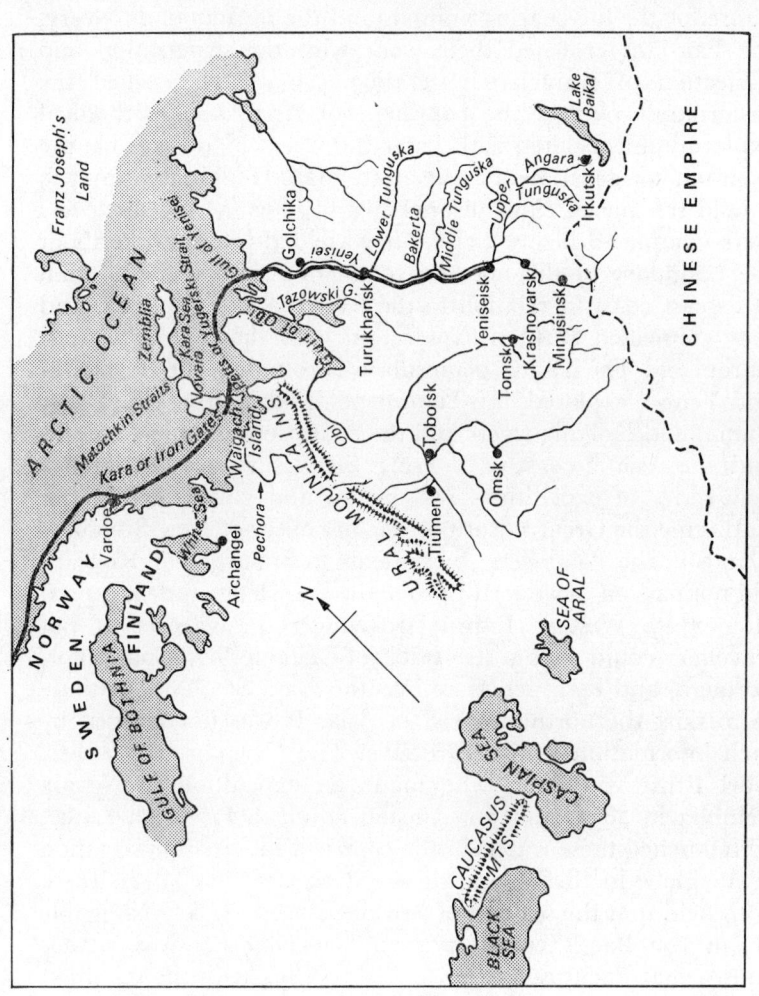

MAP 5. The Kara Sea
(based on Morier's own sketch-map)

1697.[1] Led on, as the French had been in Canada, by the desire for the fur-bearing animals and the instinct of discovery, the Russians crowned their work with the penetration and subjection of Kamchatka in 1697. They had reached the easternmost part of the continent of Asia. The methodical exploration associated with Peter the Great made possible the eventual construction of an accurate map. He initiated in 1725 a bold scheme of eight distinct sets of journeys of which few were completed before 1742. They yielded information about the boundary of the northern coast of Asia and the position of its east coast in relation to the west coast of America, and they connected Russian exploration with that of the western Europeans. The Yamul peninsula was rounded, the rivers Obi and Yenisei explored, the Taimur peninsula skirted, the Lena, Yama, and Kolyma rivers and the coast between their mouths and the Asiatic coast of Behring Strait surveyed. In 1760 a new series of expeditions was begun and culminated,[2] after Catherine the Great's death, in the discovery of New Siberia— islands in the Polar Sea—by an exile in Siberia. The Russians did not pass on to western Europe the knowledge they acquired after 1725. Western Europe was uncertain whether or not travellers could follow the track of Willoughby, Chancellor, Borough, and Pett, penetrate into the Kara Sea, and continue so to skirt the northern coast of Asia. It was discouraged by such information as it did receive. The German geographer, Karl Ernst von Baer, who made an expedition to Novaia Zemblia in 1837, and the Russian admiral, Friedrich Lutke, who touched these waters in the course of his circumnavigation of the globe in 1826–9 and surveyed part of the coast in 1840, both held that the sea east of Novaia Zemblia was unnavigable or, in von Baer's words, was an 'ice-cellar'. It was further known that Pachtusov, who started in 1832 with the intention of reaching the Yenisei, had failed and returned after wintering on Novaia Zemblia. Even after the use of steam had shortened the time of the journey, it could not be accomplished, it was said, because of the presence of ice all the year round in the

[1] Adolf Eric Nordenskiöld, *The Voyage of the* Vega *round Asia and Europe*, trans. A. Leslie (2 vols., 1881), ii, ch. xiii, pp. 159 ff. has a detailed account of Russian exploration and the gradual accumulation of knowledge about the northern coast of Asia.
[2] Between 1805 and 1811.

Kara Sea and in the three straits which gave access to it from the White Sea. Yet the course which it was conjectured the Gulf-stream followed round the North Cape, through the White Sea, and into the Kara Sea south of Novaia Zemblia suggested a contrary view.

In 1844 Lieut.-Col. G. Sabine translated into English from the German, which in turn came from a Russian manuscript, Admiral Ferdinand von Wrangell's *Narrative of an Expedition to the Polar Sea in 1820-23*. Von Wrangell had explored the sea, starting from Siberia, in an unsuccessful search for the land which was subsequently given his name. His book contained a history of Russian exploration and thus brought to western Europe that knowledge which the Russians had so far kept to themselves. Above all it established the falsity of the notion of continuous ice in this sea.

Von Wrangell's book was a godsend to Captain Joseph Wiggins. He was a Norfolk-born seaman, who had been in the service of a shipowning uncle of Sunderland and, after a pioneer voyage to Iceland in 1866, had become absorbed in the problems which ice creates for seamen. Von Wrangell confirmed notions which Captain Wiggins already entertained. He had brooded over them during a spell of shore service as examiner in navigation and seamanship between 1869 and 1874. Wiggins opened a correspondence with von Wrangell. His conviction that Siberia beyond the Urals was accessible by sea remained only to be proved by sailing there. In 1874 when he was 42 he was ready to risk the small fortune he had saved in proving that the Kara Sea was open for three months every year and that by sailing from England in June the voyage could be accomplished, with time to trade, and the return made before October. Under his command, the *Diana*, the *Whim*, the *Thames*, and the *Warkworth* attempted the voyage in the years 1874, 1875, 1876, and 1878 respectively. Not all voyages were equally successful. But it was proved that the Kara Sea was relatively ice-free—at least free long enough for the mouths of the rivers Obi and Yenisei to be reached. The *Diana* reached the mouth of the Obi; the *Thames* worked its way up the Yenisei and wintered in the river, but was lost in July 1877 at the beginning of her homeward journey; the *Warkworth* was the most successful, for she unloaded a cargo of salt, Sheffield steel goods, and porcelain at the mouth of the Obi and returned to London laden with a cargo of Siberian wheat. Captain Wiggins had by now not only spent the whole of his fortune, but exhausted the help which Sunderland friends were able to give him. He was afraid of speculators and dropped the active pursuit of his projects. Without his special knowledge and experience nothing more could be done from Britain.

Meanwhile in 1875 Baron Nordenskiöld, a Swedish scientist and polar explorer, had led the expedition of the *Pröven*. This was a small sailing-vessel of only seventy tons burden. Leaving Tromsø at midsummer it entered the Kara Sea by the Ugor Straits and reached the mouth of the Yenisei. Nordenskiöld himself disembarked here and proceeded by a Nordland boat up the river to Dudina and thence by a Russian steamer, *Alexander*, to Yeniseisk and so overland to Ekatrinenburg and Moscow. The *Pröven* meanwhile returned home, reaching Hammerfest by 29 September. Nordenskiöld wrote: 'I thus inaugurated . . . a new and important route for the commerce of the world.'[1] It was an irritating claim after the English voyages, but had to be tolerated because the *Diana* had only reached the Obi, the *Whim* had failed, and he had forestalled the *Warkworth* in linking the sea and river routes. Nordenskiöld, who had an established reputation, attracted public attention to the exploit of the *Pröven* in a way Wiggins had not been able to do to those of the *Diana* and *Thames*. Nordenskiöld's voyage also drew attention because it coincided with three Russian land expeditions of the summer of 1875. These were thought to have established that for an aggregate expenditure of 700,000 roubles it would be possible to render the Angara, a tributary of the Yenisei, navigable and to connect the Obi and the Yenisei, and the Yenisei and the Lena, by canal.

The achievement of linking the sea and river routes was, moreover, repeated, the money being provided by a rich Siberian merchant, A. Sibiriakov, a Swedish merchant called Oscar Dickson, and the Swedish navy. No one could go to the European side of the Ugor Straits without encountering Alexandre Sibiriakov—the uncrowned king of the Somoyades,

[1] *The Arctic Voyages of Adolf Eric Nordenskiöld, 1858–1879*, ed. A. Leslie (1879), p. 37.

'the Rothschild of these parts'.[1] In the squalid settlement of poor huts at Nikolskoe he built a stone church and an enormous store. His one remaining ambition was the development of trade between Siberia and the river Pechora. For this purpose he had built a road across the Urals and set up two steamers on the river: the *Nordenskiöld* and the *Obi*. Oscar Dickson belonged to a group of commercial magnates, including Ekman and Carnegie, who had already helped to pay for arctic exploration. The *Ymer*, the *Fraser*, and the *Vega* made the voyage into or beyond the Kara Sea in 1876, 1877, and 1878-9 respectively. All three made some contact with the river trade, the *Fraser*, for instance, in 1877 when owned by Sibiriakov, carrying out sugar, tobacco, and a steam pump and, in 1878-9, carrying out iron and tobacco and bringing back wheat and tallow on Sibiriakov's account.[2] The *Vega* in 1878-9 was accompanied by three other vessels for different parts of the voyage: the *Fraser* to carry goods to the Yenisei and back, the *Express* and the *Lena* to carry coals. On the last day of August she successfully passed south of the New Siberia islands to winter east of them and reached the Taimur peninsula in 1879 with the object, which she achieved, of making the north-east passage.[3]

Sir Robert Morier had only been a few months at his new post when, early in 1886, Captain Wiggins was introduced to him. Even before Morier took up residence in St. Petersburg when, that is, he saw de Giers at Franzensbad in August 1885, he had made much of his 'close relations with the commercial community' in England.[4] The introduction to Wiggins gave him opportunity to exploit it. Russia presented itself to him as a great 'protectionist bloc' stretching from the Polar Seas to Afghanistan—one of three with whom Britain traded, France and Austria-Hungary with her Serbian, Rumanian, and Bulgarian satellites being the other two.[5] He was determined,

---

[1] V. Morier, 'A Reindeer Journey in Arctic Russia,' *Murray's Magazine* (Aug.-Sept. 1889). Victor Morier was Sir Robert Morier's son. He was born in 1867, educated abroad, and at Balliol College, Oxford which he left without his degree. He served with Rhodes's mounted police and died in 1892.
[2] *The Arctic Voyages of Adolf Eric Nordenskiöld, 1858-1879*, ed. A. Leslie (1879), pp. 38-9, 340-6.
[3] A. E. Nordenskiöld, *The Voyage of the* Vega, i, *passim*.
[4] To Salisbury, private, 1 Sept. 1885.
[5] To Salisbury, private, 18 Sept. 1885.

like an explorer or trader in the Africa of the eighties, to open it up.

To open up to international commerce [he wrote] the whole of northern Asia down to the Chinese frontiers, to add one of the richest regions of the earth many times the size of Europe and inhabited by very intelligent and very wealthy white men who require all we can furnish to them [and have minerals and timber to export] and who can only get them by water to the world's markets ought surely in this age of commercial explorations and openings up to be a matter of capital importance.[1]

Morier's large views seem less extravagant if the small scale and slow pace of the period are remembered. Expeditions of single ships were usual and ideas were entertained in the hope, not of quick returns, but of profits in ten or twenty years' time. In any event he was soon the brains, the driving-power, and the invaluable 'man of influence' behind the plan of opening up Siberia, and so remained until his death.

In 1887, H. N. Sullivan, son of Admiral Sir James Sullivan, who assisted Darwin on the *Beagle*, organized a private company called the Phoenix Merchant Adventurers Limited.[2] It was able to buy the *Phoenix*, a small iron steamer of 273 tons burden,[3] and through Morier to gain a concession from the Russian government to import into Russia free of duty. The vessel left South Shields under Captain Wiggins's command on 5 August 1887. By 29 August she had successfully passed the Ugor Straits and entered the Kara Sea. She was of small enough draught to navigate both the shallow estuary of the Yenisei, from Karaoul to Golchika, and the river itself above Golchika. By 9 October the *Phoenix* was between 1,500 and 2,000 miles up the river at Yeniseisk, where she unloaded and went into winter quarters. Here she was deep in Siberia at the fair-town for the whole of the heart of the area through which the Trans-Siberian railway was later to pass. Captain Wiggins went back by land to the Baltic port of Libau and thence home by sea. Sullivan stopped at St. Petersburg where in January he had interviews with Morier, with Vyshnegradski, the new

[1] To Grey, 22 Dec. 1889. The passage in square brackets is conjectural.
[2] Morier's Promemoria, Nov. 1890, and Henry Johnson, *The Life and Voyages of Joseph Wiggins, Modern Discoverer of the Kara Sea Route to Siberia* (1907).
[3] Johnson's figure. Morier, in writing to Grey, 22 Dec. 1889, gives 400 tons.

Russian minister of finance, and with the minister for commerce. Morier even broke the normal court rules to ask for an audience of the Tsar for Sullivan.[1] Three concessions were the outcome: leave to bring British goods from England by sea to the mouth of the Yenisei for five years, and to that of the Obi for one year, and permission to the *Phoenix* by name to bring a cargo of Siberian goods down the Yenisei and to take a cargo of goods back up-stream in 1888. The last was a particularly valued concession, since river navigation was otherwise reserved to Siberian or Russian ships.[2] These successes brought a few more shareholders to the company, but its capital was still so small as to leave no margin beyond the actual cost of the plans of 1888.

Two voyages were projected: that of the *Phoenix* with her load of goods from the interior, down the Yenisei, and that of a new vessel from the Tyne through the Kara Sea to meet the *Phoenix* at the mouth of the Yenisei. The new vessel was the *Labrador*, a fine Arctic ship built especially for the Hudson's Bay Company of wood, as pliable in ice, but plated with iron, of 300 tons burden,[3] and owned by G. W. Ashdown. She left the Tyne on 16 July 1888 under Wiggins's command and with Morier's only son, Victor,[4] on board. Reaching Vardoe on 3 August[5] she there learnt that the *Phoenix* had stuck on a sandbank and that, since the river was falling, she could not be got off in time to make the rendezvous. Captain Wiggins was able to communicate with the directors, who promptly sent out the *Seagull*, a small paddle-steamer, with goods for the river voyage. After a weary month's delay the *Labrador*, together with the *Seagull*, left Vardoe on 4 September and made for the Kara Sea. Meanwhile, the *Phoenix* had safely reached the mouth of the Yenisei—the news had much exaggerated her difficulties—only to find the *Labrador* not arrived and to be obliged to sail back up river without having transferred her cargo. The *Seagull* anyhow failed to get into the Kara Sea. Thus there was

[1] To Salisbury, 28 May 1888.
[2] See Notes of Vyshnegradski to Morier, 23 Mar. and 21 June 1888, and to Grey, 22 Dec. 1889.
[3] Victor Morier gives 500 tons.
[4] See above, p. 311 n.
[5] Victor Morier wrote 3 Sept. This must be a mistake, since that date would allow too long for the voyage.

no financial return whatever, but instead the extra cost of the *Seagull*'s voyage and of the *Labrador*'s stay at Vardoe. The Phoenix Merchant Adventurers as a company was ruined and had to go into liquidation. The two or three friends who had furnished the bulk of the capital lost heavily and Sullivan lost all his fortune. The *Phoenix*, which remained on the Yenisei, was still an asset. It was left in charge of Robert Wiggins, brother of Joseph, at Yeniseisk. Meanwhile, the latter, on the *Labrador*, had been unable to resist the temptation to prove 'the absence of ice at this time of year in the Kara Sea', and he had steamed well beyond the mouth of the Yenisei—as far as Whale Island—before returning to meet the *Seagull* at Vardoe and to take them both back to the Tyne, where they arrived by October 1888. 'The feasibility of the route', wrote Morier to Albert Grey, 'was never more brilliantly demonstrated for it was the worst year for ice ever known and the *Labrador* a really good Arctic ship made nothing of it.'[1]

Between the autumn of 1888 and the summer of 1890, Morier made tremendous exertions as a company promoter in London, an agency organizer in Siberia, and a concession seeker in St. Petersburg. He even wrote himself to Nordenskiöld to inquire whether, owing to an abnormally mild winter in 1889–90, the straits might be ice-free earlier than usual in 1890.[2] In January 1889 the Anglo-Siberian Syndicate Limited of London took over the liabilities and assets (of which the *Phoenix* was the sum total) of the Phoenix Merchant Adventurers of Newcastle. But, as Morier relates, Captain Wiggins had fallen 'into the hands of a set of scoundrels, who thought they could use his name to finance a bubble Company with a share capital of £100,000 and all the rest of it: they brought out their Company, appealed to the public and having spent £500 in advertisements obtained £27: 10. 0 from the public!'[1] At least Morier was in England when the crash came (24 July 1889). G. W. Ashdown was still prepared to put the *Labrador* at Wiggins's disposal, if he could find crew, cargo, and the cost of the voyage.

At this point in Morier's career Mackinnon, now Sir William

---

[1] To Grey, 22 Dec. 1889.
[2] From Nordenskiöld, 11 Apr. 1890, replying to Morier, shows the gist of what he asked.

and a baronet, makes a second appearance. Morier, turning anywhere for help, wrote from the Athenæum on 11 July, 1889 recalling the Goa railway to him and asking for advice. Mackinnon replied, not with advice, but with a promise of £500 to add to Morier's capital to send out the *Labrador* again. Morier used the promised sum to buy up the cargo brought back to England the previous year, in order to dispatch it again. He advanced the money out of his own pocket. When Mackinnon's sum still did not arrive, he was reduced to using money set aside to pay his household bills in St. Petersburg. He had put himself in a position that by all the standards of his day the status of an ambassador of the Crown abroad demanded he should above all others avoid. Mackinnon's money eventually arrived, but he refused Morier the advice he sought. He disassociated himself. Thus Mackinnon was important only perhaps to Morier's biographer; since Morier, trying to get his money, chanced to write to him an account of the humiliation he suffered during a meeting of 'millionaires' convened by Lord Brassey on 16 July 1889. Morier had been put in touch with Lord Brassey by Benjamin Jowett.[1] He was invited to come with Captain Wiggins and to put their case for financing a fresh voyage of the *Labrador* to a group of men whom Brassey had collected. They were cross-examined, wrote Morier, 'like a couple of swindlers' by men who would not miss the five or six thousand it would take to float his company, and in the end dismissed with empty hands; for 'the millionaires' had looked at the proposal as 'a commercial speculation' and missed its essential quality as 'a great national undertaking'.[2]

Lord Brassey having proved a broken reed, Morier turned to rich friends of his own as he had turned in 1879 to the Duke of Sutherland and the Stafford House Committee. Within ten days, with the assistance of five or six others, he had accomplished the feat of collecting upwards of £3,000. His personal friends who included the Duke of Bedford, the Duke of Westminster,[3] and Lord Derby contributed £1,700. Oliver

[1] To Jowett, 18 Nov. 1888.
[2] The Mackinnon papers, 173, fos. 9–28 contain letters to Mackinnon from London of 11, 14, 17, 18 July 1889, and 174, fos. 1–23 letters to Mackinnon from St. Petersburg of 11 Aug. 1889, in which is the account of the Brassey meeting, 1 Jan., and 19 Feb. 1890.
[3] He had been up with Morier at Balliol, see *Daily Telegraph*, 17 Nov. 1893.

Williams was Morier's chief agent and adviser in this work. He also worked on his own account with Sir Louis Mallet and W. C. Cartwright to interest the City, addressing himself especially to the bankers, Henry Hucks Gibbs and Sir John Lubbock. English merchants, such as Messrs. Hubbard, bankers, already engaged in the Russian trade, Morier had to avoid, for, as he owns, he had quarrelled with the English colony in St. Petersburg. Thus in July 1889 a new syndicate was formed comprising Lord Wenlock, the banker, as chairman, Albert Grey of the British South Africa Company, and William Grenfell, also a banker. In December 1890 Grey became chairman in place of Wenlock who had been appointed governor of Madras.[1] The company was run from 3 Brabant Court, the office of Beavan & Ollard, with a man called Wincott as managing director. Morier never liked him, thinking he was out to puff up the company's prospects in order to inflate its borrowing powers and the number of its shareholders.[2] His efforts at least enabled the *Labrador* to set sail on 2 August 1889 from London with a cargo worth £4,000.

Morier both appealed in all this to patriotic pride and offered the glamour of quickly won wealth. Let Grey, for example, put out a fly-sheet inviting subscriptions 'to back up a brave British Navigator of the old stamp, who has spent his whole fortune and all the best years of his life, almost unaided in solving practically the great problem the theoretical solution of which Nordenskiöld has declared to have been the great result of his voyage in the *Vega* . . . The motive power here is not profit but a patriotic wish that England and no other power should do this great work' of making available to mankind the enormous resources of Siberia.[3] Morier cried up the gold, graphite, and timber of Siberia. Let the trading syndicate join with a mining syndicate that was being planned; for the discovery of gold in sufficient quantities to make its working profitable would ensure a real return on the sea voyage.[4] 'I send you', he wrote on another occasion, 'the enclosed pencil— the very best pencil you can write with—made of Irkutsk

---

[1] To Grey, 23 Dec. 1890 and 2 Jan. 1891.
[2] To Grey, 11 Nov. 1890. [3] To Grey, 22 Dec. 1889.
[4] Notes and counter notes, on the present position of the Anglo-Siberian Trading Syndicate Ltd., Nov. 1890.

graphite which I have always maintained was the finest pencil lead in the world though nobody would believe me and a cargo of which would pay us ten times over.'[1] Finally the forests of Siberia were the largest virgin forests left in the world. 'Now I wish to point out that the finest of these forests are half way down the Yenisei. That if we set up steam saw mills on the river we could float timber in any quantities down to Karaoul for nearly nothing and that we could on this alone realise fabulous wealth.'[1]

Morier's organization of the Siberian agency proved little short of calamitous, but it looked very well at the beginning. He established it in June 1889 just before he left for England. It comprised three men: George Lee (son of a well-known preacher, Robert Lee), a certain Davison, and H. N. Sullivan (who did not know Russian) from the *Phoenix* enterprise.[2] In Lee Morier believed he had 'discovered a staunch old Scotchman of the very highest reputation who had been a civil engineer for 25 years working some of the greatest mines in Siberia. Married to a Siberian, so as in one way to be a native of the country, whilst remaining as regards his acuteness and thorough honesty a staunch Presbyterian of the old school.' Morier had got him to England in the winter of 1888–9 and then at his own expense sent him to the Yenisei 'with a full knowledge of English prices etc. there to study the wants and commercial conditions of exchange'.[3] Lee prepared lists of goods likely to be acceptable to the Siberian market—'his marvellous lists the admiration of the English experts'—kept good accounts, and even turned his hand to reducing the draught of the *Phoenix* to make it better suited to river conditions.[4] Davison, who acted as clerk and interpreter, was the son of Morier's new chancery servant, a man just appointed to this post of trust to replace someone alleged to have sold chancery secrets to the Russian government. The new man was an Englishman who had tried to run his own business in St. Petersburg but failed owing to want of capital. His passport to Morier's trust was membership of a dissenting chapel[5]—'a most invaluable trustworthy old nonconformist, whose children

---

[1] To Grey, 28 Nov. 1890. [2] To Grey, 30 Oct. 1890.
[3] To Grey, 22 Dec. 1889. [4] To Grey, 22 Oct. 1890.
[5] To Sanderson, private, 12 Dec. 1888, F.O. 65/1333.

are like even unto him'.¹ The young Davison's letters to his father eventually revealed all the shortcomings of George Lee. H. N. Sullivan, I assume, had gone out to the Yenisei again at his own expense, being unable to resist the lure of the enterprise. Oliver Williams, the man who had helped Morier in London and was, in 1890, to be made a director of the syndicate, also went out to Yeniseisk in July 1889. He saved the situation when Lee died and remained in charge until Arthur Medhurst replaced him in February 1891. Medhurst was vice-consul at Moscow and a businessman acting as agent for an English firm of agricultural machine-makers. He was another paragon: 'a first-rate man . . . our very best Consular officer in Russia' who might, had he had the means, have expected a diplomatic career.² The agency was not a success, partly because Morier's head man proved less good than he expected, but also because it had a fantastic task. Besides having to organize the river navigation, which was in itself difficult, it had 'to set up retail shops within a country the size of France, Germany, and Austria . . . to label each article and to put its price on it (as young Davison in a letter to his father tersely puts it from a 50 kopek doll to a 1000 rouble engine) . . . then to sit behind the counter and sell'.³

The work of concession seeker in St. Petersburg Morier found the most arduous. He spent on it 'an amount of diplomatic skill which would have made the fortune of a first class statesman at the Congress of Vienna or Berlin'.⁴ The difficulty was the dominance in Russia since the accession of Alexander III of the anti-foreign, Muscovite element in whose 'creed Nihilism and the foreign revolutionary party are one'. From the Emperor downwards all the Russians who were called upon to deal with the Siberian scheme 'hate it, hate to hear of it and with all their hearts wish it not to succeed'. To make matters worse the finance minister, Vyshnegradski, was 'the child of Moscow' who had risen to power 'on the shoulders of the commercial element' of the Panslavist reactionary party. Even if one discounts it, the drama with which Morier characteristically invested their relationship could not have been particularly

---
¹ To Grey, 14 Oct. 1890.
² To Grey, 30 Oct. and 28 Nov. 1890.   ³ Notes and counter notes, Nov. 1890.
⁴ To Grey, 5 Dec. 1890, upon which the whole of this paragraph is founded.

suited to humdrum commercial purposes. 'At the very outset of our undertaking in 1888 I had a violent quarrel with him. He is a coarse, big, violent man ... and I have got a bit of a temper myself so there was war *à outrance* betwixt us.' But Morier resorted, as with Corvo or with de Giers himself, to a secret personal understanding. According to his own account he won Vyshnegradski over by understanding his budget, praising it, and explaining it in a dispatch to the foreign secretary which he then got printed in the Foreign Office leaflets and distributed in St. Petersburg. So he 'hooked and landed' his man. 'I have had him with me ever since ... He has worked for me tooth and nail ... but the condition of his aid was that it should be *subterranean*! and that he should not appear in public as the friend of the scheme!!'

Morier's first effort was to gain the renewal of permission to the *Phoenix* by name to bring cargoes up and down the Yenisei. In this he failed, the Russians maintaining that there were Siberian ships enough to navigate both river and estuary. His second task was to gain an extension of the main five-year concession which was due to expire in 1892. He argued with the Russians that two (i.e. 1889 and 1890) of the original five years had been virtually lost owing to their failure to renew the permission to the *Phoenix*. He was justified, therefore, in asking that the lost years be made good by extension up to 1894.[1] While this request was being passed from Vyshnegradski to de Giers, and back to Vyshnegradski, then back to de Giers, and from de Giers to the Emperor, the syndicate asked for a ten years' charter.[2] Morier was in despair at this, but in January 1891 in fact gained his original request. He gave a dinner to a number of key members of the committee of ministers[3]— Howick pheasants from Lord Grey were an important feature but the decisive factor was the support of General Ammenkov. The decree authorizing the building of the Trans-Siberian railway was on the point of signature and it was 'on the cards that Ammenkov' would 'be called upon to construct it, as he engages to construct it in four years for 30 millions sterling'. Morier won him over by the hope that his English company would export by the sea and river route 'rails,

---

[1] Promemoria for the Russian government, 1890, and to Grey, 22 Nov. 1890.
[2] To Grey, 9 Dec. 1890.   [3] To Grey, 2 Jan. 1891.

boilers, parts of machinery etc.' at a cheap rate for the railway.[1] It was also important that the syndicate did not at this point hold to its demand for a ten-year charter, though it revived it later.

Other subsidiary activities of Morier included an attempt to gain the stationing of a meteorological ship, connected by telegraph with the mainland, at the entrance to the Ugor Straits in order to keep those using the sea route briefed about ice.[2] He also sought a Russian government subsidy to a Russian river company. Finally he proposed that Wenlock, the former chairman of the Anglo-Siberian Syndicate and now governor of Madras, should offer hospitality to the Cesarevitch, when he visited India, and should use his opportunity to ask that the *Phoenix* (sold by order of the bankruptcy court and registered now as a Russian vessel) might be renamed *Cesarevitch* during the Prince's prospective tour of Siberia.[3] When this visit, during which the Cesarevitch cut the first sod for the Trans-Siberian railway (4 May 1891), happened, Morier had broken his connection with the Siberian venture altogether and nothing of this sort was done.

The fruit of all this endeavour was two voyages: one in 1889 and one in 1890. The *Labrador* left London on 4 August 1889 and reached Karaoul on 4 September. A Russian river expedition successfully came down to Golchika. But success ended there. The *Labrador* drew too much water to make the estuary voyage up to Golchika and, owing to the poverty of the Company, had sailed without a steam launch to do it for her. The Russian ship with its high deck was unsuited to navigating the estuary and meeting its terrible gales. The two expeditions, therefore, failed to meet and exchange their cargoes.

The expedition of 1890 took place without Captain Wiggins, who had sailed on the *Labrador* for its owner to South America and not returned in time. It was made with some éclat by the *Thule*, the *Biscaya*, and the *Bard*. Albert Grey was responsible for the publicity and the financing. He and John D. Milburn had organized a so-called 'Local Committee for the North of England' which collected subscriptions from private persons. Thus enough money was raised to buy the *Thule* and to charter

[1] To Grey, 18 Dec. 1890.   [2] To Grey, 12 Jan. 1891.
[3] To Grey, 23 Dec. 1890.

the *Biscaya*, wooden vessels of light draught, and a powerful tug, the *Bard*. The expedition, accompanied by Julian M. Price of the *London Illustrated News*, reached Karaoul safely. The *Thule* and *Biscaya* then trans-shipped valuable cargoes on to a flotilla of river lighters and steam tugs, convoyed down river by the *Phoenix* from Yeniseisk.[1] The transfer took three weeks and the two expeditions parted again on 13 September. The *Thule* and *Biscaya* returned to London, while the *Bard* joined the river expedition and went with it up to Yeniseisk. 'Every day', during the transfer, 'a disaster or hair breadth's escape was recorded.' George Lee, who 'alone was in a position to take the command as only he could communicate with the eighty Russians whom he had brought to effect the loading and unloading of the ships', went on a drinking-bout. Young Davison had gone up river with a mining party. 'The best steam launch and several of the lighters became total wrecks; others, already half-filled with valuable merchandize dragged their moorings, and drifting towards the shore were only with difficulty saved by the *Bard*.' At the end of the operation the whole of the English company were assembled after dinner in the cabin of the *Phoenix*. 'Williams and Lee were playing chess; outside was a pitch dark night, and a howling snowstorm was proclaiming the advent of winter. Some call on deck caught Lee's ear: he said he feared they were touching ground and ran out.' Lee never returned and was presumed to have lost his balance while taking a sounding and to have been drowned. Oliver Williams now took command and brought the river expedition, with its cargo intact, safely back to Yeniseisk just ahead of the Arctic winter.[2]

Williams, in charge of the Siberian agency, had for sale goods ranging from needles, coconuts, oranges, and dolls to electric light apparatus, locomotives, and mining machinery. But his difficulties were only beginning. Lee had lived at Krasnoyarsk, some 250 miles higher up the river than Yeniseisk, and had established the offices and warehouses of the syndicate there.

[1] The account of the 1890 expedition is taken from Morier's printed letter to the shareholders in the syndicate, from which all quotations come unless otherwise indicated.
[2] For Vyshnegradski's telegram of congratulation to Morier, dated from Kokand where he was negotiating a tariff for the trans-Himalayan trade, see to Salisbury, private, 2 Oct. 1890.

Williams had not only to borrow money locally (since Lee's funds and effects had all been sealed up) in order to pay off the crew, but also to buy a building at Yeniseisk to house and display his goods. He was then confronted with the excise official. 'Though the goods were all imported free [of duty], he insisted on everything' in 700 tons of miscellaneous merchandise 'being opened, classified, and weighed, and the exact amount it would have had to pay if not duty free, registered. Till all this was done he declared he could not release the cargo. The process lasted two months.' That it did not last longer was due to Morier's gaining orders from St. Petersburg to 'put an end to all this pedantry'. The cargo released, Williams sent a portion of it up by land to Krasnoyarsk, where Lee's widow changed her house into a store and she and her three daughters sold the small goods across the counter 'at enormous profits'. The worst difficulty was to find customers and to gain payment for the large goods. With Lee's death there had 'disappeared once and for ever a whole year's work in preparing the ground for the sale of the goods and securing customers'. The Siberian market was accustomed to trading habits based on the 'eleven months" land carriage from Moscow and consequent allowance of a year's credit. These could not be quickly changed and accommodated to the four months' journey and to Williams's need for quick returns to satisfy the subscribers in England. 'Many of the smaller articles under a pound sold for ready money as quick as they could be taken out of their wrappers, and at gross profits ranging from 100 to 300 per cent.' But when it came to the machinery, not only did the credit difficulty arise, but also 'though buyers undoubtedly existed within our market of 1,500 miles diameter, they were not at Yeniseisk where the [heavy] goods were, but mainly at Irkutsk, with some at Krasnoyarsk and Minusinsk, that is respectively 1,000 and 250 and 500 miles away, and in the winter these people stick to their stoves and only begin to move about when the summer sets in and mining begins'. But this was a complaint in the circumstances 'about as rational as if a sea captain from South Africa groaned because he had been unable to sell a full grown rhinoceros to a dealer in canary birds at Brighton'.[1] In any event Williams overcame even this difficulty. Morier

[1] To Grey, 31 Dec. 1890.

describes with much elaboration how between Christmas and April Williams went to Irkutsk, and enlisting the help of everyone, from officials to political exiles, completed his task of disposing of his cargo and creating a market. This was in the spring of 1891, when the ukase for the construction of the Trans-Siberian railway was at last issued. The prospective terminal of the sea route, Krasnoyarsk, was to be one of the stations on the line. For constructing the line the sea route became 'all but indispensable' as much the cheapest way of bringing in rails—it was calculated the cost would be one-third less than by land. When the Trans-Siberian railway was complete, the syndicate would be able to export not only cereals and timber from the valley of the Yenisei, but graphite, lapis lazuli, and malachite from Lake Baikal.

It was already plain before Williams's journey to Irkutsk that definite orders in advance were not to be had for the sort of small goods that could be retailed by the syndicate itself. Every venture would, therefore, involve a risk of the same sort that had accompanied the expedition just completed. Grey, a disciple of Cecil Rhodes and director of the South Africa Company, was convinced that it was impossible to invite regular investment on the open market on this basis. 'The business of the retail merchant', he wrote, was 'one to be avoided by commercially minded men who look for a profit.'[1] He urged, therefore, that the enterprise be either enlarged or cut down: either the syndicate should become a chartered company with a ten-year concession and buy up various independent mining concerns, or it should leave the river and retail trade to the Russians and act simply as ocean carrier. Grey preferred to enlarge and Morier to cut down. Moreover, he talked over the future with Vyshnegradski, who also approved the smaller alternative and, as Morier wrote, 'considers *the* great thing to effect is the creation of the two Syndicates the English for the Ocean route, the Siberian for the River route'.[2]

Yet Grey relied on Morier to further his larger plan in St. Petersburg and Morier felt bound by gratitude to do so. Undoubtedly his imagination was caught by the larger scheme as it began to develop after 5 January 1891. On that date Grey

[1] From Grey, 7 Jan. 1891. [2] To Grey, 15 Jan. 1891.

expounded a plan for bringing Baron Günsburg, the great Russian Jewish banker and owner of the Lena gold-mines, into association with Lord Rothschild and securing their joint backing and capital for an Anglo-Russian scheme of development based on the proposed chartered company. 'The chance of approaching Günsburg thro' Rothschild', Morier replied, 'I consider *absolutely invaluable*. Therefore *do so at once* . . . If he will in any way help it would be a very great thing indeed.'[1] But he refused to act as go-between. 'It would be absolutely fatal to my position here. So marvellously contrived is Petersburg Society that I don't even know him by sight.' Moreover, Morier had so far gained all he had gained with Vyshnegradski by representing the enterprise not as a 'commercial moneymaking concern' but as 'a gentleman's fad'.[2] Albert Grey should himself come out to St. Petersburg and negotiate with Günsburg, all the more because one of the members of the syndicate, who had come out on the *Thule* and been subsequently engaged in Williams's heroic shopkeeping in Siberia, had returned by way of St. Petersburg and been put by a member of the Russian ministry of finance, Timiriashev, into touch with Günsburg.[3] Eventually, however, Morier, stung by a sentence in Grey's reply about the folly of the aloofness of ambassadors from the commercial community, called both on Günsburg, soliciting orders for mining machinery, and on Oswald Cattley, an English merchant in Russia who had got the cargo of wheat to the mouth of the Obi for the *Warkworth* in 1878 and disposed of the goods the latter had brought.[4]

Meanwhile, Morier gave most of his effort to providing cargo, markets, and orders for an 1891 expedition and to the scheme for two companies. The Russian river company was to have shares in the English ocean company and representation on its board and the English to have shares in the Russian and similar representation.[5] But it was soon clear that Grey expected Morier to drop his efforts for an 1891 expedition and to concentrate on the big scheme. 'We have got out of touch with each other', wrote Morier on 7 February, 'and are pursuing different objects. *You* want an immediate pot of money—I want the

---

[1] To Grey, 15 Jan. 1891.
[2] To Grey, 21 Jan. 1891.
[3] To Grey, 28 Jan. 1891.
[4] To Grey, 3 Feb. 1891.
[5] To Grey, 29 Jan. 1891.

route.'[1] He was especially alarmed because Grey had now found no fewer than four mining syndicates[2] which he wished to amalgamate into his big company. He could not resist this. 'Circumstances', he wrote on 10 March, 'have forced me to give you a perfectly free hand in the matter of amalgamation', but he begged that it should be done quietly. Above all he saw that it endangered the plan for the two companies. 'You have confounded', he continued in the letter of February, 'the small Russian Syndicate for working the River, which I started ... with your Charter scheme and you fancy that Günsburg has already been won for the big Charter scheme ... He has volunteered his help and has already shown how helpful he can be, in building up the small Company, and out of this small Company I think it very probable that if we don't RUSH and allow for the small growth of all things in Russia, big things may grow ...' But it was nonsense to think of his being won for a big scheme. Morier was already endangering his position as ambassador which entailed, necessarily and traditionally, refusal to aid private business ventures. 'My hand has now been forced', he complained, 'because the bringing of Günsburg into touch with Natty [Lord Rothschild] was so immensely important that I felt I must give a help—at any risk.'[1] He ended with an appeal for the small scheme. 'I can only feel an interest in the carrying out of this year's expedition which I have been building up bit by bit but with the greatest success, if I could only get some efficient interest taken in the matter in England.'

The appeal went unanswered. Meanwhile, on 8 February Morier, in compliance with Albert Grey's and Lord Rothschild's wish, had a long interview with Günsburg. He made it clear that he was negotiating in Grey's scheme and was conscious that it was quite a different one from his own. 'You and I,' he reported to Grey, 'though belonging to the same pack, have been hunting two separate foxes. You have been running after your Charter as if you were the huntsman of the Pytchley, I with a few sorry beagles have been pottering after my Siberian River Company.' Günsburg was not unreceptive,

---

[1] To Grey, 7 Feb. 1891.
[2] Those of (1) Vautin, (2) D'Arcy Becket, (3) The Barrow Haemetite Steel Company of which Lord Hartington was chairman, and (4) an Australian concern referred to as the Kangaroo, see to Grey, 8 Feb. 1891

but made it clear that further progress depended on how serious Lord Rothschild was and on the attitude of Vyshnegradski. 'I must confess, however,' wrote Morier as he concluded with yet another appeal for the 1891 expedition, 'that it is not without the gravest misgivings and *à contre-cœur* that I have opened up these negotiations with Günsburg', but since Grey had refused to come to St. Petersburg, 'it was a case of *vis major* ... There was no one but myself who could undertake the job.' He would throw himself into it heartily but '*as part of a solemn bargain* that *you* on your part at once see to *my* object ... I mean the taking in hand of this year's expedition'.[1]

Morier next saw Vyshnegradski. He persuaded him to support the big scheme and to sanction the creation of a Russian company for the exploitation of the mineral wealth of Siberia and the development of her transoceanic trade, its headquarters at Moscow or St. Petersburg, a small proportion of English capital invested in it, and English representation on its board.[2] Further appeals to Grey still failed to gain his support for an 1891 expedition and, indeed, by the end of February the plan for the creation of a Russian river company had already failed.[3]

Before this, however, two other Russians had begun to show interest in the big scheme: a millionaire mine-owner and his partner, Ratkov Rajnov and Basilewski, who wanted English capital and mining machinery. There was also Krasnoselski—'another Beit', 'the brains of the Günsburg House', and 'Günsburg's familiar'[4]—and an Englishman called Mercer, the head of a Siberian mining syndicate, who had patented a machine for crushing the quartz after it was mined and separating the gold from the quartz dust. The Russian mine-owners wished to import this machine—by the ocean route, Morier hoped. By March he was negotiating with Günsburg for an exact amount of machinery and about the importation of the quartz-crushing machine by the ocean route.[5] There was a promising correspondence between Rothschild and Günsburg, but Rothschild suddenly changed his tune and telegraphed bluntly: 'at the present moment all fresh business is really quite

---

[1] To Grey, 8 Feb. 1891.   [2] To Grey, 23 Feb. 1891.
[3] To Grey, 28 Feb. 1891.
[4] To Grey, 28 Feb. and 25 Mar. 1891.
[5] To Grey, 20 Mar. 1891.

impossible.'¹ Krasnoselski then went to London. (Before this telegram Günsburg was to have gone.)² By now Günsburg had agreed that he would take up a proportion, and do his best to persuade other Russian mine-owners to take up the remainder, of 300 tons of mining machinery to be brought out by the Anglo-Siberian Trading Syndicate at a cost of £4,000, freight to be paid on delivery.³ This would make possible an 1891 expedition. It was also hoped to bring out Mercer's quartz-crushing machine by the same expedition. But nothing happened from the London end. So there was no expedition in 1891. Morier was bitterly disappointed. Some eighteen months earlier he had written to Louis Mallet and Cartwright: 'The only thing I have left to care about is this Siberian Route. I don't think you either of you see the importance of it or can keep your minds clear of detail. It's the song of the swan ... To succeed in this is what my whole soul strives after.'⁴ Now it had failed, he was 'physically dead beat', sick with gout and worry and with no spirit left in him.¹

There was still, however, something of Grey's scheme left. Negotiations for the big amalgamation had failed, but he hoped still to purchase shares in the Ratkov Rajnov–Basilewski gold-mines, to purchase the river Abakan iron-mine and other iron-mines situated near the prospective line of the Trans-Siberian railway and perhaps turn them into a rail manufactory.⁵ In mid April Grey came out to St. Petersburg, but he failed to bring any of these negotiations to a successful conclusion. Grey's big scheme had failed and had only served to foil the expedition for 1891. In May 1891 Morier broke all his connections with plans for the Siberian ocean route. He recalled Arthur Medhurst. The remaining English interest in the *Phoenix* and the *Bard* was sold.⁶ He broke off relations with Günsburg, Krasnoselski, and Oswald Cattley. He told Vyshnegradski that 'the question having got into a purely mercantile phase and you [Grey] and Williams having come to St. Petersburg and been placed personally *en rapport* respectively with the Government and the commercial people,

¹ To Grey, 27 Mar. 1891.
² To Grey, 30 Mar. 1891.
³ Ibid. and 1 and 3 Apr. 1891, and mem. enclosed in the last.
⁴ To Mallet and Cartwright, 27 Oct. 1889.
⁵ To Grey, 3 Apr. 1891.   ⁶ To Grey, 18 May 1891.

no intervention on my part was further necessary or diplomatically possible'.[1]

One cause of failure would seem to have been Albert Grey's over-ambitious scheme, built upon shaky foundations. He had tried to use the Rothschilds without any certainty that they were interested. He had gone ahead in Russia without any certainty that Russian enterprises could attract English capital. There were, secondly, too many incompatible interests involved. The navigators and the salesmen were not easily kept together. Joseph Wiggins and Oswald Cattley had quarrelled already in 1878.[2] Nor did the salesmen and financiers see things in the same light. Oliver Williams's hard work was useless plodding to a Günsburg or a Rothschild. The gap between the diplomatic and commercial circles in St. Petersburg was not to be bridged even by a Morier. Indeed, there was a feud between himself and the whole English community there 'entirely their fault— a social question and absurd pretensions put forward by them'.[3] The chief cause of failure was that Morier had tried to do much that was beyond his power as an ambassador to do. He could not be a successful company promotor and commercial traveller and ambassador too. He had tried to be a rower in the boat, when the most that it was in his power to do was to fend it off the banks. A more conventional ambassador would not have taken the initiative in promoting the enterprise, only smoothed its way with the Russian government.[4] Morier just lived to see the enterprise renewed in 1893. The voyage of that year was the most successful of Wiggins's voyages to the Kara Sea.[5] It was run by a private syndicate in which F. Leybourne-Popham was the chief figure. Wiggins had a stated salary and a small share in the profits, in return for which he selected ships and cargoes, conducted the vessels, and kept in touch with the Russian government and Siberian officials. The principal constituent of the cargo was rails for the Trans-Siberian railway, ordered by the Russian government at the last moment. There were two wooden steamers, the *Blencathra* and the

---

[1] To Grey, 28 Apr. and 8 May 1891.   [2] To Grey, 29 Jan. 1891.
[3] To Mallet, 4 Nov. 1889.
[4] See D. C. M. Platt, *Finance, Trade, and Politics in British Foreign Policy, 1815–1914* (Oxford, 1968), pp. 55–60, 85, 97, 403–15.
[5] Henry Johnson, *The Life and Voyages of Joseph Wiggins* (1907), pp. 264 ff.; see also Helen Peel, *Polar Gleams. An Account of the Voyage on the Yacht* 'Blencathra' (1894).

Orestes, and a steel shallow-draught steam yacht, the *Minusinsk*. They were joined at Vardoe by three Russian steamers built on the Clyde, under Russian naval officers, for the river work. The expedition left Vardoe by 29 August and reached Golchika on 3 September. The *Minusinsk* and the Russian vessels took the cargo thence to Yeniseisk and the *Blencathra* and *Orestes* began the return journey to England on 20 September.

In the next year, 1894, after Morier's death, his aim of a real Anglo-Russian expedition was at last realized. The *Sterzhen*, commanded by Captain Wiggins and owned by Leybourne-Popham, was escorted to the Kara Sea by the *Windward* and accompanied by the *Pervoi* and *Vtoroi*, built at Newcastle for the Russian government. The *Sterzhen* discharged her cargo on the banks of the Yenisei and sailed for home on 15 September. The Russian ships were delivered to an agent of the board of the Siberian Railway Company and completed the fleet designed for the river service. In each of the following years until and including 1899 there were expeditions, successful deliveries of cargo, and successful loadings of return cargoes of graphite and wheat. The main exports from England were cured herrings, mining machinery, agricultural implements, locomotive boilers, furniture, and Sheffield steel goods. The expeditions were on a small scale, carefully organized, and had the co-operation of the Russian government, the Trans-Siberian Railway Company, and local Siberian merchants. One more expedition took place in 1903. But the outbreak of the Russo-Japanese War, combined with the coming into full use of the Trans-Siberian railway, was sufficient to end a trade route that at best could only have had a restricted usefulness, since it needed special vessels, careful timing, and special cargoes.

12

PERSIA AND THE PAMIRS

During Morier's last years at St. Petersburg the chances of Anglo-Russian *entente* revived, with the idea of co-operation in the economic development of Persia, but then collapsed with the Pamirs incident of 1891. The idea of developing a common policy over Persia goes back to the Russian 'overtures' of July and August 1887 (see above, pp. 247-8). They suggested to the Foreign Office the improvement of the temper of Anglo-Russian relations at Teheran.

British influence in Persia had for generations been held steady by Sir Ronald Thomson and, before him, by his brother and their father. The 'sheep-walks' on Persia's north-eastern frontier, when the Turcomans settled down to cultivation under Russian government, had, however, come by 1884–5 to represent territorial power of a more modern kind. Russia's occupation of Merv, Penjdeh, and land thence eastwards towards the Oxus meant their incorporation into a modern state. The Persian province of Khorassan was now bordered on the north by the organized power of Russia and on the east by that of Britain's protégé, the Amir of Afghanistan. The three frontiers met at Zulficar. Rivalry between Britain and Russia at Teheran had accordingly become virulent.

Already in 1874 Salisbury had reached the conclusion that Britain could 'not give *complete* assistance to Persia', and '*incomplete* and hesitating assistance was dangerous'.[1] He laid it down that Britain's course, therefore, was to encourage Persia to strengthen herself and rely upon the resolution and energy of her own government. 'Any such appearance of returning vigour should be watched for and carefully encouraged. It may not even now', he wrote, 'be too late to undertake the arduous work of internal reform, and to make the necessary preparations

[1] R. L. Greaves, *Persia and the Defence of India* (1959), p. 49.

for self-defence. The sympathy, and, so far as it can be practically given, the assistance of H.M.G. may be counted on by the Government of Persia in any such endeavours.'[1]

The policy of depending on Persia's own vitality was not the same as a policy, such as that pursued in Afghanistan, of strengthening British influence. It was better served by relaxing than by stiffening the rivalry between the British and Russian representatives at Teheran, even though its ultimate objective was anti-Russian. This explains the Foreign Office's response to the Russian 'overtures' of 1887. Currie urged upon Salisbury that the 'only chance' of helping Persia 'would be to take advantage of the friendly disposition of the Russian Govt. and try to have some kind of exchange of ideas with them'. He thought an opportunity was afforded by the outcry of the Russian press at the announcement of Sir Henry Drummond Wolff's appointment as successor to Thomson at Teheran, and advised Salisbury to open the subject with Baron de Staal in London.[2] Salisbury acted on Currie's advice, but stated British intentions in Persia to Morier rather than to de Staal.

His statement of policy began with a profession of the intention to maintain Persia's territorial integrity and went on to disclaim rivalry with Russia. It then discussed the possibility of Anglo-Russian co-operation in Persia's economic development. Three methods of development were particularly mentioned: the development of trade, which Britain was prepared to leave to Russia in northern Persia; the opening to navigation of the Karun river in the south-west, a special British interest; and the building of railways which might be considered a common interest. A warning against any violation of Khorassan's political position as part of Persia concluded the statement.[3]

Morier at once made the most of this opening. He communicated the dispatch, as he was directed to do, and in a long and cordial conversation with de Giers he enlarged upon the desirability of agreement. As might be expected, he went more

[1] Salisbury to Thomson, no. 75A, 6 Aug. 1885, F.O. 65/1248; quoted by Mrs. Greaves, op. cit., p. 88.
[2] R. L. Greaves, op. cit., p. 111; minute by Currie on Nicolson to Salisbury, no. 12 secret, 10 Jan. 1888, F.O. 65/1347.
[3] From Salisbury, nos. 51 and 52 secret, 21 Feb. 1888, F.O. 65/1347; cf. Platt, *Finance, Trade, and Politics in British Foreign Policy*, p. 224.

than half-way to meet Salisbury in a policy of agreement with Russia and, as usual, more than half-way to meet de Giers. It became at once an overture for a Russian *entente* over Persia. On his own responsibility and to please de Giers he changed a phrase, in the dispatch for communication, from 'the *assurance* of the *Emperor*'s desire to treat the Persian Government with equitable consideration', to which de Giers objected, into 'measures which would testify to the desire of the Russian Government to . . .', and in that form it was communicated to the Tsar.[1]

Meanwhile, on 15 February 1888, Russia had made a fresh start in Bulgaria and proposed to the Powers collective pressure at Constantinople to induce Turkey to declare Prince Ferdinand's position illegal. Russia's object was to bring about his deposition.[2] The proposal was rejected by Great Britain. De Giers then complained that she rejected without consideration any proposal coming from Russia. Morier answered, according to his instructions, that a British government was bound to reject interference 'with a government *de facto* which owed its existence to a nation's will'. De Giers repudiated any intention to trench upon Bulgaria's right to shape her own destinies. But the conversation left Morier 'unhappy'. 'The very great quickness with which we announced [rejection], striking the negative note 24 hours before any one else, has led the people here to believe that we took the lead in the opposition and are the intellectual authors of the fiasco—though the rage is with Crispi. But this of course reacts on the whole tone of our relations.'[3]

Russia's first reception of the overture about Persia, made nearly a week later on the Monday following this conversation, was warm and eager. Yet when de Giers eventually brought back the Emperor's reply, that de Staal would be instructed to begin an exchange of ideas with Salisbury, his tone was much less warm. Morier's explanation was that this was due to de Giers's discouragement about Bulgaria and to the belief 'that we took the lead in the opposition and are the authors of the fiasco'.[4] But it scarcely fitted the fact that the refusal of

[1] Morier to Currie, 2 Mar. 1888, F.O. 65/1330.
[2] To Salisbury, no. 60, 15 Feb. 1888, F.O. 65/1329.
[3] To Salisbury, no. 65 very confidential, 22 Feb. 1888, F.O. 65/1329.
[4] To Currie, 2 Mar. 1888, copy in the Morier papers, holograph in F.O. 65/1330.

the Bulgarian overture preceded the first conversation about Persia. One suspects that Morier's imagination, as so often, imposed a coherence on events. He saw them in the light of his *idée fixe* about the interaction of the European and Asiatic elements in Russian policy. There was possibly no deeper explanation than the cooling effect of the lapse of time, the absence of Morier's own *empressement*, and the influence of the Emperor's passivity.

All Morier's efforts to weaken Salisbury's resolution on Bulgaria were unavailing. His attempts were met squarely. 'It would be worth while', Salisbury wrote, 'to be very conciliatory about the Prince to be selected', supposing Russia succeeded in her ambition of inducing Bulgaria to depose Ferdinand, 'if by that means the thorn could be taken out. But proposals whose simple object is to knock to pieces the present government in Bulgaria are no good at all.'[1] Salisbury also made it clear that his overture about Persia did not mean any softening of the British attitude about the India frontier. In April, largely as a consequence of information collected by Drummond Wolff on his way through Transcaucasia to Persia, Morier was told 'to remind Giers that he has been several times instructed to say that Herat means war'.[2] In a long conversation with de Giers, Morier then renewed his warnings of opposition to further Russian expansion in Turkestan. Drummond Wolff's arrival at Teheran raised Persia to new importance—as, indeed, was intended[3]—in British diplomacy. Morier, who claimed in 1891 to have known Wolff for sixty years, the acquaintance having begun when they were respectively four and five on the top of the Wagern Alp, noticed in him 'especially his dogged energy and obstinacy . . . the electric current of subtlety and craftiness intellectually illuminating those brute forces . . . and his superhuman powers of push'.[4]

Meanwhile the two linked ideas, that Russia had no immediately aggressive intentions and that her very 'planlessness'

---

[1] From Salisbury, private, 29 Feb. 1888.
[2] Salisbury's minute for a dispatch to Morier on Wolff to Salisbury, separate, secret and confidential, 9 Apr. 1888, F.O. 65/1348; to Salisbury, no. 146 confidential, 18 Apr. 1888, ibid.
[3] See Platt, *Finance, Trade, and Politics in British Foreign Policy*, p. 225.
[4] To Salisbury, private, 10 June 1891.

gave the opportunity to private Russian adventurers to thrust expansion upon her, fastened their hold more and more firmly in London. On 30 May 1888 Morier reported that an inquest on a very large scale was being held in St. Petersburg into the military condition of Russia with the object of determining how far she could cope with the gigantic preparations of Germany. The outcome, surprisingly, was the Tsar's rejection of the increase proposed in the war budget for 1889. The Tsar's attitude, Morier wrote, was that of a man who, feeling himself secure from attack and perfectly able to defend himself 'if attacked, without military ambition, and desirous of peace for its own sake and for grave internal political considerations, knowing, moreover, full well that the "hasteless and restless"[1] national aspirations of his country can at present best be served by delay, is determined that he at least will not be the first to draw the sword'.[2] A private letter to Salisbury[3] insisted on the truth and importance of his information and explained that by a 'diplomatic ruse' he had ascertained that Schweinitz had reported to Berlin in the same sense.

Morier's racy account of how the editor of the *Pall Mall Gazette*, the immensely self-confident W. T. Stead, 'interviewed' the Tsar for his paper at an audience on 24 May confirmed the impression of peaceful resolutions and 'planlessness'. Salisbury gathered that the Tsar had 'scattered his promises of no war this year right and left', but the unsatisfactory part of this was 'the absence from the Emperor's mind of any definite view of policy, other than the negative one of keeping the peace'. 'From Wolff's account of what passes in Persia, and Haggard's account of what passes in Greece' he gathered further that 'there is a good deal of "planlessness" at St. Petersburg.'[4] Morier agreed,[5] but:

> I confess [he wrote] that when I have to deal with a Leviathan I ask for no better than that he should be planless. A *planful* Leviathan, consciously directing with the cunning of a baser reptile his

[1] See above, p. 198 n.
[2] To Salisbury, no. 197 secret, 30 May 1888, F.O. 65/1330; no. 214 confidential, 12 June 1888, F.O. 65/1331.
[3] To Salisbury, private, 31 May 1888.
[4] From Salisbury, private, 6 June 1888.
[5] To Salisbury, private, 13 June 1888.

gigantic resources against me is an object of no small terror . . . I am compelled, though with a disagreeable feeling that I shall probably stand alone, to regard the Emperor, with his personal aversion for war—an aversion based not only on his idiosyncracy but upon the strongest motives of internal policy—as one of the forces making for peace . . . I know I shall be met by the argument that no Russian Czar and no Russian Government can be trusted—I can only answer to this that Russia for the present is the Czar, and that Alexander III can be trusted . . . that is if you know how to make him understand that he has personally pledged himself . . . I need not say that this diagnosis applies solely to the present phase and to the actual acute symptoms of the morbus Europaicus with which alone in my humble opinion the European doctors have at present to deal. That the general pathology of the case, the growing military strength of Russia, the expansive forces within her, the avowed objects she has in view whenever the present status quo in the East has to be changed, remains unaltered, no one feels more keenly than myself.

This was a bad foundation on which to build a policy of co-operation in Persia. The conviction that Russian expansion was inevitable, unplanned, and therefore not to be stopped, Morier had discussed with Salisbury already in 1886 and 1887. It stood in the way of Anglo-Russian co-operation in Persia as it had prevented any response to the 'overtures' of 1886-7.

The passages I have quoted were part of a lengthy letter in which Morier, about to take his first four months' leave since his arrival in St. Petersburg, reviewed all he had done there. He somewhat complacently believed he could state 'honestly that I have made no serious blunder', though he returned regretfully to the hope of a *modus vivendi* with Russia on which Salisbury in 1886 had stated his 'permanent views' and made him 'discard' his own 'as outside the field of practical politics'. This mood of sober, though satisfying, self-appraisal was sharply broken. Morier reached London and the Prince of Wales communicated the accusation of passing information to Bazaine. He did not return to St. Petersburg until 21 October, when the dominant news concerned a train accident, if it was an accident, and the Tsar's narrow escape: so that from June to October 1888 Morier's diplomatic career was virtually interrupted. This interruption was the more marked as the argument between himself and Salisbury about the treatment of the

Bazaine story became sharper. In December, the publication of this story, and the renewed controversy with Salisbury which followed, meant that active diplomacy was again impossible for him. Morier's dispatches for the first quarter of 1889, in the political series, report no single conversation of political importance. They were anyhow very few and there was not a single 'secret' or 'confidential' report among them. Morier never resumed the mood of glowing optimism of June 1888. An earlier chapter shows how the Bazaine incident, though it ended in a personal victory, permanently took from him the relish for the political side of his work.

In the interval between Morier's return from London in October 1888 and the publication of the Bazaine story in December, he had had to report a renewal of the intermittent Russian 'overtures' for an understanding. In a discussion of the consequences of the accession of William II in Germany, de Giers led up to a 'somewhat forced reference' to the conversation of July 1887 about the common interest of Britain and Russia in preventing France's being *saignée à blanc* by Germany or the other way round (see above, p. 247). Giers thought the outlook was really far less peaceful than the lull in diplomacy would lead people to suppose, that

> the co-operation of England and Russia . . . was the only condition which would ensure the maintenance of peace . . . An alliance—I will not use the word alliance, because it may give rise to some misapprehension—but a cordial understanding between England and Russia to restore peace . . . would be liable to no sinister misinterpretations and excite no suspicions. I hope, therefore [concluded Morier], that there will be, between Her Majesty's Government and Russia not a mere general exchange of platitudes . . . but something more.[1]

This general discussion had a connection with Persia, for Morier and de Giers agreed that an outburst of rivalry there would be unfortunate, and Morier wished that there might be, at least, some reduction of asperity in the present Anglo-Russian argument. He telegraphed:[2]

> Could not Sir Henry Drummond Wolff put water into the Shah's

---

[1] To Salisbury, no. 397 secret, 21 Nov. 1888, F.O. 65/1333.
[2] To Salisbury, telegram, no. 69 secret, 5 Dec. 1888, F.O. 65/1334.

wine about [the] Meshed consulship and do something to show we are not opposing the Astrabad–Meshed road? Feeling here very violent . . . I have insisted that our policy is one of co-operation for material development of Persia, principally by opening up means of communication. Russia in the north, England in the south. Nevertheless they believe Sir H. Wolff is stopping the way north.

Lord Salisbury responded—on 6 December 1888—by repeating Morier's telegram to Drummond Wolff with the addition: 'Russians imagine you are preventing the admission of a Russian consul to Meshed. I do not know whether you are doing so? but I see no objection to both Russians and English having a consul there. Russia's diplomacy is so bad that we have no cause to fear its extension.'[1]

Meanwhile Britain and Russia continued to exercise conflicting pressure: Britain to induce the Shah to build a railway to the Indian Ocean from Teheran; Russia to persuade him to postpone railway-building until she was ready to join the Persian railways to her own system. Russia had, in fact, obtained an undertaking from him in 1887 not to grant any concessions for building railways or waterways to foreign companies 'before consulting His Majesty the Emperor'. The British, in ignorance, continued to press for a railway. The Russians persuaded the Persians to build roads in the north from the Caspian to Teheran and Meshed; the British induced the Shah to proclaim the river Karun, which flows through south-west Persia into the Persian Gulf, open to the navigation of all nations (30 October 1888).[2] A British company put steamers on the river and 177 miles of water-carriage were made generally available as a substitute for bad or impassable roads. A British vice-consulate was established at Mohammerah and British trade on the Karun rapidly expanded. The opening of the Karun river was an effective answer to the Russo-Persian agreement of 1887. It brought, however, renewed Anglo-Russian argument. De Giers showed 'the greatest irritation' and complained that equilibrium had been upset in Persia.[3] But characteristically it was also the occasion for the renewal, as has been shown, of 'overtures' for an understanding. The pattern of the Batum incident seemed

[1] R. L. Greaves, op. cit., pp. 149, 159.
[2] R. L. Greaves, op. cit., pp. 164–5.
[3] To Salisbury, no. 396 most secret, 21 Nov. 1888, F.O. 65/1355.

to be repeated. Giers, in fear of an actual breach, redoubled efforts to obtain an *entente*. The possibility, however, exists that it was Morier's reading of the situation, transmitted through his reports, that made it seem so.

In March 1889 Morier began to resume diplomatic activity. He was not now, however, as eager to drive forward. The incident with which he had to deal was created by Russia's alarm about the intentions of the Amir of Afghanistan, who in a punitive raid against his own subjects drew dangerously near to the Russian frontier. Morier congratulated himself for having worked so hard for the settlement of this frontier. The old note of self-satisfaction seemed to creep back as he wrote: 'Matters would have looked very different had the Amir in his bloody assizes approached an unsettled frontier respecting which we and the Russians held opposite views.'[1] The optimism did not persist. It did not survive the return of Prince Dolgorouki from Teheran to St. Petersburg; for he returned as the supposed victor over Britain. He boasted of having gained for Russia, in the face of British opposition, consular representation at Meshed—the holy city in the north from which foreigners had always been excluded until Britain gained permission to station a consul there—and the concession for a railway from Astrabad or Resht to Teheran.[2]

The next event was the Shah's visit to St. Petersburg in May 1889, followed by his visit to London in June. Salisbury prepared Morier for the visit to St. Petersburg: 'When he is there he will profess sentiments the most contemptuous of the English and will make every kind of promise to the Russians. The great thing will be to prevent his putting any of those promises into writing.' Nor did Salisbury welcome the visit to London. This negative attitude made Morier inclined to wash his hands of the business: 'I fear I shall have no means at my disposal to prevent the Shah when here signing I.O.U.'s. It will be Wolff's business to prevent his meeting them.'[3]

At the beginning of the chapter it was suggested that there

[1] To Salisbury, private, 17 Apr. 1889.
[2] To Salisbury, private, 2 Mar. 1889.
[3] From Salisbury, 10 Apr. 1889. This letter also referred to the Russian alarm about Afghanistan, 'subsequent communications have thrown little light on the Afghanistan scare. I think the Ameer must have been guilty of some impatience of which we never heard the real details'; to Salisbury, 17 Apr. 1889.

were two sides to Salisbury's policy over Persia: on one side, Britain would rely upon Persia's innate power of regeneration, and would support its economic development; on the other side, Britain would relax her rivalry with Russia for predominance at Teheran, and would support an understanding with her. Salisbury meant, however, to suggest a direction of policy but not to drive forward in it. The narrative so far suggests that the explanation for this holding back was that he did not believe that Russia had a forward policy in Persia and did not expect much from Morier in St. Petersburg. There is also an explanation stemming from his views about Persia. Whatever her capacity for economic development, in Salisbury's view, her political structure could not last. Arthur Hardinge, who had been second secretary under Morier at St. Petersburg and was now again private secretary to Salisbury, was sometimes the channel by which his new master's views reached his former master. 'Lord Salisbury seems to contemplate', he wrote to Morier, 'a break up of Persia after the Shah's death, as the most likely solution of the rivalries between the Zil[1] and the Valiahd,[2] the Zil having the Southern and the Valiahd having the Northern provinces, which latter would be practically absorbed into Russia.'[3] In 1888 Wolff was energetically supporting the Zil as the abler man and the more progressive. Salisbury let Wolff do as he wished, as if he knew nothing would come of it.

Meanwhile the Shah was in St. Petersburg. Morier wrote no private letter about the visit; for de Giers had told him nothing and said only that the Shah had 'talked generalities, which disappeared in a cloud of words and little anecdotes'.[4] As if to underline Morier's failure, it became apparent that Wolff had learnt more in Teheran. Wolff reported that railways had, in fact, been discussed and that the Tsar had 'insisted very strongly on the maintenance of the Shah's promise not to grant

[1] The Zil es Sultan, or Shadow of the King. He was Mas'ud Mirza, the eldest son by a morganatic marriage and so barred from the succession. He was governor of the southern provinces, with his capital at Ispahan.
[2] The heir apparent. He was the second son, but by a recognized marriage. He was governor of Azerbaijan with his capital at Tabriz.
[3] Hardinge to Morier, 23 Apr. 1889.
[4] To Salisbury, no. 172 confidential, 27 May 1889, F.O. 65/1361. The dispatch contains the sentence 'H.M. had telephoned at 2 a.m. to say he was coming to Giers at 9 a.m.'

Railway Concessions for five years'.[1] The Shah's sojourn in London, though attended by further talk about railways and much assiduous courtesy, seems to have had no results whatever.

During the summer of 1889 Morier was on leave in Finland. He did not take up his duties in St. Petersburg again until his return on 2 September 1889. By then a new twist in the Persian thread had occurred. Drummond Wolff appeared in person in St. Petersburg and was given an audience by the Tsar. He meant to use his visit to discuss Persia with the Russian ministers and to make sure at St. Petersburg of the policy of Anglo-Russian co-operation over Persia which he wished to see established. 'Of course, he will not touch main lines of policy,' Salisbury telegraphed to Morier, 'but he is anxious to be assured that his coming will be agreeable to you before he decides to do so.'[2] Morier would have vetoed the visit, if he could have done so. 'Wolff's visit would create an immense sensation and give rise to every kind of speculation—and Giers desires above all things that the Persian question should be kept asleep.'[3] The visit had, however, been arranged between the Prince of Wales and the Tsar at Copenhagen,[4] where they met during the summer, and Morier could not stop it without creating yet another argument with Salisbury.

The visit made abundantly clear the differences in British and Russian views about Persia. These differences were another cause of Salisbury's caution. 'There is no desire whatever', Morier wrote, 'either on his [de Giers's] part or anybody else's in Russia to ameliorate the condition of Persia or in any way to arrest the progress of decomposition, which, it is calculated, will sooner or later bring about the annexation of a larger or smaller proportion of the Shah's possessions.'[5] Britain wished 'to stiffen' Persia; Russia wished to keep her 'flabby'. Britain wished to see 'all manner of forces stirred up by the magic of capital'; Russia wished things left as they were 'so that when she entered into possession she might begin everything *de novo* in her own way'. Britain believed banks and railways would

---

[1] Wolff to Salisbury, no. 211 most confidential, 21 Nov. 1889, quoted by Mrs. Greaves, op. cit., p. 172.
[2] From Salisbury, telegram, 29 Aug., not answered until 2 Sept. 1889.
[3] To Salisbury, telegram, 4 p.m., 2 Sept. 1889.
[4] From Salisbury, private, 30 Oct. 1889.
[5] To Salisbury, private, 4 Sept. 1889.

PERSIA AND THE PAMIRS 341

revive Persia; Russia that they would break her up. Britain wanted railways for trade; Russia for military strategy.[1] It was clear that Wolff 'in his devouring activity'[2] wished to carry forward Salisbury's two-sided policy to the point of positive acts of Anglo-Russian co-operation in the economic development of Persia. His visit not only drew from Morier this clear statement of the differences between British and Russian views, but made him avow that an understanding with Russia over Persia was impossible. Morier did not see the faintest chance of co-operation in a forward policy. He would support a policy of conciliation towards Russia and of British development in Persia. He could not believe in a policy of joint Russo-British development. Indeed, by 1891 he had come to think of Wolff as the 'friend winning coup after coup at Monte Carlo and going on doubling each time' and of himself as 'the man who tries to get him away from the green table with his winnings'.[3] Morier's views by 1891 were almost exactly those of Sir Cecil Spring Rice[4] when the Anglo-Russian agreement on Persia had after all been concluded—on the basis of partition of Persia into spheres of influence—as part of the Anglo-Russian *entente* of 1907.

Even more important, Wolff's visit made clear the essential mistrust which underlay every proposal for Anglo-Russian co-operation. Wolff in his audience of the Tsar had exchanged with him assurances about both Powers being willing to discuss the economic development of Persia, on the basis of their common interests, by the opening of negotiations for railways, waterways, and industrial undertakings. Wolff sought to give to these assurances the greatest binding force possible by recording them in a report to Salisbury[5] which he was to send to Morier for reading back to the Tsar in the hope that the latter would say the record was a true one. This, Morier claimed, was a serious breach of normal conventions and he characteristically took credit to himself for compassing, by an elaborate ruse, the

[1] To Salisbury, private, 10 June 1891.
[2] To Salisbury, private, 10 Feb. 1890.
[3] To Salisbury, private, 6 Mar. 1891.
[4] G. P. Gooch and H. Temperley (eds.), *British Documents on the Origins of the War* (1927–38), iv. 450–3.
[5] Wolff to Salisbury, secret and confidential, 14 Oct. 1889, F.O. 65/1379, quoted by Mrs. Greaves, op. cit., p. 180.

object Wolff wished to achieve. He pretended to pass the record to de Giers, by a calculated indiscretion, as a secret paper for his use alone and de Giers undertook to pass it on to the Emperor, by the same sort of indiscretion, for *his* use alone.[1] This, at least, was Morier's version of what happened. The element of mistrust behind this ostensible conspiracy of frankness is evinced in Wolff's avowal that the assurances were wholly and solely to Britain's advantage; since Britain could build her share of any railways, the building of which might be assigned by Persia to Britain and Russia in common, and Russia could not. Mistrust was similarly evident in Salisbury's opposite fear that the assurances were wholly and solely to Russia's advantage; since Russia *could* build her share, while no British capital would be available for the British share. In other words, whether the policy of joint Anglo-Russian development of Persia was followed or rejected would be determined not by its possible contribution to strengthening Persia or to improving Anglo-Russian relations, but by its power to help Britain to outdo Russia. Morier, in fact, talked of Wolff's success in getting the assurances as 'thimble-rigging'.[2]

Nevertheless, a firm overture for the opening of negotiations for Anglo-Russian co-operation in the economic development of Persia followed Wolff's visit.[3] A beginning would be made in railway building, Russia building in the north and Britain in the south. Salisbury accepted with the utmost caution. 'The discussions', he wired to Wolff, 'will require careful conduct. Material development may mean only an easier way to Herat.' Nor was the basic mistrust dispelled. It soon appeared that Wolff had either charmed the Tsar into greater warmth than he really felt for the plan, or that he had misreported him. Anyhow, Russia made it clear that the negotiations were not to take place in Teheran between Wolff and Butzov, the new Russian envoy there, but directly between the Russian and British governments in either London or St. Petersburg. Later Russia also made it plain that Wolff had misunderstood references in his audience to a general understanding. It was explained that the Tsar had meant by this phrase not an under-

[1] To Salisbury, private, 8 Nov. 1889.
[2] From Salisbury, private, 30 Oct. 1889; to Salisbury, private, 8 Nov. 1889.
[3] From Salisbury, no. 307, 28 Oct. 1889, F.O. 65/1379.

standing about Asia but one about the eastern question. The context of the phrase was a sentence of the Tsar on the contrast between east and west. He had meant not to contrast Asia and Europe but to contrast eastern and western Europe.[1] Morier explained that Wolff could easily have misunderstood. 'The important thing in collating the two versions is that the Emperor's tallies exactly with all the antecedents of the case whereas Sir Henry's implies so complete a change from one pole to the other on the subject treated that it almost presupposes a kind of miracle.'[2] This summary could not have increased Salisbury's confidence in Wolff, and 'both the Emperor and de Giers', Morier was certain, had 'a profound distrust' of him too; since in his dealings with Dolgorouki, the former Russian envoy in Teheran, he had used all the Russian weapons for outdoing a rival and defeated them by their own means.

Yet Morier's reports did not weigh much with Salisbury; for the whole incident bears an uncanny resemblance to his own proceedings in Portugal of which Salisbury had been a witness when he had been secretary of state for India and during his first period as foreign secretary. Morier had planned Anglo-Portuguese co-operation in the economic development of Africa and India and in his eagerness and single-minded devotion to his plan had pressed negotiating partners further than they wished to go and had failed in the end. Salisbury never intended to commit Britain, judged Wolff's hectic schemes calmly, and made up his own mind, not much influenced by Morier's reports.

Meanwhile, British economic penetration of Persia continued. It was quite independent of the position of the British government. Although the Imperial Bank of Persia, because it was incorporated in London by royal charter, attracted more investors than it would otherwise have done, its career was entirely independent. The Persian Bank Mining Rights' Corporation obtained on its own initiative a concession to exploit Persia's mineral wealth. The railway question was the most acute. The Russian 'military party' was now alleged to be pressing for lines through Khorassan east to Herat and south

---

[1] To Salisbury, private telegram, 20 Nov. 1889.
[2] To Salisbury, very confidential, private, 20 Nov. 1889.

to Seistan and the Persian Gulf. Wolff was trying desperately to convince his government of the benefits which would accrue from 'a line to Seistan both in trade and defence'. The Tsar and de Giers refused to commit Russia, and Morier advised a similar reserve for Britain. Salisbury saw arguments both ways, but caution triumphed. 'It appears to me that the more this question of co-operated railway construction by British Companies in the South and Russian Companies in the North is considered, the more evident become its dangerous aspects from all sides.'[1] A Russian financial authority, once minister for finance, Aleksandr Abaza, presided over a commission to inquire into the question of railways and on its report depended the fate of the Puliakov–Raffaellevich syndicate which had assembled itself to build railways in the north. British Intelligence disliked their project for strategic reasons and E. G. Law disliked it as likely to ruin British trade in south Persia. In the end Morier, Vyshnegradski, and the Abaza Commission combined to defeat the Russian syndicate and plans for Russian-built railways fell to the ground. Ideas of active Anglo-Russian co-operation collapsed,[2] but Russian political influence in Teheran was stronger than ever. In September 1890 Wolff fell seriously ill and British influence in Teheran ceased to be exercised for nearly a year. In November 1890 the Shah gave a pledge to Russia that he would build no railways for the next ten years. De Giers 'bitterly'[3] denounced British practices in Persia, but Morier believed the Shah was 'dropping beyond redemption into the arms of Russia'.[4]

There was a brief epilogue in 1891. In June 1891 Wolff was still in London and the Legation at Teheran still under a chargé d'affaires. He was, however, on the road to recovery and able to explain afresh to Lord Salisbury his scheme of Anglo-Russian co-operation in the economic development of Persia. Wolff's original plan had been for a Russian railway to run through Khorassan or north Persia to Herat, a joint Anglo-Russian railway to run from Resht, in north Persia, through Teheran to the Persian Gulf, the northern part being Russian

[1] R. L. Greaves, op. cit., pp. 178–80.
[2] To Salisbury, secret, 6 Jan., 10 Feb., and 6 Mar. 1890.
[3] From Salisbury, private, 22 Oct. 1890.
[4] To Salisbury, private, 25 Dec. 1890.

and the southern British-built, and for a British railway in south-west Persia. His new plan would have kept the Russian railway away from Herat and the Anglo-Russian away from Teheran, proposing that it should run from the Caspian by Kermanshah to a village at the head of the Karun river. It was not difficult for Morier to kill the revived scheme; for Salisbury was doubtful of Russian support and 'equally doubtful whether if we obtained Russian co-operation, we should be able to obtain the still more important assistance of English capitalists'.[1] Morier made it quite clear that real and reliable Russian assistance in this plan was not to be obtained.[2] His connection with Persia now ceased.

In the early summer of 1891, Britain was on the alert over the whole Middle East, while Russia awaited Persian disintegration. The Yarmout Turkomans were in revolt against Persia in Khorassan and alleged to be armed with Russian weapons, and to be under the influence of the Russian General Kuropatkin. Fresh reports of Russian activity on the Indian frontier well to the east reached Downing Street at the same time. Already in May Russian officers on the Russo-Persian frontier of Afghanistan were 'assembling a considerable amount of war material and getting up quarrels about the Yarmouts, about the Sarakhs' water supply and the conduct of the Governor of Meshed'.[3] This activity was not supposed to be authorized from St. Petersburg, but said to be the result of local and deliberate efforts of the Russian military party 'to cause a collision'. Morier begged that he might receive instructions to open the eyes of the Emperor to what was going on in the full conviction that 'a collision is impossible if the Emperor is warned, but if he remains with his eyes shut there is no knowing to what extent a man like Kuropatkin who, from all I hear, is of the type of the Skobeleffs and Kaufmanns, may compromise his Government and force their hands'.[4]

These alarms were still fresh in mid July when news arrived in London—through the German ambassador—that a Russian expedition of 300 cavalry and 300 infantry had been ordered

[1] From Salisbury, private, 3 June 1891.
[2] To Salisbury, private, 10 June 1891.
[3] From Salisbury, private, 10 May 1891.
[4] To Salisbury, private, 12 May 1891.

to the Pamir plateau[1] to annex the territory east of the Russo-Afghan frontier defined in 1887. Its importance to British India was that it commanded the routes between Kashmir and Russian Turkestan. The Russians first denied the report, then made light of it, but at the end of August, had to acknowledge that it was true. By that date a telegram from the Viceroy of India had been received in London describing Colonel Francis Younghusband's encounter with the Russian force on the plateau and his expulsion at its hands.

The danger of Anglo-Russian war loomed up. With this prospect came, as one has learnt to expect, renewed overtures from Russia for an understanding. Morier tells the story of Vyshnegradski's and de Giers's overtures in his usual dramatic manner. The way the conversation with Vyshnegradski began

was by his taking me aside at a party and saying in a very earnest way and totally unlike his usual manner, 'It is true you are going away and how soon are you coming back?' I said it is true and I mean to remain away as long as I possibly can. '*Ne faites pas cela*,' he said, '*revenez le plus tôt possible.*' I was so puzzled by his manner that I answered 'What on earth should I come back for and why do you wish to rob me of my holiday . . .' He said, 'It is the *political* situation.'

After some talk about the danger from Germany and of William II's visit to England, Vyshnegradski came to the heart of the matter with an appeal to Morier to stay. 'You have a great position here', Morier reports him as saying, 'because people *know* that you have the maintenance of good relations with Russia for the sake of peace at heart' and that you are strong enough '*pour empêcher les bêtises* . . . C'est une aptitude à nous autres Russes de faire les choses dans la direction tout contraire à celle où nous voulons aller — et alors nous nous étonnons des résultats'.[2] De Giers on another occasion added his appeal using similar language. He spoke of *ennuis* as Vyshnegradski spoke of *bêtises*.

Morier had expected the result of William II's journey to

[1] For a vivid description of the geography of this area, see G. J. Alder, *British India's Northern Frontier* (1963), pp. 7–12; and for the events leading up to Younghusband's expulsion in 1891, ibid., pp. 217–24.

[2] 'To prevent stupid things from being done . . . We Russians have a talent for doing things so that we go in the opposite direction to that in which we wish to go, and then we are surprized at the results,' to Salisbury, private, 23 July 1891.

England, the visit of the French fleet to Kronstadt, and the visit of the King of Serbia to St. Petersburg to be 'a great outburst of national exuberance and revivifying of Ignatieff'. What actually happened was a further advance in Central Asia, the arrest of Lieutenant Davison, and the expulsion of the Younghusband expedition. The 'overtures' for an understanding came within a week of this news reaching London. Morier called them 'overtures', but he had nothing more concrete to report than the language of Vyshnegradski and de Giers that I have quoted. Nor did anything come of them.

In December 1891 Morier was again offered the embassy at Rome which he had refused in 1887.[1] He accepted, then withdrew his acceptance, because of a further Russian appeal.

Giers expressed such deep regret at my transfer to Rome and insisted so strongly on the public disadvantage of my leaving St. Petersburg, that I said that if he took steps, which I fancied he was contemplating, to ask that I might remain, I would consent to do so. I am making a very great sacrifice, but if it is a case of public duty, it must take precedence over private considerations.[2]

Morier stayed in St. Petersburg in order to deal with the consequences of the Pamir clash and to avert the danger that 'we should have to swallow a second Penjdeh and ratify a very distinct step forward on the part of Russia in her advance to our frontier'.[3] He stayed, with fatal consequences for his health, in the conviction that 'I am the only person really fitted to handle the negotiations on this question here'.[4] It was far worse than the mere *bêtises* of the military party adumbrated in July. He was perfectly certain that we had 'not got to deal with a wild escapade of a Cossack Tam O'Shanter, but with a carefully worked out scheme of the War Office'.[5] General Vrevski, the governor-general of Russian Turkestan, he reported, was under orders from General Vanovski, the minister of war, and General Obruchev, the chief of staff. Colonel Jonov, the

---

[1] Lord Dufferin was to be moved from Rome to succeed Lord Lytton in Paris. When Morier declined, Lord Vivian was appointed.
[2] To Salisbury, telegram, private and confidential, 4.30 p.m., 23 Dec. 1891.
[3] To General Brackenbury, 15 Feb. 1892.
[4] To Salisbury, private, 4 Jan. 1892. Salisbury sent the letter to the Queen without comment. The Queen returned it remarking, 'he must have a real belief in his powers of negotiation', R.A. H 46/2 and Salisbury papers, A 68/98.
[5] To Salisbury, private, 4 Jan. 1892.

commander in the field of the Pamir expedition, was under Vrevski's orders. Reports had been daily forwarded for telegraphic transmission to St. Petersburg. The expedition had had a distinct political object: 'to make a sensational demonstration throughout the Pamir country ... in the character of proprietors'. The demarcation of 1873 having assigned exclusive influence to Russia north of a line from the confluence of the Kokcha with the Oxus and east to Lake Victoria, Russia intended to sweep out of her area all foreign elements, whether English, Chinese, or Afghan, that might be met with. It was a faithful reproduction of the campaigns which had carried Russian power over the Turkoman steppes to Merv and the Russians were 'in a very nasty frame of mind'. Salisbury treated Morier's request to stay with some scepticism, but three considerations moved him to agree. The Pamir negotiation really had assumed an unexpected importance and a new ambassador could not quickly pick up its threads; de Staal had spoken to him of the Emperor's fancy to keep Morier; the German ambassador had spoken to him of the Italian displeasure at the prospect of Morier's appointment to Rome.[1]

Morier now set himself two tasks: first, to contrive an agreement with Russia; second, to clear away some of the fog of illusion about the permanent defences of the Indian frontier. He was prepared to pay for the settlement, on his constantly proclaimed principle of *do ut des*. Thus in February 1892 he obtained an apology from Russia for the expulsion of Younghusband and arrest of Lieutenant Davison at the price of agreement in principle to the delimitation of the Pamir Indian boundary. He had not, however, reckoned with Salisbury's invincible objection to delimitation. This was even stronger in 1892 than in 1886–7 and the reasons for it were much plainer. Salisbury refused to proceed with actual delimitation on the ground.

The apology itself had not been obtained without difficulties. Morier had begun by presenting a note asking for a disavowal of Jonov's acts and an expression of regret.[2] The reply had been unsatisfactory and had convinced Morier that he could not

---

[1] Salisbury to the Queen, 12 Jan. 1892, R.A. A 68/99; see also Hatzfeldt to Holstein, private telegram, 15 Dec. 1891, Auswärtiges Amt Archiv., Bonn, London Embassy, 3971 i.

[2] To de Giers enclosed in Morier to Salisbury, no. 3, 2 Jan. 1892, F.O. 65/1434.

expect a written apology.¹ He had, therefore, inquired whether his government would be satisfied with a verbal disavowal and expression of regret.² To this Salisbury had agreed and on 3 February Morier had submitted a formula: 'Le governement impérial désavoue les verbes et gestes du Colonel Jonow et les regrette.' De Giers had, in fact, already gone further than this and instructed de Staal in London that he was authorized by the Emperor to declare that the Russian government considered Jonov's acts illegal and to express regret.³ De Staal, who 'had the peculiarity of never finishing a sentence, so that he was a good channel for an awkward apology, was nevertheless understood by Lord Salisbury to say that Jonov had acted without the Russian Government's knowledge and his action could not be justified and was regrettable'.⁴ The word 'illegal', with its implication that Russia renounced territorial claims in the Pamirs, de Staal had, however, avoided. Morier had determined, then, to get the fulfilment of de Giers's instructions. As usual he prided himself on the device to which he had resorted. He had embodied his own formula in an imaginary answer by Salisbury to a parliamentary question and asked de Giers whether he would accept it as faithfully representing the Russian position. De Giers had replied with approval.⁵ This approval was, however, contained in a private letter from de Giers to Morier and could not, any more than de Giers's instructions to de Staal, be published. Anyhow, Salisbury declined to arrange the parliamentary question to which this pre-concerted reply could be given.⁶

It is perhaps worth pausing on Morier's dispatch in which he relished his 'triumph' in gaining the apology, because it is so characteristic. He describes how he hoped to take the Russians by their weak side in addressing himself to Vyshnegradski, who for financial reasons was determined to avoid war. He recounts how, by describing Jonov's exploits as those of an irresponsible

---

[1] De Giers to Morier, 23 Jan., enclosed in Morier to Salisbury, no. 24, 24 Jan. 1892, F.O. 65/1434.
[2] To Salisbury, no. 28 secret, 28 Jan. 1892, F.O. 65/1434.
[3] To Salisbury, no. 36 very confidential, 3 Feb. 1892, F.O. 65/1435.
[4] Cf. Baron Alexandre de Meyendorff, *Correspondance diplomatique de M. de Staal*, (1929), ii. 162. From Salisbury, telegram no. 9, 12 Feb. 1892, F.O. 65/1435.
[5] To Salisbury, telegram no. 20, 15 Feb. 1892, F.O. 65/1435.
[6] From Salisbury, telegram, 20 Feb. 1892, F.O. 65/1435.

hothead, he had given the Russians an opportunity to apologize without loss of dignity; and how they had perversely declined to take it, thus keeping the grounds which would justify the British government in taking offence. Once, said Morier (he reports himself talking to Vyshnegradski), this would have meant war; it could still mean a breach of diplomatic relations; it would probably mean—indeed he would recommend this—his own recall on indefinite leave. Without himself at St. Petersburg the least incident in Central Asia might lead to war. Vyshnegradski 'was fairly taken aback by the prospect I held out to him. "It is impossible," he exclaimed, "impossible that such a question should find such a solution. Believe me it can't be."' Conferences with de Giers had followed and 'capitulation' was the outcome, since Vyshnegradski dominated the divided Foreign Office and could, so Morier asserted, control the disputes between Foreign Office and Tsar.[1] Though Morier's diplomatic action may well have been, as G. J. Alder says, 'masterly', this was to magnify out of all proportion something that was of only marginal importance in the struggle for power that was proceeding on the Indian frontier.

The apology was only one side of the negotiation. The other side was, it will be recalled, British agreement to the delimitation of the boundary. This Morier failed to gain, except in principle from Salisbury, though he fought obstinately for it. 'We are in a corner,' wrote Salisbury on 5 February, adjusting his method of argument to his man,

for we have encouraged the Ameer of Afghanistan to cross the Oxus eastwards and to occupy Pamir territory, that is the province of Shignan: yet we had undertaken in 1872–73 that Afghanistan should not be deemed to extend beyond the Oxus. These two undertakings are as entirely contradictory—as hopelessly incapable of simultaneous fulfilment—as the promises of a young gentleman who has proposed to two young ladies at one ball.

Delimitation must lead either to a breach of our pledge to the Amir, or to a quarrel with Russia. 'Of the two alternatives—if we are driven to it—we must adopt the latter: but I need not say with how much misgiving and aversion: for we shall as regards Russia be evidently in the wrong.' Salisbury, therefore,

[1] To Salisbury, no. 28 secret, 28 Jan. 1892, F.O. 65/1434.

argued that actual delimitation should be put off at least until the accession of a new Amir with whom British India could make new arrangements. 'Please consider what devices can be adopted to lengthen out these negotiations as to delimitation.'[1]

The most forceful argument against delimitation was, however, the policy on which the Indian government was engaged. This was even more developed than Salisbury had suggested. Morier himself summed it up as

the policy of pushing the Chinese Westwards and the Afghans Eastwards till they meet and effectively cover the exposed corner of the Hindu Kush. The new frontier [he continued] proposed by Major Younghusband and apparently approved by the Indian Government (see map enclosed in letter from the India Office of April 22 1892) not only recognises Shignan and Roshan as Afghan territory but the whole scheme of the new frontier is based on their continuing such, seeing that the positions we are to urge the Chinese to occupy abut on those very provinces.[2]

Morier, however, continued to oppose Salisbury's Fabian policy[3] intending that delimitation should give Afghanistan part of the two provinces. He wrote to Salisbury: 'I do not quite share the feeling of the utter irreconcilability of the two factors: Agreement of 1873 and occupation of Shignan and Roshan by the Afghans.' He rejected Salisbury's simile. 'I would rather put it thus: our young friend proposed to a young lady at a ball 20 years ago and proposes to another young lady now.' (He omits to notice that his analogy would only have been exact if the first proposal had been accepted, and then it would not have proved his case.) He continues: 'He will be able to find plenty of excuses for not marrying the first young lady.' The principal 'excuse' was that it was not only on the Afghan side that effective occupations had taken place, but that the Russians also had broken the agreement of 1872–3. He, therefore, proposed to base delimitation on a bargain: Afghanistan's retention of Shignan against Russia's retention of Darwaz; Afghanistan's evacuation of Roshan against Russia's withdrawal to north of Lake Victoria, so that the Afghan

[1] From Salisbury, private, 3 Feb. 1892, and telegram no. 7, 1 Feb. 1892, F.O. 65/1435. The telegram read: 'With regard to delimitation, we should prefer to delay discussion.'
[2] To Rosebery, 5 Oct. 1892.
[3] To Salisbury, 17 Feb. 1892.

province of Wakhan might be extended to a mountain instead of a river barrier and include the caravan route. The arrangement would be completed by enforcing the Russo-Chinese frontier line laid down in a protocol of 22 May 1884 and favourable to Great Britain. This was the arrangement which Morier in the end negotiated—though not to a conclusion. He was only able to do so because Rosebery replaced Salisbury. He would never, in this instance, have overcome Salisbury's dislike of firm frontiers which, he said, we respected and the Russians disregarded. Nor would he have overcome Salisbury's wise hesitation to act, as long as the Chinese wished to withdraw (in order to avoid clashing with Russia) rather than to advance to meet Afghanistan.

In this, Morier's last negotiation, characteristic notes sound again and recall the themes of his Lisbon negotiations and reflections. He talked again of holding the threat in reserve, of using the war *in posse* to avoid the war *in esse*, and he talked again of prescribing himself a clear *objectif* before he began.

He believed he was well placed to use the threat of war, though without perhaps actually voicing the threat. The Russians 'not only dare not make a war, but they dare not risk the faintest rumour of war, because it would bring about an immediate collapse of their finances and this when the back of the country is broken with this terrible famine'.[1] Moreover, in the Pamirs, as distinct from the Heri-Rud–Oxus area, 'we can bring up forces quicker and much earlier in the season ... than they can'. Morier, therefore, proposed that his government should plan a parallel expedition to that of Jonov, aimed at the Alichur Pamirs.[2] As usual, Morier's efforts to direct policy failed—the plan was turned down by the Indian government[3]— but were not entirely without effect.

The narrative has now reached the end of Lord Salisbury's administration on 12 August 1892. The position was that 'the apology' had been made in what Morier considered an unsatisfactory form without the use of the word 'illegal', and that it had been agreed that 'delimitation' should be preceded by a

[1] To Salisbury, private, 28 Jan. 1892.
[2] To Salisbury, private, 17 Feb. 1892; to Rosebery, private, 2 Sept. 1892; these letters comment on proposals made at the end of 1891.
[3] India Office to Foreign Office, 4 Feb. 1892, F.O. 65/1435.

joint topographical commission of inquiry into geographical, historical, and ethnographical data. This Salisbury had accepted, because it would take a great deal of time and put off the evil day of delimitation.[1] It was never appointed, because in March de Giers had fallen ill and, because he was thought always to be about to recover, no one was appointed to act in his stead. Thus, as Morier had reported in May and might have repeated at any time during the summer of 1892, since he was unaware of the French side of Russian policy, 'all serious international business is at a standstill'.[2] There was a further element in the situation of which Morier was also apparently quite ignorant. Sometime in May 1892 a series of discussions took place between the war and foreign ministries in Russia. Decisions were taken which resulted in the late summer in a further Russian military advance in the Pamirs and the clash between Russians and Afghans at Somatash.[3]

On the succession of Rosebery, Morier felt his freedom. He began, much to Rosebery's irritation, as Sanderson told him, to teach the foreign secretary his business. 'You must make up your mind beforehand', he wrote, 'what it is you want to ask and that you ask what can be granted. You should never ask for more and never be content with less and keep hitting the same nail over and over again and asking for the same thing till your very presence is loathed.' A little later he wrote:

> To have a clear and previous vision before me of what I mean to obtain has always been my custom in the many negotiations I have been engaged in. It must be framed strictly according to the possibilities of the case, it must be feasible and as far as possible fair to all parties. It is astonishing the enormous advantage this gives one. . . . To have a distinct object before you which the other party does not know, but which you go doggedly for enables you to keep along a straight line amidst the infinite gyrations of your compeers.[4]

So Morier dictated the aim of the negotiation. This was to be the bargain: Afghanistan to retain Shignan and withdraw from

---

[1] From Salisbury, telegram no. 9, 12 Feb. 1892, F.O. 65/1435.

[2] To Salisbury, private, 12 Mar., and no. 60 most confidential, 12 Mar. 1892, F.O. 65/1436; no. 97, 10 May 1892, F.O. 65/1437.

[3] A. de Meyendorff, *Correspondance diplomatique de M. de Staal* (1929), ii. 176, and G. J. Alder, op. cit., pp. 248–50.

[4] To Rosebery, private, undated, before 11 Sept. 1892; to Rosebery, private, 12 Sept. 1892.

Roshan; Russia to retain Darwaz and to withdraw from an enlarged Wakhan (see above, p. 351). It suited Rosebery, to whom Morier outlined it in conversations during August when he was in London and in a memorandum of September. Rosebery liked firm outlines and was without Salisbury's subtlety and patience. The unsatisfactory character of the apology he simply disregarded, taking the view that by continuing with the negotiations for delimitation the Russians were tacitly admitting the 'illegality' of Jonov's actions. Rosebery was lucky not to be challenged. He was soon absorbed in the struggle to bring about the annexation of Uganda and always apt anyhow to treat the Pamirs flippantly. On the new basis of Morier's devising, the negotiation entered its penultimate phase.

On 26 September 1892 Morier had a conversation with Chichkine, who had for most purposes now replaced de Giers, and presented a formal note outlining the British proposal. The Russians postponed a reply until they had had Jonov's report on the part of the Pamirs that he had surveyed. By November Rosebery was impatient. 'The Pamir business is flagging—nay hung up', he wrote and asked, 'Could you jog them on a bit?'[1] Morier had come to the conclusion that a mere jog would do no good, but possibly much harm. 'The whole question', he wrote, giving a characteristic reason for this opinion,

is too amorphous [Morier, like Roseberry, had a weakness for firm outlines] and émiettée to allow of a written answer, and if we have to content ourselves with a verbal one we are almost certain to get some evasive shuffling reply which would leave matters as they are. For we must not forget that though our case has been laid before them, it has been in fragments, partly in conversation, partly in notes, partly to Giers and partly to Chichkine, but nowhere in a coherent state-paper to which answers paragraph by paragraph could be given.[2]

This was the genesis of the last phase in the negotiation, opened by Morier's note to Chichkine of 14 December 1892. It made an attempt to give a comprehensive statement of the British case and also contained a new element in the proposal

---

[1] From Rosebery, private, 14 Nov. 1892.
[2] To Rosebery, private, 23 Nov. 1892.

for spheres of influence. 'The Hindu Kush is the natural frontier of the [Indian] Empire, and we would claim as exclusively under our influence the northern slopes leading up to it.' The meaning of the claim to these northern slopes was, Morier was convinced, that Russia intended to advance southwards as far as the Hindu Kush and that the annexation of the Pamirs up to that point had been the object both of Jonov's expedition of 1891 and of the new advance of 1892. 'We are face to face with a determined effort on the part of Russia to extend herself to the Hindu Kush and . . . we have to make up our minds at once whether we will let her do so, and if we do not mean to let her do so to determine how we mean to prevent her . . .' Morier wished to let the Russians know 'that we regard the northern slopes of the Hindu Kush as under our exclusive influence, and . . . that we mean to send an expedition on our own account *le cas échéant* . . . If we remain perfectly cool, perfectly courteous and perfectly insistent we have the game in our hand', for the Russians could not contemplate the eventuality of war coming within measurable distance 'as it would send their funds down to bankruptcy point'. Morier sent a draft note home for Rosebery's sanction, containing the substance of this letter. With some verbal and softening amendments it became the note presented to Chichkine on 14 December 1892.

General Roberts, the commander-in-chief in India, had meanwhile (November) met the Amir and in conversation and subsequent correspondence had induced him to abate his claims in the Pamirs. It was a withdrawal that, from the Afghan side, was dictated by distrust of Britain and not by confidence in her.[1] Morier, however, did not shift his position and his fierce and masterful tone produced a reply from Chichkine. He was sufficiently satisfied with this to propose that the British rejoinder should insist on the appointment of a joint commission for the actual delimitation and a clear acceptance, in principle, by Russia of the two parts of the bargain upon which the delimitation was to be based. Rosebery's need to consult Lord Kimberley, the secretary of state for India, caused delay, but the British replied on these lines on 27 February 1893. This was the end of progress as far as Morier

[1] See G. J. Alder, op. cit., p. 254.

was concerned. It had been of little importance compared with what was being done from the Indian government's side.¹ The treaty, finally signed on 11 March 1895, was not his work.

At this point the negotiation tailed off in mutual recrimination between Morier and Rosebery. First, at the end of March Rosebery complained of delay.

I am not impatient. But I do not find myself materially further in this business than I was in August . . . It is the 22nd of March, and . . . in April a new expedition may be launched against the Pamirs. Meanwhile our threat of a counter expedition necessarily loses some of its force with each day that passes, as the Russians must be perfectly aware that no counter-force is being prepared in India. Altogether I chafe a good deal, as though the delay may possibly be unavoidable, one cannot help feeling that the Russians are playing with us.²

Morier, when this letter reached him, was still ill after a month in bed with influenza and in a state of desperate nervous tension, aching to get away to the south and unhappy at losing his last chance of being posted elsewhere, for Vienna had just been given to another man. This last disappointment, as Morier prophetically wrote to Currie, was *un arrêt de mort*.³ Nor must it be forgotten that the sudden death of his son on 27 May 1892, on his way back from Africa,⁴ had been a blow from which Morier never recovered. The consequence of Morier's depression that matters here, however, was that it caused him to write back angrily to Rosebery that his letter was 'unfair'. Rosebery could not have deduced the conclusion he had come to from Morier's own dispatches and therefore must have 'secret sources of information'.⁵ Thereupon, Rosebery too fired up. He was much irritated at this last phrase and at Morier's assuming the role of instructor. He remembered an earlier occasion when Morier had used words which suggested that he was the first in a line of radical foreign secretaries, with Dilke, Labouchere, and Keir Hardie to follow, and yet another occasion when he had compared a draft dispatch to a Brighton bathing woman and the finished product to Venus Aphrodite rising from the waves: the draft had been Rosebery's and the

---
¹ See G. J. Alder, op. cit., pp. 255-63.
² From Rosebery, private, 22 Mar. 1893.
³ To Currie, private, 25 Mar. 1893.   ⁴ See above, p. 311 n. 1.
⁵ To Rosebery, private, 26 Mar. 1893.

final dispatch Sanderson's.[1] When he received Currie's account of Rosebery's annoyance, Morier had already left to recuperate from his illness in the Crimea.

The negotiations were, therefore, temporarily transferred to London.[2] He came back from the Crimea, 'immensely stronger and better', and in June wrote at length to Currie, asking to be brought up to date with the Pamir negotiations and at the same time liberating his mind from a number of reflections on the subject that had accumulated in it during his holiday. A private letter of 14 June from Rosebery summarized the position to which he had brought the negotiation and answered questions in Morier's letter to Currie. The frontier east of Lake Victoria was now the subject of discussion and Rosebery told Morier that he was in a position to fix it on a line parallel with the lake, while agreeing to a partition of Shignan and Roshan, retaining as much as possible for the Afghans. With that Rosebery tried to hand back the negotiation to Morier. He was not, however, strong enough to take on the burden. Nor did the Russians wish the negotiation to come back to St. Petersburg. Their excuse was that the Tsar disliked the constant reference to him that a negotiation in St. Petersburg involved. Before 24 June Morier had again to ask for sick leave and the negotiation never came back to him.

It remains to recount Morier's effort to dispel the fog of illusion about the Indian frontier. He showed throughout his time at St. Petersburg an interest in military and strategic matters and some command of the subject. His report from St. Petersburg on Russia's military dispositions in 1887 (cf. above, pp. 198, 204, 334) well illustrates this. It was a masterly statement of conclusions from the military attaché's reports. He wrote to General Sir Henry Brackenbury (who was the military member of the Viceroy's council) when the Pamir negotiations began. His object was twofold. First, he wished to remove the general confidence in fixed frontier defences of fortified points. What was needed—here he had General Brackenbury's sympathy—was a well-equipped *corps d'armée* for offensive operations, a light and mobile column that could act quickly outside Britain's own frontiers.

[1] From Currie, 5 Apr. 1893.
[2] From Rosebery, private, 18 Apr. 1893.

I have been brought up [he wrote] in the Prussian school applicable both in diplomacy and war that a quick offensive is the best defensive and the idea that we have been spending half a million on defensive fortifications *behind* the Indus instead of using up every farthing in preparing for a rapid advance appears to me dotage.

Second, he wished to know whether it was true, as he thought, that

we had an infinitely superior strategic position to that of Russia in the eastern part of the frontier, first, because the struggle for the Pamirs could only be fought out with a few thousand, not to say a few hundred men, a side, secondly, because the bone of contention lying to the south of the Pamirs, our base is much nearer than the Russians' who are separated by those appalling sheep walks.

In short, would there be any difficulty in sending up 500 Gurkhas through the Alichur Pamirs?[1] Brackenbury replied that owing to the difficulty of the passes from Gilgit, the nearness of the British base would have to be discounted; that Russia, for whom the approach was easier, might well be at an advantage; and that the Indian government was very unlikely to send an expedition to the Alichur Pamirs. Morier had to jettison the idea of a retaliatory expedition to the Alichur Pamirs, but at least another dangerous illusion was cleared out of the way.

What are we to conclude about Morier's years in St. Petersburg? There were three themes in his career there. The theme of *entente* recurs most frequently. The theme of economic development was more sporadic. The most persistent, though except at the time of the Bazaine incident the least prominent, was that of failure and self-mistrust. They are in essence the same themes that ran through his years at Lisbon and Madrid.

The impression Morier's repeated reports of Russian overtures[2] for an understanding leaves upon one is that of a recurring pattern. This mechanical quality may indicate that from the Russian side, they had more to do with means than ends. The cumulative effect of reading all Morier's letters and dispatches from St. Petersburg is to bring home to one the extraordinary strength of his wish for an understanding. It

[1] To Brackenbury, 15 Feb. 1892.
[2] July 1886, Oct. 1886, July–Aug. 1887, Nov. 1888, and 1891.

would, after all, have been the greatest diplomatic triumph of the century had he been able to reverse at one stroke the Russophobia that had dominated British foreign policy since 1833. It would perhaps have been impossible to have done in seven or eight years—and those the years following the Russian 'victory' at Penjdeh—what it finally took nearly a generation and Russia's defeat at the hands of Japan to accomplish. Only the strength of Morier's wish to do it made it seem possible. What matters in any assessment of Morier is the strength of the wish. It suggests two things. First, it must have been quite as evident to the Russians at the time as it is to a modern reader of Morier's letters and dispatches. It was open to them to use this wish in order to keep Anglo-Russian relations relatively relaxed despite the numberless causes of Anglo-Russian tension. One may well be justified, then, in thinking of the 'overtures' as never meant to commit the Russians far. They were rather one way in which they used Morier's wish for an understanding. In the second place, the strength of Morier's wish for an *entente* reminds one of the way he combined an abnormally strong imaginative power, so that at times he seems to have more insight than most intelligent men, with a much weaker reasoning faculty, so that at times he seems unusually obtuse. He had the power to see the general principle with visionary clarity. He never had the power, or perhaps patience, to think out implications or other men's reactions. One cannot avoid the conclusion that the Russians sometimes threw dust in his eyes. Yet in the general principle he was right.

Again, one cannot avoid the conclusion that seeing one thing, the desirability of reversing British Russophobia, so clearly, he missed nearly everything else. His complete failure even to sense the developing Russo-French *entente*—the only thing of real importance in Russian foreign policy between 1889 and 1893— is then to his discredit. But it is so only if one expects an ambassador to surmount the limitations of ordinary men. Morier's letters so often spurn the opinions of the British philistine and claim special insight that their cumulative effect is to make one expect precisely this. One forgets that at least one other public figure of great ability shared both his vision of Anglo-Russian agreement and his insensitivity to those needs of Russia which made her look elsewhere for an ally. Lord

Randolph Churchill had, like Morier, the air of a lone crusader on the subject of Anglo-Russian friendship. Morier first wrote to him in December 1885 when he was secretary of state for India. Lord Randolph replied on 6 January 1886, agreeing on the desirability of improving relations with Russia on the Indian frontier and on the transcendent importance of the Asian as compared with the European element in Anglo-Russian contacts. Morier happened to be away from his post when Lord Randolph, now the 'fallen politician' of 1887-8, arrived in St. Petersburg, was received in audience by the Tsar, and had an interview with de Giers. Arthur Hardinge, the chargé d'affaires, reported what had passed on the basis of Lord Randolph's own notes. Before this 'outsider', as Morier called him, left, however, Morier returned, and since the visit was 'so exceptional a performance', he also wrote privately to Salisbury about it. He said he believed he had played his part in keeping Lord Randolph in the Unionist fold by assuring him that Britain had not joined the Triple Alliance and that Salisbury's foreign policy still left open the way to agreement with Russia. Morier called the visit 'an escapade' and spoke of the 'endless legends and myths' it had generated.[1] He and Lord Randolph were thus never acknowledged allies, and the relationship between them is only worth recalling because it helps to set Morier's desire for an Anglo-Russian *entente* in its proper perspective.

To some extent the same combination of vision and obtuseness as characterized Morier's view of Anglo-Russian relations marks the Siberian plan, which was the form his ideas of economic development principally took in relation to Russia. Morier had the vitality of imagination to picture to himself a flow of English machines through the Polar regions into the heart of Siberia and a return flow of gold, grain, and timber. Yet in his dealings with those who commanded real financial resources he showed himself uncertain and timid. He was not equipped with the combination of precision, care for detail, patience, and boldness that the business world demanded. Indeed, the Siberian ventures of Morier show clearly the gulf that, even in the imperialist nineties, divided political society from the business community. Morier's care to present the scheme to the Russians as an amateur venture, like his care to

[1] To Salisbury, second letter, most secret, 25 Jan. 1888.

emphasize the political purpose and to disparage the profit-making side of the Goa railway, testifies to this. It testifies, more interestingly, to the existence in the eighties of accepted frontiers to an ambassador's functions. In his evidence before the Parliamentary Committee of Enquiry into the Diplomatic Service in 1870, Morier had spoken of the 'very much greater attention given to commercial questions during the last few years'.[1] The Foreign Office and the Diplomatic Service might open up opportunities for trade. The promotion of particular commercial ventures or the interests of individual firms still, however, lay outside the boundaries they observed. What was promoted was a policy, not money-making; the public interest, not private profit. In practice it might be difficult sometimes to see the difference. Yet Morier's language over the Goa and Siberian plans shows that for him the distinction had clear meaning.

An illustration of what an ambassador, who was resolved to go beyond the immediate and political demands of his post, could do is afforded by the private letters on German internal conditions which Morier continued to write to Salisbury throughout his period at St. Petersburg. Perhaps only an ambassador like Morier could have turned this kind of higher journalism to the service of foreign policy. Malet at Berlin, reporting the government view in a divided country, was unlikely to do so. Two examples must suffice. In 1885 Morier wrote of 'the national force and energy' evoked by the wars of 1866 and 1870. 'The surplus steam has almost exclusively . . . gone into commercial enterprise. On this field they [the Germans] found themselves encountered by a rival not so easily thrown out of the saddle as Austria and France had [been] and to beat England commercially as they had beaten the former on the field of battle became a sort of national craze.' If one recollected that this feeling was tinctured with the chauvinism of a military nation, whose 'commercial classes from the richest banker to [the] commercial traveller' had all done military service, one could understand the demented commercial jealousy with which the Germans were influenced against Britain.[2] The second example comes from September

[1] *Parliamentary Papers* (1870), vii. 628.
[2] To Salisbury, private and confidential, 18 Sept. 1885.

1890 when Morier wrote of the socialist question 'which engrossed men's minds' in Germany. He wrote of the deep cleavage which the social question had wrought in the party groups and the dread among more responsible men provoked 'by the daily increase of symptoms of a close alliance between . . . several of the largest employers of labour' and the late chancellor, Prince Bismarck. 'On the other hand,' he continued, 'the Roman Catholic clergy have identified themselves with the interests of the working classes and that not on the basis of the *modus vivendi* which the Emperor is working for, but on advanced socialist demands.'[1] But such reporting had its dangers too; for to give information for which he was not asked was to increase a sense that he was not listened to. It helped to create his sense of failure.

Morier set himself objectives which he did not achieve. He had a policy of his own at St. Petersburg as at Lisbon and Madrid. On one side, he sought to bring about an Anglo-Russian *entente* and shift the emphasis in Anglo-Russian relations from Constantinople to the Indian frontier, to Persia and Tibet—where it eventually fell in 1905–7. On the other side, he sought to counter the influence of Bismarck and all he stood for. Neither objective was possible to achieve from the relatively subordinate position that an ambassador holds. He is designed to be the tool that executes policy and not the mind that creates it. To this extent Morier failed. Yet he was a success, in so far as his period at St. Petersburg saw an improvement in Anglo-Russian relations which left Salisbury free to restore the over-all balance of British foreign policy that had been lost during the early eighties, and to create for Britain a strong position in the Mediterranean, so that she could hold her own in the partition of Africa. Yet because Morier had objectives of his own, he was professionally less accomplished than either Lord Ampthill or Lord Lyons, to name his greatest contemporaries. He was too often at cross purposes with the Foreign Office and he caused trouble with the Queen. He was hectoring and overbearing with those he disliked and too sensitive to flattery from those he liked. With the first tendency in mind, Lord Granville wrote, when it was a question of appointing an ambassador to Constantinople: 'It would serve the Sultan right

[1] To Salisbury, private, 18 Sept. 1890.

to give him Morier, but the latter's habit of turning small things into great is dangerous.'[1] That Morier was bewitched by the Russians was a common opinion and not only that of the Queen. Yet the attraction was not all on one side. The Queen herself admitted: 'His wittiness gains him much sympathy among the Russians who cannot resist this quality.'[2] He had the power, too, of attaching the affections of many able men, from Lord Goschen and Sir Louis Mallet to Arthur Hardinge and Charles Eliot. Above all, he had an uncanny capacity to catch, as if out of the air, and to formulate the economic element in the imperialist idealism of his day. Nor was he without recognition. The knighthood and G.C.B. conferred on him have already been mentioned. He was also made a privy councillor in 1885 and in 1889 an honorary D.C.L. of his own university. Perhaps the last word should rest with Benjamin Jowett. He wrote to Rosebery in 1886 to persuade him to make Morier's closer acquaintance.

He is very able, and full of ideas, and has a great command of facts and an extraordinary knowledge of persons. I have never met with any one who seemed to me to have so much insight into foreign affairs. He is a strong advocate for free trade and for treaties where free trade is not to be had. I do not think him 'vain', but he is impetuous and confident about matters which he knows, and very impatient of the delays of diplomacy when they thwart an important purpose.

All men, like him, have a twofold reputation: they are greatly admired by their friends and depreciated by persons who do not understand them . . .[3]

Jowett died on 1 October 1893, and just over a month later, on Thursday, 16 November at 3 o'clock in the afternoon, Morier followed him. He ended his life where he began it: in Switzerland. He had gone there in September to the Hotel National in Montreux. He had been ill for most of the time, to quote the information given to the press,[4] 'of various internal

---

[1] Granville to Gladstone, 14 Sept. 1884, A. Ramm (ed.), *The Political Correspondence of Mr. Gladstone and Lord Granville* (1962), ii. 256.
[2] The Queen to Rosebery, 9 Apr. 1886, Rosebery papers, box. 51.
[3] Benjamin Jowett to Rosebery, 11 Apr. 1886, Rosebery papers, box 63.
[4] Central News telegram, Berne.

complications of an ill-defined character arising, it was believed, from gout'. But the end came unexpectedly and the final phase of his illness was brief. He was buried in the churchyard at Northwood, near Rickmansworth, where Batchworth Heath House belonged to his widow. His daughter went back to St. Petersburg to say farewell and to remove their possessions from the embassy. Sir Nicholas O'Connor replaced him there, but not until 1895.

BIBLIOGRAPHY

THIS study was begun when I was editing *The Political Correspondence of Mr. Gladstone and Lord Granville* and finished while I was writing *Germany 1789–1919*. It has profited from the variety of historical sources which this work brought to my knowledge. It is, however, directly based on the papers —letters to him and copies which he kept of many letters that he wrote— which Morier left in the possession of his daughter, who became Lady Wester Wemyss. They were put at my disposal with the greatest possible generosity by his granddaughter, the Hon. Alice Wemyss, now Mrs. F. H. Cunnack. They are now at Balliol College, Oxford. I was not able to find among them many of Jowett's letters to him, but many survive in the Jowett papers, also at Balliol, and nineteen of them are printed in Abott and Campbell (see below). His own to Jowett exist in a typed version—the series is not complete —which Lady Wemyss had had prepared for the continuation of her own book, *Memoirs and Letters of Sir Robert Morier, 1826–76* (2 vols., 1911). I have drawn also upon her draft of the opening chapters for this continuation.

Wherever I have not named the source of a document to which I refer, the Morier papers are to be understood as that source.

I have used Morier's official dispatches and telegrams in the Foreign Office archives. F.O. 63 Portugal, F.O. 65 Russia, F.O. 72 Spain, and F.O. 84 slave-trade (for Africa) were the relevant classes of document here.

Two microfilms (GFM 10/200 and GFM 10/180) made from the German Foreign Office archives, captured in 1945, contained material relating to Morier. I read these in the Foreign Office Library.

By the gracious permission of Her Majesty The Queen, I have been able to use the material in the Royal Archives (referred to by the letters R.A. with index numbers).

At one time or another I have consulted the private papers of the following:

Lord Cranbrook	Ipswich County Record Office
Lord Cross	British Museum
W. E. Gladstone	British Museum
Lord Granville	Public Record Office
E. W. Hamilton	British Museum
Lord Iddesleigh	British Museum
A. H. Layard	British Museum
Sir William Mackinnon	School of Oriental and African Studies, London
Lord Rosebery	National Library of Scotland, Edinburgh
Lord Odo Russell (later Lord Ampthill)	Public Record Office
Lord Salisbury	Christ Church, Oxford
Sir William White	Transcripts by Dr. C. L. Smith

I have also been allowed, by the kindness of Miss S. Crowe, to use letters of her father, Sir Eyre Crowe. I owe the reference on p. 348, n. 1 to the German Foreign Office archives at Bonn to Dr. P. M. Kennedy.

BIBLIOGRAPHY

PARLIAMENTARY PAPERS

(1861)	xliii	The East India and Other Government Guarantees on Railways.
(1863)	xliv	Correspondence ... on Cotton Cultivation.
(1870)	vii	Report from the Select Committee on the Diplomatic and Consular Services.
(1870)	lxvii	Reports of H.M. Representatives respecting the Tenure of Land in the Several Countries of Europe.
(1871)	lxxii	Treaties of Guarantee under which this Country is Engaged to Interfere by Force of Arms.
(1874)	xlix	Report to the Secretary of State for India in Council on Railways in India.
(1880)	lxxix	Treaty of Commerce and Extradition between Her Majesty and the King of Portugal with reference to their Indian Possessions.
(1882)	lxxxi	Correspondence respecting Commercial Relations between Spain and Great Britain.
(1883)	xlviii	Correspondence respecting Tariffs in Portuguese Possessions in Africa, 1877–82.
(1883)	xlviii	Correspondence respecting the Territory on the West Coast of Africa lying between 5° 12′ and 8° South Latitude, 1847–77.
(1884)	lvi	Correspondence relating to the Negotiations between the Governments of Great Britain and Portugal for Conclusion of the Congo Treaty.
(1884)	lvi	Dispatch to H.M. Minister at Lisbon enclosing the Congo Treaty and Corrected Translation of the Mozambique Tariff, 1877.
(1884)	lvi	Further Papers relating to the Congo Treaty.
(1884)	lxxxvii	Protocol of Agreement and Declaration between the Governments of Great Britain and Spain respecting the Commercial Relations of the Two Countries.
(1884)	lxxxvii	Correspondence respecting the Commercial Relations between Great Britain and Spain.
(1884)	lxxxvii	Memorial from the Association of Chambers of Commerce.
(1884)	lxxxvii	Dispatch to H.M. Chargé d'Affaires ... respecting the Commercial Relations of Great Britain and Spain.
(1884–5)	lxxxvii	Telegram from Lieutenant-General Sir Peter Lumsden.
(1884–5)	lxxxvii	Further Correspondence respecting Central Asia.
(1884–5)	lxxxvii	Maps.
(1884–5)	lxxxvii	Declaration between Great Britain and Spain relative to Commerce, 21 December 1884.

(1884–5)   lxxxvii   Further Correspondence.
(1886)   lxxiii   Correspondence respecting the Port of Batoum.
(1886)   lxxiv   Collective Notes presented to the Hellenic Government and Replies thereto.
(1886)   lxxiv   Further Correspondence.
(1886)   lxxv   Correspondence respecting the Affairs of Eastern Roumelia and Bulgaria.
(1887)   lxiii   Further Correspondence respecting the Affairs of Central Asia.
(1888)   lxxvii   Further Correspondence respecting the Affairs of Central Asia.
(1888)   cix   Dispatch from Sir R. Morier and other Correspondence respecting Attempts to establish Commercial Relations with Siberia through the Kara Sea.
(1895)   cix   Agreement between Great Britain and Russia on the Pamirs, 11 March 1895.

MORIER'S WRITINGS

The Dano-German Conflict and Lord Russell's Despatch of September 1862 (1863), anonymous pamphlet.

'Reconstruction in Germany', *North British Review*, li (1869), 253.

The Agrarian Legislation of Prussia during the Present Century (1870), pamphlet published by the Cobden Club.

Local Government in Germany and England with Special Reference to Recent Legislation on the Subject in Prussia (1875), pamphlet published by the Cobden Club.

'Prussia and the Vatican', in four parts, *Macmillan's Magazine*, xxx (1874), 464–559; xxxi (1874–5), 72–261.

OTHER ARTICLES IN PERIODICALS

Anon. (attributed to W. T. Stead by the Wellesley Index of Victorian Periodicals), 'The Bismarck Dynasty', *Contemporary Review* (Feb. 1889), pp. 157–78.

Victor Morier, 'A Reindeer Journey to Arctic Russia', *Murray's Magazine* (1889).

BOOKS WITH DOCUMENTARY MATERIAL OF IMPORTANCE FOR THIS STUDY

G. E. Buckle (ed.), *Letters of Queen Victoria*, 2nd ser., vol. iii (1928); 3rd ser., vols. i–ii (1930).

Baron Alexandre de Meyendorff (ed.), *Correspondance diplomatique de M. de Staal* (2 vols., Paris, 1929).

Documents diplomatiques français (Paris, 1929–62).

J. Lepsius, A. M. Bartholdy, and F. Thimme (eds.), *Die große Politik der europäischen Kabinette* (Berlin, 1922–7).

G. P. Gooch and H. Temperley, *British Documents on the Origins of the War* (1927–38).

Lady Gwendolen Cecil, *The Life of Robert Marquis of Salisbury* (4 vols., 1921–31).

W. S. Churchill, *Lord Randolph Churchill* (2 vols., 1906).

A SELECTION OF OTHER BOOKS AND ARTICLES

Abbott, E. and Campbell, L. (eds.), *Life and Letters of Benjamin Jowett* (2 vols., 1899).

Alder, G. J., *British India's Northern Frontier, 1865–95* (1963).

Almeida, F. de, *Historia de Portugal* (Coimbra, 1922–57), vol. vi.

Erik Amburger, *Geschichte der Behördenorganisation Russlands von Peter dem Grossen bis 1917* (Leiden, 1966).

Anstey, R., *Britain and the Congo in the Nineteenth Century* (Oxford, 1962).

Bains, I., 'British Guarantee to Portugal', *Bulletin of the Institute of Historical Research* (1942–3), p. 95.

Balfour, Lady Betty, *Lord Lytton's India Administration* (1899).

Black, C. E., *The Establishment of Constitutional Government in Bulgaria* (Princeton, 1943).

Carr, R., *Spain 1808–1939* (1966).

Curato, F., *La questione marocchina e gli accordi italo-spagnoli* (2 vols., Milan, 1961, 1964).

Faber, G., *Jowett* (1957).

Greaves, R. L., *Persia and the Defence of India* (1959).

Hennessy, C. A. M., *The Federal Republic in Spain* (Oxford, 1962).

Hollyday, F. B. M. ' "Love Your Enemies! Otherwise Bite Them!" Bismarck, Herbert, and the Morier Affair, 1888–1889', *Central European History*, i (1968), 56–79. Dr. P. M. Kennedy drew my attention to this article but unfortunately after my own chapter 10 was written.

Johnson, H., *The Life and Voyages of Joseph Wiggins, Modern Discoverer of the Kara Sea Route to Siberia* (1907).

Langer, W. L., *European Alliances and Alignments* (New York, 1937, new ed. 1950).

F. Latour da Veiga Pinto, *Le Portugal et le Congo au xixe Siècle* (Paris, 1972).

Leslie, A. (ed.), *The Arctic Voyages of Adolf Nordenskiöld* (1879).

Lowe, C. J., *Salisbury and the Mediterranean, 1886–96* (1965).

Macpherson, W. J., 'Investment in Indian Railways', *Economic History Review* (1955–6), p. 177.

Nordenskiöld, A. E., *The Voyage of the Vega round Asia and Europe* (2 vols., 1881).

Peel, H., *Polar Gleams. An Account of a Voyage on the Yacht 'Blencathra'* (1894).

Peres, D. A., *História de Portugal* (Barcelona, 1928–38), vol. vii.

Platt, D. C. M., *Finance, Trade, and Politics in British Foreign Policy, 1815–1914*, (Oxford, 1968).
Ponsonby, Sir F. (ed.), *Letters of the Empress Frederick* (1928).
Rich, N. and Fisher, M. H. (editors), *The Holstein Papers* (Cambridge, 1955–63).
Rich, N., *Friedrich von Holstein* (Cambridge, 1965).
Schreuder, D. M., *Gladstone and Kruger. Liberal Government and Colonial 'Home Rule', 1880–85* (1969).
Smith, C. L., *The Embassy of Sir William White at Constantinople* (Oxford, 1957).
Sumner, B. H., *Russia and the Balkans* (Oxford, 1937).
Taffs, W., 'The War Scare of 1875', *Slavonic Review* (Dec. 1930).
Temperley, H., 'British Policy towards Parliamentary Rule and Constitutionalism in Turkey', *Cambridge Historical Journal*, iv (1932–3), 156.
—— and Penson, L. M., *Foundations of British Foreign Policy* (1938).

INDEX

Abbreviations used in the Index

Amb.	Ambassador	Gen.	General
Bd.	Board	Gov.	Governor
Chanc.	Chancellor	I.O.	India Office
C.O.	Colonial Office	Lib.	Liberal
Cons.	Conservative	Min.	Minister and Ministry
Dau.	Daughter	Priv.	Private
Dept.	Department	Sec.	Secretary
For.	Foreign	Und.	Under
F.O.	Foreign Office		

Abaza, Aleksandr (1821–95), Russian min. for finance *1880–1*, 344.

Afghan frontier with Russia: Anglo-Russian agreements on, *1869–73*, 253, 267, 348, 350, 351, *1885* (Mar.) 254, (May) 254–5, (Sept.) 255, 267, *1887* (July) 247–8, 262, 269, 348; demarcation of, *1885–6*, 231–2, 242, 255, 258–61, 268–9; Salisbury against settling, 263–4, 267–8, 350–3; negotiations in St. Petersburg on, 264–8, 351–2, 353–7.

Afghanistan, 206, 236–8, 330–1, 338, 350 (*see also* Central Asian question).

Africa, 4; Anglo-Portuguese relations in, 19–21, 27, 73–6, 80–7, 89, 106; England's 'bad debt', 84–5; partition of, 97, 105–6, 109, 110.

Aguiar, António Augusto de (1838–87), member of Portuguese Chamber of Deputies *1879–83*, friend of Corvo, member of committee to supervise the Goa railway, min. for Public Works *1883*, 144.

Aksakov, Ivan Sergeyevich (1823–86), 201.

Albert (1819–61), Prince Consort, 280.

Alexander II (1818–81), Emperor of Russia *1855–81*, 195, 205.

Alexander III (1845–94), Emperor of Russia *1881–94*: character and policy of, 196–7, 201, 202, 318, 332, 333, 335; attempted assassination of, 230–1, 246; and Bulgaria, 209–11, 219, 276, 280; and Batum, 224, 225; and Anglo-Russian relations, 234–6, 239, 241, 242, 246; and Reinsurance treaty, 250 and n.; and Central Asia, 266, 268; and Shah of Persia, 338–40; audience to H. N. Sullivan, 313, to W. T. Stead, 334; to Sir H. Drummond Wolff, 340–3; to Lord Randolph Churchill, 360.

Alexander of Battenberg (1857–93), Prince of Bulgaria *1879–86*, 209–12, 217–18, 220, 221, 228–31, 234, 240, 273, 276–9, 281; a 'six shooter', 222.

Alfonso XII (1857–85), King of Spain *1874–85*, 25, 160, 161, 163, 179–81.

Alsace-Lorraine, 6, 71, 123, 241, 270, 283.

Amadeo of Savoy (1845–90), King of Spain *1870–3*, 160.

Ammenkov, Ivan Vasilievich, Russian General, 207, 319.

Ampthill, *see* Russell, Lord Odo.

Anderson, Sir Henry Percy (1831–96), head of the African dept. in the F.O. *1883–96*, 112.

Andrássy, Gyula (1823–90), Count, Austro-Hungarian for. min. *1871–9*, 51, 65.

Andrássy Note *1875*, 51, 59.

Anglo-Siberian Syndicate Ltd., 314, 316 n., 319–21, 327.

Anstey, Roger, historian, 95, 97, 100, 101, 106, 112.

INDEX

Antas, Miguel Martins d', Portuguese min. in London *1877–81, 1881–90*, 26, 40, 99–100, 103, 108–9, 111, 156–7; for. min. May *1881*, 18, 108.

Appert, Félix Antoine (1817–91), French General, amb. in St. Petersburg *1883–6*, 202, 225.

Arbuthnot, Sir Alexander John (1822–1907), Indian civil servant, member of council of Madras *1862–72*, of Viceroy's council *1875–80*, its president *1878–9*, 36, 38.

Argyll, George Douglas (1823–1900), eighth Duke of, 53.

Armand, Ernest (1829–98), Count, French min. in Lisbon *1870–7*, 22.

Armijo, *see* Vega de.

Arnold, Matthew, 3.

Ashdown, G. W., 313, 314.

Athenaeum Club, 4, 315.

Austria and Austria–Hungary, 4, 35, 51, 65, 136, 208, 213, 219, 229, 240, 243–51 (*see also* Vienna).

Ávila e Bolama, António José de (1806–81), Marquis (after *1878*, Duke), Portuguese premier *1877–8*, 14–16, 39, 47, 74, 113, 119, 149.

Balliol College, Oxford, 2–3, 53 n., 66.

Baring, Walter (1844–1915), younger brother of Lord Cromer, sec. of legation at Lisbon *1881–5*, 11, 109.

Barjona de Freitas, Augusto Cesar (1834–1900), Portuguese min. for Justice *1878–9*, 15.

Barrington, Bernard Eric Edward (1847–1918), after *1902* Sir Eric, priv. sec. to Salisbury *1878–80, 1885–6, 1887–92, 1895–1900* and to Iddesleigh *1886–7*, 205, 303–4.

Barros e Cunha, João Gualberto de, Portuguese min. for Public Works *1877–8*, 15, 149–51.

Batum, 129, 205, 223–6, 264, 275, 357.

Bazaine, Achille (1811–88), French Marshal, 288–93.

Bazaine Incident *1888–9*, 38, 204, 295–301, 303, 304, 335–6, 358.

Bazley, Thomas (1787–1885), Bart. *1869*, manufacturer, lib. M.P. *1858–80*, 44.

Beach, Sir Michael Hicks (1837–1916), first Viscount St. Aldwyn *1905*, col. sec. *1878–80*, 89, 92, 93.

Bedford, Francis Charles Hastings (1819–91), ninth Duke of, 315.

Belgium, 8, 18–19, 24.

Bento da Silva, Carlos, Portuguese min. for finance *1877–8*, 15.

Berlin, 3, 4, 5, 188.

Berlin, congress of *1878*, 27–8, 146–8.

Berlin memorandum *1876*, 51, 58–9, 124.

Berlin, treaty of *1878*, 209, 210, 213, 217–18, 223, 225.

Berlin West Africa Conference *1884–5*, 112, 191.

Bismarck, Herbert von (1849–1904), Count, eldest son of the chanc., served in London embassy *1882–4*, in German F.O. *1885–90*, 218, 249, 272, 280, 287, 292–303.

Bismarck-Schönhausen, Otto Edward Leopold von (1815–98), Prince, chanc. of the German Empire *1871–90*: methods of, 25–6, 271–2; and Morier, 275–7, 281, 286–7, 293, 302; Morier and, 5–6, 71, 112, 188, 204, 218–19, 221, 241, 250, 284, 304; and war scare *1875*, 7–9; and Spain, 25; and eastern question *1878*, 59, 65, 117–18, *1885–7*, 210, 212; and Congo treaty *1884*, 112; and Catholic ultramontane party, 117–18; and colonies, 191; and Anglo-Russian relations, 234–5; and Russia, 128, 209, 241, 243, 250, 264, 280; and Crispi, 286; charges against O'Connor, 247 n.; opposition to, in Germany, 271, 287; sordid end of his régime, 303.

Black Sea, Russian repudiation of neutrality of, 140, 223–4.

Blowitz, Henri Stefan Opper de (1825–1903), correspondent of *The Times* in Paris *1871–1902*, 119.

Bonham, Sir George Francis (1847–1927), second Bart., second sec. at Lisbon *1876–7*, at Madrid *1877–80*, 11.

Bosnia, 50, 54, 55.

Braamcamp, Anselmo José (1817–85), Portuguese premier and for. min.

INDEX 373

1879–81, 15, 17, 22, 46, 47, 98–100, 102–5, 155, 157.
Brassey, Thomas (1836–1918), first Baron *1886*, first Earl *1911*, 315.
Brazza, Pierre Savorgnan de (1852–1905), African explorer, 97, 109, 110.
Bright, John (1811–89), radical M.P. *1847–89*, 64, 123, 125.
Bryce, James (1838–1922), first Viscount *1914*, 224 n.
Bulgaria: *1875–8*, 51–3, 56, 59, 60–2, 67, 123; *1885–7*, 205–14, 222, 228–35, 238–40, 243–4, 246–9, 251, 255, 258, 259, 265, 280; *1888*, 332; Turco-Bulgarian negotiations, 213, 217–20, 221–2, 259; Bismarck said to have urged Russia to occupy, 250, 280; satellite of Austria–Hungary in trade, 311.
Bülow, Bernhard (1849–1929), Count, after *1905* Prince, German sec. of embassy, sometime chargé d'affaires at St. Petersburg *1884–8*, for. sec. *1897–1900*, chanc. of the German Empire *1900–9*, 276, 279, 283.
Bunge, Nikolai Christianovich (1823–95), Russian min. for finance *1881–7*, 198, 209.
Bunsen, Georg von (1824–95), Baron, lib. member of the Prussian parliament, 6.
Bunsen, Maurice de (1852–1932), third, then second, sec. at Madrid *1882–6*, amb. at Madrid *1906–13*, at Vienna *1913–14*, 165, 192.
Burgers, Thomas François (1834–81), president of the South African Republic *1872–7*, 92.
Butzov, Eugen Karlovich (1837–1904), Russian min. at Teheran *1889–97*, 342.

Camacho, Juan Francisco (1817–96), Spanish min. for finance *1881–3*, 163, 164, 173–7.
Cameron, Verney Lovett (1844–94), African explorer, 95.
Camoens, Luis Vaz de (*c.* 1524–80), 102.
Campbell, Frederick, company promoter, 30, 41–5.
Campos, *see* Martinez de.

Canning, George (1770–1827), for. sec. *1807–9*, *1822–7*, prime min. *1827*, 24.
Cánovas del Castille (Castillo), Antonio (1828–97), Spanish premier *1875*, *1875–9*, *1879–81*, *1884–5*, *1890–2*, etc., 148, 160, 162–4, 186–8.
Carlyle, Thomas, 3.
Carnarvon, Henry Howard Molyneux (1831–90), ninth Earl of, col. sec. *1874–8*, 78–9.
Cartwright, William Cornwallis (1826–1915), of Aynho, Oxon., lib. M.P. *1868–85*, 4–5, 316, 327.
Carvalho, Lourenço António de, Portuguese min. for Public Works *1878–9*, 15, 16.
Carvalho, Mariano de (1836–1905), member of Portuguese Chamber of Deputies *1870–86*, min. for finance *1886–91*, 22, 104.
Casa La Iglesia, — Marquis, Spanish min. in London *1875–86*, 166–8.
Castedo, Julian, 186.
Catherine of Braganza, 23, 27.
Catholic question, between ultramontane and liberal Catholics, 113–17 (see also *Kulturkampf*, Vatican).
Cattley, Oswald, English merchant in Russia, 324, 327, 328.
Central Asian question, 206, 226, 231, 246–8, 252–69, 280, 347 (*see also* Pamirs Incident).
Cetewayo (d. 1884), Zulu king *1873–9*, *1883–4*, 87.
Chamberlain, Joseph (1836–1914), president Bd. of Trade *1880–5*, etc., 170, 216 n.
Charivaria, 102.
Chernayev, Mikhail Gregorovich (1826–98), Russian General, 52.
Chichkine, Nikolai Pavlovich (1830–1912), Russian deputy for. min. *1891–7*, 199, 200, 354, 355.
Childers, Hugh Culling Eardley (1827–96), chanc. of the exchequer *1882–5*, 170, 189, 192.
Churchill, Lord Randolph Henry Spencer (1849–95), chanc. of the exchequer *1886*, 205, 279, 360.
Clarendon, George William Frederick (1800–70), eighth Earl of, for. sec. *1853–8*, *1865–6*, *1868–70*, 55.

Clarke, Sir Andrew (1824-1902), Colonel, served with the Royal Engineers *1844–86*, member of the Indian Council *1875–80*, 36.
Clough, Arthur Hugh, 3.
Cobden, Richard (1804-65), radical M.P. *1841–65*, 4, 64, 123, 133, 135, 136, 138.
Cobden Club, 4, 5, 6 n., 164.
Cobden Treaty with France *1860*, 133 and n., 169.
Cobdenite Foreign Policy, Morier on, 64, 123-4, 130, 135-9.
Commercial Treaties: Gladstone hates, 189; Anglo-Austrian *1865*, 4, 35; Anglo-Portuguese, 19, 28-49 (*see also* Lorenço Marques); Anglo-Spanish, instructions to negotiate, 171; negotiations, 177-8, 181-5; negotiations fail, 186; terms of, 171 n.; protocol and declaration instead, 183-8, 192, 193; Franco-Portuguese, 169; Franco-Spanish, 170, 173-4; Spanish with several European countries, 178.
Commercio de Porto, 26, 144, 152.
Congo Conference *1884–5*, see Berlin West Africa Conference.
Congo Free State, 112.
Congo, river, free navigation of, 362-3.
Congo territory, Portuguese claims to, 21, 27, 94-7, 99, 101, 105-7.
Congo treaty, Morier's draft *1881*, 22, 105-7; dropped, 108-9; Granville's draft *1882*, 110-11; Andersonn's draft *1883*, 112.
Constantinople, question of Morier's appointment to, 10, 72, 362-3; conference at *1876*, 50, 60-70, *1885*, 212-13, 259; Russian threat to, 122, 207, 217, 234, 236-8, 274, 279.
Contemporary Review, 301.
Corvo, João de Andrade (1824-90), Professor in Portuguese Agricultural Institute, for. min. *1871–7*, *1878–9*, also min. for Colonies *1872–7*, *Mar.-June 1879*, 13-20, 22, 39-41, 50, 86, 87; fall of his govt., *30 May 1879*, 16, 94, 157-8; on Iberian union, 24; on fishing dispute with Spain, 150-1; Morier and, 145; and Morier, 148.
Cosmopolitan Club, 4.
Cranbrook, Gathorne (1814-1906), first Viscount *1878*, sec. for India *1878–80*, 36, 37.
Crimean War, 54, 57, 68, 125, 127, 140, 288-90.
Crispi, Francesco (1819-1901), Italian risorgimento leader, premier *1887–91*, *1893–6*, 203, 286, 332.
Cross, Sir Richard Assheton (1823-1914), first Viscount *1886*, sec. for India *1886–92*, 231 n., 266, 286.
Crowe, Sir Eyre A. B. W. (1864-1925), served in the F.O. *1884–1925*, permanent und. sec. *1920–5*, 278.
Crowe, Sir Joseph Archer (1825-96), father of above, consul-gen. at Düsseldorf *1872–80*, commercial attaché at Berlin and Vienna *1880–2*; at Paris *1882–96*, 192, 286 n., 290 n.
Cuba, insurrection of, against Spain, 25, 148, 163.
Cuban refugees, question of, 189.
Cuesta, Pelago, Spanish min. for finance *1883–4*, 164.
Currie, Philip Henry Wodehouse (1834-1906), first Baron *1899*, priv. sec. to Granville *1870–4*, *1880–5*, assistant und. sec. *1885–9*, und. sec. in the F.O. *1889–94*, 38, 205, 262, 266, 268, 284, 331, 332 n., 356, 357.

Daily News, 126.
Daily Telegraph, 131, 301.
Davison, —, —, employed by the Anglo-Siberian Syndicate Ltd., 317-18, 321.
Davison, —, —, Lieutenant, 347, 348.
Deines, Adolf von (b. 1845), Major, later General, German military attaché in Madrid *1883–6*; in Vienna *1886–94*, 290-3, 297 n., 298, 301.
Delagoa Bay, see Lorenço Marques.
Delagoa Bay Railway, 83-4, 86-92, 99, 109.
Delianov, Ivan Davidov (1818-97), Count, Russian min. for public instruction *1882–97*, 201.
Democracy, Morier's views on, 134-5.
Derby, Edward Henry (1826-93), for. sec. *1866–8*, *1874–8*, col. sec. *1882–5*: appointment of Morier to Lisbon, 7, 9-10, to Madrid, 159, 189, to St. Petersburg, 189; on Morier, 30, 152, 153; Morier on, 52, 54, 119, 124, 141-2; Morier's autobiographical

INDEX

letter to, 188–9; helps Morier over Siberia, 315; conversation with Morier at Baden-Baden, 18–19, 24; and war scare *1875*, 8–10; and alliance with Portugal, 24–7; vigilant in limiting obligations, 35; mentioned, 28, 30, 34, 39, 55, 95, 97, 139, 188.

Derby, Mary (dau. of fifth Earl De la Warr, dowager Marchioness of Salisbury) after *1870* Countess of, wife of above, 9, 24, 50, 52, 55–9, 93–4, 121, 141, 158–9, 165, 186–9.

Dering, Sir Henry Neville (1839–1906), ninth Bart., sec. of embassy at St. Petersburg *1886–8*, 204.

Dickson, Oscar, Swedish merchant in Russia, 310–11.

Dilke, Sir Charles Wentworth (1843–1911), second Bart., lib. M.P., parliamentary und. sec. for for. affairs *1880–2*, 165, 170, 171, 173, 175–8.

Disraeli, Benjamin (1804–81), first Earl of Beaconsfield *1876*, prime min. *1874–80*, 9, 52, 58; co-ordination in his cabinet, 89; speeches of, *17 Jan. 1878*, 124, *Apr. 1878*, 146.

Dolgor[o]uk[i]ov, Nikolai Sergeyevich (1840–1913), Prince, Russian General, min. at Teheran *1886–9*, 338, 343.

Dondukov-Korsakov [Doudakoff-Korsakoff] Aleksandr Mikhailovich (1822–89), Prince, Russian General, 258.

Dufferin, Frederick Temple (1826–1902), first Marquis of Dufferin and Ava, gov. gen. of Canada *1872–8*, amb. at St. Petersburg *1879–81*, Constantinople *1881–4*, Viceroy of India *1884–8*, amb. at Rome *1888–91*, 159, 205, 284, 286, 347 n.

Eastern question: *1875–8*, 26, 31, 50–2, 60–1, 119–20, 245, *1885–7*, 243; in general, 227, 246, 249 (*see also* Turkey, Russia, etc.).

Eastern Rumelia: reunion with Bulgaria, 208–10, 255; recovers Rhodope territory, 217–19.

Edinburgh, Alfred Ernest Albert (1844–1900), Duke of, second son of Queen Victoria, married to Marie, dau. of Alexander II, 63, 239.

Egypt: importance of, 84; British occupation of, 61, 167, 190, 279.

Elduayen, José, Marquis del Pazo de la Mercedi, Spanish for. min. *1884–5*, etc., 164.

Eliot, Sir Charles N. E. (1864–1931), third sec. at St. Petersburg *1887–93*, amb. at Tokyo, *1919–26*, 204–5, 363.

Elliot, Sir Henry George (1817–1907), amb. at Constantinople *1867–77*, at Vienna *1877–84*, 65, 71.

Elton, Frederick (d. 1878), Captain, consul at Mozambique *1875–8*, 77.

Ely, Marchioness of (1821–90), Lady of the Bedchamber *1851–89*, 180–1.

Eugénie, Empress of the French (1826–1920), 298.

Fairlie, Robert Francis (1831–85), civil engineer, inventor, 43–4.

Fane, after *1899* Sir, Edmund Douglas Veitch (1837–1900), sec. of legation at Madrid *1881–5*, min. at Belgrade *1893–1900*, etc., 165, 192.

Fawcett, Henry (1833–84), radical M.P. *1865–84*, 53.

Ferdinand of Saxe-Coburg and Gotha (1861–1948), Prince, after *1908* King, of Bulgaria *1887–1918*, 229, 247.

Fergusson, Sir James (1832–1907), sixth Bart., cons. M.P. *1854–7*, *1859–68*, *1885–1905*, gov. of Bombay *1880–5*, 36.

Flourens, Émile (1841–1920), French for. min. *1886–8*, 241.

Fontes, Pereira de Melo, Falecido António Maria de (1819–87), Portuguese General, min. for Colonies *1851*, premier *1871–7*, *1878–9*, *1881–6*, 12–18, 39, 41, 105, 144, 157–8.

Foreign Office: Morier's complaints against, 35, 37–8, 53, 62–3, 69, 120–1, 139–40, 165–6, 189, 205–6; complaints against Morier, 37–8, 41, 55, 151–5, 191–2, 295, 362–3; commercial dept. of, 37, 170, 185.

Forsyth, Sir Thomas Douglas (1827–86), Indian civil servant, commissioner of the Punjab *1860–72*, envoy to Kashgar *1873*, 45, 48.

Fortescue, Chichester Samuel (1823–98), first Baron Carlingford *1874*, lib. M.P., chief sec. Ireland, president Bd. of Trade, lord privy seal, lord president, etc., 4.

Fortnightly Review, 139, 205 n.
France: war scare *1875*, 7–8, 118; friendship with Portugal, 22; and Congo, 109–10, 112; Morier on, after war of *1870–1*, 71, 122–3; Morier on ultramontanes and radicals in, 117–19, 122; and Morocco, 165–8; trade relations with Britain, Portugal and Spain, 168–71, 173–4, 177; visit of King Alfonso to, 179–80; and naval demonstration *1886*, 216; return of Orleanist monarchy, 227–8; Salisbury on, 237; war scare *1886–7*, 241, 243; *entente* with Russia, 201–3, 241, 359–60; interest of Britain and Russia in preserving, 247, 336; visit of her fleet to Kronstadt, 347.
Franco-Prussian War, 71, 160, 288, 290–3.
Franzensbad, 199, 211, 255–6, 264, 311.
Frederick, Crown Prince of Prussia (1831–88), Frederick III *1888*, commander of armies of S. German states *1870–1*, 6–9, 58, 271, 273, 287, 291–3, 296, 299, 300; visit of, to Madrid, 184–5, 191.
Frederick Charles (1828–85), Prince, nephew of William I, German Field-Marshal, commander of Prussian second army *1870*, 290–2.
Free trade, 75, 131, 132, 135, 164, 167, 172–6, 181–2, 191, 192 (*see also* Manchester School).
Freitas, *see* Barjona de.
Frere, Sir Henry Bartle Edward (1815–84), high commissioner for S. Africa *1877–80*, 87–8.
Freycinet, Charles de Saulces de (1828–1923), French premier *1882*, etc., 167.
Freytag, Gustav (1816–95), German lib., novelist and journalist, 6.
Froude, James Anthony (1818–94), historian, 3.

Gambetta, Léon (1838–82), French radical politician, premier *1881–2*, 117, 167.
Geffcken, Heinrich (1830–96), professor at Strasbourg, German lib., 6, 8, 9, 271, 274, 278, 296, 299, 301.
Germany: Morier's attitude to, 6, 51, 71, 117, 143, 270–1; his reports of conditions in, 361–2; war scare *1875*, 7–8, 118; and Congo treaty, 112; relations with Portugal, 115–16; with Spain, 25, 164, 178–80, 184; with France *1884*, 191; with Britain, 191, 214, 218–21, 233, 240, 249, 251, 286, 303, 336; with Russia, 201, 218–19, 228, 240–3, 251, 336; war scare *1886–7*, 241, 243, 287; military preparations of, 334; against Orleanist restoration in France, 228 (*see also* Berlin, Bismarck, *Kulturkampf*, Reinsurance treaty).
Gibbs, Henry Hucks (1819–1907), first Baron Aldenham *1896*, merchant banker, 316.
Gibraltar: importance of friendship with Portugal for, 18; smuggling through, 170–3, 176, 183.
Giers, Nikolai Karlovich de (1820–95), Russian assistant min., then min. for for. affairs *1875–95*; Morier's 'pact' with, 145, 199, 211, 268; conversations with Morier: at Franzensbad *1885*, 199, 211, 255–6; on Batum, 225; *1886*, 238–9, 265; *1887*, 247, 249; *1886–7* on Afghan frontier, 262, 264–5, 268–9; *1888* on Persia, 331–2, on Turkestan, 333, on Anglo-Russian relations, 336–8; *1891*, 346–7; *1892*, 349–50; a Protestant, 200; on Rosebery, 222; Shuvalov's attack on, 250–1.
Gladstone, William Ewart (1809–98), prime min. *1868–74*, *1880–5*, *1886*, *1892–4*, 51–4, 67–8, 125, 130, 140, 170, 173, 175–7, 187–9, 192, 211, 221, 223, 233, 253–4; Morier's views on, 53–4, 189.
Glinka, Dmitri Grigorovich (1808–83), Russian min. in Lisbon *1871–83*, 50, 189–90.
Goa, 27–8, 48.
Goa Railway, 30–3, 36–49, 315, 361.
Goa treaty: negotiation of, 28–9, 33–5, 38–42, 152–3; failure of *1877*, 39, 155; terms of, 29–31; signed 26 *Dec. 1878*, 42; before the Cortes, 42, 46–7; ratified *1879*, 47, 88, 154.
Golchika, Siberian town, 312, 320, 329.
Gold Coast, proposed Portuguese surrender of territory on, 110, 111.
Gómez, Ruiz, Spanish for. min. *1883–4*, 164, 184–6.

INDEX

Gonnear, —, —, Portuguese min. for Colonies, 43.

Gorchakov, Aleksandr Mikhailovich (1798–1883), Prince, Russian chanc. and for. min. *1856–82*, 141, 198, 199; conversation with Morier on connection between Russia's Asiatic and Turkish policies, 216–17.

Goschen, George Joachim (1831–1907), first Viscount *1900*, lib. later unionist M.P., mission to Constantinople *1880–1*, chanc. of the exchequer *1887–92*, 5, 122, 295, 303, 363; Morier's autobiographical letter to, quoted, 145, 206–7, 211, 216, 222, 256.

Gosling, Audley Charles (d. 1913), sec. of embassy at St. Petersburg *1888–90*, 204.

Gould, Gerald Francis (d. 1883), sec. of legation at Lisbon *1876–8*, min. at Belgrade *1878–81*, 11.

Granville, Granville George (1815–91), second Earl, for. sec. *1870–4, 1880–5*, col. sec. *1868–70, 1886*: on Morier, 10, 158–9, 188, 362–3; Morier and, 11, 84 n., 104, 154, 156; Morier asks him for a knighthood, 154–5; writes to him on Bazaine's visit, 289; and alliance with Portugal, 24, 25; and Russian repudiation of Black Sea clauses, 140; and Lorenço Marques treaty, 103–5, 107–9, 156–7; and Congo treaty, 101–2, 105, 107, 109–12; and Morocco, 166–8; and commercial negotiations with Spain, 171–8, 181–4.

Greece, 210, 213–17, 221–3, 259, 334.

Green, Henry (1838–1900), senior partner in R. and H. Green & Co., director of E. and W. India Dock Co., lib. M.P. *1885–6*, 44–5.

Grenfell, William Henry (1855–1945), first Baron Desborough *1905*, merchant banker, 316.

Greppi, Giuseppe, Count, Italian amb. at St. Petersburg *1884–7*, 203.

Grévy, François-Paul-Jules (1813–91), president of the French Republic *1879–87*, 180.

Grey, Albert Henry George (1851–1917), fourth Earl *1894*, 316, 320, 323–8.

Grosvenor, Thomas George (1842–86), son of Baron Ebury, sec. of embassy at St. Petersburg *1885–6*, 204, 206 n., 265.

Günsburg (*also* Ginzburg) David, Baron, Russian financier, 324–8.

Hamilton, Sir Edward Walter (1847–1908), priv. sec. to Gladstone, *Diary* quoted, 220 n., 224.

Hamilton, Lord George Francis (1845–1907), first lord of the Admiralty *1885–6, 1886–92*, 279.

Hamilton, Port, 254.

Hardinge, Arthur Henry (1859–1933), third sec. at Madrid *1884*, priv. sec. to Salisbury *1885–6, 1890–2*, second sec. at St. Petersburg *1886–9*, min. at Teheran *1900–6*, 165, 204–5, 211, 229, 235, 238, 239, 339, 360, 363.

Hardinge, Charles (1858–1944), first Baron Hardinge of Penshurst *1910*, cousin of above, amb. at St. Petersburg *1904–6*, permanent und. sec. at the F.O. *1906–10*, 235.

Harford, Frederick Dundas (1862–1931), attaché, later third sec. at St. Petersburg *1885–90*, 205.

Hartington, Spencer Compton (1833–1903), styled Marquis of, eighth Duke of Devonshire *1891*, sec. for war *1882–5*, etc., 289.

Hatzfeldt, Paul von (1831–1901), Count, German amb. in London *1885–1901*, 249, 272, 276, 279, 286, 302, 345, 348.

Hay, Sir John Charles Dalrymple (1821–1912), Admiral, 215.

Herat, 206–7, 256, 333, 342, 343–5.

Herbert, Ivor John Caradoc (1851–1917), Lieutenant-Colonel, later General Sir, military attaché at St. Petersburg *1886–90*, 198, 203 n., 204.

Herbert, Robert G. W. (1831–1905), und. sec. in C.O. *1870–92*, 154.

Hertslet, after *1878* Sir, Edward (1824–1902), librarian in the F.O. *1857–94*, 34.

Herzegovina, 51, 55.

Hewett, Sir William Nathan Wright (1834–88), Vice-Admiral, Commodore West Coast of Africa *1873–6*, etc., 95.

Hinzpeter, Georg (1827–1907), tutor to William II, 7, 288 n., 290, 298.
Hohenzollern-Sigmaringen, Prince Charles of (1839–1914), Prince of Rumania *1866–81*, King Carol I of Rumania *1881–1914*, 58.
Hohenzollern-Sigmaringen, Prince Leopold of (1835–1905), 160.
Holstein, Friedrich von (1837–1909), served in German F.O. *1878–1906*, 249.
Hope, after *1886* Sir, Theodore Cracraft (1831–1915), Indian civil servant, member of Viceroy's council *1877–87*, 36 n., 38, 39, 41, 49.
Howard, Henry (1843–1921), attached to joint high commission on Anglo-American claims *1871*, etc., sec. of embassy at St. Petersburg *1891–4*, 204.
Howden, John Herbert (1799–1873), second Baron, min. at Madrid *1850–8*, 34.
Hubbard, Messrs, bankers, 316.
Hudson, Sir James (1810–85), min. at Turin *1851–63*, 63, 71.
Humbert, King of Italy *1878–1900*, 116.
Hutton, James F., West Africa merchant of Manchester, 112.
Huxley, Thomas Henry (1825–96), scientist, president of the Royal Society *1883–5*, 4.

Iberian Union, 18, 19, 24, 179.
Iddesleigh, until *1885* Sir Stafford Northcote (1818–87), first Earl of, for. sec. *1886–7*, 228, 229, 231, 235, 242, 262, 263, 265, 276–9.
Ignatiev, Nikolai Pavlovich (1832–1908), after *1878* Count, Russian min., after *1867* amb., at Constantinople *1864–81*, min. of the interior *1881–2*, 52, 53, 70, 122, 197, 347.
India: Anglo-Portuguese relations in, 19–20, 27–8, 34, 77, 89; railway building in, 31–3; Morier on importance of, 64, 217, 233–4, 275, 280, 360; Salisbury on, 236; Indian frontier defence, 348, 357–8; delimitation of frontier in Pamirs, 348, 350–7; policy of Indian govt. in Central Asia, 351, 356 (*see also* Tariffs, Goa Railway).

Isandlwha, battle of *1879*, 91.
Italy: agreement with Portugal on papal election, 115; and Morocco, 163–4; Salisbury's policy towards, 248–50, 285–6; mentioned, 51, 114.

Jenkyns, Richard (1782–1854), Master of Balliol College, Oxford *1819–54*, 66.
João I, King of Portugal *1358–90*, 23.
João V, King of Portugal *1689–1750*, 114.
Jomini, Aleksandr Henrikhovich (1817–88), Baron, senior counsellor in Russian ministry for for. affairs and sometime deputy for. min. *1856–88*, 199–200, 239, 241.
Jonov, —, —, Russian Colonel, 348–9, 352, 354, 355.
Jowett, Benjamin (1817–93), tutor at, from *1870* Master of, Balliol College, Oxford, Regius Professor of Greek *1855*, 2, 5 n., 12, 13 n., 18, 27, 33 n., 53–5, 66–72, 119–24, 139–43, 302 315, 363.

Kaffir tribes, 78–80, 83.
Kaffir war, 80.
Kálnoky von Köröspatak, Gustav (1832–98), Count, Austro-Hungarian min. for for. affairs *1881–95*, 245.
Kapnist, Dmitri Alekseievich (1837–1904), head of Asiatic dept. in Russian F.O. *1891–7*, 199, 200.
Kara Sea, 308–14, 328.
Karaoul, Siberian town, 312, 317, 320, 321.
Karavelov, Petko (1840–1904), regent in Bulgaria *1886–7*, 229–30, 240, 244, 246–7.
Karun, river, 331, 337, 345.
Katkov, Mikhail (1818–87), Russian writer and journalist, 199, 201–2, 231, 241.
Kaufmann, Konstantin Petrovich, Russian General, gov. gen. of Turkestan *1867–83*, 345.
Kaulbars, Nikolai Vasilievich (1842–1905), Russian General, missions to Bulgaria *1886* and *1889*, 229–30.
Kennedy, Charles Malcolm (1832–1908), head of commercial dept. in the F.O. *1872–94*, 38, 170, 185, 187 n.

INDEX

Kennedy, Sir Michael Kavanagh (d. 1898), General, Indian civil servant, chief engineer and sec. to Bombay govt. Public Works and Railway dept. *1863–79*, member of Viceroy's council *1879*, 36.
Kerr, William Walter Ralegh (1863–1942), hon. attaché at St. Petersburg *1888–90*, 205.
Khamiab, district of, 260–3, 265, 267–9.
Kimberley, John (1826–1900), third Baron and first Earl of, col. sec. *1870–4*, *1880–2*, sec. for India *1882–5*, *1886*, *1892–4*, 105, 107, 110, 170, 173, 355.
Kölnische Zeitung, 8, 299–302.
Krasnoselski, —, —, Russian banker, 326, 327.
Krasnoyarsk, Siberian town, 321–3.
Kulturkampf, 6, 7, 113, 118.
Kuropatkin, Aleksei Nikolaievich (1848–1925), Russian General, 345.

Laboulaye, Antoine Paul René Lefebvre de (1833–1905), Count, French min. at Lisbon *1877–86*, amb. at St. Petersburg *1886–91*, 22, 202–3, 241.
Langley, Henry Fitzroy (d. 1884), second sec. at Madrid *1880–4*, 165.
Lascelles, after *1886* Sir, Frank Cavendish (1841–1920), consul-gen. at Sofia *1879–87*, min. at Bucharest *1887–91*, Teheran *1891–4*, amb. in Berlin *1895–1908*, 205, 228.
Law, E. G. F., 205, 344.
Layard, after *1878* Sir, Austen Henry (1817–94), 'Layard of Nineveh', lib. M.P., min. at Madrid *1869–77*, amb. at Constantinople *1877–80*, 4.
Lee, George, employed by the Anglo-Siberian Syndicate Ltd., 317, 318, 321, 322.
Lennep, Clara van, grandmother of Morier, 1.
Lennep, David van, great-grandfather of Morier, 1.
Leo XIII, pope *1878–1903*, 116–17.
Leopold II, King of the Belgians *1865–1909*, 95, 97, 112.
Lessar, Pavel Mikhailovich (1851–1905), Russian engineer, adviser on Afghan frontier to Russian amb. in London, member of Afghan demarcation commission, 255, 266.
Leybourne-Popham, Francis William (1862–1907), Wilts. landowner, 328, 329.
Lindsay claim against Portugal, 18.
Lingen, Ralph Robert Wheeler (1819–1905), first Baron *1885*, sec. to the treasury *1870–85*, 4.
Lisbon: Britain's need to use its harbour, 18–19; archbishop of, 113–14; faction fights in, 144; mentioned, 3, 4, 7, 9, 10.
Lister, after *1885* Sir, Thomas Villiers (1833–1902), assistant und. sec. in the F.O. *1873–94*, 35, 37–9, 41, 153, 248 n.
Livingstone, David (1813–73), African explorer, 73, 81, 108.
Loë, Walter von (1828–1908), Baron, German Field-Marshal, 6.
Lorenço Marques, 27, 83–4, 86–7, 91.
Lorenço Marques treaty: negotiation of, 84, 87–8, 92–4, 155–6; terms of, 89, 94 n.; signed, 94, 155–6; before Chamber of Deputies, 98–100, 102–3, 105, 155; withdrawn from Chamber of Peers, 107–9, 155–6; opposition to, in Portugal, 22, 94, 102, 104–5, 108; article 5 of, 90–1, 154.
Loris-Melikov, Mikhail Tarielovich (1825–88), Count, Russian General, min. of the interior *1880–1*, 195–7.
Lowe, Robert (1811–92), first Viscount Sherbrooke *1880*, lib. M.P. *1852–74*, chanc. of the exchequer *1868–73*, home sec. *1873–4*, 53.
Lowther, James (1840–1904), third Bart., parliamentary und. sec. for the colonies *1874–8*, 77.
Lubbock, Sir John (1834–1913), first Baron Avebury *1900*, banker and naturalist, 316.
Luis I (1838–89), King of Portugal *1861–89*, 10, 12, 24, 25, 77, 103, 113–15, 117–18, 145, 148–51, 272.
Lumley, Sir John Savile (1818–96), first Baron Savile *1888*, amb. in Rome *1883–8*, 284–5.
Lumsden, Sir Peter Stark (1829–1918), Major General, 253–4.
Luxemburg Guarantee, 35.
Lyons, Richard Bickerton Pennell

(1817–87), second Baron, Viscount *1881*, Earl *1887*, amb. in Paris *1867–87*, 167, 292, 362.
Lytton, Edward Robert (1831–91), second Baron, first Earl of *1880*, min. at Lisbon *1874–6*, Viceroy of India *1876–80*, amb. in Paris *1887–91*, 9, 11, 12 n., 27, 28, 30, 32–6, 39, 132.

Maçao, 18.
Mackenzie, Dr., later Sir, Morell, English surgeon to Frederick III, 296.
Mackinnon, Sir William (1823–93), first Bart. *1889*, founder of British East Africa Company, 44–5, 112, 314–15.
MacMahon, M. E. P. M. de (1808–1903), Count, Marshal, president of the French Republic, *1873–9*, 76, 117–19.
Macmillan's Magazine, 6 n.
Macpherson, William (d. 1898), vice-consul, after *1885* consul, and assistant to the legation at Madrid *1868–90*, 165, 185, 294–6.
Madrid: Morier appointed to, 18, 158–9; convention of, on Morocco *1880*, 165.
Maine, Sir Henry James Sumner (1822–88), jurist, 4.
Majuba Hill, battle of *1881*, 156.
Makoko treaty, 97, 109–10.
Malet, Sir Edward Baldwin (1837–1908), consul-gen. in Egypt *1879–83*, amb. in Berlin *1884–95*, 188, 219, 276, 280, 292–4, 296, 297, 300–2.
Mallet, Sir Louis (1823–90), served in the Bd. of Trade *1847–72*, member of the Indian Council *1872–4*, und. sec. in the I.O. *1874–83*, 4, 10, 19, 35, 37, 39, 59–64, 129–39, 153, 155, 316, 327, 328 n., 363.
Manchester School, 130, 138 (*see also* Cobdenite Foreign Policy).
Mancini, Pasquale Stanislao (1817–88), Italian min. for Justice *1876–8*, 117, 118.
Maria Cristina of Habsburg, wife of Alfonso XII, 160.
Martinez, Alonzo, Spanish min. for Justice *1881–3*, 163.
Martinez de Campos, Arsenio (1831–1900), Spanish General and politician, 25, 163.

Martos, C. (1890–3), Spanish democratic politician, 164.
Max Müller, Friedrich (1823–1900), orientalist and philologist, 2.
Medhurst, Arthur F. Hastings, vice-consul in Moscow *1889–95*, 318, 327.
Mediterranean Agreements *1887*, 244–6, 248–51, 284–6.
Mercer, —, —, English businessman in Russia, 326, 327.
Merv, 253, 260, 330, 348.
Midhat (1822–84), Pasha, Turkish vizier *1860–71*, grand vizier *1871*, *1876–7*, 58.
Milan Obrenovich (1854–1901), Prince, after *1882* King, of Serbia, 212.
Milburn, John Davison (1851–1907), first Bart. *1905*, Northumberland shipowner, 320.
Mingrelia, Prince of, 229 n., 230.
Minusinsk, Siberian town, 322.
Mohrenheim, Arthur Pavlovich (1824–1906), Baron, Russian amb. in London *1882–4*, in Paris *1884–97*, 202, 225, 241.
Montenegro, 50–2, 54, 210, 215.
Moore, A. W., served in the I.O., 39.
Moret Y Prendergast, Segismundo (1838–1913), Spanish lib., min. of the interior *1883–4*, 161, 164, 175.
Morier, Alice (d. 1903), *née* Peel, wife of Morier, 4, 9, 50, 91, 181.
Morier, David Richard (1784–1877), father of Morier, min. at Berne *1832–47*, 1–2, 11, 39, 142.
Morier, Isaac (1750–1817), grandfather of Morier, 1.
Morier, James Justin (1782–1849), uncle of Morier, sec. of embassy at Teheran, author of *The Adventures of Hadji Baba*, 1.
Morier, Robert Burnet David (1826–93): early career of, 1–6; appointment to Lisbon, 7–8, 9–10, 189; to Madrid, 18, 158–9, 189; to St. Petersburg, 188–91, 272; appointment considered to Constantinople, 10, 72, 362–3; to Rome, 284–6, 347, 348; to Vienna, 188, 286, 356; knighthood (K.C.B.) *1882*, 154, 159; G.C.B. *1887*, 285; Bismarck on, 275–7, 281, 286–7, 293, 302; Crown Princess on, 274, 277, 280, 282–3; Derby on, 30,

152, 153; Granville on, 10, 158–9, 188, 362–3; Jowett on, 363; Mallet on, 35–6, 37 and n., 131–2; Rosebery on, 220 and n., 274, 356–7; Salisbury on, 41, 153, 155, 303, 343; Queen Victoria on, 159, 181, 189, 191, 207, 273–84, 363 (for Morier's views, see subject headings).

Morier, Victor (1867–92), only son of Morier, 311 and n., 313, 356.

Morier, Victoria Mary A., only dau. of Morier, see Wester Wemyss.

Morley, John (1838–1923), first Viscount Morley of Blackburn, editor of the *Fortnightly Review*, etc., radical M.P. *1883–95, 1896–1908*, chief sec. for Ireland *1886, 1892–5*, etc., 4, 139.

Morocco, 165–8, 190.

Moscow: party of, 196, 198–201, 209–10, 318; university of, 201; merchants of, 202.

Moscow Gazette, 201, 203 n., 231.

Münster, Georg Herbert (1820–1902), Count, German amb. in London *1873–85*, in Paris *1885–1900*, 8, 159.

Mutkurov, Colonel, regent in Bulgaria *1886–7*, 229–30, 240, 244, 246–7.

Napier, the Hon. William John George (1846–1913), master of Napier, eleventh Baron *1898*, sec. of legation at Lisbon *1877–83*, 11.

Natal, 78, 80, 84 (*see also* Tariffs).

Nelidov, Aleksandr Ivanovich (1837–1910), Russian amb. in Constantinople *1883–97*, 209–10.

Nesselrode, Karl Vasilievich (1780–1862), Count, Russian chanc. and for. min. *1816–56*, 199.

Nicholas I (1796–1855), Emperor of Russia *1825–55*, 196, 205.

Norddeutsche Allgemeine Zeitung, 272, 300, 304.

Nordenskiöld, Adolf Eric (1832–1901), arctic explorer, 308 n., 310, 314, 316.

North British Review, 270.

Nyasa [Nyassa], 73, 74, 81, 113.

Obi, river, 309, 310, 313, 324.

Obruchev, Nikolai Nikolaievich (1830–1904), General, Chief of the Russian General Staff *1881–97*, 202, 348.

O'Connor, after *1895* Sir, Nicholas Roderick (1843–1908), consul-gen. at Sofia *1887–92*, min. at Pekin *1892–5*, amb. at St. Petersburg *1895–8*, 247–8, 364.

Ottoman Empire, see Turkey, Eastern question, Bulgaria.

Oxford, University of, 2–3, 363.

Palgrave, W. Coates, agent of Cape Colony and Special Commissioner to the Tribes North of the Orange River, 82.

Pall Mall Gazette, 126, 131, 300, 334.

Palmerston, Henry John Temple (1784–1865), third Viscount, for. sec. *1830–4, 1835–41, 1846–51*, prime min. *1855–8, 1859–65*, 2, 3, 69, 95.

Pamirs Incident *1891*, 330, 346–57; Morier recommends British expedition to Alichur Pamirs, 352, 355, 358.

Panslavism and Panslavist Party, 52, 201–2, 229, 230–1, 318.

Paris, peace of *1856*, 140, 146–7, 223.

Pauncefote, after *1874* Sir, Julian (1828–1902), first Baron *1899*, assistant und. sec. in the F.O. *1876–82*, und. sec. *1882–9*, min., after *1893* amb., in Washington *1889–1902*, 34, 38, 102, 205, 280.

Peel, Arthur Robert (1861–1952), son of Frederick, second son of the prime min., attaché, later third sec. at St. Petersburg, etc., 205.

Peel, Jonathan (1799–1879), Lieut.-General, brother of the prime min., father-in-law of Morier, 9 n., 91.

Penjdeh, 233, 254, 256, 258, 268, 330, 347, 359.

Persia: generally, 330–45; Russo-Persian agreement *1887*, 337; British economic penetration of, 343–4 (*see also* Karun river, Railways).

Persia, Nasir ad Din, Shah of *1848–96*, 336–40, 344.

Phoenix Merchant Adventurers Ltd., 312–14.

Pimental, see Serpa Pimentel.

Pius VI, pope *1775–99*, 114.

Pius IX, pope *1846–78*, 114–17.

INDEX

Pobiedonostsev, Konstantin Petrovich (1827–1907), Procurator of the Russian Holy Synod *1880–1905*, 199, 200–1.

Ponsonby, after *1879* Sir, Henry Frederick (1825–95), priv. sec. to Queen Victoria *1870–95*, 4 n., 122, 124–9, 157, 158, 181, 189 and n., 205, 217 and n., 256–7, 273, 274, 281, 300, 302, 303.

Portugal: 'ancient alliance' with, 17, 18, 20, 23–7, 34–5; Anglo-Portuguese co-operation in Africa, 19–20, 40, 73–6, 80–1; Anglo-Portuguese relations in India, 19–20, 27–31, 35–6, 39–42, 46–9; Britain disliked by, 18, 20–2, 26, 27, 76, 81–3, 102, 107–8, 157; British proposal to buy Portuguese Indian colonies, 27–8; a liberal Catholic country, 114–15; claim to exercise veto at papal elections, 114–16; and Congo, 94–8, 100–12; Congress of Berlin, representation at, 26–7; disorders in *1881*, 17, 107; and France, 21–2, 116, 117–19, 169–70; Goa railway, concession for, 30, 31, 41–6; and Lorenço Marques treaty, 83–4, 87–9, 91, 94, 98–100, 102–9; Morier's arrival in, 10; Morier's grand project for co-operation with, 19–20, 27, 31, 89; Morier's three letters to Portuguese newspaper, 77–80; political parties in, 13–16; a small Power, 18; Spain, fear of, 18, 24–6; fishing dispute with *1877*, 148–52; unbusinesslike ways of, 152; attitude during Zulu War, 86–7, 91.

Posada Herrera, J. (1815–85), Spanish premier *1883–4*, 164.

Post, Berlin newspaper, 8, 301.

Prieto, Raffaele, 185–6.

Progresso, Lisbon newspaper, 144.

Prussia, 6, 270–1 (*see also* Germany).

Railways: generally, 4; in India, 31–3; in Africa, 85; in Russia, 196, 199; in Persia, 331, 337–42, 344–5 (*see also* Delagoa Railway, Goa Railway, Trans-Siberian Railway).

Reeve, Henry (1813–95), registrar of the Privy Council *1853–87*, editor of the *Edinburgh Review 1855–95*, 5.

Reinsurance treaty, *July 1887*, 241–2, 246, 247, 250.

Ribeiro Ferreira, Tomás António, Count, Portuguese min. for Colonies *1878–9*, 15, 16, 99.

Ridgeway, after *1886* Sir, Joseph West (1844–1930), commissioner for the Afghan frontier *1885–6*, negotiator in St. Petersburg *1887*, 255, 260, 262, 263, 265–8.

Roberts, Frederick Sleigh (1832–1914), first Earl *1901*, General, commander-in-chief in India *1885–93*, etc., 355.

Roggenbach, Franz von (1825–1907), Baron, German lib., 4 n., 6, 7, 58, 59, 204.

Rome, 4, 5 (*see also* Vatican); Morier, and embassy at, 284–6, 347, 348.

Rosebery, Archibald Philip (1847–1929), fifth Earl of, for. sec. *1886*, *1892–4*, prime min. *1894–5*, 5 n.; on Morier, 220 and n., 274, 356–7; rebukes Morier, 219–20, 273–4; Morier on, 215, 216, 222, 233, 353, 356–7; Morier begins priv. correspondence with, 218; Sanderson on, 221; and naval demonstration against Greece, 214–16; his 'blood and iron' policy, 216; and Bismarck, 218; and sanctity of treaties, 224–5; and reform of reports to F.O., 305–6; and return to F.O. *1892*, 305, 352; and Pamirs, 353–7.

Rosenbach, Nikolai (1836–1901), Russian General, gov. gen. of Turkestan *1884–9*, 258.

Rothschild, Nathan Meyer de (1840–1915), first Baron *1885*, 324–6, 328.

Rumania, 234, 241, 311; Elizabeth, known as Carmen Sylva, Queen of, 6, 58.

Russell, Lord Arthur Edward John (1825–92), elder brother of Lord Odo, lib. M.P. *1857–85*, 4–5.

Russell, Lord Odo William Leopold (1829–84), first Baron Ampthill *1881*, special envoy to Rome *1858–70*, amb. in Berlin *1871–84*, 5, 9, 51, 143, 188, 362.

Russell, Lady William, mother of above, 5.

Russia: alliance policy of, 201–3, 241, 359–60; Anglo-Russian agreement

INDEX

31 May 1878, 136; Anglo-Russian crises *1885–6*, 211, 213, 215, 217–18, 221–2; Penjdeh, 254; Anglo-Russian mistrust, 341–2; Anglo-Russian occupation of Turkey-in-Europe, 59–64; **Anglo-Russian understanding**: Morier on, 50–2, 64–5, 207, 211, 214, 216, 232, 234–5, 242, 256–7, 282–3, 285; Iddesleigh's questions on, 242; over Persia, 330–3, 335, 340–5; Queen Victoria on, 273–6; Russian 'overtures' for, *July 1886*, 226–8, 335, *Oct. 1886*, 228, 238–9, 335, *July–Aug. 1887*, 247–9, 335, *Nov. 1888*, 336, *1891*, 346–7, considered generally, 358–60, 362–3; army of, 198, 201, 204, 236, 334, 357; European and Asiatic policies of, linked, 216–17, 231–2, 353, 360; expansion of: like an ocean tide, 232–3, 235–6; 'planless', 333–5; finances of, 208–9; policy discussions in *1892*, 353; press in, 203 and n.; revolution threatening, 209; trade concessions gained by Morier from, 312–13, 318–19; and war scare *1875*, 9.
Russo-Turkish War *1877–8*, 53, 59, 63–6, 68–70, 119–22, 233.
Rylands, Peter (1820–87), pacifist, lib. M.P., 138 and n.

Sagasta, Práxedes Mateo (1827–1903), Spanish premier *1881–3*, *1885–90*, 162–4, 174, 175.
St. Petersburg: city described, 195–6; Morier's appointment to, 188–9, 272, 299; university of, 201; newspapers of, 203; Afghan frontier negotiations transferred to, 263–6; business community in, British, 316, 328, Russian, 324, 328, 360.
Salcedo, Alba, 190.
Salisbury, Robert (1830–1903), third Marquis of, sec. for India *1866–7*, *1874–7*, for. sec. *1878–80*, *1885–6*, *1887–92*, *1895–1900*, prime min. *1886–92*, *1895–1902*: on Morier, 41, 153, 155, 303, 343; Morier on, 62–3, 93, 211, 214; **receives letters from Morier**: on eastern question, 59–62; on Anglo-Portuguese relations, 73–4; on Anglo-Russian understanding, 233–5; on Afghan frontier, 265–6; on calumnies, 281, 284; reviewing work *1885–8*, 335; on Ld. R. Churchill, 360; **argues with Morier**: on Bazaine incident, 295–7, 300–1, 335–6; on Anglo-Russian understanding, 228, 235–8, 244–6, 334–6; warns Morier against spies, 280; and Africa 'England's bad debt', 84; and Bazaine incident, 298, 299, 303; Bulgaria, stiff on, 333 (*see also* and Russia *below*); Congo treaty, disapproves Morier's proposal, 101; at Constantinople conference, 37, 59–60; demarcation of Afghan frontier, regrets and recommends Fabian policy, 238, 263–4, 267–8, 348, 350–3; and Germany, conversation with Hatzfeldt *1887*, 249; unwilling to quarrel with the Bismarcks, 296; and Goa treaty, 39 and n., 40, 89–90, 155; and Lorenço Marques treaty, disapproves Morier's draft, 90, responds to his appeal on, 91–2; and Persia, 330–1, 333, 337, 339, 340, 344; and Russia, 208–9, 213, 235–8, 244, 248–9; mentioned, 4, 9.
Salisbury, Lady, wife of above, invites Morier to Hatfield, 295.
Sampaio, António Rodrigues (1806–82), Portuguese lib. and journalist, min. for the interior *1878–9*, premier *1881–2*, 15, 17–18, 105, 107, 108, 144, 157.
Sanderson, Thomas Henry (1841–1913), first Baron *1905*, assistant und. sec. *1889–94*, und. sec. in the F.O. *1894–1906*, 38, 205, 220, 221, 262; on Rosebery, 221.
San Stefano, treaty of, 119, 141.
San Thomé, 18, 21.
Sarakhs tribes, 261–2, 267, 269, 345.
Saurin, Dudley Edward (d. 1901), in the diplomatic service *1856–85*, sec. of legation at Lisbon *1878–82*, 11, 154.
Schleswig-Holstein, 6, 270.
Schnaebele Incident, 283.
Schweinitz, Hans Lothar von (1822–1901), German General, amb. in Vienna *1871–6*, in St. Petersburg *1876–93*, 202, 218–19, 221, 247, 250, 283, 285, 334.
Sekukuni, Kaffir king, 79–80.

Serbia, 50–2, 54, 210, 213, 217, 234; defeated at Slivnitsa, 212; satellite of Austria–Hungary in trade, 311; visit of King of, to St. Petersburg, 347.
Serpa Pimentel, António de (1825–1900), Portuguese min. for finance *1871–7, 1878–9*, for. min. *1882*, representative at Berlin West Africa Conference *1884–5*, 13–16, 109.
Serrano, *see* Torre, Duke de la.
Shepstone, Sir Theophilus (1817–93), South African statesman, administrator of the Transvaal *1877–9*, 78 n., 80, 88.
Shiré, river, 73–4, 81.
Shuvalov, Paul Andreievich (1830–1908), Count, Russian amb. in Berlin *1885–94*, 242, 250.
Shuvalov, Peter Andreievich (1827–89), Count, Russian amb. in London *1874–9*, 9, 241–4, 250–1.
Siberia, 204; Russian exploration and conquest of, 306–9; sea route to, opened, 310, and developed, 311–13, 320–3, 328–9; Morier's plan for trade to, 312, 316–17, 324, 360–1; Grey's plan for trade to, 325–7, 328.
Sibiriakov, Aleksandre, Siberian merchant, 310–11.
Simon, Jules François (1814–96), French lib. philosopher, min. of education *1870–3*, premier *1876–7*, 117–19.
Skobelev, Mikhail Dmitrievich (1843–82), Russian General, 345.
Slave-Trade, 21, 27, 75, 85, 101, 106, 110–11.
Slave-Trade classification in F.O., 154.
Smith, William Henry (1825–91), sec. for war *1886–92*, 279, 303.
Smyrna, 1.
Soares, Duarte Gustave Nogueira, Portuguese civil servant in India, 38, 39, 41.
Solms-Braunfels von, Prince Louis (*b. 1847*), Austro-Hungarian vice-consel at Madrid, 292, 298.
Somatash, battle of *1892*, 353.
Spain: fishing dispute with Portugal *1877*, 148–52; *turnismo* in, 160–1; political parties in, 161, 164–5; army of, 161–2; and Britain: overture for closer relations, 179–80; diplomatic questions with, 189; on occupation of Egypt by, 190 (*see also* Commercial Treaties); and France, 180; and Germany, 164, 179, 180, 272; and Morocco, 165–8.
Staal, Georges de (1822–1907), Baron, Russian amb. in London *1884–1902*, 212, 225, 255 n., 265, 266, 272, 278, 331, 332, 348, 349.
Stafford House Committee, 154, 315.
Stambulov, Stefan Nikolov (1854–94), regent in Bulgaria *1886–7*, 229–30, 240, 244, 246–7.
Stanley, Arthur Penrhyn (1815–81), dean of Westminster, 201.
Stanley, Sir Henry Morton (1814–1904), African explorer, 97, 109.
Stead, William Thomas (1849–1912), assistant editor, after *1883* editor, of the *Pall Mall Gazette 1880–90*, 302 n., 334.
Stockmar, Christian Friedrich von (1787–1863), Baron, 6, 280.
Stockmar, Ernst von (1823–86), Baron, son of above, jurist and historian, 6–8, 221, 275, 280.
Stosch, Albrecht von (1818–96), General, head of Prussian (German) Admiralty, opponent of Bismarck after *1877*, 6.
Suda Bay, 215, 222.
Sullivan, H. N., 312–14, 317, 318.
Surat, British factory at, 28, 29, 30–1.
Sutherland, George Granville William (1828–92), third Duke of, 44–5, 315.
Switzerland, 1, 2, 363–4.

Tariffs: generally, 4, 20, 25, 311; Cape Colony's, 88; Indian, 28, 29; Mozambique, 73–4, 87; Natal, 74, 87–8; Russian, 223; Spanish, 163, 168.
Teheran, 1, 330–3, 337–9, 342, 344.
Temple, Sir Richard (1827–1902), first Bart, *1876*, Indian civil servant, finance min. of India *1868–74*, gov. of Bombay *1877–80*, 36.
Tenterden, Charles Stuart Aubrey (1834–82), third Baron, und. sec. in F.O. *1873–82*, 37, 38, 101–2, 152, 154, 205.
The Times, 119, 121, 126, 127, 140, 274, 278, 279, 300, 301.

Thomar, — de, Count, Portuguese min., later amb., in Rome *1870–85*, 114–16.

Thomson, Sir Ronald Ferguson (1830–88), served at Teheran *1848–87*, as min. and consul-gen. *1879–87*, 330, 331.

Thornton, Sir Edward (1817–1906), min. in Washington *1867–81*, amb. at St. Petersburg *1881–5*, at Constantinople *1885–7*, 72, 254.

Thornton, Edward (d. 1904), third, later second, sec. at St. Petersburg *1881–Oct. 1885*, *1889–94*, 205.

Timiriashev, Vasili Ivanovich (1849–1919), served in Russian min. for finance, especially concerned with trade and industry, first min. for trade and industry *1905–6*, 324.

Tolstoy, Dmitri Alekseyevich (1823–89), Count, Russian min. for public instruction *1866–80*, min. for the interior *1882–9*, 197.

Torre, Francisco Serrano de la (1810–85), Duke, Spanish Marshal, lib., head of provisional govt. *1869–70*, premier *1870–1*, 161.

Trans-Siberian Railway, 312, 319–20, 323, 327–9.

Transvaal: annexation of, 40, 76–80, 113; insurrection in *1880–1*, 104, 156.

Treaties, sanctity of, 146–7, 223–4.

Trench, Frederick Chenevix- (1837–94), Colonel, later Major-General, military attaché at St. Petersburg *1883–86*, 204.

Triple Alliance *1882*, 251, 360.

Turkey: Morier on British relations with, 50, 52, 54, 66–7, 121–2, 124–6, 132; on reform of, 55–8, 60, 127; on Anglo-Russian occupation of, 60–3; on loan to, 61; and Bulgaria, 209–13, 217–20, 229, 240, 248, 332; Anglo-Russian co-operation to preserve, 227, 235; Anglo-Turkish convention *1878*, 136.

Valbom, — de, Count, Portuguese min. in Madrid *1878*, 149.

Vanovski, Peter Semiovich (1822–1904), General, Russian min. of war *1881–98*, 198, 209, 347.

Vansittart, Arthur Gordon (1854–1901), third sec. at Lisbon *1879–81*, 11.

Varna, Russian expedition to, 246.

Vatican, 4, 114–15.

Vatican Council *1870*, 4.

Vatican party in Lisbon, 113–14.

Vega de Armijo, Antonio Aguilar Y Correa de la, Marquis, Spanish for. min. *1881–3*, *1888–9*, *1890–3*, 163–4, 174–6, 178–81.

Velasco, Bonifacio Ruiz de, 186.

Victor Emanuel, King of Italy *1860–78*, 8, 12, 114–15, 117, 119.

Victoria (1840–1901), Crown Princess of Prussia, German Empress *1888*, eldest dau. of Queen Victoria, md. Crown Prince of Prussia *1858*, 6–8, 58, 221, 271, 274, 275, 277, 279, 280, 282, 283, 286, 287, 290 n., 293, 296, 297.

Victoria, Queen, 6, 9, 124, 125, 129, 152, 159, **179–81**, **189**, **191**, 207, 211, **221**, 228, 240, 242, **273–84**, 288, 293–5, 363.

Vienna, 3, 4; Morier's work in *1865–7*, 1, 4, 35, 188; question of Morier's appointment to, 188, 286, 356.

Vlangali [Vlangally], Aleksandr Georgievich (1823–1908), Russian deputy for. min. *1888–91*, amb. in Rome *1891–7*, 199, 200, 278.

Vorontsov-Dachkov, Ilarion Ivanovich (1837–1916), Count, 197.

Vrevski, Aleksandr Boriseivich (1834–1910), Baron, Russian gov. gen. of Turkestan *1889–98*, 347, 348.

Vyshnegradski, Ivan Alekseievich (1830–95), Russian min. for finance *1887–92*, 198–9, 312, 318–19, 321 n., 323, 324, 326, 327, 344, 346–7, 349, 350.

Waddington, William Henry (1826–94), French for. min. *1877–9*, amb. in London *1883–93*, 116.

Wales, Edward, Prince of, later Edward VII, 10, 157; Morier's champion with the Queen, 287–8, 293–5; H. Bismarck tells him the Bazaine story, 293; quarrel with William II, 287, 296.

Walfisch Bay, annexation of, by Cape Colony, 82–3.

INDEX

Walsham, Sir John (1850–1905), second Bart., sec. of legation at Madrid *1875–8*, sec. of embassy in Berlin *1878–83*, etc., 168 n., 185.

War, Morier on diplomatic use of threat of, 62–3, 67, 69, 127, 130, 135–7, 138, 206, 332.

War scare: *1875*, 7–10, 117–18; *1886–7*, 241, 243, 287.

Watson, Robert Grant (d. 1892), served in Indian army and Middle East *1856–69*, etc., sec. of legation at Lisbon *1876*, 11.

Wenlock, Beilby (1849–1912), third Baron, 316, 320.

West, Lionel Sackville (1827–1908), min. at Madrid *1872–81*, 169.

Wester Wemyss, Victoria Mary A. (1865–1945), only dau. of Morier, md. *1903* Rosslyn Erskine-Wemyss, first Baron Wester-Wemyss *1919*, First Sea Lord *1917–19*, Admiral of the Fleet (d. 1933), preface, 10, 38, 364; extracts from her draft continuation of Morier's *Memoirs*, 9, 11–12, 38, 52, 136.

Westminster, Hugh Lupus (1825–99), first Duke of, 315.

White, after *1885* Sir, William Arthur (1824–91), consul-gen. at Belgrade *1875–9*, min. at Bucharest *1879–85*, min., later amb., at Constantinople *1885–91*, 50, 55, 63–5, 205, 220, 222, 227.

Wied, Elizabeth of (Carmen Sylva), 58.

Wied, Dowager Princess of, 6, 58.

Wiggins, Joseph (1832–1905), Captain in the merchant navy, 309–15, 320, 328, 329.

Wiggins, Robert, brother of above, 314.

William I (1797–1888), King of Prussia, German Emperor *1871*, 202 n., 287.

William II (1859–1941), German Emperor *1888–1918*, 7, 8, 296, 298, 336, 346–7.

Williams, Oliver, employed by the Anglo-Siberian Syndicate Ltd., 315–16, 318, 321–3, 327, 328.

Wine Duties: Indian, 29–30, 53; British, 168–71, 176, 177, 182.

Witte, Serge Yulievich (1849–1915), Count, Russian min. for finance *1892–1903*, premier *1905–6*, 198, 209.

Wolff, Sir Henry Drummond (1830–1908), cons. M.P. *1874–85*, min. at Teheran *1887–91*, Bucharest *1891*, amb. at Madrid *1892–1900*, 331, 333, 334, 336–44.

Wolkenstein-Trostburg, Anton von (1832–1913), Count, Austro-Hungarian amb. at St. Petersburg *1882–94*, 202, 247, 283.

Wrangell, Ferdinand Petrovich von (1797–1870), Baron, Admiral, Russian navigator, 309.

Wyke, Sir Charles Lennox (1815–97), min. at Lisbon *1881–4*, 170.

Wylde, William Henry (1819–1909), served in the slave-trade dept. in the F.O. *1838–80*, head *1869–80*, 95.

Yenisei, river, 308–14, 317–18, 321–3, 329.

Yeniseisk, Siberian town, 310, 312, 318, 321, 322, 329.

Youle, Frederick, chairman of the London County Bank, 44–5.

Young, Edward Daniel, Scottish missionary, established 'Livingstonia', 81–2.

Younghusband, after *1904* Sir, Francis Edward (1863–1942), Lieutenant-Colonel Indian Army, mission to Lhasa *1903*, etc., 346–8.

Zambesi, river, 73–4, 81, 89, 110–11.

Zamora waterworks, 189–90.

Zinoviev, Ivan Alekseievich (1835–1917), head of the Asiatic dept. in Russian F.O. *1884–91*, min. at Stockholm *1891–7*, amb. at Constantinople *1897–1909*, 199, 200, 262, 267, 268.

Zollverein, between Portuguese and British India, 29–30; between successor states to Turkey-in-Europe, 143; German, 143.

Zulficar Pass, 254, 255, 330.

Zulu threat to Transvaal, 77, 78.

Zululand, importance of direct access to, 91–2.

Zulu War *1879*, 83, 86–7, 91–2, 98–9, 153.

Soc
DA
46
M7
R35